Medical Ethics

A focus on the interplay between medical law and medical ethics makes this refreshing new textbook the most balanced approach available to students of law and medicine. By offering a unique chapter structure which gives equal weight to both the legal and ethical issues, it allows for an appreciation of all factors at play in the field of medical law. In addition, its student-friendly writing style combined with critical analysis gives students the tools to engage with key issues and form their own understanding. Accompanying online case studies convey the law in practice, and encourage students to consider their own views and arguments in terms of legal analysis and ethical consideration. Coverage of recent judicial cases and statutes, with a good balance of factual detail and critical analysis, allows students to engage with this evolving discipline.

NILS HOPPE is Professor of Life Sciences Regulation at Leibniz Universitaet, Hannover, a Director of the Centre for Ethics and Law in the Life Sciences. He is also a group leader in the research cluster REBIRTH – From Regenerative Biology to Reconstructive Therapy, specializing in technology regulation and bioethics.

JOSÉ MIOLA is Professor of Medical Law at the School of Law, University of Leicester. He has published widely in the area and is on the editorial boards of the *Medical Law Review*, *Clinical Ethics* and the *UK Clinical Ethics Network*.

MEDICAL LAW AND

Medical Ethics

Nils Hoppe and José Miola

CAMBRIDGE
UNIVERSITY PRESS

CAMBRIDGE
UNIVERSITY PRESS

University Printing House, Cambridge CB2 8BS, United Kingdom

Cambridge University Press is part of the University of Cambridge.

It furthers the University's mission by disseminating knowledge in the pursuit of education, learning and research at the highest international levels of excellence.

www.cambridge.org
Information on this title: www.cambridge.org/9781107015227

First published 2014

Printed in the United Kingdom by TJ International Ltd, Padstow Cornwall

A catalogue record for this publication is available from the British Library

Library of Congress Cataloguing in Publication data
Hoppe, Nils, author.
Medical law and medical ethics / Nils Hoppe and Jose Miola.
    p.   ;   cm.
Includes bibliographical references and index.
ISBN 978-1-107-01522-7 (hardback) – ISBN 978-1-107-61237-2 (paperback)
I. Miola, José, author.   II. Title.
[DNLM: 1. Legislation, Medical – Great Britain.   2. Bioethical Issues – Great Britain.   3. Ethics, Medical – Great Britain. W 32.5 FA1]
R725.5
174.2–dc23

2013040517

ISBN 978-1-107-01522-7 Hardback
ISBN 978-1-107-61237-2 Paperback

CONTENTS

PREFACE

This book is not aimed at one group in particular. Despite the fact that it considers the law, it is not designed to cater solely for lawyers any more than the fact that it considers the ethics should limit it to philosophers. Rather, we have attempted to make both the legal and ethical discussions as accessible to all disciplines as possible. That said, the ethical discussion will relate to the legal rules, and so provide something of an ethical commentary surrounding the law. This approach results in several consequences. First, we do not claim to consider each and every issue in detail within each legal topic. Rather, we concentrate on those with an ethical component and those that we feel are the most important. Moreover, we have tried to avoid legal minutiae, which we feel would have the effect of making the book less accessible to non-lawyers in particular. We do, however, provide suggested further reading for both law and ethics at the end of each chapter to direct readers towards more detailed consideration of the topics.

We have also tried not to use more cases than we need to – we want this book to be about issues rather than cases, and there are already several other textbooks available that provide a comprehensive account of case law, and we do not wish to merely repeat what they have done, particularly since they have done it very well. Nevertheless, we do of course cover the major cases. Again, the further reading suggested at the end of each chapter will direct readers who wish to look at more case law to sources where this is provided for.

Indeed, it is crucial that students in particular realise that this book – as with *all* textbooks – is not seen as the beginning and end of what must be read. Textbooks are merely a jumping-off point, and their function is usually to give the reader a basic knowledge of the area so that when they read more specific, challenging material later they have a broad knowledge base that helps them to understand it. In other words, it is merely the base camp at the bottom of the mountain that lays the foundation that will make possible the climb to the top. That is certainly the way in which we have designed this book, and how we envision it being used. We hope that readers will leave with an appreciation of the general legal rules, and some of the legal controversies, and also with an appreciation of the ethical difficulties and debates that surround those rules. For those who wish to seek out more detail, the suggested further reading will cater for that. Above all, however, we hope that readers will share our fascination with medical law and ethics, and that the book helps them to appreciate the controversies and inspires them to delve deeper.

ACKNOWLEDGMENTS

Books are hard to write. Quite apart from the fact that they take a lot of time to write, they also place a strain on friends and family members who have to watch us work at weekends, listen to our moaning about the process and, in some cases, read and provide comments on chapters. We would first like to thank our wives, Nina and Tania, for their support. They bore the brunt of the moaning, and even had to put up with us visiting each other to work in the same room rather than in different countries. They kept us sane, as did our family and friends. We could not have done it without them.

Cambridge University Press has been nothing but understanding and helpful throughout, and we would particularly like to thank Sinead Moloney, who really helped to make this project run in the first place. We remain very grateful for her professionalism and understanding, and for being a friendly contact point for us.

Some people have read chapters, made comments or have been available for debate. These friends and colleagues have helped greatly. We would therefore like to thank Katharina Beier, Tracey Elliott, Sara Fovargue, Simon Lohse, Thomas Reydon and Stephen Smith. We are particularly grateful to Jasjote Grewal for selfless, last minute assistance with the manuscript.

All errors, of course, remain our own.

Hannover and Leicester

TABLE OF CASES

TABLE OF LEGISLATION

ABBREVIATIONS

AG Attorney General
AHA Area Health Authority
ANH artificial nutrition and hydration
ART assisted reproductive technology
BMA British Medical Association
BMC Medical Ethics *Biomedcentral Medical Ethics*
BMC Medicine *Biomedcentral Medicine*
BMJ *British Medical Journal*
BPAS British Pregnancy Advisory Service
CPS Crown Prosecution Service
DCA Department for Constitutional Affairs
DNAR do not attempt resuscitation
DoH Department of Health
DPP Director of Public Prosecutions
ECHR European Convention on Human Rights
ECT Electro Convulsive Therapy
ECtHR European Court of Human Rights
EMA European Medicines Agency
EU European Union
GCP good clinical practice
GMC General Medical Council
GMP good manufacturing practice
GP general practitioner
HA Health Authority
hESC human embryonic stem cell
HFEA Human Fertilisation and Embryology Act
HSR health service research
HTA Human Tissue Authority
HTA 2004 Human Tissue Act 2004
ICSI intracytoplasmic sperm injection

ICU	intensive care unit
ILPA	Infant Life (Preservation) Act 1929
IMP	investigational medicinal product
IRB	institutional review board
IUI	intrauterine insemination
IVF	in vitro fertilisation
LPA	lasting powers of attorney
MCA	Mental Capacity Act 2005
MCS	minimally conscious state
Med. L. Rev.	*Medical Law Review*
MHRA	Medicines and Healthcare Products Regulatory Agency
MLR	*Modern Law Review*
MMR	Measles, Mumps, Rubella
NHS	National Health Service
NICE	National Institute for Health and Clinical Excellence
OAPA	Offences Against the Person Act 1861
OJ	Official Journal (of the European Union)
PGD	pre-implantation genetic diagnostics
PVS	persistent vegetative state
QALYs	Quality Adjusted Life Years
RCN	Royal College of Nursing
RCOG	Royal College of Obstetricians and Gynaecologists
REC	research ethics committee
RHA	Regional Health Authority
RLF	retrolental fibroplasia
SOP	standard operating procedure
STD	Sexually transmitted disease
vCJD	variant Creutzfeldt-Jacob disease
WMA	World Medical Association

1 Introduction

The approach that we take in this book is one that considers medical law and ethics. The book seeks to make clear distinctions when speaking of 'law', 'morals' and 'ethics', but what do we mean when we use these terms? It seems self-evident that these words do not mean the same things and it is vital to be certain of their meaning before embarking on working with medico-legal and medical ethics literature (and with this book for that matter). We will outline our use of these terms in the context of this book in this chapter in a way which, hopefully, will give the reader an appreciation of the delineation and overlap of these concepts. We do, of course, realise that these terms, and their exact relationship, are the subject of much debate. At the end of this chapter – as with all chapters – we have provided references for further reading that will illuminate the scope of that debate and allow the reader to delve deeper if he or she wishes to do so. For the purposes of this textbook, however, it is prudent to identify and define how *we* use these terms so that our discussion of their relationship can make sense to the reader.

On a very fundamental level, by 'law' we mean a framework of rules developed, codified and enforced by society in some way. 'Morals' refers to a more diffuse set of shared values and norms which inform our ability to decide between what is right and wrong in certain contexts. These values and norms might be cultural or religious. 'Ethics' is a systematic method for reflecting, arguing and justifying what a wrong or a right decision might be. In this book, we are concerned with medical ethics, which is a subset of applied ethics, and which follows slightly different rules from, for example, conventional moral philosophy. By and large, medical ethics looks at distinct case constellations from biomedical practice and seeks to make a normative statement about how one should behave in such cases. We are not suggesting that these three concepts of law, morals and ethics are the same types of categories. The law often enshrines moral notions (respect for the autonomy of a patient by way of requiring consent, for example), but not all laws are necessarily based on a moral notion. Ethics systematically uses moral notions to develop an argument for or against a certain course of action, so ethics would not function without morals. Morals, on the other hand, are initially independent of law and ethics.

While it seems clear that there is a conceptual hierarchy at work here, the three terms we refer to do have something in common: they create a web of duties, obligations, rights and recommendations. A legal duty, for example, is clearly one that is prescribed by law – in some way, shape or form. This might mean a statutory duty, or one that is established through precedent or by way of guidelines that have been given binding character (by a legislator, a court or in some cases even a professional body). A moral obligation is one that an individual is thought to have towards others in a society,[1] based on shared sets of values, but which does not, necessarily, amount to a legal duty. In the area of medicine, we regularly touch upon issues that raise both types of obligations – a legal obligation as well as a moral obligation. This is why law and ethics (as the arbiter of morals) in medicine interact to a much greater extent than you might see in other areas of law – this is particularly visible when you try to get an appreciation of the formidable spectrum of different types of regulation you find in this specialised area: from primary law all the way down to standard operating procedures (SOPs) in laboratories and operating theatres. All of these instruments form part of the body of *regulation* that is medical law and medical ethics.

Most of the time, the foremost question that we are dealing with in this book is how an individual (for example a doctor) is supposed to act in certain (mostly very difficult, or life-and-death) circumstances. Consider the following case:

Patient X is diagnosed as HIV positive by his GP. During the course of the post-diagnostic discussion, it becomes obvious that X intends to keep this diagnosis secret and will continue to have unprotected sex with his partner, who is currently not HIV positive.

Cases such as this one raise issues that can be looked at through the lens of law and that of morals. There may be a legal duty for the GP to act in such circumstances (for example, to prevent harm to X's partner) in the same way as there might be a legal duty for the GP not to act (for example, to protect X's privacy and to maintain confidentiality). At the same time, there might be a moral duty for the GP to act (in order to prevent harm to one or more others) or not to act (in order to respect X's autonomous decision-making, even if it seems poorly justified) in such circumstances. It is clear that it is not the law's job to enshrine all moral obligations we might care to think of – the law will merely try to encompass those moral obligations that are considered most weighty, although this assessment can clearly be contentious. A legal duty does not always correspond to a moral duty, and vice versa. In

---

[1] Contemplate how moral aspects might actually come into play in a fictitious situation where there is only one person and no others. Might we need more than one person in order to give rise to moral contemplations, or is there such a thing as being moral towards yourself?

fact, sometimes the moral and the legal duties conflict – for example where a doctor knows that an individual does not wish to be resuscitated, but the lack of appropriate documentation compels her to do just that in order to avoid liability. Law and morals, therefore, are not the same thing, but – to some extent – they overlap.

The next question is how law and ethics interact. Georg Jellinek, an important German legal positivist from the early twentieth century,[2] very eloquently defined the scope of the law as the 'ethical minimum', and even if we do not agree with all of his views, Jellinek's way of describing the relationship between law and ethics is compelling:

> Law is nothing other than the *ethical minimum*. Objectively speaking, these are the maintaining conditions of society, to the extent that they are dependent on man's free will, i.e. the existential minimum of ethical norms. Subjectively speaking, it is the minimum of equitable activity and disposition demanded from members of this society.[3]

So it is clear that, in the sense that Jellinek is using the term, the scope of ethics goes over and beyond the law. The law merely covers the minimum that is required to 'keep going' in terms of societal cohesion. We have discussed law and morals, but what is meant here when the term 'ethics' is used? 'Ethics' is the reflective process that asks the question of what a moral norm really intends to achieve, what is 'right' and what is 'wrong' in certain circumstances. While both the law and morals, therefore, are frameworks of norms of differing binding quality and pedigree, 'ethics' can be the process which is used to reflect what course of action is appropriate in terms of moral obligations (much in the same way as we use certain methods to work out how to apply abstract law in individual circumstances). This means that the tools of medical ethics help us go over and beyond the interpretation of mere legal or technical norms in order to try and work out 'how to get it right'. After this first look at our three terms, we will now look at these three concepts – 'law', 'morals' and 'ethics' – in more detail to see how we use them in this book.

The special quality of human interaction in the field of biomedicine means that the scope of medical law already covers far more than mere matters of technical medical skill. Indeed, one of the peculiarities of the subject, which grew out of something of a tort and criminal law hybrid, is the fact that areas of ethical controversy (i.e. 'how to get a morally difficult decision-making process right') are ubiquitous. Abortion, euthanasia, the sterilisation of adults with serious mental disabilities: all of these are topics where moral questions are intrinsic and feelings

---

[2] Legal positivism is a school of thought that, by and large, propagates the idea that whatever is stipulated as law by a recognised source of law at any given time ought to be followed – even where moral norms, or natural law, suggest that this law might be unjust. Legal positivists, such as H. L. A. Hart, have suggested that some of the crimes perpetrated during the Nazi regime in Germany were legally (not morally) justifiable as long as they were in accordance with the law at the time. Law is therefore seen as a purely social construction by positivists.

[3] G. Jellinek, *Die sozialethische Bedeutung von Recht, Unrecht und Strafe* [The socio-ethical significance of justice, injustice and punishment], 2nd edn (Berlin: O. Häring, 1908), p. 45. (emphasis in original, our translation).

run deep. Even the fundamentals of medical law in the shape of capacity, consent and confidentiality are based on significant moral issues, so it is no surprise that medical law cannot avoid ethical discussion – and in some cases (such as in *Re. W*, which we also discuss later in this chapter), we can see that deliberate moral wriggle room is left by the law to acknowledge the difficult ethical dimension of legal decision-making in medicine. In this book, we recognise this fact by giving full consideration to both the legal and ethical issues behind each topic that we consider.

LAW AND LEGAL DECISION-MAKING

We begin by looking at how the law is shaping up in the areas that we cover. When a decision is legal in nature, this means that certain behaviour by a medical practitioner is either demanded or prohibited by the law. For example, a doctor who has begun an operation will be under a legal duty to complete it (in the absence of, for example, finding a replacement to do so); equally, doctors owe their patients a duty of confidence and may not in normal circumstances disclose information to others about them. These are rules that are prescribed by the law, and they are obligatory. A failure to follow them will result in civil or criminal sanctions being imposed on the transgressor independent of any professional sanction or authorisation of the act. This gives legal stipulations a certain – 'hard' – quality.

What we shall see is that in most cases where the law takes control and classifies the decision as legal in nature, it does so to protect patient autonomy (which is a moral concept underpinning much of the corresponding medical ethics discussion, as we shall see). Indeed, a fundamental aspect of this category is that the law identifies and protects what it sees as a fundamental right, almost always pertaining to the patient.

A good example of this is the case of *Ms B*.[4] The case concerned a paralysed woman who could not live without artificial ventilation. She made a decision that she no longer wished to live, and thus asked for the ventilator to be disconnected so that she could die. The doctors treating her refused to do so, despite the fact that she was legally able to make her own decisions. This, they said, was because they viewed their purpose as being to maintain rather than end life, and therefore that to disconnect the ventilator would be unethical. The court disagreed, and said that Ms B had a fundamental right to self-determination that must trump the doctors' views. It therefore ordered that the ventilator be disconnected in accordance with Ms B's wishes, thus bringing the force of the law to support her rights.

---

[4] *Ms B* v. *An NHS Hospital Trust* [2002] EWHC 429.

MORALS, DECISION-MAKING AND COMMONLY HELD VIEWS

'Moral' concepts initially seem far easier to define in the context of clinical decision-making. A decision might be classed as moral if it may be decided by the conscience of the individual medical practitioner. This is effectively the opposite of a legal decision, in that the normative weight of the decision-making process rests not at a macro level (i.e. legislation), or at the professional level (i.e. conduct mandated by a professional body with a sanction for non-compliance), but instead at a micro-level (i.e. with individual decision-makers, such as a doctor). This also means that there is usually no sanction in the same way that a legally relevant decision or activity might trigger a sanction, which in turn results in a situation where the ultimate choice often belongs to the medical practitioner, rather than the patient. Often, moral decisions pertain to controversial individual issues and the categorisation allows the doctor to opt out of involvement in a given practice. Notably, this is normally only possible where the patient will not be harmed by the doctor's choice. A classic example of this is the conscience clause in the Abortion Act 1967, which allows medical practitioners to choose not to participate in abortions if they have a conscientious objection to it.[5] This therefore prioritises the doctor's conscience over the patient's desire for the procedure. In much the same way, a medical practitioner (be this a doctor or other care staff) cannot be compelled to end life-supporting treatment for an individual, even where this is the clear wish of the individual. The limit of that individual's ability to give effect to her autonomy therefore lies somewhere where the autonomy of others is touched upon. This is a point worth remembering when looking at how different protagonists' interests are assessed by the law throughout this book.

The notable deviation from this concept of an exception based upon the doctor's conscience is that it does not apply where the life of the patient is at risk, or where not to perform the termination may lead to serious, permanent harm to the patient. Rather, in such emergency situations the welfare of the patient must come before the moral views of the doctor. The framework which underpins these types of decisions is one of shared sets of values and principles, at societal level ('first, do no harm'), at community level ('always help those who present at A&E') or at individual level ('always counsel against an abortion'). This framework might come from religious values, from traditional convention or from other strongly held beliefs – the distinguishing factor is that they are not prescribed by society in a 'hard' way, but expected or desired in a 'soft' way and left up to the individual to make her mind up about them. The process for making up the mind in such circumstances, then, is that of 'medical ethics' as used in this book.

---

[5] Abortion Act 1967 s. 4.

MEDICAL ETHICS, GUIDANCE AND DISCOURSE

'(Medical) ethics' can operate in more than one way. We outline two ways here, but do not make representations that these are the only (or even the most significant) ways. The unifying characteristic for both of these is the fact that 'ethics' means that a moral decision-making process is left to an individual, on the basis of guidance and shared values. The first of these ways in which ethics operates is regulatory in nature. The medical profession is a self-regulating one, and under the Medical Act 1983 the regulator is the General Medical Council (GMC). In order to be able to practise medicine, a doctor must be registered with the GMC, and this registration may be suspended or even permanently deleted from the register (hence doctors being referred to as having been 'struck off') in the event of misconduct. This misconduct can include both technical and ethical deficiencies in performance. Indeed, under section 35 of the Act, the GMC also has the power to give ethical advice to the profession. It provides that:

The powers of the General Council shall include the power to provide, in such manner as the Council think fit, advice for members of the medical profession on –
(a) standards of professional conduct;
(b) standards of professional performance; or
(c) medical ethics.

Thus, the GMC publishes documents relating to a range of issues, from consent to doctors' use of social media, which are available to all on its website.[6] As might be expected from guidance issued by a regulator, it is prescriptive. To give an example, at the beginning of the guidance on consent, readers are advised of the following:

In this guidance the terms 'you must' and 'you should' are used in the following ways:
    'you must' is used for an overriding duty or principle
    'you should' is used when we are providing an explanation of how you will meet the overriding duty
    'you should' is also used where the duty or principle will not apply in all situations or circumstances, or where there are factors outside your control that affect whether or how you can comply with the guidance.[7]

The sanctions for failure to comply are also clearly set out, as doctors are warned that '[s]erious or persistent failure to follow this guidance will put your registration at risk. You must, therefore, be prepared to explain and justify your actions.'[8]

---

[6] www.gmc-uk.org/guidance/index.asp.
[7] GMC, 'Consent: Patients and Doctors Making Decisions Together' (GMC, 2008), www.gmc-uk.org/Consent___English_0513.pdf_48903482.pdf.
[8] GMC, 'Consent'.

The ability to explain and justify actions, in the light of guidance that (a) is outside the spectrum of what 'law' encompasses, (b) is within what we consider to be 'moral' (such as issues of consent) and (c) has regulatory character is what we consider much of medical ethics to be about. It is also evident that the translational process of moral and ethical norms into delegated regulation changes the 'hardness' of the norm: from a relatively soft and broad moral sentiment to a codified and enshrined professional norm, armed with sanctions.

Therefore, the GMC guidance must be seen as having a regulatory function in a similar way to the law in that it provides standards that must be met and penalties for non-compliance. In this sense, the GMC's guidance is unique as it is the only body that has control over the medical register and therefore the only one that can discipline doctors and ultimately decides who can legitimately practise. Nevertheless, doctors are also provided with a plethora of advice on ethical matters from other medical bodies. Most notably the British Medical Association (BMA) – the doctors' trade union – and the Royal Colleges publish books, booklets and pamphlets on all of the issues covered by the GMC. In the case of the BMA, this is even more voluminous in nature. It is worth repeating that these professional bodies have influence over who may, and may not, practise this particular profession. A prohibition from this self-regulated body of professionals amounts to an occupational ban, which is a very strong (indeed, 'hard') sanction.

Given the prestigious nature of the organisations which provide this documentation, it is no surprise that this is also taken very seriously by the medical profession. It is also taken seriously by the law, and indeed there have not only been cases where such guidance has been cited by the courts, but also others where it has been used by judges as evidence of what the legal standard may be.[9] This is even the case when deciding such an intrinsically ethical matter as whether a medical practitioner should be allowed to remove life support from a patient in a coma despite the objection of the patient's relatives.[10] At other times, the courts will assume that regulatory medical ethics is an effective policeman of medical conduct. A good illustration of this is the case of *Re. W*.[11] The issue was the refusal of medical treatment by minors. Lord Donaldson MR had, in an earlier case, held that where a mature minor refuses consent to medical treatment, the doctor could still proceed legally where there was consent by one or both parents.[12] The decision was criticised by academics and others as potentially allowing for serious and contentious treatments to be allowed by law to be forced on older minors. His Lordship

---

[9] See, e.g., *Airedale NHS Trust* v. *Bland* [1993] 1 All ER 821; [1993] AC 789; and *Re. G (Persistent Vegetative State)* [1995] 2 FCR 46.
[10] This was the issue in the case of *Re. G*.
[11] *Re. W (A Minor) (Medical Treatment: Court's Jurisdiction)* [1992] 4 All ER 627.
[12] *Re. R (A Minor) (Wardship: Medical Treatment)* [1992] Fam 11; [1991] 4 All ER 177.

met this criticism directly in *Re. W*, and noted that he was happy to leave a legal lacuna due to his faith in medical ethics as a regulatory tool:

> Hair-raising possibilities were canvassed of abortions being carried out by doctors in reliance upon the consent of the parents and despite the refusal of consent by 16 or 17 year olds. *Whilst this may be possible as a matter of law, I do not see any likelihood, taking account of medical ethics [that it should be allowed to occur].*[13]

However, professional bodies are not the only source of medical ethics discourse. The second way in which ethical discourse works and influences the law is as a result of the overwhelming variety of opinion and debate contributed by philosophers, lawyers, sociologists and others – including, of course, this book – which seeks not to *regulate*, but rather to *discuss*. In short, these contributions do not claim to provide 'answers' and are thus more discursive than they are normative in nature.[14] Sometimes referred to as 'critical' or 'philosophical' medical ethics, this discourse has also been referred to by the courts, but has one obvious flaw: if it does not seek to provide answers, then it can only be used to guide rather than regulate, as it has no way of choosing between competing answers to questions. As Ranaan Gillon asked rhetorically,

> if Dr A's conscience tells him to transfuse a Jehovah's Witness regardless of her own views and Dr B's conscience tells him not to transfuse such a patient, where stands medical ethics? Which position is right and why? Are both right? Why? Is no resolution or even attempt at resolution possible or desirable?[15]

While this is in line with our principal understanding of the meaning of 'ethics' (i.e. it being the skillset required to adequately reflect competing moral theories in difficult individual circumstances), it is sometimes of little assistance when applied in a context where a normative statement is required. Therefore, this type of discursive ethics is most likely to be used by judges to justify decisions that they have already come to – most notably if there is no settled law in the area or the judges wish to reshape the existing legal rules. This is not uncommon, and occurs on several occasions in cases referred to in this book.[16] In *Chester* v. *Afshar*, for example, the House of Lords wished to change the law so as to prioritise patient autonomy (and thus make the decision 'legal' in nature). It justified this, in part, by quoting the following piece of work by the legal philosopher Ronald Dworkin to demonstrate the principle that it wished to uphold:

---

[13] *Re. W*, at 635. Our emphasis.
[14] Of course, as these discursive dealings with medical ethics usually end up suggesting that one course of action might be more justifiable than another, there is also a weak normative element to them.
[15] R. Gillon, *Philosophical Medical Ethics* (Chichester: John Wiley & Sons, 1986), p. 31.
[16] See, for the former, *Chester* v. *Afshar* [2004] UKHL 41; [2005] 1 AC 134; and, for the latter, *Airedale NHS Trust* v. *Bland* [1993] 1 All ER 821.

The most plausible [account] emphasizes the integrity rather than the welfare of the choosing agent; the value of autonomy, on this view, derives from the capacity it protects: the capacity to express one's own character – values, commitments, convictions, and critical as well as experiential interests – in the life one leads. Recognizing an individual right of autonomy makes self-creation possible. It allows each of us to be responsible for shaping our lives according to our own coherent or incoherent-but, in any case, distinctive-personality. It allows us to lead our own lives rather than be led along them, so that each of us can be, to the extent a scheme of rights can make this possible, what we have made of ourselves. We allow someone to choose death over radical amputation or a blood transfusion, if that is his informed wish, because we acknowledge his right to a life structured by his own values.[17]

However, we must also be careful to ensure that we distinguish between a decision that is ethical in nature and one that is best left to medical ethics. In particular, it is important to remember that the latter does not automatically follow from the former. Thus, a decision regarding whether abortion should be legal – which is one that is almost universally considered to be ethical in nature – is not necessarily one that should be decided by the medical profession. Indeed, we would argue the opposite, which is that decisions that are ethical in nature provide the law with more rather than less legitimacy to make itself the final arbiter. This is because by their very nature ethical decisions are not matters of technical medical skill, and therefore doctors are not uniquely competent to make these decisions. In fact, it might be argued that the law rather than the medical profession is the proper forum for the resolution of ethical issues and conflicts. Certainly, the pattern of medical law in the recent past has been one of movement towards greater judicial activism, as we detail below, but medical ethics in both its regulatory and discursive forms still remains of great significance both inside and outside of the courtroom.

When we consider medical ethics in this book, we refer to the second type of ethics described here. In other words, we discuss the theoretical elements rather than what the guidelines have to say. Morals have a much greater role to play, and we seek to examine what principles are at play rather than what conduct the profession demands.

THE LAW'S ROLE IN DECISION-MAKING

It is undeniable that the law has adopted a more interventionist stance over the past fifteen years. The old *Bolam* test from 1957, which we discuss in detail in Chapter 3 on errors and fault, used to provide that as long as the defendant doctor could provide some expert witnesses willing to testify that they might have acted in the same way as

---

[17] R. Dworkin, *Life's Dominion: An Argument about Abortion, Euthanasia, and Individual Freedom* (New York: Vintage Books, 1993), cited in *Chester* v. *Afshar* at para. 18, *per* Lord Steyn.

she did, then it was not then open to the judge to find their conduct to fall below the legally required standard of care.[18] In such circumstances, the law would refuse to intervene to censure the doctor's conduct. It takes little imagination to see how this represented an almost insurmountable hurdle for plaintiffs to leap over. Almost unbelievably, this interpretation of doctors' legal duties was applied by judges until 1997. Even since then, courts are only to be allowed to find doctors liable if the expert evidence on their behalf was unable to withstand logical analysis – which makes it possible but still very hard for plaintiffs to succeed.[19] Even more worryingly, *Bolam*, which was principally intended to relate to medical negligence (which most often *does* involve the application of technical medical skill), grew to be almost ubiquitous in medical law. Thus, questions surrounding, for example, whether to remove life-sustaining treatment from patients in a persistent vegetative state and whether to sterilise adults with learning disabilities came to be governed by what was known as the *Bolam* test. In other words, *Bolam* also crept into the resolution of ethical matters – thus failing to distinguish between ethical issues and issues that should be governed by medical ethics. This was seen by many, such as Sheila McLean, as an abrogation of responsibility on the part of the law:

No matter the quality of medicine practised, and no matter the doubts of doctors themselves about the appropriateness of their involvement, human life is increasingly medicalised. In part, this is the result of the growing professionalism of medicine, in part our responsibility for asking too much of doctors. In part, however, it is also because the buffer which might be expected to stand between medicalisation and human rights – namely the law – has proved unwilling, unable or inefficient when asked to adjudicate on or control issues which are at best tangentially medical.[20]

While *Bolam* has been reined back in and its reach outside of negligence may be seen as contracting (through, for example, the Mental Capacity Act 2005 as we discuss in Chapter 5), its influence remains and medical law retains many instances of decisions effectively being made by doctors through medical ethics rather than the law.

THEORIES OF ETHICS

While we have, in this book, put the focus of our ethical discussion on the pertinent issues identified in the corresponding legal discussion, a number of recurring themes will become apparent. These themes can, by and large, be

---

[18] *Bolam* v. *Friern Hospital Management Committee* [1957] 1 WLR 582. While it is unlikely that this is the way in which the judge in *Bolam* intended his judgment to be interpreted, this is how it was applied by future courts. See M. Brazier and J. Miola, 'Bye-Bye Bolam: A Medical Litigation Revolution?' (2000) 8(1) *Med. L. Rev.* 85–114.

[19] See *Bolitho (Deceased)* v. *City and Hackney HA* [1998] AC 232.

[20] S. MacLean, *Old Law, New Medicine: Medical Ethics and Human Rights* (London: Pandora Press, 1999), p. 2.

attributed to a small cluster of theories which are usually discussed when attempting to categorise schools of thought. We will briefly introduce these terms and their basic meaning here and refer back to them in more detail when we encounter them in each chapter. In essence, the question of whether doing something is 'right' can be separated into considerations in relation to the action itself and of the type of person we should strive to be. In the former category, we find consequentialist ethical theories (often oversimplified as 'utilitarian' theories) and deontological theories. In the latter category, we are concerned with what makes a good person, because what that person would do would in any situation be the right thing to do. This is often referred to as 'virtue ethics'. We will look at consequentialist theories (which are particularly relevant when looking at legal decision-making) and deontological theories, and very briefly at virtue ethics. Before we do this, it is worth highlighting a particularly important set of principles which are deployed regularly in medical ethics and which we cannot do without in this book.

The four principles

The four principles are described by Tom Beauchamp and James Childress in their book *Principles of Biomedical Ethics*.[21] They have proved to be one significant yardstick by which the discipline of medical ethics measures difficult issues. The four principles are: (1) Respect for autonomy; (2) Beneficence; (3) Non-maleficence; and (4) Justice.

> *Respect for autonomy* – this principle encompasses the notion of respect for the ability of autonomous individuals to make decisions on their own behalf. It includes the concept of enabling individuals to deploy their autonomy and it significantly overlaps with the legal notion of autonomy.
> *Beneficence* – means essentially that the doctor needs to carefully balance risks and benefits to ensure that whatever he or she does is benefiting the patient.
> *Non-maleficence* – the doctor must not cause harm to the patient. Again, this is a point where the doctor needs to balance risks and benefits (as most medical interventions cause some type of harm). The harm must not be, however, disproportionate.
> *Justice* – includes a notion of fairness and equality. Those in equal need should be treated equally. Benefits should be distributed fairly across patient populations.

We will encounter the first principle (respect for autonomy) in every chapter. Beneficence is a principle often encountered where there is a difficult decision in relation to whether or not to treat a patient (think 'withdrawal of treatment').

---

[21] T. Beauchamp and J. Childress, *Principles of Biomedical Ethics*, 5th edn (New York: Oxford University Press, 2001).

Non-maleficence appears, for example, when we speak of research using healthy volunteers. Justice, again, does appear in many of the chapters in this book, but none more than when we discuss resource allocation (in Chapter 6). The important point to remember is that these principles, in varying constellations, play a role in pretty much every area of medical law – the reasons for this are obvious: questions of consent (i.e. autonomy) are paramount throughout medical law; principles of beneficence and non-maleficence go to the core of the self-perception of doctors and other health care staff (these are the types of characteristics doctors ought to have, in order to be fit for purpose); and justice is a theme which in the dealings between individuals, particularly between individuals of differing bargaining powers, is fundamental in prioritising interests. The interesting questions arise where, in our discussions in the subsequent chapters, these principles are potentially in conflict with one another – where beneficence may involve ostensibly harming a patient, or where consent is overruled in order to be just.

Consequentialism

Consequentialists are concerned with the consequence of a certain act, not – initially – with the act itself. It is a broad label that tries to detach itself from the sometimes unsavoury connotations that other, historically more established, terminology might evoke. One of these terms is 'utilitarianism'. Utilitarianism is a school of thought which is concerned with the 'utility' of a certain action (hence the name). This means that the primary concern of those subscribing to this theory is whether what they are doing is particularly efficient in achieving a certain outcome – for example, whether a certain activity produces more or less 'happiness' than another activity. Following this idea, the appropriate thing to do is therefore the thing which produces the most 'happiness'. What can be understood to be meant by the label 'happiness' is a question under contention even among utilitarians. Hedonistic utilitarianism, for example (such as that essentially postulated by Jeremy Bentham), is concerned with maximising pleasure (even if called 'happiness') and minimising pain. Some utilitarians will argue that the thing which we seek to maximise needs to be more carefully defined and should hinge on preferences and desires. Finnis argues that a revised version of utilitarianism, cleansed of the potential for seeking to give effect to all desires (including spurious ones), would concern itself with rational choices, rather than mere desires.[22]

---

[22] J. Finnis, *Fundamentals of Ethics* (Washington, DC: Georgetown University Press, 1983), pp. 81–2.

He also discusses the subset of 'proportionalism' which, in the context of legal philosophy, rightly takes an elevated position. Finnis cites Thomas Aquinas and illustrates the 'principle of proportionality', using the example of the difference between murder and self-defence:

'An act done with a good intention', says Aquinas, 'can be rendered morally bad by being disproportionate to its end. [And so if someone, in order to defend his own life, uses more violence than is necessary [. . .], his act is immoral.]'[23]

This is eminently interesting in the setting of medical law, as Aquinas is generally thought to have first introduced the principle of 'double effect' to which we return in Chapter 11 when we discuss euthanasia. Consequentialism, whether you encounter it in its incarnation as plain utilitarianism, continental teleology or proportionalism, plays an important role in legal decision-making. The reasons for this are no doubt manifold, but one very compelling point is that the aims of the law (assess conduct to arrive at an outcome which either maximises societal benefit or minimises societal disruption) is clearly extremely close to the methodology favoured by consequentialists.

Deontology

The classic continental distinction in ethics was that of teleological ('telos' being the Greek word for 'aim' or 'outcome') and deontological ethics ('deon' is the Greek word for 'duty'). The former aligns roughly with our discussion of consequentialism above, the latter is concerned not with the outcome, but with how the activity that leads to the outcome is conducted. In other words, the end does not necessarily suffice to justify the means: there are, according to this, rational duties and principles which guide behaviour. The 'goodness' of the behaviour therefore lies in the path taken rather than the destination sought. In contrast, in consequentialism there is generally little concern about how we achieve a desirable goal. An important proponent of deontological ethics was Immanuel Kant (whom we will encounter when we discuss organ and tissue transplantation). He postulated, for example, that human beings are always ends in themselves, never merely means to an end (see our discussion in Chapter 9).

Virtue ethics

Virtue ethics is not so much concerned with the outcome of our activities, nor with the duties we might encounter when making choices when acting. It is instead focussed on what our acts mean in relation to our status as moral

---

[23] Thomas Aquinas, *Summa Theologica II-II*, q. 64, a. 7c. quoted in Finnis, *Fundamentals of Ethics*, p. 85.

individuals. This means that virtue ethics resides in a category of its own and is not really in conflict with other theories of ethics. The outcome of ethical deliberation might be identical, but in the case of virtue ethics there is an assumption that one's personal (virtuous) characteristics make the choice for the right approach more straightforward. The main point to bear in mind here is that, while other ethical theories are concerned with actions and their moral meaning, in virtue ethics we are concerned with individuals and how they *are*, morally. Virtue ethics is a fundamental component of how the development of self-perception of medical professionals can be assessed, as it judges an individual on her character rather than on her acts. In an ideal world, the physician acts to help, out of a deep-seated desire to do good and to assist. Some commentators argue, therefore, that virtue ethics is particularly suitable to resolve moral dilemmas in this area, as this might be the only way to encompass the necessary components of emotions and motivations in the biomedical context.[24]

All of these theories, and others, have an important role to play when trying to assess the moral status of a decision. In many cases, particularly the very difficult ones, it is very much worth trying to see through the lenses of all of them to get the best possible picture. At the same time, this book will make it reasonably clear that the majority of moral questions that are encountered in the biomedical context are approached by way of consequentialist approaches and the four principles. The overlap of these notions and principles with legal notions and principles is immense (think of 'justice' and 'proportionalism' in a legal and an ethical sense). What we can therefore see is that there is no consistent structural mechanism used by the law to distinguish between issues that are appropriately legal, those that are appropriately ethical and those that are appropriately moral. The – in our view necessary and overdue – conversation to settle this has yet to be had. It is therefore critical that anyone with an interest in medical law is aware of both the legal obligations *and* the ethical arguments inherent in the topics that we cover. Quite apart from the fact that such knowledge of the ethics will help to provide a more rounded picture of what should most appropriately be done, in many instances the law still leaves decisions at the discretion of medical practitioners and their very personal ethics. So, for doctors (and medical students) reading this book, the discussions of the ethical components are of more than simply academic value. For lawyers, law students and other non-doctors, they also not only provide a juxtaposition to the law, but also raise questions regarding the appropriateness of the law's claims to control or delegation of responsibility to ethics or morals, as the case may be.

---

[24] P. Gardiner, 'A Virtue Ethics Approach to Moral Dilemmas in Medicine' (2003) 29(5) *Journal of Medical Ethics*, 297–302.

ADDITIONAL READING

Law

R. Dworkin, *Life's Dominion: An Argument about Abortion, Euthanasia, and Individual Freedom* (New York: Vintage Books, 1993)

S. MacLean, *Old Law, New Medicine: Medical Ethics and Human Rights* (London: Pandora Press, 1999)

J. Miola, *Medical Ethics and Medical Law: A Symbiotic Relationship* (Oxford: Hart, 2007)

K. Veitch, *The Jurisdiction of Medical Law* (Aldershot: Ashgate, 2007)

Ethics

T. Beauchamp and J. Childress, *Principles of Biomedical Ethics*, 7th edn (New York: Oxford University Press, 2012)

J. Finnis, *Fundamentals of Ethics* (Washington, DC: Georgetown University Press, 1983)

L. Francis, A. Silvers and R. Rhodes (eds.), *The Blackwell Guide to Medical Ethics* (Hoboken: Wiley-Blackwell, 2008)

T. Hope, *Medical Ethics: A Very Short Introduction* (Oxford University Press, 2004)

H. Kuhse and P. Singer (eds.), *Bioethics: An Anthology* (Hoboken: Blackwell, 2006)

2 Confidentiality and access to information

When one thinks of different types of information, there is a clear intuition to feel that medical information touches upon a personal sense of privacy in a way that makes it inherently private and confidential. As we will see from the approach of the courts which we discuss in this chapter, there is no question that medical information is deemed confidential, and this is true both in legal and ethical terms. Historically, in medical ethics the confidential nature of medical information (and the duties on doctors that this imposes) has been asserted from the Hippocratic Oath to the World Medical Association's Declaration of Geneva to the General Medical Council's guidelines in the United Kingdom. Indeed, the GMC considered the doctor's duty of confidence so important that at one point in the 1990s it was one of only four issues specifically covered in its 'Duties of a Doctor' guidance.[1] In legal terms, the confidential status of medical information has been repeatedly asserted by the courts, to the extent that it was held to be 'well recognised as confidential' by the House of Lords in the case of *Campbell* v. *Mirror Group Newspapers.*[2] Obviously, this means that there is a prima facie duty imposed on the doctor not to disclose information inappropriately.

However, this duty is subject to various caveats and definitions that we explore in this chapter. First, we must remember that while we all live as individuals, we do so within a society, and so there may be circumstances in which a patient's medical information gives rise to concerns about public safety, or the safety of individual

---

[1] The 1995 version of 'Duties of a Doctor' was a folder containing four documents: GMC, *Good Medical Practice* (GMC, 1995) – updated in 1998; GMC, *Advertising* (GMC, 1995) – replaced in 1997; GMC, *HIV and AIDS: The Ethical Considerations* (GMC, 1995) – replaced in 1997; and GMC, *Confidentiality* (GMC, 1995) – replaced in 2000. These documents, and a full archive of the GMC's guidance from the past and present, can be found at: www.gmc-uk.org/guidance/archive.asp.

[2] [2004] 2 All ER 995 at 1018.

third parties, which may require the interests of society and others to be given priority over those of the patient. The most obvious example is that of contagious disease or a psychiatric patient who poses a danger to the public (or, for that matter, a specific individual). Secondly, there is an argument that we owe a duty – given the benefit that we gain from the NHS – to allow our information to be used to help ameliorate treatments and techniques for others. Indeed, information regarding outcomes may be used to compile data sets that can be used to develop evidence-based approaches to help the NHS act efficiently. Finally, and on a related note, if there are legal rules and ethical guidelines which control the disclosure of 'medical information', then it is first important to define what 'medical information' is, as it may be possible to achieve the aims of society (particularly relating to research) without compromising the dignity or integrity of the patient, such as by releasing information in an anonymous fashion – and it might be argued that this removes the confidential nature of the information.

Essentially, there are three ways in which the law will allow for the disclosure of medical information about a patient by a doctor to a third party. The first is uncontroversial, and is where the patient consents to the disclosure. Needless to say, the disclosure is only justified insofar as it keeps to the boundaries provided by that consent (this is a fundamental legal tenet of processing personal data – see the discussion of data protection law in this chapter). The second and third exceptions require a little further analysis, and are considered below: they are that disclosure may be justified where it is in the public interest (through both domestic law and the European Convention on Human Rights (ECHR)) and when there is a statutory exception to the general rule (we consider the Data Protection Act below as the most significant statute relating to medical information). We then continue by examining what makes medical information confidential, and in particular the question of whether anonymisation removes its confidential nature. A further quirk relating to the law in this area is the fact that, due to its nature, it is one of the few areas of medical law where prospective rather than retrospective relief may be sought – the claimant may seek an injunction preventing disclosure rather than merely seeking damages after the event. We begin, however, by considering the exceptions to the rule that medical information cannot be disclosed.

EXCEPTIONS TO THE RULE – CONSENT

One exception to the rule that medical information must remain confidential is, obviously, that disclosure is permitted where the patient has given consent. As mentioned above, this exception is also mirrored in the provisions of data protection law (more on this later). This is uncontroversial, and the normal rules of consent apply. The only aspect that needs to be emphasised is that the boundaries of that consent need to be respected. Thus, if a patient consents to disclosure to one party, that consent is limited to that party only. Equally, if the consent is given for one purpose (such as research), it cannot be used for another. This raises important and difficult problems in relation to the extent and quality of consent (which we deal with in more depth as part of Chapter 10 on research).

EXCEPTIONS TO THE RULE – THE PUBLIC INTEREST

Domestic law

How the courts conceptualise and apply the public interest exception is demonstrated well by the decision in the case of *X* v. *Y*.[3] The facts are that in 1987 one or more employees of a health authority provided a national newspaper with information from hospital records which showed that two GPs who had HIV were continuing to practise medicine. The newspaper published a headline, 'Scandal of Docs with AIDS', which alleged that there were doctors who continued to practise despite having contracted AIDS, and that the Department of Health and Social Security (as it was then) was trying to suppress this fact.[4] It wished to publish a further article naming the two doctors, who in turn (through the health authority) sought an injunction preventing publication of their names. The question for the court was whether the proposed article was in the 'public interest' and thus the names of the doctors were allowed to be disclosed.

Rose J., in considering the public interest, was at pains to emphasise that the starting point should be that it would be in the interests of society as a whole that confidence be maintained. Thus, he quoted approvingly from a witness, who stated that:

> In the long run, preservation of confidentiality is the only way of securing public health; otherwise doctors will be discredited as a source of education, for future individual patients 'will not come forward if doctors are going to squeal on them'.[5]

Thus, it is for the party seeking disclosure to justify the disclosure, as the initial assumption is in favour of there being no public interest in that course of action. What is interesting in the above quote is that Rose J. also justifies the protection of an individual right to confidentiality with a more utilitarian concern for the maintenance of public health. In other words, the patient's right to confidentiality

---

[3] *X* v. *Y* [1988] 2 All ER 648.
[4] See C. Dyer, 'Doctors with AIDS and the "News of the World"' (1987) 295 *BMJ* 1339.   [5] *X* v. *Y* at 653.

is protected not with reference to individual interests, but instead due to the wider concern to protect the public. With this underlying philosophy in mind, the judge continued by considering whether it was in the public interest to disclose the names of the two doctors. He found that it was not:

> On the one hand, there are the public interests in having a free press and an informed public debate; on the other, it is in the public interest that actual or potential AIDS sufferers should be able to resort to hospitals without fear of this being revealed [. . .] [b]ut in my judgement those public interests [in disclosure] are substantially outweighed when measured against the public interests in relation to loyalty and confidentiality both generally and with particular reference to AIDS patients' hospital records.[6]

Given that the issue was already being debated in the press (not least by way of the newspaper's initial article), it is clear that they could not show that it was necessary to disclose the names of the doctors in order to begin or continue a discussion. However, what is interesting here is the way in which the legal test is essentially turned on its head. This is because the public interest – which is supposed to provide an exception to the rule that medical information is confidential – is actually utilised as a concept that *strengthens* the duty of confidence. In other words, instead of being used to justify disclosure, it is used to justify the *non-disclosure* of the information. Also noteworthy is the extremely wide scope of the test, which is so wide as to be almost meaningless: Rose J. is saying that it will be in the public interest to disclose information if the interests in disclosure outweigh the interests in non-disclosure. The test therefore merely asks the court to balance the interests in disclosure against the interests in non-disclosure. This essentially allows the court the free-dom to decide cases on an individual basis, and there is little in the way of guidance regarding what sorts of factors the court must employ in making its decision.

Further guidance regarding the public interest was to be provided by the Court of Appeal in the case of *W* v. *Egdell*.[7] W had shot and killed five people, and wounded two others. He was found to have mental problems, and was hence sent to a secure hospital rather than a prison. Ten years later, he applied to a mental health tribunal to be discharged, or at least to be transferred to a regional secure unit with a view to a subsequent discharge. His medical officer at the unit supported the application, although the Home Secretary opposed it. W's solicitor instructed a consultant psychiatrist, Dr Egdell, to examine W with a view to using the report at the tribunal in support of W's case. Unfortunately for W, Dr Egdell opposed the application, finding that W still had an unhealthy interest in firearms and explosives. He therefore disagreed that W was no longer a danger to society. Dr Egdell sent the report back to the solicitors, believing that it would be used at the tribunal. The solicitors withdrew the application in view of the report. When Dr Egdell learned of

---

[6] *X* v. *Y* at 660.   [7] *W* v. *Egdell* [1990] Ch 359.

this, and that the report had therefore been kept from the tribunal members and the secure hospital doctors, he passed on a copy to the medical director at the hospital and asked him to forward copies to the Home Secretary and the tribunal, for consideration if W applied again and had a different, more favourable report to back up his application. This the medical director did. W's solicitors sued, among other things, for breach of confidence. The Court of Appeal agreed with the trial judge regarding the central issues in the case:

> The question in the present case is not whether Dr Egdell was under a duty of confidence; he plainly was. The question is as to the breadth of that duty. Did the duty extend so as to bar disclosure of the report to the medical director of the hospital? Did it bar disclosure to the Home Office? ... [A]lthough the basis of the law's protection of confidence is that there is a public interest that confidences should be preserved and protected by the law, nevertheless that public interest may be outweighed by some other countervailing public interest which favours disclosure.[8]

What can be seen here is the court, first, clearly identifying that the information is confidential and asking itself whether there was therefore a justification in the disclosure. Of note is the way in which it asks this question in relation to *each and every person* to whom the information is disclosed. This makes sense – just because disclosure is warranted to one person, it does not justify disclosure to anyone else since being able to disclose to one person does not remove the confidential nature of the information. The Court of Appeal concluded that the threat to public safety sufficed as such a justification. However, what is interesting about the way in which the court did this was that it seemed to equate this justification with the doctor having acted in accordance with the GMC guidance of the time:

> In this case the number and nature of the killings by W must inevitably give rise to the gravest concern for the safety of the public. The authorities responsible for W's treatment and management must be entitled to the fullest relevant information concerning his condition. It is clear that Dr Egdell did have highly relevant information about W's condition which reflected on his dangerousness. In my judgement the position came within the terms of r. 81(g) of the GMC's rules. Furthermore, Dr Egdell amply justified his actions within the terms of r. 82. The suppression of the material contained in his report would have deprived both the hospital and the Secretary of State of vital information, directly relevant to questions of public safety. Although it may be said that Dr Egdell's action in disclosing his report to Dr Hunter fell within the letter of r. 81(b), the judge in fact based his conclusion on what he termed 'broader considerations', that is to say the safety of the public. I agree with him.[9]

This conflation of the legal and professional ethical standards (in this case, the GMC's guidelines) has been noted by others,[10] and is perhaps reflective of the

---

[8] *W* v. *Egdell* at 411.   [9] *W* v. *Egdell* at 416.

[10] See R. Lee, 'Deathly Silence' in R. Lee and D. Morgan (eds.), *Death Rites: Law and Ethics at the End of Life* (London: Routledge, 1994).

acquiescent attitude of judges of the time towards the medical profession. Nevertheless, it remains significant that the court essentially adopted the ethical guidance as the legal standard. In terms of the public interest, it is difficult to argue with the reasoning in the case. Indeed, it will almost certainly be enough to demonstrate a potential risk to an individual, rather than society as a whole,[11] which is entirely appropriate. The Court of Appeal confirmed the test in *X* v. *Y* and the philosophy behind it, and applied it appropriately, emphasising the need for the disclosure to be justified in relation to each party.[12] What the cases tell us about the public interest exception is that it is wide, and contains a high level of judicial discretion. It can be used both to justify disclosure and also to justify non-disclosure. Moreover, it is interesting to note that the philosophy behind the rule is different from many topics in medical law: while the patient's interests are protected, the reason for that is a concern that people would stop seeing their doctors if they could not be sure of confidentiality being respected, to the detriment of public health. This, recurring, argument can be shown to be a fundamentally consequentialist approach and thereby a deviation from the individualistic, autonomy-based approach normally taken (though one that can be seen regularly in public health contexts). However, the rights of individuals are protected by the ECHR, which the Human Rights Act 1998 brings into English law, and the Convention has had an impact on the law in this area.

The human rights approach

Article 8 of the ECHR protects the right to a private and family life, subject to certain exceptions:

1. Everyone has a right to respect for his private and family life, his home and correspondence.
2. There shall be no interference by a public authority with the exercise of this right except such that is in accordance with the law and is necessary in a democratic society in the interests of national security, public safety or the economic well being of the country, for the prevention of disorder or crime, for the protection of health or morals, or for the protection of the rights and freedoms of others.

This has been held to confer a right to privacy on the part of the patient (Article 8(1)), which is subject to the limitations that are provided for in Article 8(2). Article 8 has been used to fill in a legal gap in England and Wales, where traditionally tort

---

[11] See M. Jones, 'Medical Confidentiality and the Public Interest' (1990) 6 *Professional Negligence* 16.
[12] This is consistent with the early authority of *Initial Services* v. *Putterill* [1967] 3 All ER 145.

law has not recognised an explicit right to privacy.[13] This approach differs from that in *X* v. *Y* and *Egdell*, in that it considers the issue not from the perspective of the discloser's *duty* of confidence as those cases do, but instead from that of the patient's *right* to privacy. Medical information has always (and uncontroversially) been held to fall within the ambit of Article 8, and therefore any medical information will, prima facie, be classed as 'private'.[14] Therefore, any disclosure of that information must be justified under Article 8(2). Essentially, the approach is similar to that relating to the duty of confidentiality – the information is, unless there is some justification in disclosure, confidential – and the key question is the same: when can disclosure be justified?

This was considered by the English courts in the case of *A Health Authority* v. *X and others*.[15] During care proceedings in the courts in 2000, certain facts emerged about the conduct of Dr X and other members of his GPs' practice. The local authority felt that these matters were for the relevant health authority to consider. In other words, the local authority felt that Dr X and his colleagues should be disciplined and wanted to refer the matter, including the relevant information, to the health authority.

In fact, they had four initial areas of complaint about the practice with regard to the medical treatment it gave the patients in care. They were:

1. serious over-dispensing of medicines;
2. completeness of the medical records. In fact, it was said that in one case the records were missing for the last fifteen years, which clearly has the potential to have a deleterious effect on the quality of treatment for that patient;
3. inappropriate delegation of medical care of the patients; and
4. adequacy of the consent sought before performing medical procedures, in particular the sterilisation of a particular patient.

As Munby J. pointed out, this list was not even exhaustive as the local authority had only been able to gather up the facts that were disclosed at the care proceedings. The confidentiality of the patients' medical records prevented passing these records on to the local authority. The local authority therefore wanted the disclosure of two types of documents: first, specific documents which were relevant to the care proceedings in 2000; secondly, GP records of seventeen patients and former patients of Dr X's practice. The purpose of this was to obtain these documents with a view to

---

[13] See, e.g., M. Arden, 'Human Rights and Civil Wrongs: Tort Law under the Spotlight' (2010) *Public Law* 140. However, it should also be noted that privacy was protected in other ways (ibid.).

[14] This is made clear in all of the cases, whether they be decided by the 'English' approach (as with *Egdell*) or the 'human rights' approach (as with *Campbell*).

[15] *A Health Authority* v. *X and others* [2001] WL 513038. The case was appealed, unsuccessfully (see *A Health Authority* v. *X and others* [2001] EWCA Civ 2014), but the most comprehensive consideration remains that of Munby J. at first instance.

commencing disciplinary proceedings against Dr X and his practice, and the question for the court was whether it was justifiable to disclose them. Munby J. had no problem in deciding that both sets of documents could be disclosed, but it is the method that he used to reach that conclusion that is of interest to us in this chapter.

Clearly, the information contained within both sets of documents was confidential. Therefore, some justification was required before they could be disclosed. Perhaps unsurprisingly, the court also chose to consider European Court of Human Rights (ECtHR) cases to justify its decision. In particular, it took guidance from the ECtHR decision in *Z* v. *Finland*.[16] In that case, partially involving the confidentiality of medical records and, in particular, the HIV+ status of the applicant, the court had to determine when it was justifiable to allow the disclosure of this information. The starting point for the court was identical to that in *X* v. *Y* – it recognised that public health may be at risk if confidentiality is not maintained:

> It is crucial not only to respect the sense of privacy of a patient but also to preserve his or her confidence in the medical profession and the health services in general. Without such protection, those in need of medical assistance may be deterred from revealing such information of a personal and intimate nature as may be necessary in order to receive appropriate treatment and, even, from seeking such assistance, thereby endangering their own health and, in the case of communicable diseases, that of the community.[17]

For this reason, then, there could be no disclosure of the information without justification, and the court turned its attention to the question of when it might be justifiable to disclose; in other words, when Article 8(2) would apply. In the following quote, the words 'necessary in a democratic society' are a reference to the wording of Article 8(2). The court outlines here when it would be appropriate to justify disclosure under that heading:

> In determining whether the impugned measures were 'necessary in a democratic society', the court will consider whether, in the light of the case as a whole, the reasons adduced to justify them were relevant and sufficient and whether the measures were proportionate to the legitimate aims pursued.[18]

What can be seen from the above is that the test is in two parts. First, it must be 'relevant and sufficient' to disclose the information. This means that, in order to justify disclosure, the putative discloser must demonstrate that the reason for the disclosure matches one of those listed as being 'necessary in a democratic society' in Article 8(2). In other words, it must be relevant to one of the aims listed in Article 8(2), and sufficient to satisfy it. The second part of the test refers to proportionality. This means that the disclosure must be the minimum required to fulfil the aim in the first part of the test. Thus, *only* the parts of the information required to satisfy the

---

[16] *Z* v. *Finland* (1997) 25 EHRR 371.   [17] *Z* v. *Finland* at para. 2.   [18] *Z* v. *Finland* at para. 94.

first part of the test may be disclosed. It might be said that the first part of the test establishes *whether* any disclosure is justified, and the second (should the first be satisfied) relates to *how much*. The operation of this test can be seen in the way in which it was applied by the court in *A Health Authority* v. *X and others* in relation to the documents from the original care proceedings. Munby J. quoted the case of *Woolgar* approvingly, where the judge had stated that:

> disclosure is 'necessary in a democratic society in the interests of . . . public safety or . . . for the protection of health or morals, or for the protection of the rights or freedoms of others'. Even if there is no request from the regulatory body, it seems to me that if the police come into possession of confidential information which, in their reasonable view, in the interests of public health or safety, should be considered by a professional or regulatory body, then the police are free to pass that information to the relevant regulatory body for its consideration.[19]

Public safety, protection of health or morals and the protection of the rights and freedoms of others were selected from the list in Article 8(2) as being applicable. Thus, the first part of the test was satisfied and there was a justification in disclosing some of the information. However, in order to satisfy the second part of the test, Munby J. felt that he had to impose some limitations. He thus held that only the parts of the medical records that related to the conduct that was being examined by the regulatory body could be disclosed. He also specified that the records should be anonymised – as there was nothing in the justification for disclosure that required the names of the patients.[20]

It must be said that this test is substantially the same as the 'public interest' test traditionally used by the English courts. Indeed, there is very little to distinguish the human rights 'privacy' approach in substantive terms from the English courts' traditional 'duty of confidence'. Both look at whether it is justifiable to disclose at all, then seek to limit disclosure to the smallest amount necessary – and in both cases the policy considerations seem to be the same. Even the philosophy behind the legal rules is identical: confidentiality is required not solely to protect the rights and integrity of the individual patient, but also (perhaps primarily) because if patients are not certain that their information will be kept confidential, they will not see their doctors and as a result diseases will spread to the detriment of public health. It is worth noting the quirkiness of this rule. We see in other chapters of this book that medical law has tended to prioritise the individual rights of patients. However, this area of law is different in that the protection of the rights of the patient can almost be seen as a mere vehicle for the achievement of the overall aim – which is to safeguard public health. In this way, it may be

---

[19] *A Health Authority* v. *X and others* at para. 47, quoting Kennedy LJ in *Woolgar* v. *Chief Constable of Sussex Police* [2000] 1 WLR 25, at 36.

[20] *A Health Authority* v. *X and others* at paras. 50–6 for 'List A' documents, and para. 71 for 'List B' documents.

argued that individual rights (and thus a more deontological philosophy behind the law) are tangential to the law's purpose, which is a consequentialist concern for the overall health of society. If this analysis is accepted, then the protection of individual rights is therefore little more than a deontological means to a teleological end.

AN IMPORTANT STATUTORY EXCEPTION: THE DATA PROTECTION ACT 1998

Medical information is also protected through the Data Protection Act 1998, which has a particular effect on information held by the NHS. It is not intended to replace the common law (it is therefore a requirement that *both* the provisions of the Act and the common law are complied with), but instead to implement an EU Directive.[21] The Data Protection Act regulates the storage, use, disclosure and obtaining of information relating to individuals.[22] Critically, it applies both to information that is held electronically and to that in hard copy. Under section 2(e), any information about a person's 'physical or mental health or condition' is classed as sensitive personal data, which means that extra rules (as we shall see, contained in Schedule 3 of the Act) apply to it. Essentially, the Data Protection Act 1998 operates through the application of eight data protection principles, which are set out in Schedule 1 Part I:

1. Personal data shall be processed fairly and lawfully and, in particular, shall not be processed unless –
   (a) at least one of the conditions in Schedule 2 is met, and
   (b) in the case of sensitive personal data, at least one of the conditions in Schedule 3 is also met.
2. Personal data shall be obtained only for one or more specified and lawful purposes, and shall not be further processed in any manner incompatible with that purpose or those purposes.
3. Personal data shall be adequate, relevant and not excessive in relation to the purpose or purposes for which they are processed.
4. Personal data shall be accurate and, where necessary, kept up to date.
5. Personal data processed for any purpose or purposes shall not be kept for longer than is necessary for that purpose or those purposes.
6. Personal data shall be processed in accordance with the rights of data subjects under this Act.

---

[21] Directive 95/46/EC, the Data Protection Directive.   [22] For basic definitions of the terms, see s. 1(1).

7. Appropriate technical and organisational measures shall be taken against unauthorised or unlawful processing of personal data and against accidental loss or destruction of, or damage to, personal data.
8. Personal data shall not be transferred to a country or territory outside the European Economic Area unless that country or territory ensures an adequate level of protection for the rights and freedoms of data subjects in relation to the processing of personal data.

The most important principle for our purposes is clearly the first. Part II of Schedule 1 provides further guidance for the interpretation of each of the principles, so we shall consider each principle relevant to medical law in turn.

Principle 1: personal data shall be processed fairly and lawfully.
It will be remembered that Schedule 1 Part I provides that for this principle any use or processing of the information must fulfil at least one of the criteria in Schedule 2, and *also* one in Schedule 3 (as medical information is classed as sensitive personal data). This principle may sound somewhat tautologous, in the sense that the Act appears to state that the processing of the information is lawful if it is lawful; and indeed it is not a very well-defined principle, despite its description in Schedule 1 Part II being the most comprehensive. Schedule 2 provides the following wide-ranging criteria:

1. The data subject has given his consent to the processing.
2. The processing is necessary –
    (a) for the performance of a contract to which the data subject is a party, or
    (b) for the taking of steps at the request of the data subject with a view to enter into a contract.
3. The processing is necessary for compliance with any legal obligation to which the data controller is subject, other than an obligation imposed by contract.
4. The processing is necessary in order to protect the vital interests of the data subject.
5. The processing is necessary –
    (a) for the administration of justice,
    (aa) for the exercise of any functions of either House of Parliament,
    (b) for the exercise of any functions conferred on any person by or under any enactment,
    (c) for the exercise of any functions of the Crown, a Minister of the Crown or a government department, or
    (d) for the exercise of any other functions of a public nature exercised in the public interest by any person.
6. (1) The processing is necessary for the purposes of legitimate interests pursued by the data controller or by the third party or parties to whom the data are disclosed, except where the processing is unwarranted in any particular case by reason of prejudice to the rights and freedoms or legitimate interests of the data subject.
    (2) The Secretary of State may by order specify particular circumstances in which this condition is, or is not, to be taken to be satisfied.

Schedule 3 contains a lot of repetition of Schedule 2's requirements, so that, for example, the individual's consent can satisfy both schedules as required for sensitive data such as medical information. The ones that are distinct from those in

Schedule 2 and of most relevance to medical information are paragraphs 3 and 8. Paragraph 3 provides for processing for the welfare of the individual or someone else if it is necessary

(a) in order to protect the vital interests of the data subject or another person, in a case where –
  (i) consent cannot be given by or on behalf of the data subject, or
  (ii) the data controller cannot reasonably be expected to obtain the consent of the data subject, or
(b) in order to protect the vital interests of another person, in a case where consent by or on behalf of the data subject has been unreasonably withheld.

Paragraph 8 more explicitly allows information to be processed for health reasons – although the beneficiary does not have to be the data subject:
(1) The processing is necessary for medical purposes and is undertaken by –
  (a) a health professional, or
  (b) a person who in the circumstances owes a duty of confidentiality which is equivalent to that which would arise if that person were a health professional.
(2) In this paragraph 'medical purposes' includes the purposes of preventative medicine, medical diagnosis, medical research, the provision of care and treatment and the management of healthcare services.[23]

Principle 2: Personal data shall be obtained only for one or more specified and lawful purposes, and shall not be further processed in any manner incompatible with that purpose or those purposes.

Just as the common law provides in *Egdell*, the information does not lose its confidential status because it is justifiable to disclose it to one person (or, in this case, for one reason). All processing must be for reasons authorised by the Data Protection Act 1998.

Principle 5: Personal data processed for any purpose or purposes shall not be kept for longer than is necessary for that purpose or those purposes.

Once the information is no longer needed, it must be destroyed.

Principle 8: Personal data shall not be transferred to a country or territory outside the European Economic Area unless that country or territory ensures an adequate level of protection for the rights and freedoms of data subjects in relation to the processing of personal data.

This provision, usually referred to as the 'safe-harbour principle', exists to prevent data from being moved abroad, to places where the rules relating to processing may be less stringent, and subsequently used for purposes that would not be authorised under the Act – thus strengthening Principle 2.

---

[23] The Data Protection (Processing of Sensitive Personal Data) Order 2000 should also be noted. This expanded Schedule 3 to include justifications for processing if it is in the substantial public interest (the Order can be downloaded at www.legislation.gov.uk/uksi/2000/417/schedule/made).

What can be seen from the Data Protection Act 1998 is a comprehensive frame-work for protecting the data of individuals even when it is held by organisations such as the NHS. However, it should be noted that reform is on the horizon at EU level, with a proposal to replace the old Directive from which the 1998 Act derives with a Data Protection Regulation. The rationale behind this is set out in the explanatory memorandum:

Rapid technological developments have brought new challenges for the protection of personal data. The scale of data sharing and collecting has increased dramatically. Technology allows both private companies and public authorities to make use of personal data on an unprecedented scale in order to pursue their activities. Individuals increasingly make personal information available publicly and globally. Technology has transformed both the economy and social life.[24]

The Commission was concerned that in particular the digital age was rendering some of the old Directive obsolete, and that while the

current framework remains sound as far as its objectives and principles are concerned [...] it has not prevented fragmentation in the way personal data protection is implemented across the Union, legal uncertainty and a widespread public perception that there are significant risks associated notably with online activity.[25]

We can thus expect increased detail relating to digital records, but little change in the fundamental principles behind the Directive and therefore the Data Protection Act 1998. What has changed is that the instrument of choice is now a European Regulation, which means that it is no longer subject to a process of domestic implementation in the member states. Regulations have direct effect and are equivalent to national laws.

WHAT IS CONFIDENTIAL ABOUT MEDICAL INFORMATION?

We have seen so far that it is considered uncontroversial that medical information is deemed confidential per se. Indeed, whether we use English law's 'duty of confidence' approach or the ECHR's 'privacy' approach, all are agreed that this is a fundamental legal fact. However, it is important to spend some time examining what it is about medical information that makes it confidential. On the one hand, it might be argued that confidentiality is a part of the relationship of trust

---

[24] European Commission, 'Proposal for a Regulation of the European Parliament and the Council on the protection of individuals with regard to the processing of personal data and on the free movement of such data (General Data Protection Regulation)' {SEC 2012 73 Final}, p. 2. The page can be downloaded at: http://ec.europa.eu/justice/data-protection/document/review2012/com_2012_11_en.pdf.
[25] European Commission, 'Proposal for a Regulation of the European Parliament and the Council', p. 3.

that must exist between doctor and patient. Equally, it might be said that the patient has a right to privacy, since medical information satisfies the legal test of being information that the patient has a reasonable expectation of being kept private. Indeed, to divulge medical information may be seen as a violation of the patient's integrity akin to treatment without consent. However, there are equally arguments in favour of disclosing information in certain circumstances. It might be argued, for example, that the rights of the individual may be protected only as long as they do not threaten the safety of others (communicable diseases come to mind here), or that within the NHS our medical information should be used to help create more effective treatments (this is known as 'health service research' (HSR)).[26]

However, there is another aspect to medical information that may have a bearing on whether it should be classed as confidential: anonymisation and pseudonymisation. In anonymisation, all identifying characteristics of a data set are permanently and irrevocably removed (such as is the case when documents are redacted, or 'blacked out'). In pseudonymisation (which is the more common procedure, especially in biomedical research), the information is 'coded' so as to make it unidentifiable for the time being, with someone holding the key to decode the information again should it be necessary to identify the patient in question (we deal with this aspect in more detail in Chapter 10 on research). In both procedures, the aim is to unlink the information from the individual whose rights might be at stake. The argument here is, as long as we do not ascribe property rights to information about ourselves, then as long as the information is anonymised and therefore does not reveal the identity of the patient, it ceases to be confidential and may be used for any purpose. Following this argument, the integrity of the patient would not be infringed, his or her privacy protected and society could benefit from the research that needs the information to be completed. This was considered by the Court of Appeal in the case of *R* v. *Department of Health, ex p. Source Informatics*.[27] Source Informatics (we will refer to them as 'SI' here) was a company that gathered data about the prescribing habits of doctors, for the purpose of selling that information to pharmaceutical companies, who would then use it to help them to target their marketing. In order to obtain the information, SI required participating pharmacists to run the prescription forms through a specially designed computer program. Essentially, prescription forms contain the names of the doctor and patient, the date of the prescription, what was prescribed and in what quantity. SI were not interested in the identity of

---

[26] For an argument that such research should be able to proceed without the prior consent of the patients to whom the information pertains see, e.g., J. Cassell and A. Young, 'Why We Should Not Seek Individual Informed Consent for Participation in Health Service Research' (2002) 28 *Journal of Medical Ethics* 313.

[27] *R* v. *Department of Health, ex p. Source Informatics Ltd (No. 1)* [2001] QB 424.

the patients, and thus their computer program would remove that information before sending it to SI, where it would be aggregated and sold on to the pharmaceutical companies. In return for their cooperation, SI offered a modest payment to GPs and pharmacists. Patients were not aware of their involvement, and needless to say had not therefore consented to it. The Department of Health issued a policy document that stated that this might put both GPs and pharmacists at risk of actions for breach of confidence:

Anonymisation (with or without aggregation) does not, in our view, remove the duty of confidence towards the patients who are the subject of the data ... the patient would not have entrusted the information to the GP or pharmacist for it to be provided to the data company. The patient would not be aware of or have consented to the information being given to the data company, but would have given it to be used in connection with his care and treatment and wider NHS purposes. *Anonymisation of the data (with or without aggregation) would not obviate a breach of confidence.*[28]

SI sought a judicial review of the document, arguing that it was not an accurate assessment of the law, and that the anonymisation process removed the confidential nature of the information. In essence, they were arguing that it was the identification of the information to a patient, rather than the information itself, that made it confidential.[29] At first instance SI lost, and appealed to the Court of Appeal. The problem for the court was that this was not an issue that had been considered before. Moreover, each side was able to present an example from a previous case that would appear to support its own arguments. Thus, counsel for SI presented a quote from *Egdell*, where Bingham LJ implies that anonymisation would remove the confidential nature of medical information:

It has never been doubted that the circumstances were such as to impose on Dr Egdell a duty of confidence owed to W. He could not lawfully sell the contents of his report to a newspaper, as the judge held. Nor could he, without a breach of the law as well as professional etiquette, discuss the case in a learned article or in his memoirs or in gossiping with friends, unless he took appropriate steps to conceal the identity of W. It is not an issue here that a duty of confidence existed.[30]

Of course, the implication is that had the doctor taken such steps he could have discussed the case. Equally, counsel for the Department of Health found the following quote within the judgment of Rose J. in *X* v. *Y* that seemed to suggest the opposite:

---

[28] *Source Informatics* at 431.
[29] See A. Grubb, 'Breach of Confidence: Anonymised Information' (2000) 8 *Med. L. Rev.* 115.
[30] In *Source Informatics* at 434. Emphasis added.

... detriment in the use of the information is not a necessary precondition to injunctive relief ... [u]se of the information ... in a way which identifies neither the hospital nor the patients does not mean that the patients have suffered no detriment ... The risk of identification is only one factor in assessing whether to permit the use of confidential information.[31]

So Simon Brown LJ had a decision to make, and given the conflicting nature of the precedents it would seem that he could come to either conclusion. He decided that he would return to first principles and decide the case from there. He began by noting that the function of the law was to protect the privacy of the patient. Given that anonymisation removed this concern, he agreed with SI that this removed the confidential nature of the information, since the patient had no proprietorial claim to it:

The patient has no proprietorial claim to the prescription form or to the information it contains. Of course he can bestow or withhold his custom as he pleases – the pharmacist, note, has no such right: he is by law bound to dispense to whoever presents a prescription. But that gives the patient no property in the information and no right to control its use provided only and always that his privacy is not put at risk ... If, as I conclude, his only legitimate interest is in the protection of his privacy and that is safeguarded, I fail to see how his will could be thwarted or his personal integrity undermined.[32]

He concluded that nothing that SI, the GPs or the pharmacists were doing infringed the privacy of the patient, and therefore the anonymised information should not be classed as confidential. SI's argument that the Department of Health's guidance was not an accurate statement of the law was accepted. On one level (although not, we would suggest, for the reasons given by Simon Brown LJ), the decision can be supported. SI was not interested in patients or their information. Rather, it was interested in the information about doctors and their prescribing habits. Thus, it might be argued that the information was information *about doctors* rather than *about patients*. The patient may be considered tangential to the enterprise at best.

However, that is not to say that the patient is simply an incidental figure, for without her there would be no prescription. The information, it might be said more accurately, really pertains to *both* doctor *and* patient. Furthermore, patients may also have more than a passing interest in what is done with that information. To this end, Mason, McCall Smith and Laurie have argued that the decision ignores fundamental issues such as the 'role of consent in legitimising uses of information, the concept of reasonable expectations and

---

[31] In *Source Informatics* at 435.   [32] *Source Informatics* at 440.

the use and ... importance of maintaining a *prima facie* respect for confidences'.[33] Moreover, there are other objections that can be made. For example, as Beyleveld and Histed note, a patient may not wish to be involved with SI's business because

he or she has deep ethical concerns about contributing to the profit making of large pharmaceutical manufacturers, based on knowledge of those very manufacturers' lack of ethical concerns in other, less advanced countries.[34]

Equally, Herring has argued that some research might indirectly harm patients (such as research that might find an elevated propensity to certain conditions in certain ethnic groups, leading to increased insurance costs), which would be another, self-interested reason to object to the use of one's information being used.[35] However, even Simon Brown LJ's own reasoning – that there is no invasion of privacy – can be called into question. Herring challenges the implication that privacy is an objective concept that is external to the patient. Instead, he argues that it is subjective and that anonymisation does not necessarily result in no loss of privacy. He gives the example of someone having a nude picture of their body, without the head being shown so nobody could identify them. Herring's argument is that, despite their identity not being known, it would be perfectly legitimate for that person to feel that their privacy has been violated.[36] Indeed, '[t]heir private and intimate space had been invaded, even if no one else but them realized it. Could not the same thing be said about someone's private medical details?'[37]

Finally, it is also perhaps worth noting that the decision in *Source Informatics* does not quite fit with the human rights approach adopted in *A Health Authority* v. *X and others*. In *A Health Authority*, the question of the patient's identity was only considered with respect to the proportionality arm of the test – in other words, to determine *how much* information could be disclosed. It played no part in deciding *whether* the information might be disclosed at all, and is certainly nothing close to the determinative factor that was presented as being in *Source Informatics*. Given that *Source Informatics* places privacy at the heart of its construction of the law, this might be problematic in the future.

---

[33] J. K. Mason, A. McCall Smith and G. Laurie, *Law and Medical Ethics*, 7th edn (Oxford University Press, 2007), p. 280.
[34] D. Beyleveld and E. Histed, 'Betrayal of Confidence in the Court of Appeal' (2000) 4 *Medical Law International* 277, 295.
[35] J. Herring, *Medical Law and Ethics*, 4th edn (Oxford University Press, 2012), p. 237.
[36] Herring, *Medical Law and Ethics*, p. 237.
[37] Herring, *Medical Law and Ethics*, p. 237. See also J. Miola, 'Owning Information – Anonymity, Confidentiality and Human Rights' (2008) 3 *Clinical Ethics* 116.

CONCLUDING REMARKS ON LAW

The law relating to confidentiality clearly demonstrates that it takes the notion seriously. This is most clearly demonstrated in relation to the rules regarding the public interest exception to the general rule that medical information may not be disclosed. In particular, it is noticeable that not only did the courts uphold the general rule, but they also used the concept of the public interest and the philosophy behind it – that it benefits society that patients should feel that their information is secure – and used it not only to frame the exception to the rule, but also as a further justification for the rule itself. In other words, instead of using the public interest merely as an exception to confidentiality, the court in *X* v. *Y* also used it to bolster confidentiality by stating that it is also in the public interest to keep medical information confidential.

The human rights approach that relies on Article 8 of the European Convention adopts the same philosophy – and also protects the rights of the individual principally on utilitarian grounds. The 'necessity and proportionality' test used by the court in *Z* v. *Finland* and *MS* v. *Sweden* also demonstrates a robust approach to protecting patient confidentiality. Other than the fact that it considers the issue from the perspective of the patient's rights rather than the duties of the doctor (the latter being as the domestic courts in England do), the human rights approach is very similar in content and philosophy to that of the English courts. Indeed, one of the most striking elements is how similar the two tests are, despite coming at the issue from diametrically opposed positions. Moreover, both appear to recognise the importance not just to patients, but to *society as a whole*, in protecting confidentiality, and indeed the utilitarian justification seems at times to be the root of the protection rather than its deontological equivalent.

The robustness of the legal framework is echoed by the Data Protection Act 1998, which adds yet more layers of protection. As can be seen from both its origins as a response to an EU Directive, and indeed the proposals for reform that intend to better reflect the challenges of the clinical age, it is clear that the European Union takes data protection as seriously as the courts, and that there will be no tension between them. Confidentiality is taken very seriously by the law, and this is unlikely to change in the near future.

ETHICS

The law on confidentiality of medical information raises a similar range of moral questions regarding how we view individuals' control rights over information – in particular in the context of their relationship to others and society as a whole. We

Some might argue that this is doubly the case where that information is anonymised. Indeed, it might be said that much of the objection to the decision in *Source Informatics* is based on the status of the company as a private, profit-making entity. Yet, we could argue that there is more than an instinctive objection to the behaviour of Source: the fact that the direct benefit of the data would go to the company in the form of profits. This can be distinguished from, for example, HSR, which uses data from hospitals regarding how patients respond to certain treatments for certain conditions and helps to create evidence bases for the future. This benefits us all indirectly, particularly within the NHS. There is at least an argument that the normal rules of confidentiality should not apply in such cases. Alternatively, at the very least it should be recognised that this situation is different from the usual doctor-patient relationship setting. The Data Protection Act, and the proposed new EU rules, if anything extend the protectionist stance in relation to data, but we must be careful not to inhibit important research. That is not to say that we should disregard patient confidentiality totally where data is anonymised, but that we must be careful to strike the correct balance between protecting the individual and society. This balance is difficult to achieve, and it is not the last time that balancing the rights of individuals with the interests of others will feature in this book.

ADDITIONAL READING

 ### Law

M. Arden, 'Human Rights and Civil Wrongs: Tort Law under the Spotlight' (2010) *Public Law* 140

D. Beyleveld and E. Histed, 'Betrayal of Confidence in the Court of Appeal' (2000) 4 *Medical Law International* 277

P. Case, 'Confidence Matters: The Rise and Fall of Informational Autonomy in Medical Law' (2003) 11(2) *Medical Law Review* 208

R. Gilbar, 'Medical Confidentiality within the Family: The Doctor's Duty Reconsidered' (2004) 18(2) *International Journal of Law, Policy and the Family* 195

M. Taylor, 'Health Research, Data Protection and the Public Interest in Notification' (2011) 19(2) *Medical Law Review* 267

Ethics

T. Hope, J. Savulescu and J. Hendrick, *Medical Ethics and Law: The Core Curriculum*, 2nd edn (Edinburgh: Churchill Livingstone, 2008), chapter 7.

B. Lo, *Resolving Ethical Dilemmas: A Guide for Clinicians*, 4th edn (Philadelphia: Wolters Kluwer, 2009), chapter 5.

G. Niveau, S. Burkhardt and S. Chiesa, 'Medical Confidentiality and the Competent Patient' (2013) *Journal of Medical Ethics*, doi: 10.1136/medethics-2012-100947

M. Rothstein, 'Is Deidentification Sufficient to Protect Health Privacy in Research?' (2009) 10(9) *American Journal of Bioethics* 3

A. Slowther, 'Sharing Information in Health Care: The Nature and Limits of Confidentiality' (2006) 1(2) *Clinical Ethics* 82

Case studies from this chapter are available online at www.cambridge.org/hoppe.

3 Errors and fault

Occasionally, even the best doctors make mistakes. Sometimes, the mistake will lead to an injury to the patient, while at other times the parties are lucky in that there is no adverse consequence following the error. There are also times where a patient may *feel* that the doctor has made a mistake, such as when he or she does not recover from a procedure as fully as he or she would have expected or hoped, or has reacted badly to a drug. In all of these scenarios, we are not concerned with any bad faith or intention on the part of the doctor, but instead a potential display of a lack of skill in treating the patient. In this chapter, then, we examine how the law seeks to respond to a doctor who it deems to have fallen below the standards expected of him or her.

The first question, of course, is whether the doctor has indeed acted in a way that is unacceptable at all. Therefore, we shall begin this chapter by outlining the law relating to negligence. This discussion will not only take in the general elements of the law (duty, breach and causation), but also the role of guidelines and evidence-based medicine in determining and encouraging good practice. We shall also consider the issue of systemic fault and whether it would be right for the law to punish that. Finally, we shall examine the concept of no-fault compensation, which is generally seen as the most likely alternative to the use of negligence to compensate the victims of medical misadventure. In this chapter, we are therefore concerned with errors and fault, rather than mere negligence. However, since negligence constitutes the current method in English law for considering suboptimal treatment, the majority of our analysis will begin with and concentrate on that.

NEGLIGENCE – INTRODUCTION

The tort of negligence may be the appropriate forum for redress when a patient has been injured due to a mistake by the doctor. It does not apply when the patient suffers injury due to a deliberate act – and it therefore concerns lack of skill (or application of that skill) rather than intentional harm. As a part of tort law (although, as we shall see, the rules relating to doctors were for some time unique and did not correspond with how other professions were treated), the direct purpose is not to 'punish' the doctor, but to compensate the patient. The aim of the exercise is therefore *restitution*: to return the wronged party as much as possible to the state he or she was in before the wrong took place, although at times exemplary damages may be awarded. Thus, the patient may only sue for negligence if he or she has suffered some injury, and the compensation will reflect the gravity of the damage rather than that of the error. In terms of proving negligence, then, there are three elements to examine. First, the patient must be owed a 'duty of care' by the doctor. This duty must be breached (in other words, the doctor's conduct must fall below the standard of care prescribed by the law) and, finally, the breach of duty must have caused the harm that is being litigated. Each of these elements shall be considered in turn.

THE DUTY OF CARE

The imposition of a duty of care by the law means precisely that: that a person is under a duty to take care in relation to another, whose welfare they should have in reasonable contemplation. Therefore, the question of whether a doctor owes a patient a duty of care relates to the question of whether there is sufficient *relationship* between the parties to make the imposition of such a duty fair. Although in the general law of tort this can be a problematic concept,[1] in the doctor-patient relationship the fact that a doctor is treating a patient means that we can virtually take as read that the imposition of such a duty is appropriate. Put bluntly: it is almost trite to observe that a surgeon operating on a patient will have enough of a relationship to owe a duty of care. The question thus becomes, in most cases, *when* rather than *if* a duty exists.

In general terms, a duty of care is established when the doctor undertakes the task of treating the patient or otherwise assumes responsibility for him or her. At this point, the patient's welfare should be uppermost in the doctor's mind, and the patient should reasonably be able to expect that they will receive treatment. This is demonstrated by Denning LJ in the case of *Cassidy* v. *Ministry of Health*:

Whenever they accept a patient for treatment, they must use reasonable care and skill to cure him of his ailment ... Once they undertake the task, they come under a duty to use care in the doing of it, and that is so whether they do it for reward or not.[2]

---

[1] See, e.g., M. Lunney and K. Oliphant, *Tort Law: Text, Cases and Materials*, 4th edn (Oxford University Press, 2010), ch. 3.
[2] *Cassidy* v. *Ministry of Health* [1951] 2 KB 343 at 359.

Of particular note in the quote is also the final sentence, which makes clear that this applies to private doctors as well as those in the NHS. This is unsurprising given that the concept assesses the relationship between the parties rather than any financial obligation or service bought. Indeed, the principles involved in the establishment of a duty of care (and some further guidance) are exemplified by the case of *Barnett* v. *Chelsea and Kensington Hospital Management Committee*.[3] Three night watchmen fell ill after drinking tea, and attended their local casualty department. A doctor was called by telephone but refused to see the men, stating that they should go home and see their GPs in the morning. It transpired that the tea had been laced with arsenic, and one of the men died. The case turned on causation – and for that reason we shall return to it later in this chapter – but the court did also consider when a duty of care was established between the doctor and the patients. Nield J. stated that:

This is not a case of a casualty department which closes its doors and says that no patients can be received. The three watchmen entered the defendant's hospital without hindrance, they made complaints to the nurse who received them and she in turn passed those complaints on to the casualty officer, and he sent a message through the nurse purporting to advise the three men.[4]

He held that the duty was established once they were allowed to enter the casualty department 'without hindrance'. This, it should be made clear, is due to the unique role played by such departments, and this would not have been the case at another department where patients are not seen without prior appointments. However, even had this not been the case, once the doctor purported to advise the men by discussing their case with the nurse over the telephone the duty would have been created, as he would have undertaken responsibility for them (or, in the words of Denning LJ in *Cassidy*, 'undertaken the task' of treating them). In the case of *Kent* v. *Griffiths*, a similar approach was taken by the court to the ambulance service.[5] In that case, an ambulance was called when a man suffered an asthma attack but was found to have arrived with an unreasonably long delay, during which he suffered respiratory failure. In the Court of Appeal, Lord Woolf MR held that a duty of care was owed from the moment that the 999 call was accepted. Interestingly, this is a different approach from that taken towards the police and fire brigade.[6] The (in our view debatable) difference found was that the police and fire brigade were 'rescue' services, while the ambulance was a part of the health service. What can therefore

---

[3]   *Barnett* v. *Chelsea and Kensington Hospital Management Committee* [1969] 1 QB 428.
[4]   *Barnett* v. *Chelsea and Kensington Hospital Management Committee* at 435.
[5]   *Kent* v. *Griffiths* [2000] 2 WLR 1158. See K. Williams, 'Litigation against English NHS Ambulance Services and the Rule in *Kent v Griffiths*' (2007) 15(2) *Med. L. Rev.* 153; and K. Williams, 'Emergency Services to the Rescue' (2008) *Journal of Personal Injury Law* 202.
[6]   See Williams, 'Emergency Services to the Rescue'. See also R. Lewis, 'The Liability of the Emergency and Rescue Services' (2000) *Journal of Personal Injury Law* 198.

be seen is that the general rules relating to the establishment of a duty of care are both simple and easily triggered. In almost all cases, it will be unproblematic to demonstrate that a duty existed. There are, however, some specific issues that merit brief consideration.

Organisational issues

Sometimes, a hospital might fail to provide an adequate level of service due to the fact that they simply lack the money to do so. In the Court of Appeal in *Wilsher* v. *Essex Area Health Authority* (a case to which we shall return in more detail later), it was suggested by the court that it might be possible that a health authority might be itself liable in negligence if it inadequately utilised its resources, as the authority may be under a duty to adequately use them.[7] The comments were obiter, although there have been some subsequent attempts to argue this – some successful, such as in the case of *Bull* v. *Devon Area Health Authority*.[8] However, the courts are understandably reluctant to encourage such litigation, not least due to the logical progression that might argue that responsibility goes beyond the NHS and may lie at the hands of the government. This was put forward in the case of *Re. HIV Haemophiliac Litigation*, where haemophiliac patients infected with HIV through blood used for transfusions tried to sue the Secretary of State for Health. An initial hearing to see whether a full trial might be appropriate went to the Court of Appeal, which accepted that there was sufficient proximity in relationship between the parties that the plaintiff's argument was not so outlandish as to make a full hearing pointless, and thus authorised the procession to it.[9] However, the parties themselves settled the case, and the full hearing therefore never went ahead.

Can a duty be owed to a party other than the patient?

As we have seen, the concept of the duty of care relates to the relationship between the parties. In some cases, this relationship can be wider than the two parties involved in the interaction, as there may be others who can easily be identified as potentially being affected. In the general law of tort, where a small number of people can easily be identified, the courts have found that a duty of care might be established – such as in the case of *White* v. *Jones*,[10] where a solicitor who negligently processed a will (and whose relationship would have been with the client rather than the beneficiaries) was held to owe the beneficiaries (as an identifiable class of persons) a duty of care. A simple example of this in the medical context can be seen in 'failed sterilisation' cases, where two cases can be

---

[7] *Wilsher* v. *Essex AHA* [1987] QB 730.   [8] *Bull* v. *Devon AHA* (1989) 22 BMLR 79.
[9] *Re. HIV Haemophiliac Litigation* (1998) 41 BMLR 171.   [10] [1995] 1 All ER 691.

juxtaposed. In *McFarlane* v. *Tayside Health Board*, a doctor who negligently failed to tell a patient about the risk of a sterilisation reversing itself was also held to owe a duty of care to the patient's wife.[11] This is because she was an easily identifiable person – or class of persons – whom the doctor should have in reasonable contemplation. However, in the case of *Goodwill* v. *BPAS*, concerning the same issue, the doctor was not held to owe a duty to a woman who started a sexual relationship with the patient *after* his sterilisation – the 'class of persons' at the time of the negligent warning ('potential future sexual partners of the patient') would have comprised of far too many women to be classed as an identifiable class of persons with a close enough relationship with the patient that it be reasonable to impose a duty of care.[12]

In short, then, the concept of a duty of care is one that measures whether a relationship has been formed between the claimant and the defendant. If it has, then the latter has a duty *to take care* – in other words, to act in a manner that takes the welfare of the claimant into account. This examination of the conduct itself we consider in the next section.

BREACH OF DUTY

Breach of duty relates to the defendant's actions themselves. Sometimes this arm of the test for negligence is known as the 'standard of care', since it normatively assesses the quality of the conduct. Put another way, in order for his or her act or omission not to be negligent, the defendant's conduct must not fall below the *standard* demanded by the law. If it does, then the defendant is in *breach* of his or her duty of care. In this section we shall examine how we define the standard of care for doctors. This is important because, as we shall see in later chapters of this book, various topics within medical law became highly reliant on this test in order to determine a myriad of questions – many unrelated to matters of technical medical skill, but instead to ethical decisions. In general terms, the standard of care required by law is that a person acts in a manner consistent with that of a 'reasonable man'. The question thus becomes: how do we ascertain how a reasonable man would act? This is less easy to answer than it may appear, as much has hinged on how the courts have interpreted the test, which is outlined in the case of *Bolam* v. *Friern Hospital Management Committee*.[13]

---

[11] *McFarlane* v. *Tayside Health Board* [2000] 2 AC 59. In some very rare cases (estimated at 1 in 500 – see A. Grubb, 'Failed Sterilisation: Is a Claim in Contract or Negligence a Guarantee of Success?' (1986) 45(2) *CLJ* 197), the patient may be very unlucky and the disconnected 'tubes' may reconnect themselves, thus naturally reversing the sterilisation.
[12] *Goodwill* v. *BPAS* (1996) 31 BMLR 83.   [13] *Bolam* v. *Friern Hospital Management Committee* [1957] 1 WLR 582.

THE *BOLAM* CASE

Bolam became, arguably, the most important case in medical law. As Michael Davies noted, there was a time when the judicial attitude was 'if in doubt, *Bolam*ise'.[14] Yet the case is a somewhat unlikely candidate for this accolade, given that it is a first instance decision, from 1957 (in a subject that is fast moving), and not even a judgment but a direction to a jury. Nevertheless, it would come to be vital. The facts are that Mr John Bolam, a voluntary patient at a psychiatric hospital, was offered Electro Convulsive Therapy (ECT) as treatment for depression. He consented to the treatment, but was not warned of the risk of fracture that is inherent in the treatment; nor was he given relaxant drugs, which would have lessened the chances of injury. As a result of the treatment, he suffered several injuries, including dislocation of hip joints, and fractures to his pelvis on both sides caused by the femur on both sides being driven through the cup of the pelvis. He claimed damages from the hospital, arguing in part that the ECT without relaxant drugs, or at least manual restraint, amounted to negligence. However, a complicating factor was that the doctor who performed the ECT, Dr Allfrey, had performed the procedure in exactly the way that he had been taught to do so. Moreover, the medical evidence was divided, with each party bringing forward experts who supported their case. The question for the jury was whether the doctor's conduct was of the requisite legal standard. In directing the jury, McNair J. began from first principles, outlining how the standard of care was to be determined:

in an ordinary case which does not involve any special skill, negligence in law means a failure to do some act which a reasonable man in the circumstances would do, or doing some act which in the circumstances a reasonable man would not do ... How do you test whether this act or failure is negligent? In an ordinary case it is generally said, that you judge that by the action of the man on the street. He is the ordinary man. In one case it has been said that you judge it by the conduct of the man at the top of the Clapham omnibus ... But where you get a situation which involves the use of some special skill or competence, then the test whether there has been negligence or not ... is the standard of the ordinary skilled man exercising and professing to have that special skill ... A man need not possess the highest skill at the risk of being found negligent ... [I]t is sufficient if he exercises the ordinary skill of an ordinary competent man exercising that particular art.[15]

Thus, when dealing with a professional, the standard changes to that of a reasonable member of that profession – in the case of doctors, then, this is the 'reasonable doctor'. But how do we determine whether a doctor has been acting reasonably?

---

[14] M. Davies, The "New *Bolam*": Another False Dawn for Medical Negligence?' (1996) 12 *Professional Negligence* 10, 10.
[15] *Bolam* at 586.

The key, according to McNair J., is the evidence from experts called by either side. As he explained to the jury:

A doctor is not guilty of negligence if he has acted in accordance with a practice accepted as proper by a responsible body of medical men skilled in that particular art . . . Putting it the other way round, a doctor is not negligent, if he is acting in accordance with such a practice, merely because there is a body of opinion that takes the contrary view.[16]

So as long as there is a *responsible* body of medical opinion that would do as the doctor did, then the doctor will have satisfied the legal standard of care. It is noteworthy that the judge also informs the jury that a doctor is not negligent simply because there are other doctors who might have acted differently. Indeed, McNair J. cited with approval this quote from a Scottish case:

In the realm of diagnosis and treatment there is ample scope for genuine difference of opinion, and one man clearly is not negligent merely because his conclusion differs from that of other professional men, or because he has displayed less skill or knowledge than others would have shown. *The true test for establishing negligence in diagnosis or treatment on the part of the doctor is whether he has been proved to be guilty of such failure as no doctor of ordinary skill would be guilty of if acting with ordinary care.*[17]

Thus, the error must be one that *no* 'ordinary doctor of ordinary skill' would make, which suggests that as long as the doctor can adduce *some* evidence that other doctors might have acted as he or she did, then he or she is not negligent. However, it is not that simple, as the judgment is littered with the use of the words 'reasonable', 'responsible', 'respectable' and 'ordinary'. As Norrie has noted, there is a difference in category between the first three words and the last.[18] The word 'ordinary' is *descriptive*, which suggests that as long as the doctor does what other doctors do, then the mere existence of expert evidence stating that others may have acted as the defendant doctor did is enough to satisfy the test. However, the other words are *normative*, as they allow the court to examine the conduct. In other words, a body of opinion may be 'reasonable' or it may be '*un*reasonable' – we test this by assessing the evidence itself rather than whether it is simply there. Thus, a test of 'reasonable care' 'necessarily carries with it a connotation which allows the court to say what *ought to have been done* in the circumstances'.[19]

This is very important, as it determines whether the court is merely a rubber stamp, or retains ultimate control of the standard of care. From the direction that McNair J. gave to the jury, it would seem that he was intending a normative approach:

---

[16] *Bolam* at 587.   [17] *Bolam* at 587. Emphasis added.
[18] K. Norrie, 'Common Practice and the Standard of Care in Medical Negligence' (1985) *Juridical Review* 145.
[19] Norrie, 'Common Practice', 152.

[I]t is not essential for you to decide which of two practices is the better practice, as long as you accept that what Dr Allfrey [the doctor who actually performed the ECT] did was in accordance with a practice accepted by responsible persons; but if the result of the evidence is that you are satisfied that this practice is better than the practice spoken of on the other side, then it is a stronger case.[20]

As can be seen here, he is clearly telling the jury that, should they wish to find Dr Allfrey liable in negligence, it is their right to do so – and thus to find that he had breached his duty despite the existence of evidence from other doctors stating that they might have done the same as he did. However, for fully forty years the courts in England did not agree, and instead interpreted *Bolam* in a descriptive way.

'Old' Bolam

It is well documented in the literature that *Bolam* was interpreted in a descriptive manner after it was decided, so it is thus not necessary to chart this in too much detail.[21] Although there were some cases where the courts did seek to assert their authority in relation to the medical profession, by and large the courts instead preferred to simply defer to medical evidence.[22] Perhaps the clearest example of the approach of the courts can be seen in the House of Lords decision in *Maynard* v. *West Midlands Regional Health Authority*, which considered the issue of how to treat medical evidence directly.[23] In that case, two consultants were treating the claimant for a chest infection. They believed that she was suffering from tuberculosis, but thought that there was a possibility that she was suffering from Hodgkin's disease, which is fatal unless treated early. As a result, the consultants decided not to wait for the tests to see whether she had tuberculosis, and instead conducted an exploratory operation to test for Hodgkin's. The operation was carried out properly, and showed that she had tuberculosis rather than Hodgkin's. The plaintiff sued on the basis that the decision not to wait for the tests for tuberculosis had been negligent. The judge at first instance was very impressed with the plaintiff's expert witness, who said that the case had almost certainly been one of tuberculosis, and that to carry out the operation before the results of the tests for it had been dangerous and wrong. As a result, he found for the plaintiffs. The Court of Appeal reversed this decision, and the plaintiff appealed to the House of Lords.

The issue for the House of Lords was quite simple: was the judge *entitled* to find for the claimant despite the existence of medical evidence for the defendant? Essentially, the court was asked to rule on whether *Bolam* should be interpreted

---

[20] *Bolam* at 587–8.
[21] See, e.g., M. Brazier and J. Miola, 'Bye-Bye Bolam: A Medical Litigation Revolution?' (2000) 8(1) *Med. L. Rev.* 85.
[22] For an example of a challenge to this prevailing judicial attitude, see *Hucks* v. *Cole* [1993] 4 Med LR 393 (although the case was only reported in 1993, it was actually decided in 1968).
[23] *Maynard* v. *West Midlands RHA* [1984] 1 WLR 634.

normatively or descriptively. The House of Lords, through Lord Scarman, was explicit in its view that it was *not* open to the judge to choose, and therefore that the existence of medical evidence for the defendant was determinative. All that was needed was that the evidence was provided by experts and in good faith:

> I have to say that a judge's 'preference' for one body of distinguished professional opinion to another also professionally distinguished is not sufficient to establish negligence in a practitioner whose actions have received the seal of approval of those whose opinions, honestly expressed, honestly held, were not preferred. If this was the real reason for the judge's finding, he erred in law ... For in the realm of diagnosis and treatment, negligence is not established by preferring one respectable body of professional opinion to another. Failure to exercise the ordinary skill of a doctor (in the appropriate specialty, if he be a specialist) is necessary.[24]

Essentially, then, as long as the witnesses were experts, and their evidence was honest, it was not open to the court to reject it. Needless to say, this state of affairs is easy to criticise. To begin with, the medical profession is essentially able to set its own standard of care – and the law, rather than providing oversight and protecting patients, becomes nothing more than a rubber stamp.[25] Moreover, doctors were the only profession that enjoyed this interpretation of the law. For all other professions, the courts retained the right to declare even the unanimous practice of the profession to be a breach of duty.[26] Clearly, this difference in treatment was unsustainable, and the only surprise was that it took so long for it to change.

'New' Bolam

Towards the end of 1997, forty years after the decision in *Bolam*, the House of Lords had a further opportunity to consider its interpretation of the judgment of McNair J. This time, their Lordships were to change the way in which they approached the issue of expert evidence in the case of *Bolitho* v. *City and Hackney Health Authority*.[27] Patrick Bolitho was 2 years old and, suffering from a bout of croup, he went to the hospital. He was released, but returned the following day due to breathing difficulties. He had further treatment, and appeared to be progressing well. The day after that, he suffered two episodes where his breathing appeared to be obstructed, and the nurse called the senior paediatrician and the Senior House Officer (junior doctor). Neither of these came to the patient. He suffered a third episode, where again they did not attend, and this led to a cardiac arrest and brain damage. The defendants accepted that there was a breach of duty in not attending Patrick. However, their case rested on causation – stating that even if they *had* attended, they would not have intubated Patrick (which the medical evidence

---

[24] *Maynard* at 639.   [25] See Brazier and Miola, 'Bye-Bye Bolam'.
[26] *Edward Wong Finance Co.* v. *Johnson, Stokes and Master* [1984] 1 AC 296 (solicitors); *Re. Herald of Free Enterprise, Appeal by Captain Lewry* (1987) *The Independent*, 18 December (commercial ship captain).
[27] *Bolitho (Deceased)* v. *City and Hackney HA* [1998] AC 232.

stated would have been the only course of action that could have prevented the cardiac arrest). The question for the court was whether it would have been reasonable not to have intubated. As is often the case, both sides provided experts who would support their case. Under 'old' *Bolam*, this would be the end of the matter. However, Lord Browne-Wilkinson and the House of Lords took a different view, and decided to interpret *Bolam* in a different way. He said that:

> the court is not bound to hold that a defendant doctor escapes liability for negligent treatment or diagnosis just because he leads evidence from a number of medical experts who are genuinely of the opinion that the defendant's treatment or diagnosis accorded with sound medical practice.[28]

It is important to note that he was not seeking to overrule *Bolam* in saying this. Rather, he used *Bolam* itself as his justification, essentially recognising that how *Bolam* had been interpreted before was a misrepresentation of McNair J.'s intentions:

> In the Bolam case itself, McNair J stated . . . that the defendant had to have acted in accordance with a practice accepted as proper by a 'responsible body of medical men'. Later . . . he referred to 'a standard of practice accepted as proper by a competent reasonable body of opinion'.[29]

Therefore, it *would* be open to the court to analyse the medical evidence:

> the court has to be satisfied that the exponents of the body of opinion relied upon can demonstrate that such opinion has a logical basis . . . [I]f, in a rare case, it can be demonstrated that the professional opinion is not capable of withstanding logical analysis, the judge is entitled to hold that the body of opinion is not reasonable or responsible.[30]

It is thus open to the judge – *in a rare case, where the evidence is unable to withstand logical analysis* – to reject even the unanimous practice of the medical profession. The decision was met with some optimism in legal commentary,[31] and even senior members of the judiciary noted that the medical profession had previously been treated with too much deference by the courts.[32] However, it is a case that should not be oversold. First, it is vital to remember that Lord Browne-Wilkinson refers to *rare* cases – *Bolitho* is not intended to be used where the judge simply prefers the plaintiff's experts, only when the defendant's experts provide evidence that is *unable to withstand logical analysis*. This test is designed to be difficult to satisfy. Secondly, if the problem with *Bolam* was not the judgment itself,

---

[28] *Bolitho* at 241.   [29] Bolitho at 241.   [30] *Bolitho* at 241–2.

[31] See Brazier and Miola, 'Bye-Bye Bolam'; and, in particular, A. Grubb, 'Negligence, Causation and *Bolam*' (1998) 6(3) *Med. L. Rev.* 378, who begins the commentary section of his casenote on *Bolitho* by exclaiming 'Eureka! The courts have got it at last' (at 380).

[32] See Lord Woolf, 'Are the Courts Excessively Deferential to the Medical Profession?' (2001) 9(1) *Med. L. Rev.* 1, who argues that the courts had for a variety of reasons been overly deferential – a state of affairs that the profession can get used to (see, e.g., J. Miola, *Medical Ethics and Medical Law: A Symbiotic Relationship* (Oxford: Hart, 2007), pp. 43–6).

but the way in which it was interpreted by the courts, the same is true of *Bolitho*. It is worth mentioning, then, that the feared deluge of judgments finding doctors negligent despite medical evidence on their behalf has not materialised.

At first, results were mixed. In 2002, almost five years after the decision by the House of Lords, Alasdair Maclean undertook research into how *Bolitho* was being utilised by the courts.[33] He found that the courts were inconsistent in their application of *Bolitho*, with the Court of Appeal more frequently utilising 'old' *Bolam* than the 'new' version.[34] More recently, Rachael Mulheron's 2010 analysis has had a larger base from which to draw conclusions. She felt that *Bolitho* had had an impact, even if it was not openly acknowledged in cases:

> Another intriguing aspect of *Bolitho* is that its operation is generally regarded as a 'rare' occurrence, only to apply in exceptional circumstances where 'the evidence shows that a lacuna in professional practice exists', and 'extreme'. It has variously been said that peer professional opinion 'should not lightly be set aside', and that it would have to display a degree of '*Wednesbury* unreasonableness' in order for *Bolitho* to be triggered. However . . . the *Bolitho* test, while not *commonly* trumping *Bolam*, has certainly changed the outcome of medical negligence lawsuits in more cases than perhaps the label of 'rarity' would suggest.[35]

Mulheron identified seven factors which would make the application of *Bolitho* (in other words, the rejection of the defendant's expert's evidence) more likely. These factors state that *Bolitho* is more likely to be applied where:

1. the peer professional opinion has overlooked that a 'clear precaution' to avoid the adverse outcome for the patient was available;
2. there is a question of resources and conflicts of duty;
3. there is a failure to weigh the comparative risks and benefits of the chosen course of conduct;
4. the accepted medical practice contravenes widespread public opinion;
5. the doctor's peer medical opinion cannot be correct when taken in the context of the whole factual evidence;
6. the doctor's expert medical opinion is not internally consistent;
7. the peer professional opinion has adhered to the wrong legal test.[36]

Indeed, many of the cases where *Bolitho* has been used 'in anger' can be related to Mulheron's points. The most frequently cited are the decisions in *Penney*, *Reynolds*, *Richards* and *AB* v. *Leeds*, which provide a flavour of the approach currently taken

---

[33] A. Maclean, 'Beyond *Bolam* and *Bolitho*' (2002) 5 *Medical Law International* 205.

[34] Maclean, 'Beyond *Bolam* and *Bolitho*', 224.

[35] R. Mulheron, 'Trumping Bolam: A Critical Legal Analysis of Bolitho's "Gloss"' (2010) 69 *Cambridge Law Journal* 609, 618. References removed.

[36] Mulheron, 'Trumping Bolam', 610–37.

by the courts.[37] *Penney* concerned tests for cancer on cervical smears. There were abnormalities found on a number of slides, but they were not retested and labelled 'negative' (rather than 'borderline' or 'inadequate'), which led to some women not being identified as having cervical cancer at an early stage. Eight women died as a result of these 'false negative' results. Despite medical evidence on the part of the defendants, the court at first instance found that it was not reasonable or responsible for the screeners to have labelled the slides as 'negative' (applying *Bolam* and *Bolitho*), and the Court of Appeal, led by Lord Woolf, dismissed the hospital's appeal.[38] *Reynolds* involved the rejection of medical evidence to the effect that not to conduct a vaginal examination of a woman during childbirth (on the basis that there was a risk of infection) was reasonable. Gross J. held that this was not logically defensible as the approach did not properly weigh the risks and benefits of performing the examination (essentially, the risk was low and the consequences of not doing so – cerebral palsy following the baby's asphyxia – were serious).

In *Richards*, the court held that not to follow the NICE guidelines (relating to the length of time taken to perform an emergency caesarean once the decision to perform the procedure had been taken) was held not to be reasonable. We shall return to this case later. Finally, in *AB* v. *Leeds*, the courts found what was substantially the practice of the whole of the medical profession not to be reasonable. Here, essentially, hospitals were taking the organs of dead babies without the knowledge or consent of the parents and using them for research, a practice that was widespread, but ultimately deemed unacceptable by the judiciary. These cases all utilise *Bolitho* correctly. They assess the evidence of the experts, and find for the claimants due to a perceived fault *in the evidence*, whether it be the lack of following guidelines set by the profession (*Richards*), or an inadequate risk/benefit analysis (*Reynolds* and *Penney*). However, there are some other general comments that may be made about this group of cases. First, it is noticeable that they tend not to concern matters of technical skill. In all of the cases, the 'error' has been a decision made rather than the inadequate execution of skill. Indeed in *Penney*, *Reynolds* and *AB* v. *Leeds*, the issues can be said to be far removed from technical matters – they relate to questions of *whether* to do something rather than *how*. In the other case, *Richards*, the finding of breach of duty was made on the basis that the performance had not reached the standards set out in the professional guidance. Also, once again with the exception of *Richards*, there was little additional cost involved in acting in the way in which the court found to be reasonable. In general tort law, the courts will look at issues such as the likelihood and severity of

---

[37]   *Penney* v. *East Kent HA* [2000] Lloyd's Rep Med 41; *Reynolds* v. *North Tyneside HA* [2002] Lloyd's Rep Med 459; *Richards* v. *Swansea NHS Trust* [2007] EWHC 487; *AB* v. *Leeds Teaching Hospital NHS Trust* [2004] EWHC 644.

[38]   See J. Tingle and M. E. Rogers, 'Clinical Guidelines, NICE and the Court of Appeal' (1999) *Nottingham Law Journal* 95.

potential injury, the risks in acting to prevent it and the cost of doing so.[39] Here they seem to be adopting the same approach, and indeed did so openly in *Reynolds*. This would tend to suggest that the courts will be very careful not to involve themselves too much in matters of technical medical skill and, we argue, this strikes the right balance between oversight and interference.

However, the courts must also be careful not to utilise *Bolitho* wrongly. The duty of the court is to assess whether the evidence itself can be logically supported (as it did in the above cases). This should not be confused with the question of whether the experts are well qualified. In other words, the courts must ensure that they assess the *evidence* rather than the *expert*, and it is therefore not determinative that the defendant's expert might be a leader in his or her field.

ADHERENCE TO GUIDELINES

Given the rise in evidence-based medicine and the proliferation of guidelines, the legal consequences of such guidance must also be examined. Essentially, guidance from professional bodies or NICE may constitute an indication of what might be termed a 'gold standard'. That does not mean to say that not adhering to the guidelines will constitute a breach of duty (not least since the standard of care does not require a gold standard of service, just a level of skill that might reasonably be expected). Nevertheless, it is obvious that a departure from the guidance will not benefit the defendant's case, and may be used to justify a finding of a breach in the duty of care – as the court did in *Richards*. Nevertheless, we must also be careful not to assume that mere adherence to the guidelines will in itself defeat a claim in negligence. This would lead us back to an effective 'old' *Bolam* way of determining reasonableness. Furthermore, as we note above, a proper application of *Bolitho* tasks the judge with examining the conduct itself, not the evidence regarding whether others would have recommended that course of action. That said, it would be a brave court that found a defendant following reputable guidance to be in breach of his or her duty. Also, as we discuss in the ethics section, it does not necessarily follow that a slavish devotion to guidelines is a positive development.[40]

---

[39] A good non-medical example of this in practice is the case of *Bolton* v. *Stone* (1951) 1 All ER 1078. The case concerned a man who sued a cricket club after being injured by a cricket ball being hit out of the ground by a player. In assessing whether the club had satisfied the standard of care required with respect to protecting people and property outside the ground, the court balanced how often balls had been hit out of the ground, how serious the injuries were and how expensive it would be to build higher walls. See generally Lunney and Oliphant, *Tort Law*, ch. 4.

[40] See A. Samanta, M. Mello, C. Foster, J. Tingle and J. Samanta, 'The Role of Guidelines in Medical Negligence Litigation: A Shift from the *Bolam* Standard' (2006) *Med. L. Rev.* 321 for an excellent discussion.

INEXPERIENCE

It is clear that with increasing experience, doctors become better at their jobs and fewer errors are the result.[41] Junior doctors learn 'on the job', and can be expected to be placed in situations with which they may not be able to deal as effectively as a more senior colleague. How far, if at all, should the standard of care take into account the defendant's experience and qualifications? This was considered by the Court of Appeal in the case of *Wilsher* v. *Essex AHA*.[42] Martin Wilsher was born prematurely, given a low chance of survival, and placed in a specialist unit. It was necessary to monitor his oxygen levels through catheterisation as he was suffering from an oxygen deficiency. Unfortunately, a junior doctor mistakenly inserted the catheter into the umbilical vein rather than through the umbilical artery into the aorta, which led to a reading that suggested that he had insufficient oxygen in his system. An X-ray, which showed the mistake, was mis-read by the junior doctor. A registrar then made the same mistake (and also misinterpreted the X-ray images), and this resulted in Martin being given too much oxygen, and suffering from complete blindness in one eye and partial blindness in the other.[43] The question for the Court of Appeal that concerns us at this point is whether there was a breach of duty by either or both the junior doctor or the registrar, and whether the inexperience of the junior doctor made any difference to the standard to which he was expected to conform. The court found that it did not, and that the standard depends on the act rather than the actor and therefore turns on the function that the person is carrying out. This is because to modify the standard of care according to the qualifications and experience of the individual practitioner would not be fair to the patient. According to Mustill LJ:

> it would be a false step to subordinate the legitimate expectation of the patient that he will receive from each person concerned with his care a degree of skill appropriate to the task which he undertakes to an understandable wish to minimise the psychological and financial pressures on hard-pressed young doctors.[44]

However, that is not to say that no account will be taken of the inexperience of a junior doctor. Indeed, the Court of Appeal held that while the mistake was one which no reasonable registrar would make, the junior doctor was entitled to rely on

---

[41] As an illustration, see A. J. Epstein *et al.*, 'Association between Physicians' Experience after Training and Maternal Obstetrical Outcomes: Cohort Study' (2013) 346 *BMJ* 596, a study which – on the basis of evidence gathered from nearly 7 million deliveries – showed that maternal complications decreased in the first thirty years post-training.

[42] [1987] QB 730.

[43] The case went to the House of Lords on the question of whether it was the excess oxygen that caused the blindness, and this is examined in the section on causation below.

[44] *Wilsher* at 751.

his work being checked by a more senior colleague – and he expressly did so in this case, thus absolving himself of liability, even though the Court of Appeal was tempted to conclude that the mistake was one that no reasonable junior doctor would make.[45] We can therefore see that a state of inexperience does not help the defendant by lowering the standard of care, but that he or she can absolve him- or herself of liability by recognising that inexperience and asking for a more senior colleague to check his or her work.

CAUSATION

The final element in an action for negligence is known as causation. This requires that the breach of duty has caused some harm. It will be remembered that the purpose of an action for negligence is not to punish bad behaviour, but instead to compensate the claimant for any loss or harm suffered. Therefore, causation is the bridge between the defendant owing and breaching the duty of care (and therefore being responsible for any harm), and the harm itself. In its simplest form, causation asks whether 'but for' the defendant's negligence, the claimant would have suffered the harm. If not, then the defendant is deemed to have caused that harm. Therefore, a breach of duty is not, in itself, actionable. This is most simply illustrated with reference to one of the landmark cases in causation, *Barnett* v. *Chelsea and Kensington Management Committee*, a case that we considered in the context of the establishment of a duty of care earlier in this chapter.[46] You will remember that in this case three night watchmen presented themselves at the hospital complaining of stomach aches, but were sent home after the doctor (who did not see them, but only talked about the case over the telephone) said that they should see their GP in the morning. It transpired that this was bad advice, and that the tea had been laced with arsenic. One of the men died. Despite the fact that a duty of care was owed to the men, and it had been breached, it was nevertheless held that the claim for damages should fail. This is because the levels of arsenic in the dead man's system were such that, even if he had been treated properly, he would still have died. Therefore, the damage (death) was not *caused by the breach of duty* (not being examined and treated at the hospital that night). In other words, the claimant could not show that 'but for' the breach of duty he would not have suffered the harm. The burden of proof is set at the civil standard – that is to say, it must be shown that there was *more than* a 50 per cent chance ('on the balance of probabilities') that the

---

[45] *Wilsher* at 757.   [46] *Barnett* v. *Chelsea and Kensington Hospital Management Committee* [1968] 1 All ER 1068.

harm was caused by the breach.[47] However, there is of course more to causation than this simple application. As we shall see in the following sections, there are issues surrounding multiple causes and loss of a chance of recovery. Each shall be dealt with in turn.

Single and multiple causes

However, matters may be complicated when there is more than one causal agent combining to cause harm, or if the injury might be as a result of one of several factors. Such issues appeared in the case of *Wilsher*, which we discussed earlier with respect to the effect on the standard of care of inexperience. In that case, the Court of Appeal considered the breach of duty issue, but the case was appealed to the House of Lords on the question of causation.[48] Essentially, the question was whether the excess oxygen given to Martin Wilsher had caused the blindness. Remember that in that case the junior doctor who was asked to put a catheter into the umbilical artery of Martin Wilsher hit a vein instead. The consultant checked it, and made the same mistake. As a result, there were false readings about his blood oxygen levels, and too much oxygen was given to him, and he ended up almost completely blind. In the House of Lords, Lord Bridge delivered the leading judgment, with all of the other lords giving short speeches voicing their agreement with his decision. He began with the tort case of *Bonnington Castings* v. *Wardlaw*,[49] which concerned a worker who inhaled particles of silica over a period of several years. Some of the dust, which the court called 'innocent' dust, would have been there even without negligence. The 'guilty' dust was inhaled due to a breach of statutory duty by the defendants. The House of Lords in *Bonnington Castings* had a difficult decision to make as to causation, because the two sets of dust combined to cause the lung problems suffered by the plaintiff. Lord Reid's judgment sets out the general rule of causation: the plaintiff must show that 'on a balance of probabilities, the breach of duty caused, or materially contributed to, his injury'.[50]

But what does 'materially contributed to the injury' actually mean? Basically, it is a question of fact, and it is not all that well defined. But, of course, in *Bonnington Castings*, the inhalation of the 'guilty' silica dust certainly did the plaintiff no good, and the fact that he was exposed to so much of it means that it is likely that it at least made a significant contribution to his developing lung problems. A contributory factor will therefore be said to have 'materially contributed' to the injury as long as it is outside of the de minimis range of factors.[51] Indeed, it does not have to

---

[47] It is important to note that the burden is *more than* 50 per cent. 50 per cent precisely will not satisfy the causation requirement, a point to which we shall return later in this chapter.
[48] *Wilsher* v. *Essex AHA* [1988] 1 All ER 871 (HL).   [49] *Bonnington Castings* v. *Wardlaw* [1956] AC 613.
[50] *Bonnington Castings* at 620.   [51] *Bonnington Castings* at 621.

be the only or even the main cause of the injury. But what has this to do with *Wilsher*? The problem in *Wilsher* was that the medical evidence could not lead to any firm conclusions as to whether or not the excess oxygen had caused the blindness. In fact, there were five possible causes of the blindness, if we include the excess oxygen. Counsel for the claimant tried to argue that, if we follow the logic of *Bonnington Castings*, then there was a 20 per cent chance that the blindness was caused by the excess oxygen, and that this would surely therefore constitute a material contribution. The House of Lords, however, did not accept this argument. Lord Bridge agreed with the analysis of Sir Nicholas Browne-Wilkinson VC in the Court of Appeal that there was a big distinction between what happened in the *Wilsher* case and what happened in *Bonnington Castings*. In *Bonnington Castings*, the 'innocent' silica dust and the 'guilty' silica dust had a *cumulative* effect, while the injury sustained by Martin Wilsher was caused by one, but only one, of the five possible causes. As the then Vice-Chancellor said:

> To my mind, the occurrence of RLF [the injury] following a failure to take a necessary precaution to prevent excess oxygen causing RLF provides no evidence and raises no presumption that it was excess oxygen rather than one or more of the four other agents which caused or contributed to RLF in this case.[52]

As a result, the House of Lords decided that it was impossible to say that the excess oxygen definitely either caused or materially contributed to the blindness of Martin Wilsher, and they ordered a retrial. But what do we take from this case? Well, if the cause of a disease is between a few cumulative causes, then it is very possible that the negligent cause materially contributed to the injury. But, if the causes are *separate*, and only one could have caused the injury, then the plaintiff has to prove on the balance of probabilities (a *more than* 50 per cent chance) that it was the breach of duty that led to the injury.

Loss of a chance of recovery

However, there are also times where the doctor's conduct does not cause injury per se, but instead removes the chances of the patient recovering from a pre-existing condition. This is exemplified by the facts in the case of *Hotson v. East Berkshire HA*.[53] In *Hotson*, the plaintiff, a 13-year-old boy, fell from a tree and injured his hip. He was taken to a hospital, where his injury was misdiagnosed, and he was told to go home. He did this, and stayed there, in severe pain, for the next five days. After this time, he returned to the hospital, where they carried out an X-ray, and found that he had fractured his hip. The very next day he underwent an operation to pin the joint, but this did not prevent him from suffering avascular necrosis, which

---

[52] *Wilsher* (CA) at 779.   [53] *Hotson* v. *East Berkshire HA* [1987] 2 All ER 909 (HL).

led to a deformity of the hip joint and, by the time he was 20, this had left him with a permanent disability. The plaintiffs sued on the basis that there was negligence on the part of the hospital in not giving him an X-ray the first time he was there. The hospital admitted negligence with regard to the misdiagnosis and consequent failure to conduct an X-ray, but argued that there was no causation between the delay and the avascular necrosis. In fact, the medical evidence showed that, even without the delay, there was a 75 per cent chance that the avascular necrosis would have developed anyway. The trial judge accepted this, but found that since the boy had lost a 25 per cent chance of recovery, he should receive 25 per cent of the damages. The health authority appealed unsuccessfully to the Court of Appeal, and then appealed to the House of Lords.

The House of Lords decided the case using a strict application of the laws of causation, and thus allowed the hospital's appeal. It began by stating that, in order to prove causation, the plaintiff had to demonstrate that there was more than a 50 per cent chance that the avascular necrosis might have been avoided had he not been misdiagnosed and had he been provided with an X-ray at the correct time. Given that he could not demonstrate this (there was only a 25 per cent chance of the necrosis being avoided even with correct treatment), there was no causation and thus no liability. Had he done so, he would have been able to claim for 100 per cent of the damages, but given that he could not he got nothing. This argument is well explained by Croom-Johnson LJ in the Court of Appeal:

If it is proved statistically that 25% of the population has a chance of recovery from a certain injury and 75% does not, it does not mean that someone who suffers that injury and who does not recover from it has lost a 25% chance. He may have lost nothing at all. What he has to do is prove that he was one of the 25% and that his loss was caused by the defendant's negligence. To be a figure in a statistic does not in itself give him a cause of action. If the plaintiff succeeds in proving that he was one of the 25% and that the defendant took away that chance, the logical result would be to award him 100% of his damages and not only a quarter.[54]

This 'all or nothing' approach is not uncontroversial, and we shall return to it below, but there are other reasons why *Hotson* may be criticised. First, the House of Lords did not really actually engage with the claimant's argument, and in fact they did not engage with or settle the question of whether someone could claim for a loss of a chance. Indeed, the claimant's argument was not that the 'damage' was the avascular necrosis, as the House of Lords assumed. Rather, the claimants were arguing that the damage was actually the *loss of the chance to avoid necrosis*, or in other words the loss of the benefit of timely treatment. The figure of 25 per cent of full damages is thus merely an appropriate figure of compensation, and not partial compensation for a claimant who has failed to fully prove causation. Secondly, the

---

[54] *Hotson* v. *East Berkshire HA* [1987] 2 WLR 287 at 303.

approach is particularly unfair as the claimant was prevented from proving causation by the breach of duty itself. Had timely treatment been provided, he could
have shown whether or not he would have been in the 25 per cent; but without the
timely treatment he had no chance of avoiding necrosis – it is inequitable and
ironic that it is the very breach of duty that he is claiming against that prevents
him from doing so. Finally, as Scott argues, the 'all or nothing' approach is fairest
when the chances of injury are close to 100 per cent, but gets progressively less fair
the closer we come to 51 per cent.[55] This is exacerbated by the fact that it can often
be difficult to assess the likelihood of something happening to within a single
percentage point.

The House of Lords had a further opportunity to consider these points in the case
of *Gregg* v. *Scott*.[56] Here, the claimant developed a lump under his left arm, went to
see his GP, Dr Scott, and was told that it was a benign collection of fatty tissue, and
not to worry about it. The following year, Mr Gregg moved house and registered
with another doctor. When this doctor saw the lump, he immediately sent Mr Gregg
to have it examined at a hospital, where it was found to be cancerous. By this time,
the cancer had spread to Mr Gregg's chest. The medical evidence was that his
chances of survival (which they defined as being alive in ten years) were lowered
from 42 to 25 per cent by the delay in treatment. On the normal rules of causation,
the claim would fail, despite the defendant admitting breach of duty, as his chances
of being alive in ten years were under 51 per cent to begin with. The claimant
therefore tried two different arguments.

The first was what was called the 'quantification argument'. This provides that
the spread of the tumour was, in itself, physical damage that was caused by
the breach of duty. Once this is accepted, the only thing left to talk about is the
quantification of damages – which would most fairly be the proportion of the
chance of survival that Mr Gregg lost due to the breach of duty. Note that this does
not apply to a case such as *Hotson*, because there was no additional harm that could
be considered 'physical damage'. This approach, popular with Latham LJ in the
Court of Appeal, was rejected by the majority. Lord Hoffman noted that it could not
work in isolation, and still relied on compensation for loss of a chance to be
accepted – it was essentially loss of a chance under another name (which is correct,
as it is essentially the argument made by the claimant in *Hotson* itself). Thus, if we
reject the notion of compensating for loss of a chance, then we must also reject this
argument. As he put it:

[55] W. Scott, 'Causation in Medico-Legal Practice: A Doctor's Approach to the "Lost Opportunity" Cases' (1992) 55 *MLR* 521. See also A. Grubb, 'Medical Negligence: Causation' (1996) 4(1) *Med. L. Rev.* 92; and T. Hill, 'A Lost Chance of Compensation in the Tort of Negligence by the House of Lords' (1991) 54 *MLR* 511.
[56] *Gregg* v. *Scott* [2005] 2 AC 176.

It is true that the delay caused an early spread of the cancer and that this reduced his percentage chance of survival for more than 10 years. But to say that the claimant can therefore obtain damages for the reduction in his chances of survival assumes in his favour that a reduction in the chance of survival is a recoverable head of damage.[57]

The second argument was loss of a chance itself – the House of Lords were asked to reconsider the judgment in *Hotson* and allow claims for loss of a chance. The House of Lords was split between the idealistic minority and the legalistic majority. The view of the minority was best summed up by Lord Nicholls, who argued that it was quite simply not fair to the plaintiff:

It cannot be right to adopt a procedure having the effect that, in law, a patient's prospects of recovery are treated as non-existent whenever they exist but fall short of 50%. If the law were to proceed in this way it would deserve to be likened to the proverbial ass. Where a patient's condition is attended with such uncertainty that medical opinion assesses the patient's recovery prospects in percentage terms, the law should do likewise. The law should not, by adopting the all-or-nothing balance of probability approach, assume certainty where none in truth exists.[58]

The majority, however, felt that having a certain legal principle was more important than compensating a man who probably deserved compensation. Thus, for Lord Hoffman:

What these cases show is that, as Helen Reece points out in an illuminating article ('Losses of Chances in the Law' (1996) 59 MLR 188) the law regards the world as in principle bound by laws of causality. Everything has a determinate cause, even if we do not know what it is. The blood-starved hip joint in Hotson, the blindness in Wilsher . . . each had its cause and it was for the plaintiff to prove that it was an act or omission for which the defendant was responsible. The fact that proof is rendered difficult or impossible because no examination was made at the time, as in Hotson, or because medical science cannot provide the answer, as in Wilsher, makes no difference.[59]

So the House of Lords had a chance to choose to compensate for a loss of a chance of recovery, and it chose not to. The issue is as close as it has been since *Hotson* to being settled, although given that the decision was split, it is clear that there is at least some appetite within the judiciary for allowing such claims.

NO-FAULT LIABILITY

A fundamental defect, if you will, of liability in the conventional sense, is that there is usually (excepting instances of strict liability) always the expectation that someone is at fault. This raises two significant hurdles making it more difficult to swiftly

---

[57] *Gregg* v. *Scott* at 194, *per* Lord Hoffman.   [58] *Gregg* v. *Scott* at 189, *per* Lord Nicholls.
[59] *Gregg* v. *Scott* at 196, *per* Lord Hoffman.

resolve disputes surrounding medical mishaps: the first is more or less a technical problem; the second involves the human element.

First, insurance companies underwriting the risk of running a hospital generally require that there be no admission of liability, as it is the purportedly harmed patient who has to prove that those treating him or her fell below an acceptable standard of medical care. Were the hospital or the doctors to say 'yes, we got it wrong – we're sorry', this would in many cases invalidate the relevant liability insurance cover. This results in there being a fundamentally contentious environment in which these types of claims have to be fought out, which – some argue – is counterproductive.[60] It also means that in order to simply hear the word 'sorry', patients have to successfully litigate. It seems plausible that many patients actually simply want an apology and appropriate assistance in dealing with the fallout of the mishap, and few patients are actually after revenge or damages at a punitive level.

Secondly, a clinical culture in which it is inappropriate to directly accept responsibility for mistakes does not foster a professional culture which is able to horizon-scan for potential mistakes. Near-misses are kept secret as it would not do to speak of errors in the clinical context – doctors want to be seen as not making mistakes. It takes a charismatic (and usually quite old and experienced) doctor to acknowledge and come to terms with the concept that mistakes happen the whole time. Most doctors will tell you in confidence that they have a personal tally of patients whom they have harmed as the result of a mistake – and this should neither be surprising nor shocking. It is a simple fact of life that in the context of medicine, errors happen and people are hurt. The outcome of these errors is sometimes trivial, sometimes severe. At the same time, the transparent communication and discussion of this type of information is vital to prevent harm in the future – organisations and individuals need to be in a position to learn from mistakes and near-mistakes.

Against this backdrop, there has been (for a very long time) a lively discussion of alternative models for resolving disputes surrounding errors in medicine that lead to harm to patients.[61] One of the most prominent propositions has been that of 'no-fault-liability', which does not require a patient to prove that someone has actually been at fault, but simply that there is causation between the treatment and the harm. Compensation may then become available if the harm could have been avoided if best practice had been followed (which still falls below the bar of having

---

[60] M. McKinney, 'Going beyond Saying You're Sorry: More Hospitals Using Quick Remediation Strategies Following Medical Errors' (2011) 41(13) *Modern Healthcare* 32.

[61] D. Rubsamen, 'No-Fault Liability for Adverse Medical Results – Is It a Reasonable Alternative to the Present Tort System?' (1972) 117 *California Medicine* 78.

to prove actual negligence). The advantages and drawbacks of this system have been discussed widely. A good summary is this:

No state presently uses a no-fault system for the broad run of medical patients. Florida and Virginia have instituted a no-fault system for patients with neonatal brain injury. New Zealand and Sweden have long-standing programs in conjunction with broad public health insurance coverage. Studies have indicated that a broad no-fault program could be instituted within a reasonable cost, but compensation would have to be limited in various ways, such as a four- or eight-week disability threshold or a bar to recovery of non-economic damages.

The no-fault medical liability system offers the theoretical prospect of compensating injured patients with substantial savings of time and money. By giving a broad scope to expert determination of medical avoidability, no-fault may be the alternative that would best foster continuous improvement in medical practice. At the same time, institution of such a system for the broad run of medical patients would represent a radical departure without a track record of success in any other state. Such a system could change nearly every aspect of injury finding and resolution – the standard of care and coverage, the rules of damages, the forum and process of decision making, and the bearer of financial risk.[62]

This means that the concept is very similar to that of strict liability, which comes into play when it is in the public interest to not require individuals to prove that there was fault on the part of a provider of goods or services. It is a system designed to underpin trust (as all protagonists are protected in what they are doing – the doctor can treat without fear of failure and the patient knows that he or she will be compensated in case a mishap does occur). It also opens the door to hospitals and doctors being able to admit mishaps and apologise, without compromising their position on liability. The downside is that there will usually have to be some centralised compensation scheme, which is likely to result in lower compensation payouts.

CONCLUDING REMARKS ON LAW

English medical law has had a long way to travel since 1957 and the decision in *Bolam*, but it has certainly done so. The problem has never been establishing that there was sufficient relationship between doctor and patient for a duty of care to be owed, but rather that the courts were far too reluctant to intervene to police medical conduct. *Bolam* was *mis*applied to prohibit courts from examining medical conduct, and the profession was effectively allowed to set its own standard of care. This unique power on the part of a profession was one of the reasons for medical

---

[62]   Advisory Committee on Medical Professional Liability, 'Medical Professional Liability Reform for the 21st Century: A Review of Policy Options. General Assembly of the Commonwealth of Pennsylvania' (2005), http://jsg.legis.state. pa.us/resources/documents/ftp/publications/2005-42-Med%20Mal.pdf.

negligence being seen as distinct from the general tort of negligence, and helped create medical law as a subject. The recalibration of the law imposed by *Bolitho* was not just right but necessary, and few would argue that the law is now too onerous for doctors. This is particularly the case given the growth of *Bolam* out of negligence and into ethical issues that will be evident in later chapters of this book.

The difficulties faced by patients continue with causation, where the House of Lords has made it clear that loss of a chance of recovery will not constitute a recoverable head of damages. This is a difficult area, given that there is a need both to protect and compensate patients, but also to afford equal protection to doctors who are in virtually all cases trying to do their best for patients. It is important to remember that the doctor is not necessarily to blame just because the patient is injured or has not recovered. Striking this balance is even more difficult where it can be notoriously difficult to establish precise likelihoods for an event being a direct consequence of a patient's treatment.

Given this, no-fault compensation systems appear to be an attractive alternative to the need to prove negligence. They avoid the problem – in theory at least – of balancing stigmatisation of doctors with protection of patients, and they encourage a more collaborative relationship between hospital and patient once the latter has been injured. But it is important to note that such systems do not solve the problems inherent in causation. While the headline issue for negligence has always been the standard of care, it should not be forgotten that causation also represents a significant hurdle for patients. It is one that would not be solved by the adoption of a no-fault system – which therefore should not be seen as a panacea. Indeed, the key is the balance of protection and that is devilishly difficult to achieve in any system.

ETHICS

Errors happen and are part and parcel of the general type of context we are seeking to explore in this book.[63] At the same time, the margin for acceptable error is at its thinnest in medicine: actors perform in a stressful high-stakes environment and many small errors will lead to serious consequences.[64] In order to not provide a disincentive for individuals to act in this environment, the law has sensibly

---

[63] S. Gorovitz and A. MacIntyre, 'Toward a Theory of Medical Fallibility' (1975) 5(6) *Hastings Center Report* 13, 14 and 19.

[64] N. Hoppe, 'Medical Ethics and Patient Safety' in J. Tingle and P. Bark (eds.), *Patient Safety, Law Policy and Practice* (Oxford: Routledge, 2011), at 60.

developed high thresholds before something is deemed to have been so erroneous that it gives rise to a claim.

What we have seen when we looked at the law in relation to errors and faults is a concentration on a specific constellation and interdependence of parameters to establish whether a patient is entitled to be compensated for a harm: duty, breach of that duty, and the causation of harm by the breach. The ethical issues can be charted along very much the same lines, with the most significant parameter being, of course, that of the duty owed by the doctor to the patient. You will remember that we said in this chapter that the fact that there is such a duty is nearly self-evident. The reason for this might be that the legal analysis picks up where medical ethics has already done much of the heavy lifting, namely laying the foundations of a common-sense presumption of a (moral) obligation.[65] But why is there such an obligation and what principles is this founded on? We will look first at what kind of obligations we can identify in medicine. We then discuss why such obligations should be binding on the actors in the sense of giving rise to a positive duty, before considering the special status of medical professionals and the medical context.

Duties and principles – obligations in medicine

We have taken recourse, on occasion, to the Hippocratic Oath to demonstrate certain aspects of promises made by physicians when entering their profession. It is important to understand that we do not use or see the Hippocratic Oath as a normative instrument which ultimately establishes those promises as obligations (it certainly no longer has that quality), but as an illustration of the long-standing nature of certain notions about the roles and duties of physicians – the oath has been around for nearly 2,500 years and can serve as an indication of how long-established certain (self-)perceptions are in the medical community.

This time, we need not look at an individual stipulation of the Hippocratic Oath, or of the Nuremberg Code or the Declaration of Helsinki, to show that certain aspects of medical obligations are well established. It is the mere existence of these oaths, codes and declarations in the first place which tells us something about the positioning of the physician in relation to patients' needs. The assumption that the relationship between a doctor and a patient is of a special nature, and gives rise to moral obligations, comes both from the roles that each person assumes in this relationship (the seeker of assistance and the provider of assistance, often in a situation of acute need) and from explicit promises that are made (representing to be a specialist). Where I am the incumbent of the role of doctor, I signal that I am in the position of the helper, in a situation of need. Quite explicitly, in many

[65]   For an overview, see M. Kottow, 'Medical Confidentiality: An Intransigent and Absolute Obligation' (1986) 12 *Journal of Medical Ethics* 117.

circumstances, I also make a promise to assist in a way which is state-of-the-art. Beauchamp and Childress write:

> Obligations of specific beneficence [...] typically derive from special moral relationships with persons frequently through institutional roles and contractual arrangements. These obligations arise from implicit end explicit commitments, such as promises and roles, as well as from the acceptance of specific benefits. Both our 'stations and duties' and our promises impose obligations. For example, a lifeguard on duty is obligated to try to rescue a drowning swimmer, despite personal risk, just as a physician is obligated to meet the needs of his or her patients, despite potential health risks. *The claims that we make on each other as parents, spouses, and friends stem not only from interpersonal encounters, but from settled rules, roles, and relations that constitute the matrix of social obligations and role-derived obligations.*[66]

Beauchamp and Childress' principles of biomedical ethics provide a good primer for the question of how interactions between doctors and patients are guided by special obligations.[67] They introduce a set of principles (which we have looked at in Chapter 1), not all of which seem to intuitively be appropriate to our question: (1) respect for autonomy; (2) non-maleficence; (3) beneficence; and (4) justice. In this chapter, we will look at the first three principles to see how each of these plays, to some extent, a role in the way in which we assess duties, breaches of duty and causation.

Autonomy

The principle of 'respect for autonomy' means that the patient's wishes are paramount. How does this fit into the category of errors and faults? The greatest risk to the patient's autonomy is, surely, not where a genuine error is made, but where an intentional harm might be caused, or the doctor substitutes his or her own ideals and wishes for those of the patient. It may also play a significant role where a doctor fails to take an opportunity to involve the patient in the decision-making process, even if this is done in error:

> Institutions which, as a matter of policy, do not inform patients of material risks certainly do harm to patients' autonomy by depriving them of an opportunity to base their decisions on appropriately detailed information. The same is true for harm where the patient is left in the dark about the [medical origin] of the harm – the patient is excluded from participating in the decision-making processes in relation to his further treatment.[68]

---

[66] Beauchamp and Childress, *Principles of Biomedical Ethics*, p. 175 (emphasis added).

[67] Beauchamp and Childress, *Principles of Biomedical Ethics*. Tom Beauchamp and James Childress' approach to this issue is not uncontroversial and a debate has gone on for a long time in literature on whether their system is sufficient, trivial, etc. This is acknowledged here and if you wish to delve deeper into this debate, the following papers might be of interest: K. Page, 'The Four Principles: Can They Be Measured and Do They Predict Ethical Decision-Making?' (2012) 13 *BMC Medical Ethics* 10; R. Gillon, 'When Four Principles Are Too Many: A Commentary' (2012) 38(4) *Journal of Medical Ethics* 197. At the same time, the four principles approach is a starting point which will suffice to illustrate the issues for the purposes of this chapter.

[68] Hoppe, 'Medical Ethics and Patient Safety', 57.

In the case of *Hotson* v. *East Berkshire HA*, the case where the boy fell out of a tree injuring his hip, the interference with the patient's autonomy consisted of erroneously (though not deliberately) misrepresenting the facts to the patient in a way that prevented additional treatment steps from being taken, thereby ruling out a participatory involvement in the process. This idea also plays an important role when we look at the issues raised by the 'but for' test: even if it is clear, *ex post*, that there is a very good chance that the harm would have occurred anyway, the loss of the chance to direct one's own therapy represents an interference with the individual's autonomy. The alternative would be to accept a system where doctors can make an educated guess as to the likelihood of a patient changing their mind on the basis of additional information or a potential misdiagnosis – if it is generally likely that the outcome would be the same, then the (risk of a) misdiagnosis would have no consequences. This seems to be true in law, but certainly not in ethics – causation represents a *factum interveniens*, breaking the legal culpability of the individual, but it does not heal the moral implications.

Non-maleficence

The next principle, non-maleficence, which is seen as the obligation to not harm the patient – *primum non nocere* ('first, do no harm') – is an exclamation often associated with this principle (although its origins are unclear). In the context of errors and faults, it is difficult to find a place for this notion, over and beyond the statement of fact that where an error leads to harm, the principle has clearly been contravened, albeit unintentionally. In moral obligation terms, this is of little value: '[i]t is unhelpful to direct an accusation of contravening the principle of nonmaleficence at a hapless surgeon when it simply was not an intentional act [that caused the harm]'.[69] This means that, on its own, this principle does not stretch very far. Neither does this principle assist if a doctor simply fails to act in a situation where he might prevent harm if he acted. Foster describes it thus: '[the principle of nonmaleficence] will not complain if a doctor does no more than to stay in bed – as long as he is not in bed with a vulnerable patient'.[70] Combined with another principle, however, it begins to take shape as the central set of moral obligations that give rise to a duty of care.

Beneficence

The principle of beneficence can be seen as a catalyst for the principle of non-maleficence when applied to the question of errors and fault. Beneficence involves

---

[69] Hoppe, 'Medical Ethics and Patient Safety', 58.
[70] C. Foster, *Choosing Life, Choosing Death: The Tyranny of Autonomy in Medical Ethics and Law* (Oxford: Hart, 2009), p. 18.

the expectation that a doctor not only abstains from doing something bad, but also actively contributes to the welfare and well-being of the patient. This, of course, entails that there is a duty to act and, combined with the principle of not doing harm to the patient, this strong duty to act creates an obligation to act helpfully. At the same time it is clear that – under ideal circumstances – no doctor sets out to harm the patient. The question of beneficence is therefore particularly interesting once an error has actually occurred, as there is a plausible argument that to withhold information in relation to the mishap is a violation of the principle of beneficence. In essence, the doctor is expected to act in a way which is beneficial to the patient. Withholding information and refusing to acknowledge an error and accept responsibility are difficult to reconcile with this principle, but will remain a reality as long as the system for determining liability retains a strong element of having to prove fault.

Why are these obligations duties?

We have seen that the special nature of the interaction between doctor and patient (their 'roles') gives rise to certain legitimate expectations of behaviour, including not doing any harm and doing one's best to benefit the patient. The patient entrusts herself to the care of the doctor, on the basis of a common understanding of their roles as doctors and patients:

> The relationship between physician and patient or between hospital and patient is characterised by a level of trust which is not found in the same way in another professional relationship. In showing this trust, the patient exposes himself [to risk] [. . .]. The effect is twofold: patients want to rest assured of the best possible treatment, while the medical profession uses this trust to underpin their professional confidence.[71]

The obligations, imposed to counter an asymmetry in the relationship, are augmented where there is an additional explicit or implicit promise to act in a certain way (as the courts contemplated in *Kent* v. *Griffiths* when characterising the nature of the ambulance service or a 999 call, or where an explicit contractual arrangement is made as part of admission to a hospital or mere entry into an A&E department). Some of the defining cornerstones of these roles and promises can be found in a profession's self-given codes of conduct or general frameworks which contain moral reference points (such as the Declaration of Helsinki we mentioned earlier).

Further, it is clear that a professional community which gives itself, and is given by society, codes of conduct with a very strong moral hue, also establishes significant correlating duties. These kinds of codes of conduct enforced by a professional community are action-oriented, or rule-based, systems. The danger

---

[71] Hoppe, 'Medical Ethics and Patient Safety', 59.

of relying solely on such rule-based systems is of a loss of moral self-awareness of the actors in this context. Where ethical obligations are merely seen as the product of a codified rule set of self-governance, the intrinsic motivation of the actor, which is required to fuel the principles explicated by Beauchamp and Childress, and others, no longer plays any part. This is problematic because the unchecked proliferation of 'ethical guidance' seems to, at first glance, excuse the doctor from reflecting personally about the moral consequences of his or her actions. As we have seen in the discussion of *Richards*, *Bolam* and *Bolitho*, guidelines can assist, but do not necessarily excuse. Over-reliance on guidelines, or adherence to guidelines in the face of available evidence, will not be sufficient to exculpate the doctor. Pojman summarises this in the following way: '[e]thics becomes a sort of mental plumbing, moral casuistry, a set of hair-splitting distinctions that somehow loses track of the purpose of morality altogether. But what good are such rules without the dynamo of character that propels the rules of action?'[72]

The misperception that 'ethics' is simply a set of moral, codified rules that runs alongside and supports the world of legal rules is widespread, particularly in the biomedical research community. Obligations certainly come into existence on the basis of (or better put: are discretely evidenced by) such systems, but certainly also in the context of other systems, such as virtue- and duty-based constructs. The setting of the doctor and patient relationship emphasises the blurred boundaries between these different approaches.

At the same time, making these moral obligations in some way tangible and binding for members of a certain professional community serves additional, worthwhile aims. Primarily, self-regulation is a desirably flexible way to govern within communities that represent fast-moving regulatory targets (and this, to some extent, explains the sheer scale of self-regulation in medicine). The setting of specific obligations between parties in particularly high-stakes contexts also serves to encourage engagement: from a societal perspective, it is desirable to create an environment in which individuals feel encouraged to see a doctor if they feel this might be sensible. Beauchamp and Childress recognise this and outline the issue of accepting roles and rules accordingly: 'Health care professionals typically specify and enforce obligations for their members, thereby seeking to ensure that persons who enter into relationships with these professionals will find them competent and trustworthy. The obligations that professions attempt to enforce are role obligations, that is, obligations determined by an accepted role.'[73]

Were this not the case, the interaction between doctors and patients would not function to the extent that is required for a working health system. The

---

[72] L. P. Pojman and J. Fieser, *Ethics – Discovering Right and Wrong*, 7th edn (Belmont: Wadsworth, 2012), p. 159.
[73] Beauchamp and Childress, *Principles of Biomedical Ethics*, p. 6.

presumption of a strong set of moral obligations, based on roles taken on within a 'social matrix', together with promises made in codes of conduct, ethical guidelines and contracts, create the framework in which moral obligations lay the ground-work for a legal duty of care.

The special status of medical professionals

It is worth bearing in mind that the web of duties in medical interactions is not entirely separate from everyday moral obligations. Rather, doctors enter into an advanced framework, with many interactions covered by general notions of common morality, and some interactions covered by special ethical duties for medical professionals:

> Many moral *obligations* in health care are moral *ideals* from the perspective of the common morality. Many duties in medicine and nursing are profession-relative, rather than obligations either in the common morality or in other forms of professional practice.[74]

Here, again, the blurriness of boundaries becomes evident when we try to deter-mine the exact differentiation between what is expected of a doctor, in general and on the basis of the role he or she adopts, and what can be expected of a doctor, as a specific individual:

> It is doubtful that health care professionals fail to discharge moral obligations when they fall short of the latter high standards of obligation [treating HIV patients where there is a risk of infection to the doctor], even if obligations are measured exclusively by role obligations. Confusion arises because of the indeterminate boundaries of obligations both in the common morality and in the community of health professionals.[75]

Beauchamp and Childress later give the example we have already seen above, of the lifeguard who, by virtue of showing himself to be a lifeguard, taking that role in the context of a beach where the danger of drowning cannot be ruled out, makes a promise to go over and beyond what would be required of a mere bystander in the same circumstances. This begs the question of when, and why, an individual who holds herself out to be an expert enters into an additional obligation: '. . . [P]hysicians are typically able to lend more assistance in a medical emergency than other citizens, and we can therefore ask whether the physician has a specific obligation of assistance unique to persons with such skills and training. Here we encounter a grey area between a role-specific obligation and a non-role-specific obligation.'[76]

A person holding herself out to be an expert, by way of taking on the role of that expert in an appropriate situation, goes over and beyond the non-role-specific

---

[74] Beauchamp and Childress, *Principles of Biomedical Ethics*, p. 43 (emphasis in original).
[75] Beauchamp and Childress, *Principles of Biomedical Ethics*, p. 43.
[76] Beauchamp and Childress, *Principles of Biomedical Ethics*, p. 175.

obligation that we might attribute to a bystander and assumes, additionally, the duties of the role-specific obligations, be this of a lifeguard or of an A&E doctor.

CONCLUSION

The law has come a long way. From the decision in *Bolam* in 1957 and the way in which it was interpreted until *Bolitho* in 1997, we can see a specific and deliberate judicial deference to the medical profession. It was specific because it applied *only* to the medical profession, and deliberate because the policy, as can be seen in *Maynard*, was entirely intentional and openly applied. *Bolitho* changed the tone of the law, but it also fundamentally changed who the decision-makers are. Between 1957 and 1997, in effect the medical profession policed itself, while since 1997 the courts now claim the role as ultimate arbiters of medical conduct. This is right and is to be encouraged.

Indeed, the theme of the legal and ethical discussion of negligence can be summed up by asking the question: 'Who decides?' As we note above, the fact that a doctor owes a duty to his or her patients is not controversial in terms of either the law or the ethics. The existence of the ethical codes protecting the patient is enough to demonstrate the truth of this assertion in relation to the latter. However, what the codes may also suggest is a willingness on the part of the medical profession to take control of regulation.[77] Thus, the law's conflict with the medical profession can be seen as one that asks who controls medical conduct, with the patient almost tangential in the discussion.

Nevertheless, we must also be careful not to punish doctors for things that are not their fault. For that reason, we have not just a requirement that the doctor's conduct must fall below the required standard of care, but also that it has caused harm. Here, if anything, the law has gone in the opposite direction and made it more difficult for patients. This is particularly the case in relation to the House of Lords unequivocally declaring (albeit in a majority judgment) that loss of a chance of recovery cannot be compensated. This will clearly bar some patients from claiming despite the existence of a breach of duty and a resultant harm (the loss of a chance of recovering) that many would consider tangible.

It might be argued that this is not an unreasonable ethical position to take: the standards expected of doctors are not for the medical profession to decide, but the law will demand a high level of relationship between the error and the injury. In this sense, the law might be said to protect both the patient and the doctor. Of course, this is a difficult balance to achieve, and is the one regarding how much

---

[77] For an argument to this effect, see J. Miola, *Medical Ethics and Medical Law: A Symbiotic Relationship* (Oxford: Hart, 2007), in particular chs. 2 and 3.

professional autonomy to give to doctors before asserting control. This is where no-fault compensation schemes can seem attractive: by trying to encourage a more collaborative approach following injury, the balance becomes less important as doctors are not punished and patients are compensated for harm suffered. This might, in addition, allow the profession itself to regulate the conduct of its members through internal processes rather than using the law as a proxy.

However, the key point of this chapter must be that the law has, through *Bolitho*, sought to reclaim control of medical conduct. This is important because, as we shall see in the following chapters, *Bolam* became the test used for many ethical issues and thus its interpretation by the courts is key to medical law, not least in answering the question of 'Who decides?'

ADDITIONAL READING

Law

M. Brazier and J. Miola, 'Bye-Bye Bolam: A Medical Litigation Revolution' (2000) 8(1) *Medical Law Review* 85

S. Green, 'Coherence of Medical Negligence Cases: A Case of Doctors and Purses' (2006) 14(1) *Medical Law Review* 1

A. Merry and A. McCall Smith, *Errors, Medicine and the Law* (Cambridge University Press, 2001)

R. Mulheron, 'Trumping Bolam: A Critical Legal Analysis of Bolitho's "Gloss"' (2010) 69 *Cambridge Law Journal* 609

K. Williams, 'Litigation against English NHS Ambulance Services and the Rule in *Kent v Griffiths*' (2007) 15(2) *Medical Law Review* 153

Lord Woolf, 'Are the Courts Excessively Deferential to the Medical Profession?' (2001) 9(1) *Medical Law Review* 1

Ethics

S. Buetow and G. Elwyn, 'Are Patients Morally Responsible for Their Errors?' (2006) 31 *Journal of Medical Ethics* 260

J. Dute, M. Faure and Helmut Koziol (eds.), *No-Fault Compensation in the Health Care Sector* (Vienna/New York: Springer, 2004)

B. Runciman, A. Merry and M. Walton, *Safety and Ethics in Healthcare: A Guide to Getting It Right* (Aldershot: Ashgate, 2007)

J. Saunders, 'Good People Do Bad Things' (2013) *Journal of Medical Ethics*, doi: 10.1136/medethics-2013-101460

J. Tingle and P. Bark (eds.), *Patient Safety, Law Policy and Practice* (London: Routledge, 2011)

Case studies from this chapter are available online at www.cambridge.org/hoppe

4 Consent and autonomy

INTRODUCTION

Before medical treatment may lawfully be provided to a competent patient, there must be a legally valid consent. In this chapter we consider issues surrounding the concept of consent, and then that of patients' capacity to consent. Taken together, these two topics help to determine whether the patient can legally make his or her own choices about the treatments offered, and whether he or she has received sufficient information regarding the risks, benefits and alternatives inherent in any proposed treatment. Needless to say, the prevailing theme of this chapter is *autonomy*, which ought to be distinguished carefully from the concept of *liberty* (more on this later). We begin by considering the issue of risk disclosure (also referred to as the legally substantial part of 'informed consent'), which involves the question of what information must be provided to the patient before the consent given to the proposed treatment may be valid. Obviously, a patient deprived of adequate information may make a decision that is different from the one that he or she would have made had he or she been apprised of all of the relevant facts. If the depth or range of the information is insufficient, while he or she may be at *liberty* to make his or her own decision, it will not be an *autonomous* one. The question of how the law defines a relevant fact is critical here. What we shall see here is the way in which the law has, in less than thirty years, performed a *volte face* in terms of how it sees the provision of information. It used to look at the issue from the perspective of asking what the doctor's duty should be, whereas, increasingly, it does so from a position that asks what rights the patient has and seeks to protect them. What can therefore be identified within the story of the law's development is a cultural shift that has seen the courts increasingly identify and protect the principle of autonomy as they see it. However, the liberty to express autonomy is contingent upon that person being legally competent to make it. This chapter therefore then continues by considering the question of what constitutes legal competence in adults. The position of minors and the arrangements for decision-making involving adults who lack capacity to consent is dealt with in Chapter 5. Here, while there has been law reform, the general principles utilised by both the common law and the statute-based test have remained relatively constant, and have emphasised a 'functional' test for capacity. This means that the test is designed to assess whether the person has the mental faculties that make him or her capable of making a considered decision, rather than looking at and analysing the decision itself. This concept shall be identified and discussed and leads into the next chapter, which examines the consequences of failing the test and relinquishing the right to make one's own contemporaneous decisions.

RISK DISCLOSURE AND 'INFORMED CONSENT'

Given that treatment without consent is illegal if the patient is competent, the nature of that consent is both legally and ethically critical. Doctors are required not just to ask permission before treating patients, but also to disclose to them before-hand information about risks and alternatives so that the patients can make their own informed decision. In theory, this should lead to the decision being autonomous (although, as we argue later, this does not necessarily follow). The issue of risk disclosure relates to what information a doctor must provide to a patient before the consent may be recognised as valid by the law. The term 'informed consent' is now almost universally used to refer to this process. While it is technically incorrect (as it refers specifically to the US and Canadian approaches to the law), it has now entered the legal language to such an extent that we, like others, use the phrases interchangeably.[1] In the next sections of this chapter, we shall explore the legal

---

[1] In 1960, the Supreme Court held that: 'Anglo-American law starts with the premise of thoroughgoing self-determination. It follows that each man is considered to be master of his own body, and he may, if he be of sound mind, expressly prohibit the performance of life-saving surgery or other medical treatment. A doctor might well believe that an operation or form of treatment is desirable or necessary but the law does not permit him to substitute his own judgment for that of the patient by any form of artifice or deception' (*Natanson* v. *Kline* (1960) 186 Kan 393; (1960) 350 P 2d 1093). Charles Foster quotes this case and goes on to say: 'So, as far as American law is concerned, the first sentence was something of an understatement. Not only does the American law start with that premise, it tends to end with it too. And so far as the English law was concerned, the statement was not then true, but may prove to have been prophetic" (C. Foster, *Choosing Life, Choosing Death: The Tyranny of Autonomy in Medical Ethics and Law* (Oxford: Hart, 2009), p. 101).

English judges certainly used to consider 'informed consent' to be something different from English law, which explains the frequent references in *Sidaway* to the 'transatlantic doctrine of informed consent'. For academic recognition that the law in England cannot really be couched in the term 'informed consent', see M. Jones, 'Informed Consent and Other Fairy Stories' (1999) 7 *Med. L. Rev.* 103. See also J. K. Mason and G. T. Laurie, *Mason and McCall Smith's Law and Medical Ethics*, 8th edn (Oxford University Press, 2011), pp. 106–8.

requirements concerning the provision of information necessary to make any consent legally valid.

Negligence or trespass

The law makes a distinction between a consent by the patient that is faulty due to a lack of sufficient information (where the redress is through negligence), and that where it is so substandard that it is considered to be completely invalid. In the latter case, the law considers the treatment to have been provided without the consent of the patient, so it constitutes a trespass to the person. If a patient feels that he or she has been wronged, he or she will by far prefer to sue in trespass to the person rather than negligence. This is because for trespass, all that needs to be demonstrated is (1) that there was an interference with the victim's body (and medical treatment will constitute this); and (2) that it was without the consent of the victim. In negligence, meanwhile, the test is far more onerous, with the plaintiff having to show that a duty of care existed, that it was breached (as we know, this is difficult to prove), and that the breach caused the actionable harm. No actual harm need occur for a charge of trespass to be successful. The distinction between when it is appropriate to sue in trespass and negligence is therefore important, and was discussed in the case of *Chatterton* v. *Gerson*.[2]

The facts of the case are that Mrs Chatterton was given a pain-blocking injection after suffering severe pain after a hernia operation. It worked for a while, but the pain returned and the treatment was repeated. This time the pain did not subside, and she was left with permanent numbness in her right leg and foot. She sued both in negligence and trespass. The judge, Bristow J., had to consider when each should be used. Bristow J. drew a distinction between consent that is so inadequate that the treatment should be considered to have been given without any consent at all (trespass), and consent based on insufficient disclosure of information (negligence). He held that in almost all cases negligence would be the more appropriate recourse for the patient, as 'justice requires that in order to vitiate the reality of consent there must be a greater failure in communication between doctor and patient than that involved in a breach of duty if the claim is based on negligence'.[3] Unfortunately, he did not elaborate on when this might be the case further than giving two scenarios where trespass would be appropriate: administrative error and fraud.

Administrative error is best explained by Bristow J.'s own example of the exception in action. He recounted the case of a boy in Salford in the 1940s who, due to a mix-up, was instead of a tonsillectomy given a circumcision. In such a scenario, obviously, what was performed was different from what was consented

---

[2] *Chatterton* v. *Gerson* [1981] QB 432.   [3] *Chatterton* at 442.

to, and thus in legal terms there was no consent.[4] Fraud occurs when the consent is based on information that is deliberately falsified. In this situation, the consent will be based on deception, and so it is invalidated for that reason. The one detail with invalidating consent due to fraud is that the fraud must be 'operative'. This means that the fraudulent information must have been relevant to the decision made by the patient. Otherwise, if it had no effect on what the patient decided to do, the consent would have been based on correct information. It is not therefore only the bad faith, but also the fact that it contributed to the decision made, that is necessary.

The elements of negligence

In almost all cases, of course, neither of these two factors will be present. The vast majority of litigation will therefore be in negligence which, as noted by Bristow J., is the method by which justice would best be served.[5] Indeed, it is difficult to argue that this is not the most appropriate method of dealing with a situation where, in good faith, a doctor has forgotten or decided not to inform a patient of a risk that is legally significant. Given this, the normal elements of negligence discussed in the last chapter – duty, breach and causation – must be proved. The first part is extremely simple: a doctor who warns a patient of the risks inherent in the treatment owes him or her a duty of care. The doctor's duty is to warn of all 'material risks', and not to do so is a breach of duty. As we shall see, the vast majority of cases relate to how we define a risk as 'material' or 'not material'. Finally, the breach must have caused the harm. This used to be considered to mean that the patient must demonstrate that, had he or she been warned of the risk in question, he or she would have refused consent to the procedure.[6] However, as we shall see, the law has moved away from this view, and this is no longer the case.

The materiality of risk

The issue of materiality of risk was considered in detail in the landmark case of *Sidaway* v. *Board of Governors of Bethlem Royal Hospital*.[7] The facts are simple, and constitute a classic 'informed consent' scenario. Mrs Sidaway was offered a pain-relieving operation on her back. However, there was an inherent risk of between 1 and 2 per cent of nerve damage leading to paralysis. She was not informed of the risk, and consented to the procedure. Despite the operation being properly

---

[4] *Chatterton* at 443. See also, e.g., *R* v. *Tabassum (Naveed)* [2000] 2 Cr App R 328, where the victim's consent to being intimately touched was vitiated by the mistaken nature of her belief that the defendant was carrying out a medical examination.

[5] *Chatterton* at 443.   [6] See, e.g., *Smith* v. *Barking, Havering and Brentwood HA* [1994] 5 Med LR 285.

[7] *Sidaway* v. *Bethlem Royal Hospital Governors* [1985] AC 871.

performed, the risk materialised and she was left partially paralysed. Mrs Sidaway claimed that she should have been informed of the risk, while the surgeon who provided the operation stated that he had warned her of it. The case was complicated by the fact that the surgeon died, and could therefore not be further questioned by the court. The case went all the way to the House of Lords, where Mrs Sidaway lost on two grounds. First, it was held that she could not factually prove that she was not warned of the risk. Secondly, and relevant to our purposes here, the House of Lords was unanimous in its view that the risk was not material.

However, *Sidaway* is a case that is notoriously difficult to unpick, because the five judges produced three completely incompatible definitions of the materiality of risk. Since they all came to the same conclusion, though, none is technically dissenting. The best way of understanding the judges' decisions, and the reasons for them, is in the context of whether a doctor's duty could be dissected into its component parts: diagnosis, treatment and disclosure of risk. In Lord Diplock's opinion, there was nothing to be gained by doing so. Rather, he felt that the doctor's duty was a 'single, comprehensive' one.[8] Thus, he saw absolutely no reason at all for the test for materiality of risk to be different from that relating to any other medical procedure: and that meant *Bolam* and its 'reasonable doctor' test. Given that *Sidaway* was decided in 1985, this was therefore the 'pre-*Bolitho* interpretation'. A material risk, for Lord Diplock, was therefore one that a 'reasonable doctor' would disclose to a patient.

Lords Bridge and Templeman (with Lord Keith concurring with Lord Bridge) appeared to take a less strident approach. These three judges felt that while disclosure of risk was 'primarily' a matter of clinical judgment,[9] it could be differentiated from diagnosis and treatment on the basis that it was not, unlike the other two elements of the doctor's duty, a matter of technical medical skill. Thus, they proposed a compromise solution: *Bolam* would be used in the first instance, but the courts would retain the power to declare medical practice unlawful. In the words of Lord Bridge:

> even in a case where ... no expert witness in the relevant medical field condemns the non-disclosure as being in conflict with accepted and responsible medical practice, I am of the opinion that the judge might in certain circumstances come to the conclusion that disclosure of a particular risk was so obviously necessary to an informed choice on the part of the patient that no reasonably prudent medical man would fail to make it.[10]

So they defined a material risk as one that a reasonable doctor would disclose, *but* with additional judicial oversight (lacking in the *Bolam* test as it was in 1985) in recognition of the distinction between the technical aspects of medical treatment (diagnosis and treatment) and the non-technical (disclosure of risk).

---

[8] *Sidaway* at 893.   [9] *Sidaway* at 900.   [10] *Sidaway* at 900.

For Lord Scarman, there was a clear distinction between the technical and non-technical aspects of the doctor's duty. For this reason, a test based on the doctor's duty would be inappropriate:

> It would be a strange conclusion if the courts should be led to conclude that our law, which undoubtedly recognises a right in the patient to decide whether he will accept or reject the treatment proposed, should permit the doctors to determine whether and in what circumstances a duty arises requiring the doctor to warn his patient of the risks inherent in the treatment which he proposes.[11]

Having therefore rejected a doctor-centred definition of the materiality of risk, his Lordship set about creating his own from first principles. He stated that autonomy was a 'basic human right',[12] and that the purpose of the law should therefore be to protect it. *Bolam*, he added, could not do this. Rather, the test must be based on the rights of the patient, and this led him to recommend that English law adopted the 'transatlantic doctrine of informed consent' used in Canada and the United States at the time.[13] This defined a risk as material if the reasonable *patient* in the patient's position would want to be told of it.

> In our view, the patient's right of self-decision shapes the boundaries of the duty to reveal [. . . a]nd to safeguard the patient's interest in achieving his own determination on treatment, the law must itself set the standard for adequate disclosure.[14]

Needless to say, this *Bolam*-rejecting, patient-centred test was the antithesis of that proposed by Lord Diplock, and it was driven by Lord Scarman's identification of autonomy as the purpose of the law in this area.

So, let us pause for a moment and take stock of the decision in *Sidaway*. Of the five judges in the House of Lords, four provided substantive judgments (while Lord Keith said only that he agreed with Lord Bridge). Out of these, three distinct and incompatible definitions of materiality emerge. The first is Lord Diplock's pure application of the *Bolam* test (as it was in 1985). The materiality of risk was to be decided by reference to the 'reasonable doctor', with no judicial oversight (as *Bolam* was interpreted at the time). Lords Bridge and Templeman favoured a compromise where, although materiality was determined through the reasonable doctor test, there was additional judicial oversight in recognition of the non-technical nature of such decisions. While this resembles the way in which *Bolam* would be used after *Bolitho*, it is important to remember that this is not a reinterpretation of *Bolam* on their part – just the addition of an extra safeguard given the nature of the interaction giving rise to profound ethical duties. Lord Scarman

---

[11] *Sidaway* at 882.   [12] *Sidaway* at 882.
[13] See *Canterbury* v. *Spence* 464 F2d 772 (DC Cir. 1972) in the United States; and *Reibl* v. *Hughes* [1980] 2 SCR 880 in Canada.
[14] *Canterbury* at para. 41.

completely rejected *Bolam*, seeing the issue in terms of the patient's rights rather than the doctor's duty. For this reason, he preferred to adopt the US/Canadian notion of 'informed consent'.

Given such differing views, it would always be left to future courts to unpick the judgments and follow who they preferred. While it would seem that the compromise solution of Lords Bridge (with Lord Keith concurring) and Templeman constituted the numerical majority, this was not the path that English courts were initially to take. Rather, in the cases of *Blyth* v. *Bloomsbury HA* and *Gold* v. *Haringey HA*, both decided only two years after *Sidaway*, the Court of Appeal in both cases held that Lord Diplock's judgment should be followed.[15] *Gold* concerned non-therapeutic treatment – a sterilisation sought by a woman who already had a family and wanted no more children – and it was argued that the elective nature of the procedure meant that there was no reason to exclude any facts at all from the warning of risks. The Court of Appeal rejected this, stating that to dissect the doctor's duty 'into its component parts' (diagnosis, treatment and risk disclosure) would be to 'go against the whole thrust of the majority' in *Sidaway*.[16]

Blyth was even more extreme. Here, the plaintiff had asked specific questions about the side effects of the contraceptive drug Depo-Provera, and argued that she should have been entitled to full and comprehensive answers as a result. Again, the Court of Appeal rejected the argument, holding that she had no such right:

> Neither Lord Diplock or Lord Bridge [in Sidaway] were laying down any rule of law to the effect that where questions are asked by the patient, or doubts are expressed, a doctor is under an obligation to put the patient in possession of all the information . . . The amount of information to be given must depend on the circumstances, and as a general proposition it is governed by what is called the Bolam test.[17]

It is worth noting two aspects of this pair of cases. First, there is not even a solitary mention in either of them of any 'rights' that the patient may have. They are autonomy-free zones. Rather, the judges in both cases consider only the duty of the doctor, and the patients involved are essentially treated as incidental – and this does not sit easily with the individual-centric principles of the majority of Western medical ethics. Secondly, the cases do not accurately represent the judgments in *Sidaway* that they claim to. Indeed, the notion that there is nothing in *Sidaway* that states that questions must be answered fully is, quite simply, false. Each judge (including Lord Diplock) specifically alluded to the answering of questions, and held that if questions were asked they must be answered fully.[18] Thus, English law's

---

[15] *Gold* v. *Haringey HA* [1988] 1 QB 481; [1987] 1 FLR 125; *Blyth* v. *Bloomsbury HA* [1993] 4 Med LR 151 (the case was decided in 1987, but only reported in 1993).

[16] *Gold* at 490. It should also be emphasised here that this is not the case – see J. Miola, 'On the Materiality of Risk, Paper Tigers and Panaceas' (2009) 17 *Med. L. Rev.* 76.

[17] *Per* Neill LJ, at 160.   [18] Miola, 'On the Materiality of Risk', 103–4.

first reaction to *Sidaway* was to ignore any rights that patients have, and to interpret the House of Lords' judgment in a way that was even more extreme than even Lord Diplock intended. This was to change, however, and as we shall see the definition of the materiality of risk has moved further and further away from that of Lord Diplock, and inexorably towards that of Lord Scarman. The driver for this has been an increasing recognition of the importance of patient autonomy as the underlying philosophy behind the law, and we chart this in the next section.

After Blyth and Gold – autonomy-driven change

Since those decisions by the Court of Appeal, the courts have engaged in a seemingly unstoppable process of moving as far from those decisions as possible. The first significant case is that of *Smith* v. *Tunbridge Wells HA*.[19] Mr Smith was a 28-year-old man who suffered a rectal prolapse. He was offered an operation that was not usually performed on men, and suffered from, among other things, impotence following the surgery. He was not warned of this risk, and the medical evidence stated that there were doctors who would not, at that time, have given a warning of those risks. The judge in the case, Morland J., stated that he had to use *Bolam*, but provided quotes from both the 'compromise' camp of Lords Bridge and Templeman *and* Lord Diplock, insinuating that all essentially said the same thing. He continued by rejecting the defendant's expert evidence and finding that not to warn of the risk of impotence was 'neither reasonable nor responsible'.[20] He thus found for the plaintiff. This change of direction can be attributed to a recognition that the purpose of the law is to protect the 'right' of the patient to make his or her own decision.[21]

Another notable aspect to the case is the detailed consideration given in the judgment to the High Court of Australia, which in the landmark case of *Rogers* v. *Whitaker* dispensed with *Bolam* because it was deemed to be incompatible with patient autonomy.[22] In *Rogers*, the Australian courts instead adopted a hybrid objective-subjective test that went beyond even the US/Canadian 'informed consent' model favoured by Lord Scarman in *Sidaway*. The test is as follows:

A risk is material if in the circumstances of the particular case a reasonable person in the patient's position if warned of the risk would be likely to attach significance to it; or if the medical practitioner is, or should reasonably be aware, that the particular patient, if warned of the risk, would be likely to attach significance to it.[23]

---

[19] *Smith* v. *Tunbridge Wells HA* [1994] 5 Med LR 334. See also *McAllister* v. *Lewisham and North Southwark HA* [1994] 5 Med LR 343.
[20] *McAllister* at 339. The surgeon claimed that he had warned of the risk, but the judge found as a matter of fact that he had not. This finding is, therefore, somewhat moot, but still important.
[21] In particular, Morland J. made much of the fact that the claimant was still sexually active, so would have *wanted* to be told of the risk of impotence.
[22] *Rogers* v. *Whitaker* [1992] 175 CLR 479.   [23] *Rogers* at 490.

As can be seen, the first, objective, part of the test is the 'reasonable patient' standard. However, there is then the second element, which allows the court to consider what that *particular patient* may have wanted to be informed of. It is not necessary to discuss the benefits and flaws of the test here.[24] Nevertheless, it is clear that by spending so long discussing *Rogers*, Morland J. in the judgment in *Smith* was sending something of a signal to future courts that this is what he wished that he *could* have done.[25] As a statement of intent, *Smith* may therefore be seen as a case where the concept of autonomy was reintroduced into English law, and given priority. Nevertheless, it should be noted that it was a first instance judgment, and that the plaintiff had also been successful at first instance in both *Blyth* and *Gold*.[26] The key, then, would be whether future higher courts would embrace Morland J.'s approach. They did so, and with relish. *Bolitho* helped in the sense that, even applying Lord Diplock's view that *Bolam* should be applied just as it would be for diagnosis and treatment, a 'pure' application of *Bolam* would still mean, in essence, Lords Bridge and Templeman's approach of allowing judicial scrutiny. Yet, in the first post-*Bolitho* Court of Appeal decision, the then Master of the Rolls, Lord Woolf, went even further. In the case of *Pearce*,[27] his Lordship seemed to conflate the reasonable doctor and reasonable patient tests:

> it seems to me to be the law, as indicated in the cases to which I have just referred, that if there is a significant risk which would affect the judgment of a reasonable patient, then in the normal course it is the responsibility of a doctor to inform the patient of that significant risk.[28]

The quote suggests that if there is a risk that a reasonable patient would wish to be told of, then in the ordinary course of events the reasonable doctor would inform the patient of it. In this sense, the reasonable doctor test becomes, *essentially*, the reasonable patient standard. This does not emulate the test in *Smith*: it actually threatens to go beyond it and into the definition preferred by Lord Scarman. This view was confirmed by a subsequent Court of Appeal decision. In *Wyatt* v. *Curtis*, the court had an opportunity to consider the judgment in *Pearce*.[29] Again, it was to go even further, suggesting that, if there were to be a conflict between the reasonable doctor and reasonable patient in assessing whether a particular risk is material, the latter should prevail:

---

[24] See Miola, 'On the Materiality of Risk'.
[25] In an addendum to the case in the law report, Margaret Puxon QC provided a short note, which recognised that while the court rejected *Rogers*, it nevertheless contrived to reach the same result by a different route (see *Smith* at 342). It might be argued that this therefore constitutes what the judge would have liked to have used (see Miola, 'On the Materiality of Risk', 95–9).
[26] *Blyth* v. *Bloomsbury HA* (1985) *The Times*, 24 May; *Gold* v. *Haringey HA* [1987] 1 FLR 125.
[27] *Pearce* v. *United Bristol Healthcare NHS Trust* [1999] PIQR 53.   [28] *Pearce* at 59.
[29] *Wyatt* v. *Curtis* [2003] EWCA Civ 1779.

Lord Woolf's formulation refines Lord Bridge's test by recognising that what is substantial and what is grave are questions on which the doctor's and the patient's perception may differ, and in relation to which the doctor must therefore have regard to what may be the patient's perception. To the doctor, a chance in a hundred that the patient's chickenpox may produce an abnormality in the foetus may well be an insubstantial chance . . . To the patient, a new risk . . . may well be both substantial and grave, or at least sufficiently real for her to want to make an informed decision about it.[30]

If our interpretation of this comment is correct, what the Court of Appeal is saying here essentially introduces a reasonable patient test for the materiality of risk into English law. Thus, in less than two decades the law has gone from a definition of the materiality of risk even more restrictive than that imagined by Lord Diplock to one that is essentially what was suggested by Lord Scarman. The driving force has been an increased awareness and prioritisation of autonomy. Indeed, a close reading of the cases demonstrates that the courts in cases such as *Pearce* increasingly defined autonomy as the purpose of the law. Moreover, the shadow of *Rogers*, with its own pro-autonomy philosophy, hangs above it. The direction of the law appears to be heading in the direction of dispensing with *Bolam*, just as the Australian courts did. This trend can also be seen with respect to the issue of causation.

ANCILLARY ISSUES

Informing the patient of alternatives

If the patient is to make a truly autonomous decision, the options it needs to be more wide-ranging than simply accepting or refusing the single treatment offered. Rather, the patient should also be able to consider any alternative treatments that might be available. Whether there is a duty to inform the patient of alternatives is a question that has been discussed little in the common law. The one case that confronts the issue directly is that of *Birch* v. *UCL Hospital*.[31] In that case, the patient had been offered a diagnostic test (a catheter angiography) which carried a 1 per cent chance of a stroke. However, she was not advised of an even less invasive alternative (an MRI scan) which, although not considered to be as good a test as the angiography, carried no risk of stroke. Needless to say, the claimant suffered a stroke and sued. If anything, the case epitomises the more patient-friendly approach of the courts, in that not only did Cranston J. find that there *was* a duty to inform of alternatives, but he also rejected the defendant's medical evidence (which stated that the duty was merely to inform Mrs Birch of the risks relating to the angiography).

---

[30] *Wyatt* v. *Curtis* at para. 16.   [31] *Birch* v. *UCL Hospital NHS Foundation Trust* [2008] EWHC 2237 (QB).

The reason for this was that 'unless the patient is informed of the comparative risks of different procedures *she will not be in a position to give her fully informed consent to one procedure rather than another*'.[32] Thus, information about risks in a wider sense may be required, and it is hard to disagree with the logic employed by Cranston J. Nevertheless, other authorities in support consist of, on the whole, obiter comments. Thus, as Cranston J. noted, his judgment was consistent with that in *Pearce*, where Lord Woolf held that there would also be a duty to inform of less invasive procedures.[33]

It would seem to us that, if the law is to demand that patients be given the right to information, then it is only right that 'information' is defined in a wide-ranging way, and that includes alternatives. Indeed, to do otherwise would allow for a narrow, 'yes'/'no' decision on the part of patients regarding only the treatment that is being recommended. While this may protect the patient's *liberty* to make their own decision, it would not advance their *autonomy*. Moreover, it quite simply seems to us hard to justify keeping information about alternatives from patients, particularly given the philosophy behind the law being developed by judges. Given this, we have no doubts at all that *Birch* must be considered good law.

Communication

If the doctor's duty is to 'communicate to the patient all material risks', then it is clear that virtually all of the cases have revolved around the question of what constitutes a material risk. Far less explored is the question of what constitutes a reasonable communication of the risks. One case has confronted this issue directly: *Al Hamwi* v. *Johnston*.[34] Unfortunately, it fails to adequately define the law. The case concerned a pregnant woman who spoke very little English, seeking a consultation on amniocentesis. She entered the consultation meeting being very much in favour of having the procedure. The facts are contested in terms of what was then said (complicated by the involvement of a translator) and what leaflets were provided to her, but the end result was that Mrs Al Hamwi left the meeting believing that amniocentesis carried a 75 per cent risk of harm to the foetus, when the true figure is 1 per cent. She declined the procedure, but sued when she gave birth to a disabled child.[35] The question for the court was whether Ms Kerslake (the consultant) had a duty to ensure Mrs Al Hamwi's understanding of the procedure.

The judge, Simon J., held that to impose such a duty would place a burden on doctors that would be 'too onerous'.[36] He based his decision in the case, on the

---

[32] *Birch* at para. 74. Emphasis added.   [33] *Pearce* at 58–9.
[34] *Al Hamwi* v. *Johnston and another* [2005] EWHC 206.
[35] For an account of the facts and decision, see J. Miola, 'Autonomy Rued OK?' (2006) 14 *Med. L. Rev.* 108.
[36] *Al Hamwi* at para. 69.

whole, on findings of fact, but nevertheless the underdevelopment of the legal principles in the judgment can be criticised on a number of bases. First, there is the fact that it would seem from the judgment that any requirement to adequately communicate is not emphasised. Indeed, 'the impression given is that what is important is the imparting of the information and that its effective communication – actual understanding on the part of the patient – is less critical'.[37] Certainly, the case may be seen as an exception to the general direction of the law as discussed in this chapter.

Secondly, Simon J. at no point specifies what the doctor actually has to do for the communication to be reasonable. At one point, he does note that the doctors should take 'adequate steps' to ensure understanding,[38] but there is no guidance relating to what this might be. Our view is that the adequacy or otherwise of the communication would come under the *Bolam* test, as it is the arbiter of reasonableness in professional conduct. However, if this were to be the case, then the lack of examination of the actual communication is even more inexplicable, since the GMC's guidance relating to this issue is very clear in that it mandates and emphasises discussion and interaction in order to find out what the patient's preferences are and help him or her to arrive at an autonomous choice.[39]

Thus, what we have in *Al Hamwi* is a judgment – the only one on the question of what constitutes 'reasonable' communication – that says what the legal rule is not (a duty to ensure understanding), but precious little regarding what the legal requirement *is*. Cases of this magnitude are rare and it would be preferable if the courts provided more specific guidance when such an opportunity presents itself.

Causation

In order to bring a successful claim in negligence, as we know, the plaintiff must prove that the breach of duty caused the harm that he or she is seeking compensation for. This was traditionally understood as meaning that, in terms of risk disclosure, the plaintiff had to show that had he or she been warned of the material risk, he or she would have refused consent to the procedure. If the plaintiff could not demonstrate this, then the breach would have made no difference and caused nothing at all. Indeed, this was made clear in several cases, and in some the plaintiff lost on precisely this point.[40]

However, in the case of *Chester* v. *Afshar*, the House of Lords was to effectively dispense with the need for causation at all.[41] The facts of the case are almost

---

[37] Miola, 'Autonomy Rued OK', 112.   [38] *Al Hamwi* at para. 43.   [39] See Miola, 'On the Materiality of Risk'.
[40] *Sidaway* is an example of this.
[41] *Chester* v. *Afshar* [2005] 1 AC 134. For an excellent analysis of the case, see S. Devaney, 'Autonomy Rules OK' (2005) 13 *Med. L. Rev.* 102.

identical to those in *Sidaway*. Mrs Chester was offered a pain-relieving back operation with a 1 to 2 per cent inherent risk of nerve damage. She was not informed of the risk, which materialised. Interestingly, the defendant claimed to have disclosed the risk – a claim that the court rejected – so the risk that was unanimously defined as immaterial by the House of Lords some twenty years earlier was seen as material in 2004. The complicating factor was that, with admirable honesty, Mrs Chester admitted that, had she been informed of the risk, she would have taken some extra time to think about it and sought a second opinion, but ultimately probably would have consented to the operation at a later date.

The law, in theory, was clear. Mrs Chester's claim should fail on causation. However, the courts were directed to another Australian case, *Chappel* v. *Hart*, where a plaintiff was in a similar situation.[42] In that case, the High Court of Australia held that, in order to prioritise autonomy, the patient need not demonstrate that she would refuse the procedure *forever*, it was enough to show that she would not have consented *at that time*. The fact that the same risk would occur at a later date would be relevant to the quantification of damages rather than the question of liability. The choice for the House of Lords was therefore clear: it could either apply the normal rules of causation and find for the defendant, or it could follow the Australian approach and make a 'narrow and modest departure from traditional causation principles'.[43] By a bare majority of three to two, the latter option was chosen. The traditionalist minority pointed out that the rules were there to ensure that defendants were not held responsible for damage that they did not cause. Indeed, Lord Bingham was clear on this point:

> A defendant is bound to compensate the claimant for the damage which his or her negligence has caused the claimant. But the corollaries are also true: a claimant is not entitled to be compensated, and *a defendant is not bound to compensate the claimant, for damage not caused by the negligence complained of.* The patient's right to be appropriately warned is an important right, which few doctors in the current legal and social climate would consciously or deliberately violate. I do not for my part think that the law should seek to reinforce that right by providing for the payment of potentially very large damages by a defendant whose violation of that right is not shown to have worsened the physical condition of the claimant.[44]

For the majority the key issue was, like with the materiality of risk, patient autonomy. Thus, they felt that the law must reflect and protect the principle, which was its underlying purpose. If the law did not allow for the protection of autonomy, then the law must be changed. Lord Steyn, who provided extensive quotes from Ronald Dworkin on the nature of autonomy, was open in his view that

---

[42] *Chappel* v. *Hart* (1998) 195 CLR 232.   [43] *Chester, per* Lord Steyn at 146.
[44] *Chester, per* Lord Bingham at 142. Emphasis added.

Mrs Chester's loss of autonomy must be compensated: 'I have come to the conclusion that, as a result of the surgeon's failure to warn the patient, she cannot be said to have given informed consent to the surgery in the full legal sense. Her right to autonomy and dignity can and ought to be vindicated'.[45] Similarly, for Lord Walker:

> there is no dispute that Mr Afshar owed a duty to Miss Chester to inform her of the risks that were inherent in the proposed surgery, including the risk of paralysis. The duty was owed to her so that she could make her own decision as to whether or not she should undergo the particular course of surgery which he was proposing to carry out. *That was the scope of the duty, the existence of which gave effect to her right to be informed before she consented to it. It was unaffected in its scope by the response which Miss Chester would have given had she been told of these risks.*[46]

So in this area also the law has moved towards a prioritisation of autonomy – even if it is at the expense of an established legal principle. Causation represents a further example of English law's increased attraction to the Australian approach. While this 'pro-patient' direction is laudable, it must also be acknowledged that this change is less modest than Lord Steyn would have us believe. This is because, as the quotes above demonstrate, it would seem that *any* breach of duty (i.e. not disclosing a material risk) should now be considered actionable. The logic of their Lordships applies just as much to a patient who would have consented anyway as to one who would delay the decision – their 'right' to make an informed decision will have been denied to them. Despite the fact that the damages awarded would have to be minimal, this still constitutes the wholesale removal of causation as an element of negligence – unless we define the 'damage' itself as the loss of autonomy. Either way, the change in the law is radical.

Some final words on risk disclosure

The direction that the law has been taking is very clear, and it has moved very quickly. The courts have increasingly prioritised the principle of autonomy (although whether this is an adequate conceptualisation of it is open to debate and is the subject of our discussion of the ethical aspects below), and allowed it to guide them into changing the definition of the materiality of risk. The contrast between cases such as *Gold* and *Blyth* ('pure' *Bolam*, not a single mention of patient autonomy) and *Pearce* and *Chester* (where autonomy was protected even at the expense of the law) is stark, and it is difficult to believe that the two approaches are less than twenty years apart. Essentially, we have run the full gamut between Lord Diplock's view in *Sidaway*, through that of Lord Bridge and into the approach

---

[45] *Chester, per* Lord Steyn at 146.   [46] *Chester, per* Lord Walker at 153. Emphasis added.

championed by Lord Scarman in that case. Moreover, the signs appear to be that the common law may go even further and adopt the Australian test in *Rogers*. What can therefore be seen is that the courts, having identified a problem, have acted swiftly to solve it.

VOLUNTARINESS

In order for a patient's consent to be legally valid, we know that it must be 'real'. This does not involve merely making one's own decision or being in possession of sufficient information to make a choice. Rather, it also constitutes the ability to make a *free* decision. The law therefore imposes a requirement that 'real' consent is given voluntarily. This is perhaps an obvious point, but there are nevertheless some details that merit further consideration.

First, it is important to note that a signed consent form is not in itself consent, but merely evidence of consent. We are therefore not dealing with the issue of consent itself, but merely with an issue of documenting consent.[47] Therefore, evidence may still be adduced that vitiates it. That the form was signed involuntarily will be one of the most common of such arguments seeking to annul a signed form. Needless to say, consent given following actual violence is not valid consent. Equally, consent following a *threat* of violence, or even a perceived threat, is invalid. Indeed, submission in the face of threats does not constitute consent.[48]

More complex, however, is the question of undue influence. It should first be noted that there must be a distinction made between an attempt to persuade a patient of the merits or otherwise of a certain course of action and undue influence, which crosses a boundary. Essentially, the first is desirable, while the second is unlawful. In the case of *Re. T*, a woman who had previously expressed no religious convictions refused treatment involving blood transfusions (as a Jehovah's Witness) following a meeting with her mother.[49] When her condition deteriorated, T's life was deemed to be in danger, and her boyfriend and father applied for a declaration by the court that a transfusion would be lawful (in part as the previous refusal was at a point where her life was not at risk and therefore did not apply to the new medical situation). It was granted. Addressing the question of undue influence, the then Master of the Rolls, Lord Donaldson, stated that where the other party is a close family member, or the persuasion is based on religious belief,

---

[47] Many practitioners make no appropriate terminological distinction between 'informed consent' and 'consent form'.
[48] *R* v. *Olugboja* [1982] QB 320.   [49] *Re. T (Adult: Refusal of Treatment)* [1993] Fam 95.

this makes it more likely that the patient will find it more difficult to reject the advice, and undue influence is more likely to be found.[50]

While superficially attractive – in the sense that it does contain a truism and favours dispassionate discussion over emotional blackmail – the practical application is problematic. Indeed, family and friends are precisely the people whose opinions a patient may find important, and religious convictions can be a source of comfort to many. There is a danger that, if they are discarded, decision-making will become too medicalised, in the sense that doctors on the whole could seek to persuade legally, and that will mostly be in the direction of suggesting that the patient accepts the treatment offered. Moreover, it is interesting to think about whether the question of undue influence would have been raised successfully if T's mother had persuaded her to *accept* the treatment rather than reject it. We would speculate that it would not.

ASSESSING CAPACITY TO CONSENT – THE MENTAL CAPACITY ACT 2005

All of the rights mentioned above relate to patients who are legally competent to make their own decisions. Therefore, the rights are limited to those who have passed the test for competence, now contained in the Mental Capacity Act 2005 (MCA). If they do so, they gain the *liberty* to make whatever decision they like, for whatever reason they like:

... the patient's right of choice exists whether the reasons for making that choice are rational, irrational, unknown or even non-existent. That his choice is contrary to what is to be expected of the vast majority of adults is only relevant if there are other reasons for doubting his capacity to decide. The nature of his choice or the terms in which it is expressed may then tip the balance.[51]

Of course, this liberty to make one's own decision should not be confused with autonomy. Indeed, in order to exercise the latter, one needs more than to simply have the information disclosed – one must be able to understand it and to be able to analyse it to come to a decision. Thus, there is a nexus between consent and capacity to consent, in the sense that a person who has the latter is likely to be able to properly exercise autonomy, but it should nevertheless be emphasised that liberty and autonomy are not synonymous and that the latter requires the doctor to present the information in a way that is comprehensible to the patient (enabling the exercise of autonomy in the first place) – which is why the decision in *Al Hamwi* is

---

[50] *Re. T.* [51] *Re. T* at 102.

of concern. If the patient fails the test, then an alternative method of decision-making must be found. We examine this in the next chapter. What can be seen, therefore, is that there are significant consequences relating to passing or failing the test for capacity, and it is therefore an important component of how the patient will be involved in his or her own care. The law in this area has been relatively settled for some years, despite the recent legislation in the form of the MCA. The Law Commission identified three methods available to assess a patient's capacity: the 'status' approach; the 'content/outcome' approach; and the 'functional' approach.[52] The 'status' approach merely asks whether the patient forms a part of a group that is predetermined to have capacity: an adult with no mental illness. If he or she qualifies by being a part of that group, he or she is deemed to have capacity. If he or she is not, he or she is deemed not to do so. The Law Commission noted that the obvious failing in this approach is that it is inflexible and takes no account of the fact that some people may be competent to make certain decisions, but not others.[53] The 'content/outcome' approach considers a patient's capacity in the context of his or her decision itself. Thus, what is critical is the nature of the decision itself. As the Law Commission noted in rejecting this concept, such an approach would discriminate against the eccentric, and make it too easy to equate 'wrong' decisions with incapacity.[54]

The Law Commission's preferred model is the 'functional' approach. This assesses capacity by reference to whether the patient's brain has the requisite mental functioning to allow him or her to consider all of the relevant factors and thus arrive at his or her own decision. What that decision then is is irrelevant – as it is his or her right to decide whatever he or she wishes to decide. This was also the model used by the common law, as exemplified by the case of *Re. C*.[55] In that case, a psychiatric patient developed gangrene in his leg. His capacity fluctuated, but, when lucid, he was adamant that he did not consent to his leg being amputated – stating that he would 'rather die with two legs than live with one'. The hospital sought a declaration of lawfulness allowing them to amputate his leg irrespective of his views if his condition worsened. In refusing the application, the judge developed a three-stage, functional test for capacity. The patient will be considered to *have capacity* if he or she is able to:

1. understand and retain the information necessary in order to arrive at an informed decision;

---

[52] Law Commission, *Mental Incapacity* (Law Com 231, 1995) at paras. 3.3–3.7. See also P. Wilson, 'The Law Commission's Report on Mental Incapacity: Medically Vulnerable Adults or Politically Vulnerable Law?' (1996) 4 *Med. L. Rev.* 227; and J. G. Wong *et al.*, 'Capacity to Make Health Care Decisions: Its Importance in Clinical Practice' (1999) 21 *Psychological Medicine* 437, 438–40.

[53] Law Commission, *Mental Incapacity*.   [54] Law Commission, *Mental Incapacity*.

[55] *Re. C (Adult: Refusal of Medical Treatment)* [1994] 1 WLR 290.

2. believe it; and
3. weigh it up in the balance to arrive at his or her own choice.

The key to the test is the final part – which utilised the functional approach to assess whether the patient is mentally able to think through a decision. What that actual decision ends up being is irrelevant, and indeed it is noteworthy that the test makes no reference to its content. The first two elements of the test are merely precursors to the last – clearly, a patient who cannot understand and retain the information does not have a base from which to analyse it. In terms of believing it, the case of *B v. Croydon District Health Authority* made a distinction between a patient who is 'impervious to reason, divorced from reality, or incapable of judgment after reflection' (and therefore fails the test), and one who simply disagrees with the doctor.[56]

The approach of the Mental Capacity Act is similar, in that it also adopts a functional approach to capacity. Indeed, the test is only a minor modification of the test in *Re. C*, merely formulated in the negative. The test laid out in section 3(1) of the Act comprises four elements. A person will *lack capacity* if he or she is unable:

(a) to understand the information relevant to the decision,
(b) to retain that information,
(c) to use or weigh that information as part of the process of making the decision, or
(d) to communicate his or her decision (whether by talking, using sign language or any other means).

The requirement to believe the information has been dropped, but this makes little difference as a person who refuses to believe the information will fail parts (a) or (c) of the test in any event.[57] Other than that, the first requirement of the *Re. C* test has been split into two, and the need to communicate has been added. Indeed, this sensible addition merely reflects the truth that a patient who cannot communicate his or her decision – no matter how cogently they can think – cannot physically indicate consent or refusal, so someone must do it for them.

However, the Mental Capacity Act is different in one way – it is very clear in its view that the function of the law is to allow even those who ordinarily lack capacity to make as many decisions as possible. In other words, it seeks to maximise enabling autonomy even for those who may lack capacity. This can be seen in the way in which section 3 continues:

(2) A person is not to be regarded as unable to understand the information relevant to a decision if he is able to understand an explanation of it given to him in a way that is appropriate to his circumstances (using simple language, visual aids or any other means).

---

[56] *B* v. *Croydon District HA* [1994] 22 BMLR 13 at 20.
[57] This was the view expressed by Munby J. in *Local Authority X* v. *MM* [2007] EWHC 2003 (Fam).

(3) The fact that a person is able to retain the information relevant to a decision for a short period only does not prevent him from being regarded as able to make the decision.

(4) The information relevant to a decision includes information about the reasonably foreseeable consequences of –
    (a)   deciding one way or another, or
    (b)   failing to make the decision.

Everything is done to try to facilitate the making of at least some decisions by the patient. The Code of Practice supports and encourages this approach, stating that the Act 'provides a statutory framework for people who lack capacity to make decisions for themselves'.[58] This is also reflected in the principles of the Act outlined in section 1, particularly subsections 2 to 4:

1. The principles
    (1)   The following principles apply for the purposes of this Act.
    (2)   A person must be assumed to have capacity unless it is established that he lacks capacity.
    (3)   A person is not to be treated as unable to make a decision unless all practicable steps to help him to do so have been taken without success.
    (4)   A person is not to be treated as unable to make a decision merely because he makes an unwise decision.
    (5)   An act done or decision made under this Act for or on behalf of a person who lacks capacity must be done, or made, in his best interests.
    (6)   Before the act is done, or the decision is made, regard must be had to whether the purpose for which it is needed can be as effectively achieved in a way that is less restrictive of the person's rights and freedom of action.

Thus, it is clear that the Act attempts to allow even incapable patients to make some decisions for themselves – just because a patient may lack capacity to make one (complex and serious) decision, it does not follow that he or she is incapable of making *any* decisions. Again, the key is purportedly autonomy, or at least one rather simplistic conception of it.

If the statutory test for capacity is essentially a slightly modified version of the *Re. C* test, and the functional nature of each test remains the same, the key would be how the courts would interpret the MCA. It might be thought that the MCA's emphasis on autonomy might affect the courts, but it must be remembered that in *Re. C* the court did allow C to exercise his autonomy and protected his continued right to do so. Given this, it is perhaps unsurprising that the decisions of the courts have barely changed since the passing of the MCA. One case worthy of note,

---

[58]   DCA, *Mental Capacity Act Code of Practice* (London: The Stationery Office, 2007), p. 1.

although not so much for its treatment of capacity per se as with its conflation of capacity and voluntariness, is that of *A Local Authority* v. *A*.[59] The case concerned the question of whether A had sufficient capacity to make decisions regarding contraceptive treatment, and in particular whether she should be required to be able to 'foresee the realities of parenthood' if she were to be held to have capacity.[60] The court held that she did not, and used a method of deciding the case that was similar to that before the Act: it went through the test limb by limb. The interesting aspect of the case relates to the third limb, which requires that the patient be able to weigh up the issues in the balance. Here, the judge found that A did not satisfy the requirement – not because she was functionally unable to do so, but rather because her husband was so overbearing that any choice that she made would essentially be his rather than hers given the 'unequal dynamic' in their relationship.[61] As Bodey J. noted, 'the influence of Mr A over Mrs A has been so overpowering as to leave her unable to weigh up the information and take a decision *of her free will*'.[62]

We would argue that this is a misunderstanding of the test of capacity in the MCA, and a conflation with the concept of voluntariness (or, more precisely, undue influence). The test, as we have demonstrated, is clearly and unequivocally functional in nature, and it is designed to test the ability of the patient's mental processes to make a decision, not the nature of their relationships. While we do not disagree with Bodey J. that Mr A's overpowering personality cannot be ignored, we believe that this is relevant to the voluntariness of the patient's decision, rather than her capacity to make it. Nevertheless, we do not believe that this decision is as it is due to the MCA, not least because the element of the test to which it relates was also present in the old *Re. C* test.

CONCLUDING REMARKS ON LAW

The law has been at pains to place autonomy at the heart of medical law. Whether it is a coherent and effective conception of autonomy is another matter, but what is undeniable is that the will is there. As we have seen, the evolution of the law has been to try to move away from *Bolam* and towards a more patient-centred test. The driving force in this has been an increased recognition of the ethical element to the case and an increased willingness to prioritise it. *Chester* v. *Afshar* represents the most significant manifestation of this: the court recognised the ethical component to informed consent, and determined that if the law did not protect autonomy, then the law would need to be changed. This echo of the Australian approach is

---

[59] *A Local Authority* v. *A* [2010] 1549 (Fam).   [60] *A Local Authority* v. *A* at para. 63.
[61] *A Local Authority* v. *A* at para. 73.   [62] *A Local Authority* v. *A* at para. 66. Emphasis added.

significant and we would expect that sooner or later *Rogers* will be adopted in relation to the materiality of risk just as *Chappel* was by *Chester* in causation. Moreover, the major changes in the law have come from the higher courts, so there is little prospect of them being reversed. Just as we saw in the last chapter, *Bolam* has been reassessed and is on the retreat.

The Mental Capacity Act takes a similar approach to issues, and is also based on the concept of autonomy. Just as with informed consent, the law has been at pains to emphasise and protect the concept of autonomy. This time, the impetus has come from Parliament rather than the judiciary. Nevertheless, it is clear that they think along the same lines, although it should be noted that the Mental Capacity Act's definition is little different from that which was already being employed by the common law in *Re. C.* That said, it is still worth noting that the Act provides a clear and unambiguous philosophy of encouragement and empowerment for adults who lack capacity to be able to make at least some of their own decisions.

What can therefore be seen is that the Act, just as the common law with informed consent, seeks to put patient autonomy at the top of its list of priorities. But patients can only make their own decision when they have capacity to do so. What we shall see in the next chapter are the systems put in place to allow capable adults to plan ahead for when they lack capacity, and how the law treats those who have lost capacity and left no arrangements in place. For these patients, someone has to make a decision on their behalf.

ETHICS

We have seen an interesting evolution in the courts' approach to interpreting autonomy and liberty in the context of medical treatment. Before we look at the ethical backdrop to these developments, it is worth understanding what these concepts originally mean and how they come to be applied in practice. The overarching principle is that of autonomy and we will look at this first, before discussing and contrasting subordinate and collateral aspects such as liberty and capacity.

Autonomy is a paramount principle of law as a whole – not just of medical law. We can find aspects of autonomy in every area of law that touches upon the free will of individuals (think of contractual autonomy, for example, or human rights norms which deal with physical integrity or imprisonment). It is one of the law's foremost duties to protect and enable autonomous individuals and regulate the necessary trade-offs between autonomous actors. But what do we mean when we say 'autonomy'? The term originally comes from ancient Greek and literally means 'self-governance' (*autos* means *self*, and *nomos* means *law*). The concept was originally used to describe a political context: states and cities which were in a position to enact their own laws, regulate their own affairs and act in total freedom from outside interference. This notion was subsequently applied to the idea of individuals who were free to govern their own affairs, according to their own rules and in pursuit of their own goals. The political theory of 'contractarianism' can be argued to build the bridge between the autonomous individual and the autonomous state (or other authority) by holding that the autonomous individual can be limited in his or her autonomy only by freely consenting to such a limitation. The decisive point seems to be that there needs to be a free expression of personal will to exercise autonomy in any meaningful way: either by limiting it (for example, by subjecting oneself to the power of another) or by resisting the limitation (for example, by rejecting a certain type of interference from another). Any submission to the will of an external authority by necessity entails that this authority exercises power in furtherance of the individual's well-being, freedom and equality (you can begin to see the strong nexus between these concepts and the principles of human rights and civil liberties).

On the basis of this understanding of autonomy, it is clear that expressing respect for an individual's status as a legitimate moral agent within society is paramount to the functioning of society as a whole and to sustaining order in the interaction between individuals. As a starting point, many texts refer to Immanuel Kant's proposition of each individual also being an end in themselves (as opposed to being merely a means to an end). He casts this as a moral imperative and outlines the scope of this duty to not only apply to others, but also to ourselves:

Act in such a way that you treat humanity, whether in your own person or in the person of another, always at the same time as an end and never simply as a means.[63]

He emphasises the special status of individuals and a variety of collateral contexts come to mind (such as notions of human dignity, inviolability, physical integrity), many of which have played a pivotal role in shaping contemporary human rights law (more on this below when we look at how Lord Scarman might have arrived at his view in *Sidaway*). The Kantian approach suggests that we ought to see and respect rational agents as individual sovereign authorities, capable of forming laws for themselves through their own free will:

So understood, autonomy presupposes certain deliberative and motivational capacities: the capacities to assess critically any proposed reason for action and to be motivated by reasons that are independent of one's desires and presently held values.[64]

---

[63] I. Kant, *Groundwork for the Metaphysics of Morals* (GMM 429) quoted in D. Cummiskey, *Kantian Consequentialism* (Oxford University Press, 1996), p. 62.

[64] A. Reath, 'Autonomy, Ethical' in E. Craig (ed.), *The Routledge Encyclopedia of Philosophy* (London: Routledge, 1998), p. 588.

From the Kantian perspective, therefore, the individual in question needs to be a rational agent in order to be fully autonomous (which adds an unfortunate level of complexity when we address issues of capacity later). We should probably add at this stage that, while very influential and certainly a good primer for many of the issues that merit consideration, there is no convincing argument that suggests that the Kantian stance is in any way more plausible than other approaches to defining and delimiting autonomy. At the same time, it seems clear that any modern understanding of autonomy, particularly in the medical context, requires a degree of capacity to critically reflect and weigh up choices, and to question even the most deeply held beliefs if necessary.

The proposition that individual patients ought to play a decisive role in choosing or rejecting any intervention that might be objectively necessary to improve their well-being or even save their lives therefore flows from the kernel that is the special moral status accorded to human individuals, and finds an echo in the legal concepts surrounding the doctrine of informed consent. Gerald Dworkin[65] sees this doctrine as the social normative product of underlying moral principles and acknowledges the difficulty in transferring moral duties into legal ones, and vice versa. He very helpfully writes:

[The doctrine of informed consent] is a creature of law. But my interest in the doctrine is as a moral, not, a legal view. I make this distinction, not because moral and legal contexts are sharply separated, but to remind the reader that the law has specific features (such as the need to make a decision) that do not allow one to argue directly from a legal justification to more general normative conclusions.[66]

So how do we get from abstract moral norms (even absolutely paramount ones) to useful legal norms? What we have seen at the outset of this chapter and in many other parts of this book is that questions of consent are all-pervasive in medical law and ethics: autonomous patients must, in most cases, give valid consent to make a treatment choice lawful. They must also (a) be at liberty to make that choice and (b) have the capacity to make the choice. As we have seen, autonomy therefore involves the ability of an individual to self-govern his or her affairs. This self-governance must be free from extrinsic and intrinsic interference. Extrinsic interference might be a coercive environment which curtails the individual's *liberty* to make a free choice. Intrinsic interference might be a lack of capacity to make a meaningful choice, which curtails the individual's *agency*. The Nuremberg Code, precursor to the contemporary Declaration of Helsinki and outcome of the terrible

---

[65] Note that this is *Gerald* Dworkin, not *Ronald* Dworkin, to whom Lord Steyn referred in the extracts from *Chester* above.
[66] G. Dworkin, *The Theory and Practice of Autonomy* (Cambridge University Press, 1988), p. 101.

atrocities committed by physicians and researchers in Nazi Germany, provides a first glimpse of how these different aspects of consent might fit together:

> The voluntary consent of the human subject is absolutely essential. This means that the person involved should have legal capacity to give consent; should be so situated as to be able to exercise free power of choice, without the intervention of any element of force, fraud, deceit, duress, over-reaching, or other ulterior form of constraint or coercion; and should have sufficient knowledge and comprehension of the elements of the subject matter involved as to enable him to make an understanding and enlightened decision.[67]

Unfortunately, neither the Nuremberg Code nor the Declaration of Helsinki delves to any meaningful depth in terms of giving clues as to how concepts such as autonomy, liberty and agency ought to be filled with meaning (it may well be too much to ask of these instruments in any case). The key ethical issues in this area therefore revolve around initially undefined principles of *autonomy*, *liberty* and *agency*. A good way to remember the conceptual distinctions between these three terms is to understand that *autonomy* is in many cases the product of *liberty* and *agency*.[68] We will first look at the concept of informed consent from an ethical perspective and then structure the discussion in the terms outlined above.

Introduction: elements of informed consent

Informed consent is, in principle, the outcome of a complex process by which a patient or research participant authorises a proposed intervention. Beauchamp and Faden very helpfully differentiate seven different elements of informed consent in the context of medical ethics:[69]

  I. Threshold elements (preconditions)
    1. Competence (to understand and decide)
    2. Voluntariness (in deciding)
  II. Information elements
    3. Disclosure (of material information)
    4. Recommendation (of a plan)
    5. Understanding (of terms 3 and 4)
  III. Consent elements
    6. Decision (in favour of a plan)
    7. Authorisation (of the chosen plan)

[67] Nuremberg Code, Art. 1, available at www.hhs.gov/ohrp/archive/nurcode.html.
[68] Notwithstanding an individual's capacity to limit her own liberty in the interests of enhancing her autonomy.
[69] T. Beauchamp and R. Faden, 'Meaning and Elements of Informed Consent' in W. T. Reich (ed.), *Encyclopedia of Bioethics* (New York: Simon & Schuster Macmillan, 1995), p. 1239.

Beauchamp and Faden go on to emphasise that, in ethical terms, the pr
informed consent is used in different, sometimes confusing, ways. On the   .d,
it is used in terms of the principle of self-governance (and it is in this way that we
will discuss it below). On the other hand, it is used in institutional terms, encom-
passing the regulatory framework and, we suggest, also the largely documentation-
based understanding of informed consent often used by clinicians.[70]

What seems evident from the parameters suggested by Beauchamp and Faden is
that there is a certain amount of correlation with the legal requirements of
informed consent. Issues such as 'capacity' and 'voluntariness' can be found both
in legal and in ethical terms. When illuminating the underlying principles of
autonomy, we can also find these concepts in the guise of rational agency and
freedom from interference. The moral elements of the information-giving requirements are mirrored in the legal conditions we have seen above – particularly with a
view to the discussion of cases in the section on 'materiality of risk' in this chapter,
where the questions revolved around how much information was needed to constitute a legally valid consent. A discrepancy between the ethical and the legal
assessment of these parameters is beginning to take shape. Beauchamp and
Faden's fourth and fifth elements of informed consent, for example, can easily be
developed into a forceful argument against the decision in *Al Hamwi*. This may, at
first glance, appear odd, but if you refer back to the quote by Gerald Dworkin above,
you will see that this is a feature of the relationship between law and ethics: law is
there for facilitating decisions in individual cases and it is much easier to get from
an abstract moral normative statement to a decision in law than the other way
around. Let us take a look at autonomy before trying to unpick the relationship
between the different terms used in this context.

Autonomy

It seems to be clear that there is a societal consensus that individuals' choices ought
to be subject to as little undue influence as possible. While this strong moral
entrenchment of ideas of autonomy is evident, the exact character and nature of
the notion of *autonomy* is not as well defined and agreed. Gerald Dworkin writes:

It is apparent that, although not used just as a synonym for qualities that are usually approved
of, 'autonomy' is used in an exceedingly broad fashion. It is used sometimes as an equivalent of
liberty [. . .], sometimes as equivalent to self-rule or sovereignty, sometimes as identical with
freedom of the will. It is equated with dignity, integrity, individuality, independence, responsibility, and self-knowledge. It is identified with qualities of self-assertion, with critical
reflection, with freedom from obligation, with absence of external causation, with knowledge
of one's own interests.[71]

---

[70] Also see n. 47 above.   [71] Dworkin, *The Theory and Practice of Autonomy*, p. 6.

The criticism is that the terminological confusion leads to a general untidiness within the debate on autonomy (Dworkin calls this 'intellectual disorder').[72] The danger is, very quickly, that we work on the assumption that autonomy and liberty are important concepts without understanding their meaning and functioning. That is why it is important to grasp the delineations of these principles. Dworkin goes on to give an example of the type of disorder he means by citing a US case,[73] where the court held that a prohibition of contraceptive treatment amounted to an interference with an individual's privacy:

> Whatever the misdeeds of the state of Connecticut in this matter it did not involve any attempt to get acquainted with the personal lives of its citizens. It did involve attempting to interfere with the procreative decisions of citizens, and hence raised issues of autonomy and liberty – but these are quite different issues.[74]

His explanation is that it may be the common element of interfering with an individual's status as a moral agent which may have caused the confusion, which may well explain other jurisprudential intellectual disorder in some of the cases discussed in this chapter (re-read some of the excerpts of judgments provided in this chapter and note the use of the terms 'autonomy' and 'liberty'). We will look at the plausible distinctions, made by Dworkin himself, on what constitutes 'liberty' and what 'liberty' means further below, when we discuss his famous 'Odysseus' example.   ·

It is also worth noting that, despite the very dominant prevalence of autonomy and consent in medical law, these concepts do not automatically override other moral positions.[75] Where, for example, the exercise of autonomy leads to a disproportionate risk to others, this autonomy can rightfully be limited. Furthermore, there are plausible ethical positions which limit the scope of individual autonomy in the context of giving consent and it is worth bearing in mind that there is rarely a single ethical perspective which gives the right answer. Onora O'Neill (who is very critical of individualised notions of autonomy) summarises this thus:

> The libertarian tendency in medical ethics sees informed consent as necessary and sufficient justification for action. For libertarians everything is morally permissible 'between consenting adults'. Most other ethical positions do not view consent as sufficient justification. Even if there is informed consent, we may judge surgery without medical purpose, medical practice by the unqualified, or unnecessarily risky treatment unacceptable and may think it wrong to use human tissues as commodities, as inputs to industrial processes, or as items for display. *Informed consent is one tip of the ethical iceberg: those who think otherwise overlook the rest of the iceberg.*[76]

---

[72] Dworkin, *The Theory and Practice of Autonomy*, p. 104.   [73] *Griswold* v. *Connecticut* (1965) 381 US 479.
[74] Dworkin, *The Theory and Practice of Autonomy*, p. 104.
[75] T. Beauchamp and J. Childress, *Principles of Biomedical Ethics*, 6th edn (Oxford University Press, 2009), p. 99.
[76] O. O'Neill, 'Some Limits of Informed Consent' (2003) 29(1) *Journal of Medical Ethics* 4, 5 (our emphasis).

There is, it seems, therefore, a spectrum of ethical viewpoints and stances which range from the very permissive to the very restrictive. While consenting to medical treatment is explicitly privileged as a defence (as opposed to consenting to other dangerous activities), it seems generally accepted that an individual cannot consent to every act and thereby heal that act's legal and moral impermissibility.[77] The restriction of a person's liberty to exercise her autonomy in certain circumstances is usually a serious interference with her freedom and, it is generally thought, should be sparsely applied, again with one eye on, among other things, the terrible crimes committed by Nazi doctors. Here, we have the entry point for the discussion which explains Lord Scarman's human-rights-inspired approach in *Sidaway*. As a direct consequence of the Nazi atrocities, and the Nuremberg trial of some of those doctors who had committed these crimes,[78] the medical profession developed fundamental consent-centric guidelines on medical experimentation (initially the Nuremberg Code, later developed into the Helsinki Declaration). This departure from generally paternalistic (i.e. physician-centric decision-making) to autonomy-based (i.e. patient-centric decision-making) was strongly rooted in human rights terminology and can be traced to current international human rights instruments, such as the Oviedo Convention on Human Rights and Biomedicine. Lord Scarman simply picked up a thread that had developed much earlier and had gained entry into jurisprudence across Europe and the United States/Canada already – the appreciation that the medical law's first duty is to protect the individual's liberty and not merely look after limiting the physician's liability. While the fundamental underlying principle was also visible in English law, its wholesale translation into the medical context took longer than expected:

The English law goes to great lengths to protect a person of full age and capacity from interference with his personal liberty. We have too often seen freedom disappear in other countries not only by coup d'etat but by gradual erosion; and often it is the first step that counts. So it would be unwise to make even minor concessions.[79]

It is therefore vital that there be a sufficiently liberty-imbued context within which to exercise autonomy appropriately, and we will discuss this element of autonomy in more detail below. Where there is the liberty to validly exercise autonomy to consent to a certain course of action, this also, however, entails taking on a share of the responsibility for the outcome. Capron

---

[77] An interesting case to note in this context is that of *R* v. *Brown* [1993] 1 AC 212. Here, a group of men were convicted of wounding and occasioning actual bodily harm after engaging in consensual sadomasochistic activity on the basis that it is not possible to heal the illegality of their act by providing free consent. The court saw a limit to what the men could consent to. It is generally thought that the decision was a poor one.

[78] Formally, *United States of America* v. *Karl Brandt and others* (Case I), November 21, 1946–August 20, 1947, but often referred to as the Nuremberg doctors' trials.

[79] *W* v. *Official Solicitor (acting as Guardian ad Litem for a Male Infant named PHW)* [1970] 3 All ER 107 at 111, *per* Reid LJ.

persuasively: 'The freedom to make decisions for oneself carries with it the obligation to answer for the consequences of those decisions.'[80] This aligns with fundamental legal principles such as *volenti non fit injuria*: no wrong is done to one who consents.

The next question is, then, how much information is required to enable autonomous decision-making. Recent studies seem to suggest that it is, to a significant degree, less the cognitive ability of the patient in relation to the information given in terms of informed consent, and more the emphatic and emotional context provided by the person giving the information, which is determinative of whether or not consent is given.[81] The inclusion of elements of interpersonal communication, compassion and freedom from conflicts of interest forms part of the generally non-binding (or not directly binding) professional guidance. The law concentrates, understandably, on the assessment of the extent of information provision, which is a concept that is more accessible to empirical normative definition than feelings of empathy or sympathy.

It is also important to bear in mind that, in practical terms, autonomy is not best served where we follow the fiction of a complete consent. When speaking of 'fully informed consent', we therefore need to note the clear limitations imposed by sheer pragmatism: if a patient were in a position to fully and completely understand *every little detail* of proposed medical interventions, she, bluntly put, might as well carry out the procedure herself. Instead, she quite rightly puts herself in the hands of experts because they do, in fact, know better at this stage than she does what needs to be done. The patient might have a clear view on what she wants to achieve through obtaining medical treatment (in most cases, a therapeutic intervention), but the physician is the expert who knows how to get there. On the way to that therapeutic intervention, the patient chooses alternative routes, if available, or lays down thresholds of the types of interventions she would not wish to have under any circumstances. Nonetheless, she is voluntarily in the hands of an expert who will end up making some choices for her. Beauchamp and Childress underscore this with great clarity:

> To restrict adequate decision making by patients and research subjects to the ideal of fully or completely autonomous decision making strips their acts of any meaningful place in the practical world, where people's actions are rarely, if ever, fully autonomous. A person's appreciation of information and independence from controlling influences in the context of

---

[80] A. Capron, 'Informed Consent in Catastrophic Disease Research and Treatment' (1974) 123(2) *University of Pennsylvania Law Review* 340, 365. However, the Declaration of Helsinki limits this in moral terms in the research context: '[. . .] The responsibility for the protection of research subjects must always rest with the physician or other health care professional and never the research subjects, even though they have given consent' (WMA Declaration of Helsinki, Art. 16).

[81] A. Supady *et al.*, 'How Is Informed Consent Related to Emotions and Empathy? An Exploratory Neuroethical Investigation' (2011) 37(5) *Journal of Medical Ethics* 311.

health care need not exceed, for example, a person's information and independence in making a financial investment, hiring a new employee, buying a new house, or deciding to attend a university. Such consequential decisions must be substantially autonomous, but being fully autonomous is a mythical idea.[82]

This criticism is levelled merely at the notion that it is absolutely necessary for a patient to understand everything in minute detail. Still, this notion can be found in a number of normative contexts, most crucially in instruments with a high degree of significance for the medical profession, such as the World Medical Association's (WMA) Declaration of Helsinki:

After ensuring that the potential subject has understood the information, the physician or another appropriately qualified individual must then seek the potential subject's freely-given informed consent, preferably in writing.[83]

The Declaration of Helsinki is professional guidance produced by the WMA. It does not have a direct legally binding effect, but it does deploy indirect binding effect by virtue of forming part of the professional rules for registered medical practitioners in many jurisdictions. Non-adherence to the requirements of the Declaration of Helsinki will in many cases mean an inability to practise medicine as a researcher or a physician. The concept of individual autonomy can be found in many such guidelines and declarations and therefore it forms an important part of professional rules and regulations.[84] Article 5 of the Oviedo Convention contains a similar provision calling for informed consent, although the low number of ratifications of the convention may well mean that it unfolds less binding effect than the highly persuasive Declaration of Helsinki.

Beauchamp and Childress do not go so far as to fundamentally find fault with the idea of individual autonomy (far from it). There are, however, persuasive voices in biomedical ethics who suggest that concepts of individualised autonomy are no longer appropriate in modern medical ethics and that individuals need to be seen in the context of their environments. Beauchamp and Childress, on the other hand, feel that these two conceptions do not rule each other out, but their very influential work on the principles of biomedical ethics and the implied strong causal relationship between fully informed consent and exercise of autonomy has certainly not gone unchallenged.[85]

---

[82] Beauchamp and Childress, *Principles of Biomedical Ethics*, pp. 101–2.
[83] World Medical Association, Declaration of Helsinki, Art. 24.
[84] It is worth noting that 'individual consent' is a very Western concept of medical ethics. Other parts of the world have developed other approaches more based on an individual's position in a societal network such as a family or a community.
[85] See U. Kihlbom, 'Autonomy and Negatively Informed Consent' (2008) 34(3) *Journal of Medical Ethics* 146.

Liberty

So we have seen that it is vital that a patient be at liberty to express his autonomous choices (is 'free' to act) and the distinction between 'autonomy' and 'liberty' has hopefully become a little clearer. Gerald Dworkin writes that while the distinction between autonomy and liberty is sometimes a difficult one to make, it is the principle of autonomy that most effectively grounds informed consent.[86] We disagree with Dworkin insofar as he feels that there is the need to make a choice between either one or the other to explain the significant underpinnings of informed consent. As we have outlined above, liberty and capacity form ingredients of a sufficiently empowered state of autonomy (but we also acknowledge that this definition of autonomy is not undisputed and the degree of overlap between these concepts opens the entire discussion to Dworkin's complaint of intellectual disorder). A simplistic, but for our purposes adequate, conception of liberty means the freedom from extrinsic impediments to exercising autonomous choices. John Stuart Mill, and sometimes Thomas Hobbes, are usually cited when discussing the notion of liberty as the absence of undue outside interference with an individual.

[T]he only purpose for which power can be rightfully exercised over any member of a civilized community, against his will, is to prevent harm to others. His own good, either physical or moral, is not a sufficient warrant.[87]

Others go beyond this passive understanding of liberty and insist that an appropriate concept of liberty also includes possibilities and opportunities rather than merely freedom from outside influences.[88] In other words, an autonomous individual must have both motive and opportunity to perform an act that can be said to be a true expression of autonomy. The aspect of the opportunity to exercise autonomy being a part of autonomy can, interestingly, also be found in current GMC guidance on consent, although the overall unfortunate choice of language of the guidance almost implies that the patient's wishes might have to be approved by the treating physician.[89] Dworkin provided us with an outline at the outset of the sometimes blurred distinction between the concepts of autonomy and liberty and their interaction, and he goes on to provide an excellent example, which is frequently cited in scholarship:

[86] Dworkin, *The Theory and Practice of Autonomy*, p. 105.
[87] J. S. Mill, *On Liberty*, 4th edn (London: Longman, Roberts & Freen, 1869), ch. I, p. 9.
[88] Such as Jean-Jacques Rousseau and Thomas Hill Green. Also see Dworkin, *The Theory and Practice of Autonomy*, p. 105.
[89] GMC, *Consent: Patients and Doctors Making Decisions Together* (London: GMC, 2008), p. 6. Also note that the GMC's guidance is generally wanting in terms of the extent of autonomy it seems to confer. See S. Fovargue and J. Miola, 'One Step Forward, Two Steps Back? The GMC, the Common Law and "Informed" Consent' (2010) 36(8) *Journal of Medical Ethics* 494 for a criticism of the GMC's 2008 guidance.

Not wanting to be lured onto the rocks by the siren, Odysseus commands his men to tie him to the mast and refuse all later orders he might give to set him free. He wants to have his liberty limited so that he and his men will survive. Although his behavior at the time he hears the sirens is not free – he struggles against his bonds and orders his men to free him – there is another aspect of his conduct that must be understood if we are to evaluate his situation correctly. He has a preference about his preferences, a desire not to act about certain desires. [. . .] *In limiting his liberty in accordance with his wishes we promote, not hinder, his efforts to define the contours of his life. We promote his autonomy by denying him liberty.*[90]

Odysseus makes ex ante provisions in anticipation of a time when he knows his autonomy (in this case, his ability to critically reflect and weigh up his options) is going to be diminished. This shows the degree of capacity required to be truly autonomous (it also shows, interestingly, that it is respectful of an individual's autonomy to permit the individual to make provisions limiting their autonomy at a future time; it could be argued that this is a strong argument for the ability to autonomously and irrevocably waive a right to consent). An agent can therefore be autonomous without liberty and this goes some way towards explaining our assertion that liberty is a non-essential element of autonomy.

Agency and capacity

Rather than borrowing from Homer's Odyssey, Beauchamp and Childress provide a modern-day example of an individual who is addicted to alcohol, but has a higher-order desire to cease drinking. Were she to consent to a restriction of her liberty to kick the habit, she would thereby be promoting her autonomy.[91] This example provides the key to the most convincing of systematic explanations of the element of capacity within autonomy. The alcoholic may have a first-order desire to drink (first-order desires are those that focus on desiring certain activities or objects). This, strong but not ultimate, first-order desire can (in autonomous individuals) be superseded by a higher-order desire to stop this destructive behaviour (higher-order desires are 'desires to desire something' and generally presuppose a long-term strategy or rational thinking in making long-term choices). The rational agent therefore ought to be in a position to critically reflect, question beliefs and, if necessary, give her higher-order desires preference over her first-order desires. This also means being free from external or internal influence which interferes with her ability to critically reflect:

The capacity for critical higher-order reflection is a normal feature of rational agency which may be developed to different degrees by different agents, and which can be interfered with by such factors as psychological disorder, external manipulation of an agent's deliberative

---

[90] Dworkin, *The Theory and Practice of Autonomy*, p. 106 (our emphasis).
[91] Beauchamp and Childress, *Principles of Biomedical Ethics*, p. 100.

processes, and social conditioning. A full treatment of personal autonomy must spell out the kinds of influence that undermine autonomy.[92]

The idea behind the concept of *agency* is, then, that an individual is in a factual position to exercise her autonomy appropriately. This concept captures what we described above as 'capacity'. An individual may only have a limited capacity to act as the agent of their own autonomy in circumstances where she is not free from an intrinsic impediment. A decision in relation to an individual's agency or capacity has an immediate normative effect in that it either includes or excludes an individual in vital decision-making processes. A flawed assessment in this context means that an individual is either treated disrespectfully and unfairly (where she does in fact *have capacity*, but this is not recognised) or disrespectfully and carelessly (where she *lacks capacity*, but this is not recognised). Agency is not an either-or concept: a patient may well lack capacity to decide between alternatives of invasive surgery, but is more than capable to make decisions in relation to, for example, pain medication or meal choices. Agency therefore depends on the individual and the context.

CONCLUSION

The elements of autonomy in terms of developing a legally valid informed consent take on a markedly less sharp profile when illuminated in terms of the underlying principles of medical ethics. Autonomy, as a product of liberty and agency, is only the first step towards establishing an appropriate, patient-centric regime for the purposes of decision-making in the biomedical context. It is clear that respect for a patient's or research participant's autonomy encompasses not only a respectful attitude towards that individual's self-governance, but also respectful action. This derives, in part, from the particular relationship of trust between this individual and the health care professional or researcher.[93] This means that showing respect for a patient's autonomy[94] is pivotal, particularly in the context of an inherent power imbalance between physician and patient. Only by expressing this respect, and potentially also accepting seemingly foolish decisions by the patient, do we give that patient the room to express what Kennedy so persuasively calls his personality:

if the beliefs and values of the patient, though incomprehensible to others, are of long standing and have formed the basis for all the patient's decisions about his life, there is a strong argument to suggest that the doctor should respect and give effect to a patient's decision

---

[92] Reath, 'Autonomy, Ethical', p. 589.   [93] Beauchamp and Childress, *Principles of Biomedical Ethics*, p. 102.
[94] See Beauchamp and Childress, *Principles of Biomedical Ethics*, pp. 99–148 for a detailed discussion.

based on them. That is to say that the doctor should regard such a patient as capable of consenting (or refusing). To argue otherwise would effectively be to rob the patient of his right to his own personality which may be far more serious and destructive than anything that could follow from the patient's decision as regards a particular proposed treatment.[95]

The paramount point is that any given value can be consistent with autonomy, as long as the individual in question has accepted the value as his own and is in a position to critically reflect on even the most deeply held beliefs.

Finally, it is also vital to take the time to consider the different actors' perspectives in this setting. While it is clear that the patient's welfare and autonomy (in its various forms) must form the pivotal point of concern, we also ought to bear in mind the difficult role we ask physicians to play. On the one hand, it is necessary that they in many cases view the patients dispassionately and as 'machines to be fixed' in order to do what is required; in the next moment we may ask for compassion, empathy and respect for the patient's (occasionally irrational) decision-making. This tension can conceivably lead to an occasional imbalance between the physician's decision-making and the patient's right to self-determination and it is justified that the law often takes a special view of liabilities in the context of lawful medical treatment.

ADDITIONAL READING

 Law

Department for Constitutional Affairs, *Mental Capacity Act Code of Practice* (Crown Copyright, 2007), www.dca.gov.uk/legal-policy/mental-capacity/mca-cp.pdf

M. Donnelly, 'Capacity Assessment under the Mental Capacity Act 2005: Delivering on the Functional Approach' (2009) 29(3) *Legal Studies* 464

M. Gunn, 'The Meaning of Incapacity' (1994) 2 *Medical Law Review* 8

M. Jones, 'Informed Consent and Other Fairy Stories' (1999) 7 *Medical Law Review* 103

A. Maclean, 'The Doctrine of Informed Consent: Does It Exist and Has It Crossed the Atlantic?' (2004) 24(3) *Legal Studies* 386

A. Maclean, 'Autonomy, Consent and Persuasion' (2006) 13(4) *European Journal of Health Law* 321

J. Miola, 'On the Materiality of Risk, Paper Tigers and Panaceas' (2009) 17 *Medical Law Review* 76

Ethics

T. Beauchamp and J. Childress, *Principles of Biomedical Ethics*, 5th edn (Oxford University Press, 2001), pp. 57–111

G. Dworkin, *The Theory and Practice of Autonomy* (Cambridge University Press, 1988)

[95] I. Kennedy, 'Consent to Treatment: The Capable Person' in C. Dyer (ed.), *Doctors, Patients and the Law* (Oxford: Blackwell Science, 1992), p. 56.

C. Foster, *Choosing Life, Choosing Death: The Tyranny of Autonomy in Medical Ethics and Law* (Oxford: Hart, 2009)

O. O'Neill, *Autonomy and Trust in Bioethics* (Cambridge University Press, 2002)

G. Stirrat and R. Gill, 'Autonomy in Medical Ethics after *O'Neill*' (2005) 31 *Journal of Medical Ethics* 127

Case studies from this chapter are available online at www.cambridge.org/hoppe.

5 Incapable adults and children

INTRODUCTION

Minors and incapacitated adults share one specific legal characteristic: they are unable, at least in all circumstances, to make decisions on their own behalf. This has several legal consequences. The first is that we must try as much as possible to protect the person from harm. This means acting in their interests if they cannot make decisions for themselves. Secondly, we must be careful about the decisions that they do make in order to ensure that they make only those that they are capable of making. Once again, the reason for this is so that, as much as possible, we protect the welfare of such patients. Thirdly, if the patient cannot make decisions about his medical treatment on his own behalf, there must be some mechanism for determining *who* makes the relevant choices, and yet again a major consideration is concern for the welfare of the patient. Fourthly, and finally, there must be an acknowledgment that even if the person is permanently incompetent (minors and unconscious adults, for example, may become competent at a later date), they may be able to make some decisions on their own behalf. In other words, we must strive to let them retain as much autonomy as possible – and that means allowing as many decisions as possible to be made by incapable patients. Needless to say, this final consequence may be seen as a contrast to the others, as the patient's autonomous decision may not necessarily correspond to what is in their best interests. Much of the law's development in this area relates to this tension between autonomy and welfare, and this is the focus of the legal analysis in this chapter. We shall begin by considering the legal situation for adults who have failed the test for capacity outlined in Chapter 4, before continuing by examining that for minors.

ADULTS LACKING CAPACITY

The law relating to medical treatment and adults who lack capacity tells the story of a long process of change. Initially, as we shall see, the courts took the view that the easiest route to take to protect the welfare of incapable adults was medicalisation. However, they were soon to find that one of the unintended consequences of this was that the patient's medical interests were all that mattered, and so they set about modifying the rules. In the meantime, legislation initially proposed in 1995 wound its way tortuously through the various stages before finally coming into force in 2007. This statute – the Mental Capacity Act 2005 – tried to prioritise the autonomy of incapable adults as much as possible, a far cry from the law that preceded it.

By definition, incapable adults cannot make decisions regarding medical treatment for themselves. This means that either doctors must be allowed to act despite the absence of consent, or someone else must be nominated to act on the patient's behalf and provide consent (or indeed refusal of consent) for them. Unfortunately, the law was extremely slow to provide a solution to the 'problem' created by incapacity, and it was not until 1989 that this was finally done. Before that, there was simply no legal provision for dealing with incapable adults. In the landmark case of *F* v. *West Berkshire Health Authority*, Lord Brandon recognised this fact by noting that '[t]he common law would be seriously defective if it failed to provide a solution to the problem created by such inability to consent'.[1] In that case, the House of Lords set about creating a framework through which such treatments might be legally justified. The case concerned the proposed sterilisation of a 36-year-old woman with serious learning difficulties who had begun to form a sexual relationship with another voluntary in-patient. Ensuring the appropriate use of contraceptive methods proved impossible and in order to prevent an unwanted pregnancy, the sterilisation was proposed. The question for the Lords was how (if at all) such a medical procedure might be legally justified.

The answer in the mind of the House of Lords was simple: they would medicalise the issue. Lord Brandon stated that a patient may be provided with medical treatment if they are incapable as long as that treatment was in their 'best interests'. The definition that he gave for this was so wide as to be almost meaningless:

The operation or other treatment will be in their best interests if, but only if, it is carried out in order either to save their lives or to ensure improvement or prevent deterioration in their physical or mental health.[2]

---

[1] *F* v. *West Berkshire HA* [1989] 2 All ER 545 at 551.   [2] *F* at 551.

The test for establishing whether this should be the case, according to his Lordship, should be the same as that for negligence – in other words, *Bolam*. This is despite the fact that the Court of Appeal in the case had come to the conclusion that *Bolam* was 'insufficiently stringent' to protect the welfare of incapable adults.[3] It must be borne in mind that, as this was 1989 and the courts were in the midst of *Bolam*-mania, such an approach was essentially an abrogation of responsibility to the medical profession. Indeed, this was precisely the focus of criticism of the case.[4] Needless to say, any 'rights' pertaining to the patient were not considered, including what she might have wanted. Rather, her 'interests' were firmly seen as rooted in her medical welfare, which is what *Bolam* was seen as protecting:

If doctors were to be required, in deciding whether an operation or other treatment was in the best interests of adults incompetent to give consent, to apply some test more stringent than the Bolam test, the result would be that such adults would, in some circumstances at least, be deprived of the benefit of medical treatment which adults competent to give consent would enjoy.[5]

Thus, on the first occasion that the House of Lords was able to set a framework for treating incapable adults, they handed all decision-making power to medical professionals. While this is not unusual in medical law, it proved to be such an unpopular choice that the Law Commission was asked (partly in response to this judgment) to consider the law in this area.[6] They, too, were to disagree with the House of Lords.

The Law Commission report and the road to new legislation

The Law Commission was unimpressed with the approach taken by the House of Lords in *F*, and in particular the decision that a doctor who was acting non-negligently was automatically acting in the patient's best interests. Indeed, it noted that even medical bodies were critical of the decision:

The apparent conflation of the criterion for assessing complaints about professional negligence with the criterion for treating persons unable to consent has been the butt of vehement criticism. No medical professional or body responding to Consultation Paper No 129 argued in favour of retaining such a definition of 'best interests'. Many were extremely anxious to see some clear and principled guidance given as to what 'best interests' might involve. The British Medical Association, for its part, supported our provisional proposals for statutory guidance 'without reservation'.[7]

After stating that the approach that it would recommend would constitute a significant departure from the law as it stood, the Commission provided its own

---

[3] *F* at 559–60.
[4] See, e.g., J. Shaw, 'Sterilisation of Mentally Handicapped People: Judges Rule OK' (1990) 53 *MLR* 91.
[5] *F* at 560.   [6] Law Commission, *Mental Incapacity* (Law Com 231, 1995), para. 1.4.
[7] Law Commission, *Mental Incapacity*, para. 3.26.

vision for how the law should be framed.[8] It noted that a statute was a blunt instrument, and thus that it would be impossible to legislate in such a way that would allow a person's best interests to be specifically identified; and thus opted for a non-exhaustive 'checklist' of factors which should point the way to where a patient's best interests might be said to lie.[9] The resulting checklist comprised four points:

(i) 'the ascertainable past and present wishes and feelings of the person concerned, and the factors that person would consider if able to do so';

(ii) 'the need to permit and encourage the person to participate, or to improve his or her ability to participate, as fully as possible in anything done for and any decision affecting him or her';

(iii) the views of other people who it is 'appropriate and practicable to consult about the person's wishes and feelings and what would be in his or her best interests';

(iv) whether an alternative course of action exists that would achieve the same ends 'in a manner less restrictive of the person's freedom of action'.[10]

As we can see, this is indeed a significant departure from *F*. The patient's interests are clearly distinct from her best *medical* interests, and the emphasis is on autonomy: finding out what the patient would have wanted had she been competent, and encouraging her to participate in as many decisions as possible. This was deliberate, with the Commission keen to infuse a 'substituted judgment' test (which takes the same approach), popular in Canadian and US law, into the English system.[11] This proved to be a popular recommendation, with the checklist approach and its general philosophy being supported by respondents to a subsequent consultation document.[12] The only modification was that two further items were added to the checklist. First, whether there 'is a reasonable expectation of the person recovering capacity ... in the foreseeable future'; and, secondly, the need 'to be satisfied that the wishes of the person without capacity were not the result of undue influence'.[13]

The Mental Capacity Act 2005

Progress towards the legislation being passed continued, albeit sporadically.[14] However, following a name change (to emphasise the participation of patients rather than their lack of it) – the original bill had been named the Mental Incapacity

---

[8] Law Commission, *Mental Incapacity*, para. 3.26.   [9] Law Commission, *Mental Incapacity*, para. 3.26.
[10] Law Commission, *Mental Incapacity*, para. 3.28.   [11] Law Commission, *Mental Incapacity*, para. 3.26.
[12] *Who Decides? Making Decisions on Behalf of Mentally Incapacitated Adults* (Cm 3803, 1997). The responses were collated and the consequent recommendations published as a policy document – *Making Decisions* (Cm 4465, 1999).
[13] *Making Decisions*, 1.12.
[14] See J. Miola, *Medical Ethics and Medical Law: A Symbiotic Relationship* (Oxford: Hart, 2007), ch. 6.

Bill – the Mental Capacity Act 2005 was passed and came into force in 2007. Section 4 of the Act deals with best interests,[15] and the checklist approach remains:

4 Best Interests
(1) In determining for the purposes of this Act what is in a person's best interests, the person making the determination must not make it merely on the basis of –
   (a) the person's age or appearance, or
   (b) a condition of his, or an aspect of his behaviour, which might lead others to make unjustified assumptions about what might be in his best interests.
(2) The person making the determination must consider all the relevant circumstances and, in particular, take the following steps.
(3) He must consider –
   (a) whether it is likely that the person will at some time have capacity in relation to the matter in question, and
   (b) if it appears likely that he will, when that is likely to be.
(4) He must, so far as reasonably practicable, permit and encourage the person to participate, or to improve his ability to participate, as fully as possible in any act done for him and any decision affecting him.
(5) Where the determination relates to life-sustaining treatment he must not, in considering whether the treatment is in the best interests of the person concerned, be motivated by a desire to bring about his death.
(6) He must consider, so far as is reasonably ascertainable –
   (a) the person's past and present wishes and feelings (and, in particular, any relevant written statement made by him when he had capacity),
   (b) the beliefs and values that would be likely to influence his decision if he had capacity, and
   (c) the other factors that he would be likely to consider if he were able to do so.
(7) He must take into account, if it is practicable and appropriate to consult them, the views of –
   (a) anyone named by the person as someone to be consulted on the matter in question or on matters of that kind,
   (b) anyone engaged in caring for the person or interested in his welfare,
   (c) any donee of a lasting power of attorney granted by the person, and
   (d) any deputy appointed for the person by the court,
as to what would be in the person's best interests and, in particular, as to the matters mentioned in subsection (6).

It is plain to see the approach of the Law Commission – the attempt to allow even incapacitated adults to have as much autonomy as possible – in the final version of the Act. Equally evident is the widening of the concept of best interests way beyond the bounds of merely being best *medical* interests.[16] Although many elements of substituted judgment remain, the explanatory notes accompanying the Act are at pains to point out that it is not determinative and thus that:

---

[15] Although the Act's approach has been subject to some recent criticism: see T. Hope *et al.*, 'Best Interests, Dementia and the Mental Capacity Act 2005' (2009) 35 *Journal of Medical Ethics* 733.
[16] Interestingly, while the legislative process was ongoing, the courts were similarly reforming the law, and had successfully widened the scope themselves. See, e.g., the judgments of Butler-Sloss P. in *Re. A (Medical Treatment: Male Sterilisation)* [2000] 1 FLR 549 and *Re. SL (Adult Patient: Sterilisation)* [2000] 2 FCR 452.

it requires a determination made by applying an objective test as to what would be in the person's best interests. All the relevant circumstances, including the factors mentioned in the clause must be considered, but none carries any more weight or priority than another.[17]

Nevertheless, it is a huge improvement on the decision in *F*, in that it encourages participation by adults with learning difficulties, and recognises the principle of autonomy. Moreover, it also provides alternative means for incapable adults to be able to make their own decisions in the form of advance decisions and the granting of lasting powers of attorney (LPA).

Advance decisions are covered in sections 24 to 26 of the Act. They are effectively living wills, and specify the patient's choices regarding potential future medical treatment. It is important to note that as patients cannot *demand* treatment that a medical practitioner does not consider to be in their best interests, advance decisions give effect to refusals of certain treatments. Properly constituted advance decisions must be respected by medical practitioners, otherwise they may face criminal and/or civil prosecution. In order to be properly constituted, the directive must be both valid and applicable to the situation faced by the patient. The rules regarding these elements are provided in section 25 of the Act:

(1) An advance decision does not affect the liability which a person may incur for carrying out or continuing a treatment in relation to P unless the decision is at the material time –
  (a) valid, and
  (b) applicable to the treatment.
(2) An advance decision is not valid if P –
  (a) has withdrawn the decision at a time when he had capacity to do so,
  (b) has, under a lasting power of attorney created after the advance decision was made, conferred authority on the donee (or, if more than one, any of them) to give or refuse consent to the treatment to which the advance decision relates, or
  (c) has done anything else clearly inconsistent with the advance decision remaining his fixed decision.
(3) An advance decision is not applicable to the treatment in question if at the material time P has capacity to give or refuse consent to it.
(4) An advance decision is not applicable to the treatment in question if –
  (a) that treatment is not the treatment specified in the advance decision,
  (b) any circumstances specified in the advance decision are absent, or
  (c) there are reasonable grounds for believing that circumstances exist which P did not anticipate at the time of the advance decision and which would have affected his decision had he anticipated them.

---

[17] See www.opsi.gov.uk/acts/acts2005/en/ukpgaen_20050009_en_1.htm.

(5) An advance decision is not applicable to life-sustaining treatment unless –
  (a) the decision is verified by a statement by P to the effect that it is to apply to that treatment even if life is at risk, and
  (b) the decision and statement comply with subsection (6).
(6) A decision or statement complies with this subsection only if –
  (a) it is in writing,
  (b) it is signed by P or by another person in P's presence and by P's direction,
  (c) the signature is made or acknowledged by P in the presence of a witness, and
  (d) the witness signs it, or acknowledges his signature, in P's presence.
(7) The existence of any lasting power of attorney other than one of a description mentioned in subsection (2)(b) does not prevent the advance decision from being regarded as valid and applicable.

As we can see, there is no requirement for the advance decision to be in writing unless it relates to life-sustaining treatment,[18] although it is recommended that such decisions are in written form.[19] It is also worth noting that if an LPA has been granted after the advance decision was made, *and it includes the power to give or refuse consent to the treatment to which the advance decision relates*, then the advance decision will be invalid (under section 25(2)(b)). The purpose of advance decisions is, in theory, to help the incapacitated patient make an autonomous choice by allowing her to make her decisions before she loses capacity. In this sense, the fact that it is legally binding is an important element in allowing such decisions to bite. Also noteworthy is the fact that the Code of Practice advises patients to regularly update their advance decisions, as not doing so may raise doubts about validity and applicability:

Decisions made a long time in advance are not automatically invalid or inapplicable, but they may raise doubts when deciding whether they are valid and applicable. A written decision that is regularly reviewed is more likely to be valid and applicable to current circumstances – particularly for progressive illnesses. This is because it is more likely to have taken on board changes that have occurred in a person's life since they made their decision.[20]

Again, this is a sensible attempt to protect patient autonomy – since their decision may only be said to be autonomous if it reflects what they would have wanted *at the time that the decision is made* (rather than when the directive was made). Older decisions are less likely to be representative of the patient's current feelings. The ability to make advance decisions forms one part of the two measures designed to assist in medical decision-making. The other is the ability to grant LPAs.

---

[18] See also *Mental Capacity Act Code of Practice* (London: The Stationery Office, 2007), para. 9.10.
[19] *Mental Capacity Act Code of Practice*, para. 9.18.   [20] *Mental Capacity Act Code of Practice*, para. 9.29.

Under sections 9 to 14 of the MCA, patients may appoint a person (or persons) who may make decisions on behalf of the incapacitated patient. These decisions are to be treated as if they were made by the patient herself. In theory, this should be even more autonomy-enhancing for patients as it allows, for example, an eccentric person to nominate someone who knows their views to make decisions for them. However, attorneys are able to act under one important qualification: under section 9(4)(a) decisions made are subject to 'the provisions of this Act and, in particular, sections 1 (the principles) and 4 (best interests)'. This means that the attorney's decision on behalf of an eccentric patient might be open to challenge even if they were an accurate reflection of her views. In many respects, this is a qualification that makes sense, as the attorney may benefit from the death of the patient. Nevertheless, it is inconsistent with the general philosophy behind the Act, which is about supporting and enhancing autonomy as much as possible.

Overall, the MCA's treatment of the incapacitated patient represents a huge change – in both content and philosophy – from the common law that sparked the Law Commission into action. As we have seen, the legislative framework has been one which has consistently sought to prioritise and maximise autonomy. It encourages participation, and considerably widens the scope of best interests away from a medically controlled medical best interest to, in theory at least, a wider concept that gives great weight to the views of the patient.

Post-MCA cases – the MCA in the courtroom

Just as with capacity to consent, examined in the last chapter, the key will of course be how the courts interpret the MCA. Again, it must be said that the common law was not much different from what ended up being in the MCA – and in relation to best interests in particular the development of the common law in the period between the Law Commission's report and the actual passing of the Act made it far closer to what the Law Commission envisaged. As we mentioned above, the courts had already separated *best* from *medical* interests without the MCA. Thus, again not surprisingly, there has been little discernible change in the attitude of judges. However, it may be said that the process adopted by the courts has changed. Thus, after determining that the patient lacks capacity, the courts now tend to go through the checklist of factors in the Act before reaching their conclusion. Thus, in many cases the wishes of the patient and evidence from friends and relatives regarding what the patient would have wanted are gathered together. What the patient might have wanted is then balanced with welfare considerations in a 'balance sheet' and a final decision is then made regarding the patient's best interests. However, some details are worth mentioning.

The first is that the patient retains interests even if she is in no state to appreciate them. This was the case in *Ashan* v. *University Hospitals Leicester*, where the patient was in a comatose state and one question for the court was whether it was unreasonable for the hospital not to spend extra money to provide care in accordance with her religious beliefs.[21] The hospital had argued that, since she would not be in a state to appreciate it, the extra measures would not be in her best interests. The court disagreed, and held that the public would expect that, to protect the patient's dignity, treatment should accord with their beliefs *even if they are not conscious to appreciate it*. The case is a good example of the way in which the concept of best interests has moved beyond simple *medical* interests, and also of the fact that the MCA did not necessarily move the common law on too far – *Ashan* was decided in 2006, before the Act came into force, although the court acknowledged that it would do soon so tried to anticipate it. Nevertheless, it is noticeable that it was able to reach the same decision with no legal gymnastics necessary.

Also, we should not forget that the MCA's best interest test asks not only that the patient's past feelings are taken into account, but also their *present* ones, even if they are legally incapable. Indeed, the MCA makes it clear that every effort must be made to involve the patient in decision-making. To this end, the courts have on several occasions made it clear that the feelings of incapable patients are not to be considered meaningless and should be taken into account as a part of the 'balance sheet'.[22] This is particularly the case, and the wishes should be given considerable weight, where the patient is actively refusing the treatment being offered.[23]

A further issue relates to the duty to consult others. The Code of Practice accompanying the Act states that relatives and friends should be consulted about two things: the patient's best interests and their ascertainable feelings.[24] It is difficult to understand the difference between the two, because it would seem to us to make little sense to ask relatives what *they* think should be done rather than what they think the patient would have wanted. Nevertheless, they are separated in the Code of Practice, so there must be an element of seeking the opinion of those who know the patient regarding the patient's welfare. It is not unusual for the courts to consult friends and relatives and to place great weight on their views – but in particular those relating to the views of the patient.[25] Nevertheless, such views only add to the balance sheet and do not have to be followed by the court.

Indeed, it must always be remembered that none of these is a determinative factor, and that the ultimate aim is to find the patient's best interests by going through the checklist and then constructing the balance sheet from which best

---

[21] *Ashan* v. *University Hospitals Leicester NHS Trust* [2006] EWHC 2624 (QB).

[22] See, e.g., *Re. MM (An Adult)* [2007] EWHC 2003 (Fam); and *Re. P* [2009] EWHC 163 (Ch).

[23] See M. Donnelly, 'Best Interests, Patient Participation and the Mental Capacity Act 2005' (2009) 17 *Med. L. Rev.* 1.

[24] *Mental Capacity Act Code of Practice*, para. 5.53.   [25] See, e.g., *An NHS Trust* v. *K* [2012] EWHC 2922 (COP).

interests are finally established. Needless to say, this provides the court with a large amount of latitude. Therefore, each case will essentially be decided on its own merits. A very good example of many of these factors – and an illustration of why, when very difficult decisions need to be made, the balance sheet will often prioritise welfare rather than autonomy – can be found in the recent and difficult case of *A Health Authority* v. *E*.[26]

E's case is one of a long-standing battle with anorexia. Having been seriously sexually abused as a young child, she began controlling her weight when she was 12 years old, and by the age of 15 her weight had dropped to the extent that she was sent to a specialist unit for treatment. This had a good effect on her, and she recovered sufficiently to finish school and gain a place at medical school. She attended medical school for some years, but following a bad relationship she began drinking heavily and did not complete the course. She began a new relationship with a different man and went travelling with him, but her health deteriorated and by 2006 she was admitted to specialist eating and alcohol disorder clinics on several occasions following what the court referred to as 'a continuous series of emergencies and admissions that have now lasted for six years'.[27] Between 2006 and 2010, she spent over half of her time in clinics. Since 2010, her condition had worsened:

In the past two years, she has mostly been treated in her own flat in the community as a result of the failure of the residential placements and the unavailability of further funding. This has led to a 'revolving door' series of emergency admissions for medical and psychiatric care, often after she was found in a collapsed state after drinking as much as a bottle of spirits a day. Indeed, alcohol has for some time represented her only source of calories. She has been placed under compulsory Mental Health Act section on about 10 occasions, including for one period lasting for almost 4 months.[28]

In July 2011, she signed an advance directive stating that she did not wish to be resuscitated nor receive any life-prolonging treatment. She did this again in October 2011, aided by her mother and an independent advocate. That same day, she was detained under the Mental Health Act 1983 (MHA) and placed in a specialist centre, where the consultant felt that her anorexia was severe, but that she could benefit from treatment, which she received before going back home. Yet, the following year, in March 2012, she was not eating and she was drinking heavily. On 20 March, she was again detained under the MHA, and had since then not been taking any calories at all. On 3 April, following a meeting of E's parents and the medical team, a unanimous decision was reached that there was nothing more than could be done for E and that she should be placed on a palliative

---

[26] *A Health Authority* v. *E* [2012] EWHC 1639 (COP).   [27] *A Health Authority* v. *E* at para. 16.
[28] *A Health Authority* v. *E* at para. 17.

care pathway. Essentially, the conclusion had been reached that E did not wish to live and nothing could change that. The case was referred to the court because the Official Solicitor, having taken advice from one of the consultants that there was some treatment that had not yet been tried, applied to the court to have forcible feeding and subsequent treatment declared to be in her best interests and authorised. The local authority, having initially adopted a neutral position, eventually supported the application. E's parents remained opposed to it: '[they] do not want E to die, but after years of supporting her through a series of unsuccessful treatments they believe that unless further medical intervention has a real prospect of making a difference, her wishes should be respected. For E's sake, they dread another failed effort, followed by a return to the community without adequate support'.[29] The rest of the medical staff were dubious about the merits of trying more treatment, but would support any decision of the court.

The court approached the issue in the classic post-MCA manner, asking first whether E had capacity, and whether there was an advance directive that should be considered if she lacked it. The judge, Peter Jackson J., held that as a matter of fact she lacked capacity, and that the advance directive of October 2011 was made when she lacked capacity and thus was not valid. This therefore left the final question of whether the forcible feeding was in E's best interests.

Peter Jackson J. also approached this in a classic post-MCA manner in the sense that he adhered to the checklist of factors. Thus, he had sections in the judgment considering E's past and present wishes, her beliefs and values, the views of others and her medical prognosis. He then continued by taking this information and constructing a balance sheet of factors in favour of force feeding E, and those against so doing. It is here that we can see the tension between autonomy and welfare played out, and the way in which the temptation to revert to a medical construction of best interests can become almost irresistible. The judge, in going through the checklist, established that both E and her parents were opposed to further treatment. This, as we saw above, should be strong evidence in favour of acceding to E's established wishes. Nevertheless, E's medical interests also had to be considered, and it is noticeable that Peter Jackson J. spent double the amount of time considering them than he did on the evidence regarding what E would have wanted. When it comes to the balance sheet, it is clear that the factors in favour of feeding relate to E's medical interests, while those in favour of allowing her to die relate to her autonomy. In favour of allowing E to die, Peter Jackson J. listed the following factors:

It reflects E's wishes
It respects E's personal autonomy
It spares E the risks associated with treatment

---

[29]   *A Health Authority* v. *E* at para. 36.

It avoids the harrowing aspects of treatment
It allows E to die with dignity and close to home
Treatment has limited prospects of success
E's parents and clinicians are at best sceptical about it.[30]

In favour of forcible feeding being in her best interests, the judge identified:

Without treatment, E will die
Without treatment, E will lose the chance to recover and lead a relatively normal life
There is medical opinion that E is treatable with some prospect of success
The longer E lives, the greater the opportunity for her to benefit from treatment and to revise
    her views about her future.[31]

He held that the factors were virtually at equilibrium, but the balance was tipped by the presumption in favour of life and he thus authorised one final attempt at treatment. Therefore, in a direct conflict between objective, medical interests and patient autonomy, the medical interests prevailed. We do not envy Peter Jackson J. the decision that he had to make.

It he case demonstrates several things. The first thing to note is the classic post-MCA approach to the case: assessing capacity then going through the checklist of factors to compile a balance sheet which is used to make the final decision. Also, the wide scope for discretion afforded to judges is abundantly clear here: note that all of the evidence was 'taken into account' as the MCA demands, but the final decision can go either way. On this occasion, the judge chose E's medical interests over her own wishes, but it was open to him to decide the case the other way. Indeed, it is worthy of note that the views of E's friends and relatives, and even those of E herself, carry weight, but are not determinative. It might be said, then, that while the MCA has demedicalised best interests, it has also judicialised the concept.

It would also be wrong to say that the courts will always side with the patient's medical interests over autonomy. In the case of *An NHS Trust* v. *L*, the court again had to consider whether it was in the interests of an anorexic patient to force feed her.[32] In that case, the judge held that it was not, as the treatment would be overly burdensome and very probably futile (the medical evidence was that L was almost certain not to survive the insertion of the tube under sedation). Of course, the element of futility makes the case easily distinguishable from that of E, but at the same time it also demonstrates that there are circumstances where the courts will allow the patient to die. What the cases highlight, however, is that the new construction of best interests in the MCA is neither a panacea nor much more

---

[30] *A Health Authority* v. *E* at para. 115.   [31] *A Health Authority* v. *E* at para. 116.
[32] *An NHS Trust* v. *L* [2012] EWHC 2741 (COP).

than a set of guidelines. Cases will be considered on their own merits, and a high degree of latitude will be available to judges.

Minors constitute another category of incapacitated patient, and the way in which the law treats them is very different – despite the fact that they, in contrast to some adult patients, will potentially reach a competent state at some point in the future.

Consent and minors

The complicating factor in relation to the medical treatment of minors is the fact that there are more 'interested parties' in any decision. Most medical interactions are between doctors and patients, yet here there is always the question of the views of parents. They might disagree with the recommendations of the doctor, with the decision of the patient or even with each other. In short, there is much more scope for conflict and disagreement. Also, there is a difference between how the law does (and should) treat minors of different ages. For example, while a 2-year-old child will not be able to make all but the most insignificant of decisions (such as whether he wants a red or blue sticking plaster on his cut), the same cannot be said of older children, particularly since the law defines a 'minor' as someone under 18 years of age. Thus, it is equally inconceivable that we should deprive 17-year-old patients of the right to make all but the most serious decisions (and arguably all decisions) themselves. However, as we shall see, the courts have sought to embrace autonomy for minors to a degree, but can ultimately be seen to have prioritised the protection of the child's perceived welfare over that autonomy when it has been forced to choose. This section begins with the (legally easier) situation relating to younger children before moving on to the question of how the more mature minor's interests might be protected.

YOUNG CHILDREN, PARENTS AND THE COURTS

In general terms, where the patient is a young child and thus not able to consent for herself, the consent of one or more of the parents will be required before any medical treatment may lawfully be provided (except in emergencies). The consent of only one parent will normally be required (even if the other parent does not agree).[33] There is a small group of treatments where the consent of both parents will be required, including circumcision[34] and the provision of the MMR vaccine.[35] Yet

---

[33] See *Re. W* [1992] 4 All ER 627.
[34] See *Re. J (Specific Issue Orders: Child's Religious Upbringing and Circumcision)* [2000] 1 FLR 571.
[35] See *Re. C (Welfare of Child: Immunisation)* [2003] EWCA Civ 1148.

where parents disagree, as we shall see later, the courts have tended to prioritise allowing the doctor to provide the treatment that she believes is in the interests of the child, and thus the maximisation of the number of people able to give consent presents the ideal circumstances for this to occur.

Nevertheless, one of the main difficulties in the law relating to young children occurs when the parents are seen to be acting in a manner that conflicts with what medical practitioners would see as the child's best interests. The most common scenario for this to occur is when both parents hold religious beliefs which do not allow them to accept certain treatments for their children, such as Jehovah's Witnesses and blood transfusions. In such cases, the courts may use their inherent jurisdiction to authorise treatment on her behalf. They have not been slow to do this, particularly when the treatment to which the parents object is the only realistic option. An example of this is the case of *Re. S*, where Thorpe J. delivered a judgment which encapsulates the prevailing judicial attitude. The child, whose parents were Jehovah's Witnesses, had T-cell leukaemia, but a blood transfusion was assessed as having a 50 per cent chance of successfully treating the disease. In authorising the treatment despite the parents' objections, Thorpe J. said that:

> [T]he test must remain the welfare of the child as the paramount consideration. Specifically, in this case, the choice is not between two medical procedures with similar, if differing, prospects of success. Here the stark choice is between one medical procedure with no prospect of success and one medical treatment with a prospect of success which is put at even.[36]

What can be seen here is that the court's approach is again to prioritise the medical best interests of the child, and everything else flows from that. In the context of this particular case, since the medical interests of the child pointed to only one option, the overturning of the parents' refusal of consent was the only way forward if the primary considerations were to be fulfilled.

However, where the treatment might be more painful, or have less chance of success, the courts are slightly more willing to accede to the views of the parents over those of the medical professionals. This occurred in the case of *Re. T*, where a child was born with a liver defect which required a liver transplant if the child were to live for more than a few years.[37] The parents refused consent to this, partly on the basis that surgery had previously been performed on the child's liver which was unsuccessful. At first instance, the judge authorised the procedure, but the Court of Appeal reversed the ruling. The court considered the concept of the 'welfare of the child' in much broader terms than they had in other cases, and this allowed it to move away from the medical evidence and thus agree with the parents rather than the doctors treating the child. This is a fact not lost on Fox and McHale, who noted

---

[36] *Re. S (A Minor) (Medical Treatment)* [1993] 1 FLR 376 at 380.
[37] *Re. T (A Minor) (Wardship: Medical Treatment)* [1997] 1 WLR 242; [1997] 1 All ER 906; [1997] 2 FCR 363.

that 'rather than focusing on the evidence which would have justified treatment, the judges focused on the implication for the carers should treatment be authorised against their will'.[38] But why was this so? What made the court side with the parents over the health professionals in this case? The answer, perhaps, is that the parents were health professionals themselves, so the courts were far more comfortable in seeing the parents' view as both reasonable and on a par with those of the medical professionals treating T – a state of affairs that Fox and McHale have described as 'questionable'; and certainly a presumption that is not made in favour of other parents.[39]

Essentially, then, for young children the courts are willing to intervene in order to protect the child's welfare – which they continually state is their primary consideration. In general terms, this means the child's *medical* welfare – and indeed *Re. T* must be seen as the exception to the rule that it clearly is. Of course, it is arguable that the courts are merely trying to keep the child alive until she can make her own decisions. How such minors are then to be treated is considered in the next section.

OLDER CHILDREN – THE ILLUSION OF AUTONOMY

Consenting to treatment

Once minors get older, however, it is right that they should make more of their own decisions. There are several reasons in support of such a view. One, for example, is that as they get older and become more mature, they become patients in their own right (as opposed to extensions of their parents) and deserve their own decision-making powers. Another is that it helps minors to mature if they make their own decisions as they get older – put another way, it would be undesirable for a person who is 17 years and 11 months old to be able to make *no* decisions, then a month later be expected to make *all* decisions on their own behalf. Essentially, gradually increasing the decision-making power of minors helps to ease their transition into adulthood. Once accepted, this approach places an onus on the law to recognise the rights of a minor and, perhaps even more importantly, to define when and how such rights should operate.

For minors of between 16 and 18 years of age, this is not problematic, as the law allows them to consent to treatment as if they were adults – in other words on their own behalf, without the knowledge or consent of their parents – assuming they

---

[38] M. Fox and J. McHale, 'In Whose Best Interests?' (1997) 60 *MLR* 700, 705.
[39] Fox and J. McHale, 'In Whose Best Interests?', 705.

pass the test for capacity. This is done through the Family Law Reform Act 1969, section 8, which provides that:

(1) The consent of a minor who has attained the age of sixteen years to any surgical, medical or dental treatment which, in the absence of consent, would constitute a trespass to his person, shall be as effective as it would be if he were of full age; and where a minor has by virtue of this section given an effective consent to any treatment it shall not be necessary to obtain any consent for it from his parent or guardian.

(2) In this section 'surgical, medical or dental treatment' includes any procedure undertaken for the purposes of diagnosis, and this section applies to any procedure (including, in particular, the administration of an anaesthetic) which is ancillary to any treatment as it applies to that treatment.

(3) Nothing in this section shall be construed as making ineffective any consent which would have been effective if this section had not been enacted.

Subsection 1 states that a minor can consent to treatment as if they were adults; subsection 2 defines 'treatment'; while the third subsection appears to protect some undefined person's right to consent on behalf of the minor. This section, while not relevant to *Gillick*, is important in relation to the power to *refuse* consent, and we shall return to it in due course.

For minors under the age of 16, the right to consent to treatment autonomously was achieved in the landmark case of *Gillick* in 1985, the facts of which relate directly to questions of the minor's right to consent.[40] In 1980, the Department of Health and Social Security (now the Department of Health) issued a circular to general practitioners stating that in certain, 'exceptional' circumstances, a doctor could provide contraceptive advice and treatment to a girl under the age of 16 without the knowledge or consent of her parents.[41] Mrs Victoria Gillick, who had five daughters under the age of 16, objected to this guidance and sought a declaration that it was unlawful, as well as an undertaking that none of her five daughters would receive such treatment without her prior consent being sought. Mrs Gillick lost at first instance, but won a unanimous decision in the Court of Appeal. The House of Lords found against her by a three to two majority so, while she lost the case, she can at least claim that a majority of the judges were in her favour! Nevertheless, what is of interest for our purposes is the way in which the decision was reached rather than the final decision itself.

Of the three judges who constitute the majority in the case, Lords Fraser and Scarman provided substantive judgments (although Lord Scarman declared at the

---

[40] *Gillick* v. *West Norfolk and Wisbech AHA* [1985] 3 All ER 402.
[41] Health Service Circular (interim series) (HSC (15) 32), cited in *Gillick* at 405–6.

start of his that he agreed with Lord Fraser), with Lord Bridge's shorter judgment concentrating on the public law aspects of the case. Thus, Lord Fraser's judgment is generally regarded as the leading one.[42] What the majority did was, essentially, again to medicalise the issue of whether contraceptive advice and treatment may be provided to a minor without the knowledge or consent of the parents. For Lord Fraser, then, the starting point was that, just as with younger minors, the welfare of the child must be the paramount consideration. In terms of the place of any parental rights, he noted that times had changed, and that where there was disagreement as to whether and how to proceed with medical treatment, the 'solution to the problem ... can no longer be found by referring to rigid parental rights'.[43] With parental rights not sacrosanct, his Lordship continued by asking *who* then was best placed to make such decisions. The answer was that although in the vast majority of cases the parents would be the best judges of the child's welfare, 'there may be circumstances in which the doctor is a better judge ... than [the patient's] parents'.[44] It is noticeable that he did this despite acknowledging that the decision that he was entrusting to the medical profession was not strictly medical in nature, or indeed within the bounds of medical competence:

> The medical profession have in modern times come to be entrusted with very wide discretionary powers going beyond the strict limits of clinical judgment and, in my opinion, there is nothing strange about entrusting them with this further responsibility which they alone are in a position to discharge satisfactorily.[45]

He therefore held that, as long as five conditions were satisfied, the doctor could provide such treatment without the parents' knowledge or consent. They are as follows:

1. that the minor, despite being under 16 years of age, can understand the advice;
2. that she cannot be persuaded to inform her parents;
3. that she is likely to begin or has already begun to have sexual intercourse, whether she receives the contraceptive advice and treatment or not;
4. that unless she receives the advice and treatment her physical and/or mental health are likely to suffer; and
5. that her best interests lie in the advice and treatment being given without the parents' consent.[46]

The key is the first of these conditions, which demands that the minor is able to 'understand' the advice. The concept relies on the intelligence and maturity of the

---

[42] See, e.g., E. Jackson, *Medical Law: Text, Cases and Materials*, 2nd edn (Oxford University Press, 2010), p. 265.
[43] *Gillick* at 412.   [44] *Gillick* at 412.   [45] *Gillick* at 413.   [46] *Gillick* at 413.

minor, and is known as '*Gillick* competence'. *Gillick* is settled law, and has been subsequently held to apply to all medical treatments, including abortion.[47] What can be gleaned from this landmark case is that parental control is not absolute and that it is right that, as they get older, minors may consent on their own behalf (and independently from their parents), even if they are under 16 years of age. The welfare of the minor remains paramount, but the courts seem to equate this with accepting medical treatment, and the underlying feeling is that the House of Lords was giving the doctor as much opportunity as possible to gain the consent necessary for the treatment to be lawfully administered. This view is strengthened by the way in which the courts have approached the question of whether minors should be able to refuse consent to medical treatment.

Refusal of consent

It might be thought that if a minor is sufficiently mature to consent to medical treatment on her own behalf, then she should have a corresponding right to refuse. Indeed, all of the reasons for allowing mature minors to make decisions noted above apply equally to refusal of consent. Furthermore, the House of Lords in *Gillick* referred to the competent minor's right to '*decide*' rather than merely to 'consent'. Nevertheless, the courts could not bring themselves to follow such an approach, and in two cases less than a year apart in the Court of Appeal, Lord Donaldson, then Master of the Rolls, set about systematically dismantling *Gillick*. In the cases of *Re. R* and *Re. W*, Lord Donaldson held that while minors could determinatively consent to medical treatment, they could not refuse it.[48] Rather, consent was to be seen as unlocking the door to legal treatment. According to his Lordship, the competent child and each parent held such a 'key'. If any of them were to give consent, then that was a key that unlocked the door to legal treatment, and it would be lawful to proceed – unless the court intervened to make the child a ward of court, in which case the court's decision would be final. In *Re. W*, Lord Donaldson stated that he regretted his 'keyholder' analogy (as keys can lock as well as unlock), and changed it to that of a 'legal flak jacket' protecting the doctor from the 'bullets of liability'. In legal terms, he justified his decision by using the Family Law Reform Act, section 8(3) of which, as we have seen, protected *someone's* right to consent on behalf of the child. His Lordship held that this meant that the parents (and indeed the courts) maintained their right to make decisions, even if the child was competent.

[47] See *R (on the application of Axon)* v. *Secretary of State for Health* [2006] EWHC 37 (Admin).
[48] *Re. R (A Minor) (Wardship: Medical Treatment)* [1991] 4 All ER 177; *Re. W (A Minor) (Medical Treatment: Court's Jurisdiction)* [1992] 4 All ER 627.

But why would he do this? As Ian Kennedy noted, he was essentially 'driving a coach and horses through *Gillick*'.[49] The answer perhaps lies less in legal formalism and a literal reading of the Family Law Reform Act, and more in the prioritisation of the welfare of the child and a desire to maximise the chances of the doctor being allowed to provide the treatment that he believes to be in the best interests of the patient. Thus, it is clear from the judgments that one of the primary goals of Lord Donaldson's decisions is the protection of the doctor:

If the position of the law is that upon the achievement of '*Gillick* competence' there is a transfer of the right of consent from the parents to the child and there can never be a concurrent right in both, doctors would be faced with an intolerable dilemma, particularly when the child was nearing the age of 16, if the parents consented but the child did not. *On pain, if they got it wrong, of being sued for trespass to the person or possibly being charged with a criminal assault, they would have to determine as a matter of law in whom the right of consent resided at the particular time in relation to the particular treatment. I do not believe that that is the law.*[50]

This attitude is equally evident in *Re. W*, where he held that the legal importance of consent was 'to provide those concerned in the treatment with a defence to a criminal charge of assault or battery or a civil claim for damages for trespass to the person'.[51] Moreover, the purpose of consent was defined as ensuring the patient's cooperation ('a major factor in contributing to the treatment's success'[52]), and making it easier for the doctor to administer the treatment.[53] The message is less one of respect for autonomy than of making the doctor's job easier:

These justifications did not consider the patient at all; rather, consent was apparently required to make the job of the medical practitioner easier . . . The starting point was a concern for the doctor, and in particular her ability to perform the procedures that she decided were in the best interests of the patient. She would thus have three chances to gain legally valid consent, as the competent child or either parent retained the ability to consent, and that consent was valid even if it constituted a minority of opinion amongst the three. Waiting in the wings was the judiciary, ready to consent on behalf of the child if all parties refused.[54]

This suspicion is confirmed when one considers the courts' attitude to teenagers' refusal of life-sustaining treatments. Here, all notions of autonomy are disregarded, and the welfare of the child (defined narrowly as the best *medical* interests) is without exception given priority.

Life-saving treatments

There is not, as far as we know, any case in which a child's refusal of consent to life-saving medical treatment (whether on religious grounds or otherwise) has been

---

[49] I. Kennedy, 'The Doctor, the Pill and the 15 Year Old Girl' in I. Kennedy, *Treat Me Right: Essays on Medical Law and Ethics* (Oxford University Press, 1990), p. 60.
[50] *Re. R* at 185. Emphasis added.   [51] *Re. W* at 633.   [52] *Re. W* at 633.   [53] *Re. W* at 633.
[54] J. Miola, *Medical Ethics and Medical Law: A Symbiotic Relationship* (Oxford: Hart, 2007), pp. 101–2.

treated as determinative and the child allowed to die. Of course, the state of the law which, as argued above, seeks to maximise the chances of the doctor being allowed to treat, mitigates against the chances of this happening – and the willingness of the courts to plunge in and authorise even in the absence of parental consent makes it almost impossible. Nevertheless, there have been several cases where the courts have found that the minor lacked competence simply, it seems, because they refused treatment. The level of understanding and maturity required to attain *Gillick* competence has always depended on the gravity of the consequences of the decision, and this has made it easy in such cases for the courts to argue that, while mature, such minors are simply not mature *enough*.

A good example of this is the case of *Re. E*, a 15-year-old Jehovah's Witness who was refusing a blood transfusion.[55] He was suffering from leukaemia, and the medical evidence presented to the court was that without the transfusion he had a 40 to 50 per cent chance of recovery, while with it it was 80 to 90 per cent. Based, it seems, on little substantive evidence (Ward J. stated that he was impressed by E's intelligence), he nevertheless found that E was unable to fully comprehend the manner of his decision, holding that '[h]e may have some concept of fact that he will die, but as to the manner of his death and to the extent of his and his family's suffering I find he has not the ability to turn his mind to it nor the will to do so'.[56] The latter comment regarding the parents is particularly curious, as the parents were both also Jehovah's Witnesses who supported their son's decision. Ultimately, he held that the courts should be very slow to allow minors to 'martyr them-selves',[57] and authorised the treatment on his behalf because it was 'essential for his well-being'.[58] In short, the welfare issues trumped any right to autonomy that he and his family had – even though they were of the same mind. E submitted to the transfusions until the age of 18, when he had a legal right to refuse. He did so and subsequently died of the disease.

The question that must therefore be asked is whether it is *ever* possible for a minor to be considered competent to refuse life-saving treatment. The answer may well be that it is not, as the courts have always, in the end, prioritised welfare.[59] In one case, the court even used the excuse that the minor had (deliberately) not been told the details of her prognosis to deny her the chance to make her own decision to declare her incompetent, yet did not suggest the obvious solution that she be told and then asked to reconsider.[60] The message can only be that the courts do not support autonomy for minors, but, instead, only the *illusion* of autonomy. The main concern in all of the cases appears to be the maximisation of the doctor's ability to provide the treatment that she believes to

---

[55] *Re. E (A Minor) (Wardship: Medical Treatment)* [1993] 1 FLR 386.   [56] *Re. E* at 391.   [57] *Re. E* at 394.
[58] *Re. E* at 394.   [59] See, e.g., *Re. P (A Minor)* [2003] EWHC 2327 (Fam).
[60] *Re. L (Medical Treatment: Gillick Competency)* [1998] 2 FLR 810.

be in the patient's best interests. Where this results in autonomy for the minor (when she wishes to consent), such autonomy is merely an incidental consequence. That this is the case can be seen in the way in which the law responds to the refusal of consent. When the principles of autonomy and welfare conflict, in this area of law, there is only one winner.

CONCLUDING REMARKS ON LAW

The MCA can be argued both to have made huge strides in helping even incapable patients to make their own decisions, and also to have added little to the law. On one level, we can say that providing advance directives with a statutory basis and adding LPAs undeniably aids autonomous decision-making even when capacity has been lost. On the other hand, the most visible aspect of the Act – best interests – can be argued to have added little to the law. Indeed, the common law was already making great strides in the direction that the MCA was to take, and it is at least arguable that section 4 of the MCA has changed little. It might even be argued that the equivocal wording in section 4 allows courts such latitude that the section provides little more than a suggested process for determining best interests. Perhaps even more pertinently, post-MCA cases such as *A Local Authority* v. *E* demonstrate that it is still possible for courts, when they come to balance autonomy and welfare, to choose the latter. Of course, the MCA was never *only* about autonomy – there is a welfare element also – but given the genesis of the MCA it could be argued that judges must be careful not to slip into a *re*medicalisation of the law.

A similar philosophy can be seen in relation to minors. Here, again, the law claims to provide and protect autonomous choices for those who have capacity, but all too frequently recoils when faced with hard choices where autonomy and welfare conflict. In the case of refusal of treatment, this is done openly. The law in relation to minors therefore seems to be evenly split in two: in terms of providing consent, everything is done to help minors to be able to grant permission for doctors to treat them, and their autonomy is accepted. However, when it comes to refusal of consent, the opposite is the case, and it would seem that everything is done to prevent any bar to treatment. One cannot help noticing that the common theme is that the courts actively want doctors to be able to provide treatment that they think is in the patient's best interests, and this is the case even if the parents side with the minor and refuse treatment. As mentioned above, this creates the *illusion* of autonomy rather than autonomy itself.

ETHICS

We have seen that the law aims to safeguard a number of pivotal concepts when regulating when and how decisions are made for those who cannot (or are deemed to not be able to) make these decisions themselves.[61] When we discuss the issues that arise in relation to incapacitated patients and children in ethical terms, a variety of moral theories compete for our attention. Some of these theories may look entirely at the individual whose health is at stake. Other theories will take the family's wishes fully into account. There is even room to allow for the inclusion of economical considerations in some moral theories: is it economically prudent to continue treating this person? There is an obvious distinction between moral theories and individual concepts to which these theories apply. In the following, we will look at the concepts which the law has picked to focus on and discuss the different moral dimensions of these concepts before concluding by looking at what kinds of moral theories the law seems to have adopted.

If we wish to align our ethical assessment with the law, the overriding concept to which we have to turn our attention is autonomy (as, indeed, is the case in most of the topics we cover in this text). A number of different scenarios need to be carefully separated when discussing autonomy in this context, and we shall turn to this separation in a moment. It is a particular feature of the context discussed in this chapter that the usual symmetry between autonomy and the right to self-determination is misaligned. This is because the patient is, quite rightly, still thought of as an autonomous agent – but unable to manifest his autonomy by means of self-determination *because he is incapacitated*. This means that those interacting with him must take into account his autonomy and implement an *other-determination* which resembles what his self-determination would have been as closely as possible.

The other main issues which concern us from an ethical perspective are:

(i) how we ascertain whether or not an individual is in a position to make a decision;

(ii) what constitutes welfare in that individual's case and how it is best safeguarded; and

(iii) who decides and on what basis.

---

[61] And we have expressly excluded from our assessment the inclusion of incapacitated individuals or children in biomedical research. This issue will be dealt with in Chapter 10.

Before we turn to these points we will look at the careful separation of issues mentioned above. Just as it is indispensable in law to identify who the subject is to whom we are trying to allocate an entitlement or a duty, it is as important to classify carefully who we are trying to make a moral agent or a moral patient.[62] This we will try to do in the following section, where we attempt to show the variations between the different moral patients.

Individual issues

The natural separation of issues we have discussed at the outset of this chapter is between adults and children. Within these two categories, it is necessary to distinguish those adults who are permanently incapacitated from those who are temporarily incapacitated and those whose capacity is limited. We also need to distinguish older children who can make some decisions autonomously from younger children who cannot decide for themselves and younger children who are nonetheless deemed to be competent to make certain decisions.

- Adults
  - is temporarily incapacitated;
  - has had previous capacity;
  - has never had capacity;
- Children
  - very young and unable to understand and retain information;
  - children who show sufficient maturity to take some decisions;
  - older children who are able to take some decisions.

This separation results in a consideration of whether the incapax in question *has ever had capacity* (and is therefore likely to have expressed wishes), *will regain capacity* (and is therefore in a position to take his or her own decisions at some point), *has never had and will never have capacity*, *is not mature enough to take a decision* or *is mature enough to take some or all decisions*. The recurrent theme running through all considerations here should be that in each scenario the individual should retain the maximum amount of self-determination possible.

From the viewpoint of autonomy and respect for the self-determination of the patient, it is therefore clear that any unnecessary derogation from the respect paid to the patient's wishes is unacceptable. This means that where the type of decision

---

[62] *Moral patient*, here, is a technical term in philosophy and does not refer to the person's status as a patient. See the *Blackwell Dictionary of Western Philosophy*: 'Marginal human beings, such as children and brain-damaged people, are not regarded as having moral responsibility for their behaviour, and hence are not moral agents. However, they are still the objects of moral consideration and are protected from suffering by moral laws. Accordingly they are referred to as moral patients', www.blackwellreference.com/public/tocnode?id=g9781405106795_chunk_g978140510679514_ss1-188.

which is required can be made by a patient with diminished capacity (for example, due to mental health issues), such a decision ought to be made by that patient. In the same vein, where it is to be expected that a patient will recover sufficient capacity in time to make the relevant decision, the treatment should be delayed until the patient can make the decision.

As far as children are concerned, it is clear that some treatment decisions (such as the colour of the plaster)[63] can be taken even by very young children. Just as the complexity of the treatment decision increases, so does the maturity of a child with age and experience. These two sliding variables are notoriously difficult to reconcile into a coherent, normative framework. Baines writes that:

> The decisions of non-autonomous children may be overruled by adults in a way that we would not overrule decisions made by adults.[64]

This essentially means that an adult is theoretically[65] in a position to make an irrational treatment decision (for example, refusing routine, simple, but life-saving treatment) and this decision must be respected, while at the same time, decisions made by children for the very same reasons with the very same quality would be vetoed. A case in point is that of *Re. E*, which we discussed above and will turn to again shortly.

Incapacitated adults

Any discussion relating to the issue of incapacitated adults shows a number of internal nuances which have an important impact on both the legal and the ethical assessment of whether they can take their own decisions.[66] The adult may simply be temporarily incapacitated, the adult may be incapacitated for the foreseeable future having been competent at some earlier stage or the adult may have always been and be for the foreseeable future incapacitated.

Where the adult is merely temporarily incompetent, it is clear that any decisions taken should be entirely necessary and should not be delayed until he regains capacity. Any decision taken on his behalf which is not necessary at the time of his incapacity takes away from his autonomy and diminishes his right to self-determination, rendering it *ultra vires* in a moral sense. In circumstances where the adult has had an episode of capacity preceding his incapacity, there is a fair chance that someone close to him will be in a position to assess what he would have

---

[63] Or in some cases even the fundamental decision about whether to apply a plaster or a cream to the scratch. The more trivial the choice, the more likely that a child or even an infant can be meaningfully involved in the decision-making process.

[64] P. Baines, 'Medical Ethics for Children: Applying the Four Principles to Paediatrics' (2008) 34(3) *Journal of Medical Ethics* 141, 142.

[65] See the discussion of 'autonomy' below for an important qualification.

[66] For a very controversial discussion of the notion of *capacity*, see Foster, *Choosing Life, Choosing Death: The Tyranny of Autonomy in Medical Ethics and Law* (Oxford: Hart, 2009), pp. 114–25.

wanted based on actual empirical evidence, which is a necessary condition for implementing a process which respects the patient's autonomy (see the discussion of *substituted judgment* in this chapter). Finally, the adult who has always been incapacitated will have been unable to express any desires or preferences ex ante. This means that those taking decisions on his behalf will try to take decisions which are in that patient's best interests and there is a very strong argument that society and those close to this patient have a moral obligation to promote his welfare. He is a member of a vulnerable group we seek to protect in the same way as children.

Children

The distinction between children and adults, in moral terms, seems to have difficulty holding water. It is essentially a social construction which reflects our contemporary views of how vulnerable the young are and is subject to flux.[67] We are all as familiar with young teenagers who seem mature beyond their age as we are with men and women in their early twenties who seemingly fail to demonstrate any kind of maturity. The latter are able to take decisions in relation to their health, whereas the former are not. Baines suggests that:

The abilities of some older children to absorb information, to rationalise and to communicate are perhaps the equal of an adult's, but their decisions are often overruled.[68]

They are overruled simply on the basis of the age of the patient, rather than on a functional assessment of their ability to take a (subjectively) meaningful decision. This brings us back to the case of *Re. E* (discussed above), which demonstrates that a decision taken by a minor is not necessarily of inferior quality to that of an adult. E had decided not to continue life-saving treatment and was refused the right to enforce this decision on the basis of his age. Years later, he turned 18 and enforced his decision. His reasons had not changed nor had his decision – he had simply crossed an invisible and arbitrary age threshold set by society. It is evident that setting an age limit is not a policy which is designed to underpin individual autonomy, but rather one which smacks of legalistic pragmatism. Vince and Petros convincingly summarise the ethical position thus: 'An individual's competence arises from his experiences and values, not his chronological age.'[69]

---

[67] Not so long ago, children aged 12 or 13 would have been treated as equals in the job market and in the early twentieth century it was not uncommon for children and young people aged between 14 and 16 to start their working lives. This has changed and this change can also reverse in some aspects of life (think of the discussion of giving the vote to 16 and 17 year olds). Society occasionally changes the yardstick of what is permissible at a certain age; this is indicative of a social interest to protect young people rather than a fundamental moral value.

[68] Baines, 'Medical Ethics for Children', 142.

[69] T. Vince and A. Petros, 'Should Children's Autonomy Be Respected by Telling Them of Their Imminent Death?' (2006) 32(1) *Journal of Medical Ethics* 21, 22.

With particularly young children, who are clearly not in a position to understand and retain the kind of information they need in order to make a decision, the approach seems straightforward and is easily morally defensible. Others (such as the parents or, failing that, society) take on the role of the custodian of children who need to be protected from the vagaries of life – just as we would not expect a small child to cross a dual carriageway without assistance. There is no reasonable argument to suggest that such children ought to be left to their own devices in order to be fully autonomous.[70] Exposing them to this kind of risk severely diminishes the likelihood of the child maturing to an age where they actually can live autonomously and self-determinedly. The matter becomes more difficult to argue the older and more mature the children are:

> This group of older children is more troubling because the features which separate these rational, able children who are not permitted to choose unwisely are hard to pin down, and if we were to pin them down it would be difficult to set a clear threshold to separate incompetent children from competent adults.[71]

Baines goes on to argue that *Gillick*-competent children are essentially adults. As we have seen above, this is not entirely accurate: even those children deemed to be competent to take treatment decisions by themselves cannot refuse treatment determinatively (see the discussion of *Re. R* and *Re. W* in this chapter) and therefore do not have the same rights as adults. This leads to an asymmetry of the right to consent and the right to refuse consent.[72] Ethically speaking, this requires distinct justification, as accepting and declining treatment are treated in different moral terms while being nothing short of the exact same expression of autonomy on two different ends of a scale.[73]

The important aspect to bear in mind when the patient is a child is this: treating children as a vulnerable group entitled to additional safeguards and protection at the expense of their autonomy can be robustly defended.[74] The robustness of our moral defence of disenfranchising children in decision-making processes is diminished the more mature a child is and adhering to purely arbitrary age thresholds is simply paying lip service to the social construction of *underage* and *of age*. The functional approach to determining a child's ability to control the decision is clearly the more desirable option and is certainly more representative of a regime which underpins individual autonomy.

---

[70] Society also feels that it is necessary to protect adults in circumstances where a fundamental lack of experience is imputed (think of consumer protection legislation or lay person investment banking).

[71] Baines, 'Medical Ethics for Children', 142.

[72] This might be plausibly justified using utilitarian ethics. See the discussion below.

[73] Vince and Petros, 'Should Children's Autonomy Be Respected?', 22.

[74] For an illustration, see B. Gert *et al.*, *Bioethics: A Systematic Approach*, 2nd edn (New York: Oxford University Press, 2006), ch. 10 ('Paternalism and Its Justification').

Autonomy

We have discussed the principle of autonomy[75] in detail in Chapter 4 and have also seen that the principle theoretically even extends to seemingly irrational or even objectively wrong decisions. Baines summarises this position by stating:

It is now widely accepted (at least in the UK and the USA) that a competent person's decision should be accepted (even though others believe that the person's choice is wrong).[76]

Foster goes characteristically further and asserts that the English law has a 'historic and much proclaimed determination to allow even the life-endangering eccentricity'.[77] These eccentric or irrational choices might be made for a number of reasons. Examples we have discussed include the religious convictions of Jehovah's Witnesses refusing blood transfusions. Another example might be that of a fear of needles. For those of us who give blood regularly, the notion of a mother-to-be refusing a life-saving caesarean based on her overwhelming needle-phobia seems absurd,[78] even bordering on the pathologically irrational – and this is precisely where there is a subtle line. A seemingly informed decision based on an irrational belief (a legitimate expression of autonomy) may in some circumstances be declared pathological and the threshold to incapacity thus crossed. Wheels are set in motion and decisions are made against the wishes of the patient. This is because the unfettered acceptance of the patient's autonomy leads to consequences which do not promote their welfare (we made this contrast the focus of the legal analysis of this chapter). However, if the patient's autonomy extends to taking wrong decisions, the moderation of these decisions by others on the basis that comprehensible decision-making processes are a precondition for participation is simply a derogation from the individual's autonomy and right to self-determination. The gap between theory and practice is eminently visible in this context: physicians in the heat of an emergency and judges on call at night tend to 'err on the side of life' and impute a temporary incapacity in order to enforce treatment.[79] If the law's claim to want to fully protect autonomy is true, this seems hardly plausible. It is also not entirely clear where this subtle line runs: van Staden and Krüger, for example, write at length about patients who demonstrate a 'lack of insight' into their condition and refer to the example of the patient who says:

---

[75] For a very detailed discussion of autonomy in bioethics, see B. Jennings, 'Autonomy' in B. Steinbock (ed.), The Oxford Handbook of Bioethics (Oxford University Press, 2009), pp. 72–89.

[76] Baines, 'Medical Ethics for Children', 142.   [77] Foster, Choosing Life, Choosing Death, p. 93.

[78] This was the case in Re. MB (Medical Treatment) [1997] 2 FLR 426, where the pregnant patient withdrew her consent to a caesarean, deemed to be necessary to save the life of the foetus of 40 weeks, based on her fear of needles. Both the High Court and the Court of Appeal held that the needle-phobia had negated the patient's decision-making capacity. Some commentators strongly disagree with the court's reasoning, but agree that the consequential decision (to enforce the caesarean) was morally right. See Foster, Choosing Life, Choosing Death, pp. 92–5.

[79] See also Gert et al., Bioethics: A Systematic Approach, pp. 219–20 and 223–4.

I know I am ill, I understand the proposed nature and purposes of the treatment, but I don't need treatment for it, because my illness will disappear in the near future when I will be God.[80]

This kind of assertion is deemed to be demonstrative of an inability to make treatment decisions and indicative of a mental illness. Now consider the following contention:

I know I am ill, I understand the proposed nature and purposes of the treatment, but I don't need treatment for it, because my illness will either disappear in the near future, or not, whatever God decides for me.

How this second assertion can lead to normatively different responses from the first assertion is quite unclear unless we bear in mind the cultural context.[81] Van Staden and Krüger do make it quite plain in their paper that they are referring to a context in which there is a manifestation of a mental disorder. Nevertheless, it is prudent to bear in mind the very fine line which runs between a seemingly irrational but considered refusal of consent (which ought to be respected) and a refusal of consent which is informed by mental health problems or phobias.

Decision-making

Having established that upholding the incapax's autonomy is paramount, it is necessary to determine by which kind of decision-making this is best achieved. Let us first take a look at how the law seeks to solve this dilemma. Pattinson convincingly distinguishes between the *substituted judgment approach* and the *best interests approach*.[82] We shall discuss these two approaches here in all brevity and it will quickly become clear that the substituted judgment approach is merely a mechanism for gathering evidence of what the incapax's point of view may have been in the past. The best interests approach is one which seeks to maximise the incapax's autonomy in the present with all circumstances borne in mind. It will also become clear that if we wish to fulfil the law's claim to be the protector of autonomy, self-determination and welfare, there must be an interdependency between these two principles, which the law has sought to achieve in the Mental Capacity Act.

Substituted judgment

The substituted judgment approach applies to patients who have had decision-making capacity in the past and are currently unable to make decisions, a condition

---

[80] C. W. van Staden and C. Krüger, 'Incapacity to Give Informed Consent Owing to Mental Disorder' (2003) 29(1) *Journal of Medical Ethics* 41, 42.

[81] Namely the acceptability of 'believing' in highly improbable sets of circumstances in the name of religion. It begs the question of whether if one can identify a sufficiently large number of individuals who believe that the individual in van Staden and Krüger's example really will be God, the requirements for an acceptable religious belief, rather than a personal psychotic episode, are fulfilled.

[82] S. D. Pattinson, *Medical Law and Ethics* (London: Sweet & Maxwell, 2006), pp. 146–8.

that we would respectfully suggest was not fully understood by their Lordships in *Bland*.[83] It is essentially a protocol by which those ultimately tasked with carrying out the treatment in relation to the incapacitated patient (such as the physicians) or others who are close to the incapacitated patient (relatives or nominated proxy decision-makers) may determine, to a certain extent, what the patient would have decided if he were in the position to do so. Where the nomination of a proxy decision-maker is express (for example, by means of an ex ante declaration, such as an advance decision), it is plausible that the proxy has a firm moral obligation to give effect to the incapacitated patient's wishes. This has some merit in terms of implementing a regime which shows respect for self-determination, but also has a number of serious limitations which we will address now.

First, as we have already seen, it is limited to individuals who have been competent to make treatment decisions at some stage in their lives. Secondly, whoever is called upon to substitute their judgment for that of the incapax does so on the basis of some knowledge of what the individual may have wanted up to the point where they became incapacitated.[84] This clearly means that we are limited to basic knowledge of the fundamental beliefs and principles of that individual and an abstraction of judgment from similar situations. In other words, the incapacitated patient may have said at some stage, abstractly, that if they were ever to need artificial ventilation to stay alive, they would not want this kind of intervention. They may even have communicated this to the proxy decision-maker. What of a situation where the person in question only requires a short spell on artificial ventilation after surgery with a full recovery being a certainty? It would surely not do for the proxy decision-maker to rigidly apply the incapax's assertion to any deployment of a ventilation system. This means that the principle of substituted judgment is subject to adjustment by the proxy decision-maker in order to fit in with the actual, previously unforeseen, acute treatment situation. This is, on the one hand, absolutely necessary to prevent undesirable consequences,[85] but on the other hand obviously undermines the principle of self-determination. This is simply unavoidable since we are essentially asking someone who is notoriously under-informed to take an informed decision which best represents the wishes of an individual who, in most cases, could not have envisaged the situation in question.

[83] For a discussion, see Pattinson, *Medical Law and Ethics*, p. 147; and I. Kennedy and A. Grubb, *Medical Law: Text, Cases and Materials* (London: Butterworths, 2000), p. 838.

[84] S. Bailey, 'Decision Making in Health Care: Limitations of the Substituted Judgement Principle' (2002) 9(5) *Nursing Ethics* 483. It should be noted that Bailey's incomplete distinction between autonomy and self-determination does not align with our absolute distinction in this chapter.

[85] An oft-cited example for this situation is that 'erring on the side of life' in life-threatening situations (in the face of opposite wishes of the incapax) prevents the creation of an irreversible consequence (death). This, it is argued, makes overruling the ex ante expressed wishes of an incapax in life-threatening, acute care scenarios morally defensible and quite possibly a squeaky-clean example of utilitarianism in health care decision-making. See Bailey, 'Decision Making in Health Care', 489.

Finally, in circumstances where a proxy decision-maker is called upon to decide, it is unrealistic (and some argue undesirable) to require them to adhere solely to the set of moral principles of the incapacitated patient and completely ignore their own moral principles. This leads to a predictable amount of clouding of the substituted judgment, both through injection of the proxy decision-maker's own values and morals, and through emotional distress. Bailey writes:

> Adhering to the substituted judgement principle, therefore, may be quite morally demanding for proxy decision makers. At times, these demands may be so great that the individual acting as a proxy will not be able provide a true substituted judgement. *This may be especially so in stressful situations where a decision may be clouded by emotion.*[86]

As the proxy decision-maker is usually someone who is emotionally close to the incapacitated patient, it is simply too much to ask of this individual to not let his or her own values and emotions inform the decision that is to be made. Quite the contrary: in moral terms, we are asking for a decision that is not simply a cold representation of the incapax's possible wishes, but an engagement with the very difficult situation and an emotionally warm and caring response.

The limitations we have outlined above lead to the inevitable conclusion that we cannot rely on *substituted judgment* and *best interests* (or welfare) principles in an either-or fashion. Choosing one principle over the other in individual scenarios may even serve to undermine the patient's autonomy. Bailey goes as far as suggesting (quite plausibly) that the two principles are complementary and that 'best interests' picks up where 'substituted judgment' leaves off.[87]

Best interests and welfare

The assumption in terms of decision-making on behalf of an individual who cannot decide themselves is that the decision ought to reflect what is in that individual's best interest. This assertion seems quite trivial until we subject it to some closer scrutiny. First, it is clear (and we have discussed this previously) that proxy decision-making will always include values and desires of others. This inevitably leads to a 'tainting' of the decision, taking into account the best interests of others, such as the proxy decision-maker. Vince and Petros discuss the case of a 14 year old with a terminal respiratory condition and question whether the patient should have been taken off sedation in order to inform him of his imminent death. This, they argue, would have clearly shown respect for his autonomy as an individual and given him an opportunity to say goodbye to his parents and make arrangements for his own funeral, should he wish to do so. They go on to assert:

---

[86] Bailey, 'Decision Making in Health Care', 488 (our emphasis).   [87] Bailey, 'Decision Making in Health Care', 491.

The contrasting view was that he should be kept comfortable and adequately sedated and have treatment withdrawn; to wake up the child and inform him of his death would be cruel and unnecessary. This was recognised as a paternalistic approach but felt to be in the child's best interests and was the viewpoint supported by the parents.[88]

The question of whether in the very same circumstances we would rather have a few moments to say goodbye to loved ones or never wake up to face the news of our imminent death is a very personal one. While it is clear that a decision either way can be in the best interests of the individual, this is only true where the decision is made by the individual himself. Where others take this decision for him, it is at best an educated guess at what the patient's best interests might be. This leads us to the second question we need to address: what precisely does 'best interests' as a concept encompass? In this case the best interests of the child, regardless of whether or not we consider him to be *Gillick* competent (and there is considerable evidence in the case that he was), were thought to include the expressly paternalistic notion of his parents trading his autonomy for the child not suffering distress at being told that there is no hope. In cases where we are dealing with an individual who will never regain a *compos mentis* state (i.e. not someone who is 'merely' unconscious or underage), this sort of decision-making may well be morally defensible. In cases where the autonomy of the individual has been put on hold through the use of anaesthetic or sedative, this is not so. We disagree with the evaluation of the parents and the ethics committee in our case study and are of the same mind as Vince and Petros, who conclude that '[t]he question remains, however, whether an individual's best interests can truly be respected if he is denied the opportunity to exercise his autonomy'.[89]

Some light might be shed on the exact meaning of the concept of 'best interests' if we read it to be synonymous with the term 'welfare'. Welfare, in individual terms, can take the same amorphous shape as autonomy, oscillating between that which is subjectively important to the individual in question and well-informed and objectively rational long-term choices.[90] It seems inevitable that where the individuals can decide for themselves, it is appropriate that their expression of autonomy and their understanding of their own best interest and welfare might be eccentric or outright irrational. Where others are to decide for an incapax, there is a strong expectation that their interpretation of the incapax's best interests and welfare is aligned to a rational understanding of these concepts with little or no

---

[88] Vince and Petros, 'Should Children's Autonomy Be Respected?', 21.
[89] Vince and Petros, 'Should Children's Autonomy Be Respected?', 23.
[90] See the *Blackwell Dictionary of Western Philosophy* for an explanation of the term 'welfare', which also takes into account societal issues (www.blackwellreference.com/public/tocnode?id=g9781405106795_chunk_ g978140510679524_ss2-2). See also the discussion surrounding the long-term welfare of intellectually disabled infants in D. Wilkinson, 'Is It in the Best Interests of an Intellectually Disabled Infant to Die?' (2006) 32(8) *Journal of Medical Ethics* 454.

room for the patient's eccentricity. Either way, the terms employed by the law for describing an appropriate basis for medical decision-making in this context are regrettably but possibly inevitably diffuse. It is clear that they hold little value for a moral assessment unless they are filled with life in each individual set of circumstances. Worthington suggests quite convincingly that 'the expression "best interests" enjoys a measure of legal status that I believe is disproportionate to its usefulness'.[91]

Flak jackets and paternalism

A striking element of our discussion of the law is that it seems evident that, at least to a certain point, respect for autonomy is seen as a necessary component to ensure patient compliance and to protect the physician in problematic circumstances. Patients who have been involved in decision-making processes are less likely to resist the administration of treatment. Where the patient cannot make such a decision, the next of kin are drawn into the decision-making process. On the one hand, this is reasonable as they are in the best position to assess what the patient would have wanted. On the other hand, it is in our current context also the next of kin who would create the kind of flak from which the courts would like to protect the physicians.[92] The courts' use of rhetoric such as 'flak jacket' is evidence of the perception of the physicians' role as being under constant threat from attack.

In an honest discussion of how we view patients who are unable to make their own decisions, it is necessary to also acknowledge that the consent and decision-making processes we have discussed thus far are not only an expression of respect for the patient. They are to a great extent also mechanisms by which physicians reassure themselves that what they are doing is the least controversial course of action, mechanisms by which they shift responsibility to others and mechanisms by which they protect themselves from liability when there is disagreement (and there is quite simply nothing wrong with this).[93]

Finally, an issue which ought not to go unmentioned is that of paternalism in this context. Where the patient is *compos mentis* and conscious, we have seen that there is very little room for strict paternalism. The physician can suggest a certain course of action, but cannot force it upon the fully autonomous patient – the days

---

[91] R. Worthington, 'Clinical Issues on Consent: Some Philosophical Concerns' (2002) 28(2) *Journal of Medical Ethics* 377, 379.

[92] There is also some evidence that the notion of best interest of the patient, grounded in patient beneficence, is strongly influenced by the understood wishes of the family or the next of kin. See W. Wong *et al.*, 'By-Person Factor Analysis in Clinical Ethical Decision Making: Q Methodology in End-of-Life Care Decisions' (2004) 4(3) *American Journal of Bioethics* W8.

[93] There is a good argument that the flak jacket is full of holes: guidance available on when it is permissible for physicians to derogate from, for example, the best interest test, is wanting, argues Wendler. See D. Wendler, 'Are Physicians Obligated to Always Act in the Patient's Best Interest?' (2010) 36 *Journal of Medical Ethics* 66.

when 'the doctor knows best' are well and truly over. But what of situations where the individual is diminished in their ability to make a decision, for example because of a mental disorder,[94] unconsciousness or other reasons incapacitating them? The less an individual is in a position to make decisions for themself, the more likely it is that those surrounding that individual (not just the physicians, but also the relatives and others in a relationship of proximity to the patient) inject their notion of the right course of action into proceedings. It is ethically justifiable to deploy paternalistic tactics in cases such as ours, where there is an 'evident failure of reason and will'.[95] One question should, however, be briefly touched upon in this context. The concept of paternalism means curtailing an individual's liberty in the belief that it is for that person's good or promotion of welfare, even when this is done against that individual's express wish. In cases where an individual is simply unable to make a decision, there is a reasonable question about whether that individual's liberty is in fact curtailed if they are unable to avail of their liberty in the first place. We would argue that paternalism, in a positive sense, has a robust place in medical ethics in the context of decision-making for incapacitated patients. Where this kind of paternalism is applied to children, we are very much less convinced that this is ethically justifiable.

CONCLUSION

It is clear that our discussion of medical ethics in the context of incapacitated patients and children highlights inconsistencies in the legal framework. The most obvious, and most serious, of these is the difference with which the concept of autonomy is treated with respect to minors and incapable adults. As we note above, a variance in approach based solely on the differing status of the patient is difficult to justify. Indeed, looking a level deeper at the different types of incapax we have encountered, it becomes clear that they have more in common than there are differences. In both cases, they may be temporarily incapable (the adult may be unconscious, for example, and most minors will survive to reach adulthood and legal competence), or permanently so. Equally, in both cases, their status being defined as *incapable* will be based on a functional assessment of their cognitive abilities and we have seen that, morally, a functional approach to capacity is the only robustly defensible approach.

However, the way in which the law treats the incapax following a determination that she is incompetent is different and depends on whether she is an adult or a

---

[94] See, e.g., van Staden and Krüger, 'Incapacity to Give Informed Consent', 42.
[95] J. Rawls, *A Theory of Justice*, revised edn (Oxford University Press, 1999), p. 219.

child. While in both cases others must make decisions on the patient's behalf, for adults, as we have seen, the law has evolved towards an approach that seeks to allow the patient to make as many decisions as possible for herself (through, for example, giving statutory force to advance decisions). If the patient has not made her wishes clear ex ante, she may appoint someone to make her decisions for her (through an LPA). Even where the patient's best interests are assessed, great weight is given to the patient's own views (although, as we have seen, these views are seen through the eyes of those making the ultimate decisions).

With minors, however, the situation is totally different. Here, even the explicitly expressed wishes of the competent minor may, if they constitute a refusal of treatment, be overturned by the consent of one of the parents. What the minor wants is not a legally relevant issue. Thus, any 'autonomy' granted to minors is essentially illusory – they are free to agree to the proposed medical treatment, but not to refuse it. This asymmetry between consent and refusal, as we have called it in our discussion, essentially negates the ethical value of giving a minor such a 'right': I ask you whether you are happy with an injection and you can only say 'yes' – this clearly does not amount to respect for autonomy.

Moreover, given that the decisions made on their behalf can be in total contradiction to their stated wishes and preferences, it cannot even be said that the decision-making by proxy is intended to enhance these minors' autonomy. Rather, the law openly advocates a form of paternalism that prioritises the need of the medical practitioner for valid consent over any concept of patient choice. As we mention above, the law with regard to minors seems tailored towards finding a way to allow the medical practitioner to perform the recommended treatment. In contrast, we have seen the law in relation to incapable adults change over time from one that took a similar approach to one that seeks to empower even the permanently incapable patient as much as possible. Although the law cannot pretend to be exemplary in this regard (the possibility of challenging the decision of a person granted an LPA on the grounds that it is not in the patient's best interests has the whiff of residual paternalism about it), it has steadily moved in the direction of substituted judgment and advance decision-making, both of which will help to provide real autonomy in terms of making the decisions that the patient would want to make.

The irony is that most minors will grow to become competent adults, so it would make sense to grant them the same safeguards that are granted to temporarily incapable adults – such as that the patient's best interests will lie in treating conservatively until they regain competence, then allowing them to make their own decisions. Yet the law relating to minors has remained steadfastly paternalistic and, if anything, has moved from parental to medical control. We believe that this inconsistent treatment of the incapax cannot be ethically justified.

ADDITIONAL READING

 Law

D. Archard, 'Children, Adults, Best Interests and Rights' (2013) 13(1) *Medical Law International* 55

P. Bartlett, *Blackstone's Guide to the Mental Capacity Act 2005* (Oxford University Press, 2008)

E. Cave, 'The Maximisation of a Minor's Capacity' (2011) 23(4) *Child and Family Law Quarterly* 431

E. Cave and J. Wallbank, 'Minors' Capacity to Refuse Treatment: A Reply to Gilmore and Herring' (2012) 20(3) *Medical Law Review* 423

J. Coggon, 'Best Interests, Public Interest and the Power of the Medical Profession' (2008) *Health Care Analysis* 219

DCA, *Mental Capacity Act Code of Practice* (Crown Copyright, 2007), www.dca.gov.uk/legal-policy/mental-capacity/mca-cp.pdf

M. Donnelly, 'Best Interests, Patient Participation and the Mental Capacity Act 2005' (2009) 17 *Medical Law Review* 1

S. Gilmore, 'No Is the Hardest Word: Consent and Children's Autonomy' (2011) 23(1) *Child and Family Law Quarterly* 3

J. Samanta, 'Lasting Powers of Attorney for Healthcare under the Mental Capacity Act 2005: Enhanced Prospective Self-Determination for Future Incapacity or a Simulacrum' (2009) 17(3) *Medical Law Review* 377

Ethics

T. Beauchamp and J. Childress, *Principles of Biomedical Ethics*, 5th edn (Oxford University Press, 2001), pp. 69–80

N. Cantor, *Making Decisions for the Profoundly Mentally Disabled (Basic Bioethics)* (Cambridge, MA: MIT Press, 2005)

T. Hope, J. Savulescu and J. Hendrick, *Medical Ethics and Law: The Core Curriculum*, 2nd edn (Edinburgh: Churchill Livingstone, 2008), chapters 10 and 11

B. Steinbock (ed.), *The Oxford Handbook of Bioethics* (Oxford University Press, 2007), chapter 4

C. W. van Staden and C. Krüger, 'Incapacity to Give Informed Consent Owing to Mental Disorder' (2003) 29 *Journal of Medical Ethics* 41

Case studies from this chapter are available online at www.cambridge.org/hoppe.

Resource allocation and prioritisation

INTRODUCTION

Whatever the system of health care used, whether a comprehensive service free at the point of delivery such as in the United Kingdom, or an insurance-based system such as in the United States, resources are finite. Therefore, hard choices will need to be made regarding whether individual patients can be provided with everything that they need – and that is before we get to the question of providing them with everything that they might *want*. Indeed, we should acknowledge from the beginning that all systems practise resource allocation and do not simply fund everything. In the United States, many insurance policies are not totally comprehensive, so not all conditions are covered. Equally, there may be limitations, relating to cost for example, that mean that even for a condition that is covered, unlimited treatment is not available. However, as we shall see, such rationing also occurs in the United Kingdom. The NHS does not have a bottomless pit of cash, and it is simply not possible to fund absolutely everything – the service is comprehensive rather than limitless.

In this chapter we consider, first, how the law treats and reviews decisions made by medical professionals and those managing them in the NHS, before then turning to the ethical aspects of rationing. In the legal section, we begin by examining what the NHS Constitution itself has to say about the 'right' of patients to treatment, so that we can ascertain how the NHS sees its role. We continue by then looking at the role of the National Institute for Health and Clinical Excellence (NICE), and the way in which the court has treated challenges against its decisions, before assessing the approaches taken by the courts to cases challenging rationing decisions: a human rights approach, breach of statutory duty and judicial review.

CLINICAL DISCRETION AND THE NHS CONSTITUTION – WHAT ARE PATIENTS' RIGHTS?

Fundamentally, then, what should patients be able to reasonably expect from the NHS? The NHS Constitution sets out what patients are entitled to expect from the National Health Service and the latest version, published in 2012, states that it is intended that the Constitution be reviewed every ten years, and that an accompanying handbook that elaborates on and explains the Constitution will be reviewed every three years.[1] Among other things, the Constitution provides a set of principles, rights and pledges that relate to rationing and the allocation of resources. The principles in the Constitution determine the general values that are espoused there. Rights are legally enforceable, and intended to be so. Pledges, on the other hand, are not legally enforceable, but are instead statements of what the NHS intends to achieve. The very first principle contained in the Constitution suggests that patients may expect a comprehensive service to all:

1. *The NHS provides a comprehensive service, available to all* irrespective of gender, race, disability, age, sexual orientation, religion or belief. It has a duty to each and every individual that it serves and must respect their human rights. At the same time, it has a wider social duty to promote equality through the services it provides and to pay particular attention to groups or sections of society where improvements in health and life expectancy are not keeping pace with the rest of the population.[2]

It is also made clear, in the very next paragraph, that any waiting will be based on clinical rather than financial considerations:

2. *Access to NHS services is based on clinical need, not an individual's ability to pay.* NHS services are free of charge, except in limited circumstances sanctioned by Parliament.[3]

However, that is not to say that patients may expect that the NHS will deliver everything that they want, and there is an explicit acknowledgment of the fact that resources are not unlimited:

6. *The NHS is committed to providing best value for taxpayers' money and the most effective, fair and sustainable use of finite resources.* Public funds for healthcare will be devoted solely to the benefit of the people that the NHS serves.[4]

---

[1] See NHS, *The Handbook to the NHS Constitution* (2012). Emphasis in original. This can be downloaded from the Department of Health's website at www.dh.gov.uk/prod_consum_dh/groups/dh_digitalassets/@dh/@en/documents/digitalasset/dh_132959.pdf.

[2] NHS, *The NHS Constitution* (2012), p. 3. Emphasis in original. The Constitution can be downloaded from the Department of Health's website at www.dh.gov.uk/prod_consum_dh/groups/dh_digitalassets/@dh/@en/documents/digitalasset/dh_132958.pdf.

[3] NHS, *The NHS Constitution* (2012), p. 3.   [4] NHS, *The NHS Constitution* (2012), p. 4. Emphasis in original.

There is also explicit recognition of the finite nature of resources in what the Constitution refers to as rights in relation to nationally approved treatments, drugs and programmes:

You have the right to drugs and treatments that have been recommended by NICE for use in the NHS, if your doctor says they are clinically appropriate for you.

You have the right to expect local decisions on funding of other drugs and treatments to be made rationally following a proper consideration of the evidence. If the local NHS decides not to fund a drug or treatment you and your doctor feel would be right for you, they will explain that decision to you.[5]

Indeed, there is even a pledge to 'make decisions in a clear and transparent way' in relation to access to services.[6] The Constitution therefore provides a specific message to patients: the NHS intends to provide a comprehensive, free service to all, based on need rather than ability to pay; yet patients must understand that resources are finite and that therefore not everything can be funded. Needless to say, the question of how funding decisions are made comes to the heart of the matter in this chapter. Before considering this, however, we must first define what a resource allocation decision is, and what it is not. Most fundamentally, a decision regarding resource allocation is *not* one where doctors decide that treatment is futile or has a very low chance of success and therefore do not think it is appropriate to provide it. A controversial example of this is the refusal of Cambridge Health Authority to fund leukaemia treatment for 'Child B', a 10-year-old girl. While the court case, to which we shall return later, was decided as an issue relating to the allocation of scarce resources, the hospital have always maintained that this was a misinterpretation of their position and that the decision was taken in the patient's best interests (balancing the low chance of success with the pain inherent in the treatment).[7] What the issue of resource allocation covers is the question of how to divide finite resources and adjudicate between competing claims on money. Frequent scenarios include whether to provide treatment that may have a low chance of success, or that is expensive but will lead to small extensions of good quality life. However, we must also acknowledge that resource decisions will inevitably form a part of the thinking of medical staff when considering referrals, and that thus clinical and resource issues may be inexorably linked – if funding is provided to patient A, it may mean less available for patient B (or even a potential patient who has yet to present) – allowing resource decisions to be implicitly defined as 'clinical' so as to mask their true nature.[8] This is particularly true of

---

[5] NHS, *The NHS Constitution* (2012), p. 6. Emphasis in original.   [6] NHS, *The NHS Constitution* (2012), p. 6.

[7] See *R* v. *Cambridge HA, ex p. B (A Minor)* [1995] 1 WLR 898; [1995] 2 All ER 1. For an account of the hospital's view, see S. Thornton, 'The Child B Case – Reflections of a Chief' (1997) 314 *BMJ* 1838. For a general overview, see A. Parkin, 'Allocating Health Care Resources in an Imperfect World' (1995) 58 *MLR* 867.

[8] See K. Syrett, 'Impotence or Importance? Judicial Review in an Era of Explicit NHS Rationing' (2004) 67 *MLR* 289.

GPs, who act as gatekeepers within the NHS – a role that will be expanded due to their role in local commissioning envisaged by the Health and Social Care Act 2012.[9] Moreover, the courts have themselves acknowledged that decisions regarding a particular patient in many cases cannot be separated from decisions regarding other patients, while recognising that this cannot alone justify all decisions. As Dyson J. noted in *Fisher*:

> It is absurd to suppose that, before any patient is prescribed any expensive treatment, a survey must be made of all patients who are, or might be, in need of the same treatment in the area.[10]

What can be seen, then, is that both the NHS and the courts recognise the inevitability of rationing, and also attempt to maintain some modicum of flexibility. The courts, in particular, have recognised the need for and limits of an unfettered utilitarian approach to allocating resources. This is not, perhaps, the strongest of theoretical foundations, and the Health and Social Care Act 2012 has attempted to remedy this by providing a more explicit role for NICE in the legislation. However, we first consider how someone might question resource allocation decisions in general terms.

DOMESTIC LAW – JUDICIAL REVIEW

In terms of actually challenging a decision made by a hospital or health authority, the most common method is to seek a judicial review. This works in the same way as it would with any other decision by a public body, and the law operates in the same way. Essentially, the complainant would seek to argue that the decision taken was unreasonable in the *Wednesbury* sense.[11] The most famous case in this area is that of Jaymee Bowen, known as 'Child B', to which we referred earlier in the chapter. Jaymee was 5 years old when she was diagnosed with leukaemia. She was treated and recovered, but the illness returned when she was 10 years old. The consultants treating her argued that the treatment involved, aggressive chemotherapy and a bone marrow transplant, had a low chance of success, involved excessive pain and suffering on Jaymee's behalf (particularly given the low chance of the treatment working) and was thus not in her best interests. Her father, however, found a doctor in London who was prepared to accept her as a private patient, and so he sought

---

[9] For an overview of the Health and Social Care Act 2012, see the Explanatory Notes, which can be found at: www. hsc-prof.com/Keydocs/leg/HSCA2012%20en.pdf.

[10] *R* v. *North Derbyshire HA, ex p. Fisher* (1997) 38 BMLR 76; [1997] 8 Med LR 327.

[11] *Associated Provincial Picture Houses Ltd* v. *Wednesbury Corp.* [1947] 2 All ER 680. The principle derived from the case states that a decision from a public body may be challenged if it is 'so outrageous in its defiance of logic or of accepted moral standards that no sensible person who had applied his mind to the question to be decided could have arrived at it' (*per* Lord Diplock in *Council of Civil Service Unions and others* v. *Minister for the Civil Service* [1985] AC 374 at 410).

£75,000 from the health authority to fund this treatment. When this was refused, he sought a judicial review of the decision. At first instance, Laws J. found for the family, holding that Cambridgeshire Health Authority had not justified or explained its decision, and why it did not think providing the money was appropriate. However, the Court of Appeal disagreed and stressed the fact that it was in its view undesirable for the courts to get involved in such decisions. The then Master of the Rolls, Sir Thomas Bingham, suggested that:

Difficult and agonising judgments have to be made as to how a limited budget is best allocated to the maximum advantage of the maximum number of patients. *That is not a judgment which the court can make . . . [and] it is not something that a health authority . . . can be fairly criticised for not advancing before the court.*[12]

As can be seen from the emphasised part of the quote, the court was so reluctant to become involved that it barely even required the health authority to explain its decision at all. Indeed, this is no different from the approach that courts had taken in previous cases, and has led to fierce criticism.[13]

However, this deferential approach was not to last, and later cases – perhaps significantly post *Bolitho* in date – have seen an increased willingness on the part of the courts to question resource allocation decisions. An example of this is the case of *R* v. *North West Lancashire HA, ex p. A.*[14] The case involved three transsexuals who had sought access to gender reassignment surgery, which had been refused by the Regional Health Authority. The Authority had constructed a policy which provided that gender reassignment surgery was to be given a low priority (it was placed at the bottom 10 per cent in the list of priorities), but that operations might be funded in exceptional cases. The case found its way to the Court of Appeal, where Auld LJ began by noting that, following the Jaymee Bowen case, it was settled law that authorities could and indeed should make decisions about priorities for funding, and that the courts should be reluctant to become involved in them. However, as Fennell notes in his commentary on the case, the Court of Appeal found that the Authority had to establish three things in order for their decisions to be reasonable: first, the authority has to 'accurately assess the nature and seriousness of each type of illness'; secondly, it must 'determine the effectiveness of various forms of treatment for it'; and, thirdly, it must 'give proper effect to that assessment' in the application of its policy.[15] The Court of Appeal found that the Authority had failed in all three of these requirements. Essentially, it failed to

---

[12] *R* v. *Cambridge HA, ex p. B (A Minor)* at 906. Emphasis added.
[13] See, e.g., *R* v. *Central Birmingham HA, ex p. Collier*, unreported, in C. Newdick, 'Public Health Ethics and Clinical Freedom' (1998) 14 *Journal of Contemporary Health Law and Policy* 335, 354; and *R* v. *Central Birmingham HA, ex p. Walker* (1987) 3 BMLR 32.
[14] *R* v. *North West Lancashire HA, ex p. A and others* [2000] 1 WLR 977.
[15] P. Fennell, 'Substantive Review of Decisions to Refuse Treatment' (2000) 8 *Med. L. Rev.* 129, 131.

adequately take seriously gender dysphoria as an illness, and 'drafted and applied its policy [in such a way] that no-one would receive the generally recognised treatment'.[16] Thus, the court felt able to become involved because the way in which the policy was applied *in practice* was different to the way in which it was presented. The operation of the policy effectively rendered it a blanket ban on surgery, and this was found to be unreasonable.

That said, the case should not be taken to be indicative of a complete change in approach from Jaymee Bowen's case, as all that the Court of Appeal found was that blanket bans were unreasonable, and that greater transparency regarding decision-making was needed.[17] If this were provided, then it would have been lawful to refuse to fund the treatment. Moreover, later cases have demonstrated that the threshold for complainants remains high. An example of this is the 2011 Court of Appeal case of *AC* v. *Berkshire West Primary Care Trust.*[18] This case also involved a transgendered female who was refused breast augmentation surgery by the primary care trust, although the trust did fund other gender reassignment operations and procedures, which it only did on an exceptional basis. However, in this case the Court of Appeal found for the defendant trust. The difference between this case and the situation in *North West Lancashire HA, ex p. A* is that in *AC* the trust had determined that there was no '*significant* health impairment' in not treating, and the Court of Appeal did not find its conclusion that the case did not therefore constitute an exceptional one unreasonable.[19] Indeed, it reiterated the fact that the trust 'is subject to an absolute duty to break even in each financial year',[20] and that therefore while it had some sympathy for the claimant, it also understood the trust's position:

I understand why the appellant feels aggrieved that the respondent funds the core gender reassignment procedures outlined … notwithstanding the absence of evidence of limited clinical effectiveness, but does not also fund breast augmentation surgery for persons like the appellant (given, in particular, that there is no professional consensus on the classification of core and non-core procedures for gender reassignment). But the answer in law to that feeling is that *the respondent, in exercising its statutory responsibilities, has to make very difficult choices as to what procedures to fund and not to fund and the choice made in this case is not irrational.*[21]

The message from the cases, then, is that the courts, while reticent to interfere and ever mindful of the difficult choices facing decision-makers, will find their decisions to be unreasonable on occasion, particularly if they appear to be procedurally

---

[16] Fennell, 'Substantive Review of Decisions to Refuse Treatment', 135.
[17] For an example of an earlier case finding a blanket ban to be unreasonable, see *R* v. *North Derbyshire HA, ex p. Fisher* [1997] 8 Med LR 327.
[18] *AC* v. *Berkshire West PCT* [2011] EWCA 247 (Civ).   [19] *AC* at para. 65. Emphasis in original.
[20] *AC* at para. 14.   [21] *AC* at para. 35. Emphasis added.

weak.[22] It is perhaps tempting to note that these cases coincide with the new, less deferential approach to the medical profession exhibited by the courts and exemplified by *Bolitho*. Nevertheless, it is also important to remember that findings of unreasonableness are somewhat rare, and that they will almost certainly continue to be so. It is perhaps odd, therefore, that the courts appear to have taken a more robust approach with respect to decisions made by NICE, a body which has grown in influence following the passing of the Health and Social Care Act 2012.

The role of NICE – the Health and Social Care Act 2012

The purpose of NICE is, in large part, to provide the NHS with the information that it needs to provide treatment that is both effective and a good use of resources. As it states itself:

The National Institute for Health and Clinical Excellence (NICE) is an independent organisation responsible for providing national advice ('guidance') on promoting good health and preventing and treating ill health. NICE was established in 1999 to offer NHS healthcare professionals advice on how to provide their patients with the highest attainable standards of care. In 2005, its remit was expanded to include public health (that is, health promotion and disease prevention).[23]

It does this by first looking at the evidence base and then developing guidance that reflects what has been proven to be the most efficient way of proceeding, and this can include the allocation of resources. Indeed, as its principles for development makes clear, '[m]uch of the Institute's guidance takes into account both effectiveness (how well it works) and cost effectiveness (how well it works in relation to how much it costs)'.[24] The notion of cost effectiveness is further defined in a footnote on the same page, where it is said to relate to 'value for money; a specific health care treatment is said to be "cost effective" if it gives a greater health gain than could be achieved by using the resources in other ways'.[25] Indeed, there is an entire section in the document that considers the nature of cost effectiveness and how to determine whether it is present.[26] In terms of its nature, the guidance states that:

Deciding which treatments to recommend involves balancing the needs and wishes of individuals and the groups representing them against those of the wider population. This sometimes means treatments are not recommended because they do not provide sufficient benefit to justify their cost.[27]

---

[22] However, see *R (on the application of Otley)* v. *Barking and Dagenham NHS PCT* [2007] EWHC 1927 (Admin) for an example of a case where the court found the decision to be unreasonable despite the procedural aspect having been followed.

[23] NICE, *Social Value Judgments – Principles for the Development of NICE Guidelines*, 2nd edn, 1.1. This is available to download at: www.nice.org.uk/media/C18/30/SVJ2PUBLICATION2008.pdf.

[24] NICE, *Social Value Judgments*, 1.1.   [25] NICE, *Social Value Judgments*, 1.1.

[26] NICE, *Social Value Judgments*, 4.2.   [27] NICE, *Social Value Judgments*, 4.2.

The acknowledgment that treatments may not be recommended despite being effective is made explicit in the second sentence. In terms of how to assess whether a treatment is cost effective, the section states that NICE predominantly uses Quality Adjusted Life Years (QALYs) as the measure.[28] QALYs are used because the measurement 'is a unit that combines both quantity (length) of life and health-related quality of life into a single measure of health gain'.[29] Needless to say, QALYs are a controversial form of measurement, although it might equally be argued that they are as good as any other.[30]

The significance of the work of NICE is twofold. First, there is the fact that such resource allocation assessments are meant to inform three of the four programmes for part of which NICE issues guidance, and they cover a wide variety of NHS services:

1. technology appraisals (including pharmaceuticals, devices, diagnostics, surgical and other procedures and health promotion tools);[31]
2. clinical guidelines (the 'appropriate treatment and care of patients with specific diseases and conditions');[32] and
3. public health ('[a]ctivities to promote a healthy lifestyle and prevent ill health (for example, giving advice to encourage exercise or providing support to encourage mothers to breastfeed)').[33]

The only programme that does not balance efficacy and cost effectiveness (and therefore concentrates only on efficacy) is that of interventional procedures ('[t]he safety of an "interventional procedure" and how well it works. "Interventional procedure" means any surgery, test or treatment that involves entering the body through skin, muscle, a vein or artery, or body cavity').[34]

This would be important enough, given the fact that NICE guidelines will carry much weight with courts as arbiters of reasonable conduct.[35] However, the second reason for the critical nature of NICE's guidance is that Part 8 of the Health and Social Care Act 2012 provides NICE and its guidance with statutory backing. Section 234(1) provides that NICE may be asked by commissioners to provide quality standards in relation to NHS services, public health services and social care in England. It should be noted that the latter is new and an expansion of NICE's remit. Moreover, under section 237(8)(b), bodies might be *required* to comply with

[28] NICE, *Social Value Judgments*, 4.2.   [29] NICE, *Social Value Judgments*, 4.2.
[30] See, e.g., P. Menzel, 'Some Ethical Costs of Rationing' (1992) 20 *Law, Medicine and Health Care 57*, 59–62 in particular; J. Cubbon, 'The Principle of QALY Maximisation as the Basis for Allocating Health Care Resources' (1991) 17 *Journal of Medical Ethics* 181; and J. McKie *et al.*, *The Allocation of Health Care Resources: Ethical Evaluation of the 'QALY' Approach* (London: Dartmouth Publishing Co., 1998).
[31] NICE, *Social Value Judgments* – see table 1 at p. 5.   [32] NICE, *Social Value Judgments*, p. 5, table 1.
[33] NICE, *Social Value Judgments*, p. 5, table 1.   [34] NICE, *Social Value Judgments*, p. 5, table 1.
[35] See A. Samanta *et al.*, 'The Role of Clinical Guidelines in Medical Negligence Litigation: A Shift from the *Bolam* Standard?' (2006) 14(3) *Med. L. Rev.* 321.

such guidance. Therefore, it is clear not only that NICE is an important body, but also that its remit is poised to be widened and its influence increased. It is critical, then, that NICE's guidance can be challenged; and so far there have been only two cases where this has occurred.[36]

Perhaps surprisingly, particularly given that NICE's procedures are so evidence based, the courts have not been slow to question the judgment of the organisation, and in both cases the court at least partially found against NICE. In the first of the challenges, the case of *Eisai*, the error found was somewhat procedural.[37] NICE had restricted its recommendation of an Alzheimer's drug to patients with moderate levels of the disease. Those with mild levels would not receive it. Eisai, the manufacturer of the drug, sought a judicial review of that decision, arguing that NICE's consultation had not been carried out fairly and that it had not complied with its statutory duty to have regard of equalities legislation.

At first instance, the court rejected the first point. Eisai had contended that as a part of the consultation, it had not been provided with sufficient information to be able to independently examine the cost-effectiveness model used by NICE in its assessment of the drug, and the court held that the procedure was therefore fair. However, this was overturned by the Court of Appeal, who instead allowed the appeal by emphasising the critical nature of transparency:

> ... procedural fairness does require release of the fully executable version of the model. It is true that there is already a remarkable degree of disclosure and of transparency in the consultation process; but that cuts both ways, because it also serves to underline the nature and importance of the exercise being carried out. The refusal to release the fully executable version of the model stands out as the one exception to the principle of openness and transparency that NICE has acknowledged as appropriate in this context. It does place consultees ... at a significant disadvantage in challenging the reliability of the model ... [I]t limits their ability to make an intelligent response on something that is central to the appraisal process.[38]

In a sense one could say that NICE was hoist by its own evidence-based petard by not being sufficiently transparent about the model that it used, but at the same time the judgment relates to the procedure used by NICE in consultation rather than the decision itself. Nevertheless, it does demonstrate a judicial willingness to question NICE's decision-making. This is confirmed by the case of *Servier*, where the court also accepted a challenge regarding NICE's categorisation of a drug aimed at preventing fracture in people with osteoparosis.[39] The drug, Protelos, had been approved at EU level by the European Medicines Agency (EMA). In the course of this approval, the EMA had requested from Servier further information about hip

---

[36]   Although it should be noted that the Health and Social Care Act 2012, s. 238 states that regulations should also make some provisions regarding appeals against NICE guidelines that are binding. We therefore expect that this number will rise.
[37]   *R (on the application of Eisai Ltd) v. NICE* [2008] EWCA Civ 438.   [38]   *Eisai* at para. 66.
[39]   *R (on the application of Servier Laboratories Ltd) v. NICE* [2009] EWHC 281 (Admin).

fractures in particular and the identification among a sub-group of the clinical trial participants of people who might be more at risk of hip fracture. The analysis of this data led the EMA to conclude that the drug was efficient to a considerable level. However, NICE's own analysis did not accept this conclusion and it did not recommend the drug. Servier sought a judicial review, which like in *Eisai* was rejected at first instance, but accepted on appeal. In the Court of Appeal, an extraordinary amount of weight seemed to be placed on the fact that the EMA had accepted the analysis and approved the drug. This was made clear by Wilson LJ:

> It is not suggested that NICE are bound by EMA's decision or its reasoning but the appellants are entitled to expect any decision against them to be properly reasoned, especially when it is contrary to the reasoned decision of an equally eminent body.[40]

This is, if anything, more significant than the decision in *Eisai*, as the court rejected NICE's decision itself rather than merely the procedural aspects of reaching it. Indeed, in placing so much weight on the fact that the EMA approved the drug, the court does come close to limiting NICE's power to disagree with it. Given the high-profile role of NICE following the Health and Social Care Act 2012, it is inevitable that these challenges will come more and more often, and if the courts hold to this line of reasoning it will be difficult for NICE to retain control and stem the tide of drug manufacturers who want their drugs to be approved for use within the NHS.

There are two other methods for challenging decisions: using the Human Rights Act 1998 to argue that a decision contravenes a patient's rights under the European Convention on Human Rights, and breach of statutory duty. We consider both briefly below.

ALTERNATIVES TO JUDICIAL REVIEW – THE HUMAN RIGHTS ACT 1998 AND BREACH OF STATUTORY DUTY

Some of the cases that we have already considered have also attempted to use the Human Rights Act to argue that their rights under the European Convention have been infringed. Arguments have been raised that the right to life (Article 2) has been violated by the non-provision of life-saving treatment, that to not treat constitutes torture or degrading treatment (Article 3), or even that to not treat constitutes discrimination (Article 14). These arguments have usually been rejected, and cases where the claimant has attempted to use the Human Rights Act as its principal point have invariably failed in what might be considered 'classic' resource allocation scenarios.[41] Indeed, those cases in which the Human Rights Act has been

---

[40] *Servier Laboratories* at para. 62.   [41] See, e.g., *R* v. *North West Lancashire HA, ex p. A.*

successfully applied have been less conventional.[42] But in general, the courts have remained reluctant to allow claims. In the recent case of *Condliff*, for example, the claimant attempted to argue that his Article 8 right to a private and family life involved a positive duty to treat him for morbid obesity.[43] This was rejected by the court, which held that no such positive right could be said to exist even where 'failing to provide treatment will have an impact on the quality of life and physical integrity of the person denied it', as long as the decision and its procedural aspect were not irrational.[44] In this respect, then, it can be seen that the Human Rights Act has not been a successful vehicle for claimants seeking an alternative route to judicial review.

Actions for breach of statutory duty, while possible, have met a similar fate. This is not least due to the fact that the statutes concerned, for obvious reasons, invariably stop short of promising more than the NHS can reasonably hope to deliver. Thus, for example, the National Health Service Act 1977, section 3 stated that the Secretary of State for Health was under a duty to provide medical services 'to such an extent that he considers necessary to meet all reasonable requirements'. Thus, in the case of *Hincks*, the Court of Appeal rejected a claim by patients who had spent several years on the waiting list for orthopaedic surgery, with Lord Denning MR noting that not everything could be funded and that 'the Secretary of State says that he is doing the best that he can with the financial resources available to him' to justify the decision.[45] The court was to take a similar approach in the case of *Coughlan*.[46] Section 1 of the 1977 Act imposes a duty on the Secretary of State to 'continue the promotion in England and Wales of a comprehensive health service'.[47] This was held by Lord Woolf MR in the Court of Appeal to require only that the Secretary of State 'pays due regard' to that duty and that there is no requirement for the service to be *in fact* comprehensive.[48] Indeed, he noted that 'a comprehensive health service may never, for human, financial and other resource reasons, be achievable'.[49]

That is not to say that such cases are doomed to failure. If a statute is clear enough, then a breach of duty can be, and has been, found. Nevertheless, it has been an ineffective alternative to judicial review, and must in most cases be seen as a last resort.

---

[42] See, e.g., *Price* v. *United Kingdom* (2001) 34 EHRR 1285. concerning the needs of a severely disabled prisoner (Art. 3); *Savage* v. *South Essex Partnership NHS Foundation Trust* [2008] 1 WLR 977, where the House of Lords held that if a mentally ill patient was known to be a suicide risk Art. 2 provided a duty to take positive steps to help to prevent the risk from materialising.

[43] *R (on the application of Condliff)* v. *North Staffordshire PCT* [2011] EWCA 910 (Civ).

[44] As per the judge at first instance: *R (on the application of Condliff)* v. *North Staffordshire PCT* [2011] EWHC 872 (Admin) at para. 53.

[45] *R* v. *Secretary of State for Social Services, ex p. Hincks* (1980) 1 BMLR 93 at 95.

[46] *R* v. *North and East Devon HA, ex p. Coughlan* [1999] EWCA 1871 (Civ).

[47] The Act has been superseded by the National Health Service Act 2006, but the wording is substantially the same.

[48] *R* v. *North and East Devon HA, ex p. Coughlan* at para. 25.

[49] *R* v. *North and East Devon HA, ex p. Coughlan* at para. 25.

CONCLUDING REMARKS ON LAW

The allocation of resources is just as inevitable as it is controversial. In a publically funded health service such as the NHS, difficult choices need to be made, and those on the wrong end of them will inevitably feel aggrieved. It is our contention, however, that the courts have managed to get things about right. In particular, the high threshold for questioning decisions is absolutely right, for several reasons. The first is that, fundamentally, we are concerned with decisions that reach far beyond the individual patient and her desire for (expensive) treatment. It is easy to see simply the patient who is denied, for example, life-prolonging cancer drugs, and miss the wider picture of the several patients who could have major surgery instead if that money were to be reallocated. While we are instinctively wary of an objective system such as that provided by QALYs, they at least provide the courts with some mechanism for decision-making that actually considers this wider picture.

In this regard, the increased role for NICE can only be welcomed. There will be, in theory, a thorough consideration of the issues and the courts can be helped to make evidence-based decisions. But overall, as mentioned above, we approve of the consistent approach of the courts – whether cases are brought through the Human Rights Act, breach of statutory duty or the more traditional mechanism of judicial review. The fundamental recognition that not everything can be paid for, coupled with an instinctive (though rebuttable) desire not to intervene may be the least bad option. In essence, if the courts were to take a more interventionist approach, there would be chaos, as budgets would be forced to be moved around – and these are not actions without consequences. Thus, it is only right that judicial activism is kept to an absolute minimum.

ETHICS

The fundamental starting point for our discussion of the ethical issues of resource allocation is the exact same premise upon which we started the legal discussion: it is simply a fact of life that resources are finite and rationing is inevitable.[50] A perfect solution (i.e. one where everyone is happy) is therefore an impossibility. This leaves

---

[50] See U. Reinhardt, 'Rationing Health Care: What It Is, What It Is Not, and Why We Cannot Avoid It' in S. Altman and U. Reinhardt (eds.), *Strategic Choices for a Changing Health Care System* (Chicago: Health Administration Press, 1996), pp. 63–99.

us with a situation in which we the actors must therefore try to achieve the least imperfect result when allocating resources (a situation which reminds us of the discussion of consequentialist theories in Chapter 1: the system ought to try to produce the least amount of unhappiness when deciding who gets which resource). Bearing this in mind, the discussion of allocation decisions in this chapter will lead to a surprising result when we look at how the courts have approached this issue.

What resources?

A first distinction which we need to make here is within the category of 'resource'. In the clinical setting, we are concerned not just with 'financial resources', but also with scarce commodities (for want of a better term) such as machinery (expensive or specialist diagnostic devices, for example) or individual therapeutic interventions (such as organs for transplantation). While the scarcity of devices can still, to some extent, be connected to health care spending at a macro level, the scarcity of hearts and other solid organs cannot.

Here, we simply have a situation where all the money in the world will not increase the amount of organs available (all cynical and usually ill-informed discussions about illicit organ trading aside). This splits the issue into two: allocating resources in terms of directing spending (i.e. policy decisions aimed at, for example, increasing availability of pain management facilities in the NHS at the expense of some other area of public spending for health care) and allocating resources in situations where, put simply, two or more takers exist for one intervention. The former is a policy decision which is directable and where the scarcity of a therapeutic option is an indirect result of the scarcity of funding: it is an issue of *prioritisation*, rather than allocation. The latter is a decision which is, by and large, undirectable and the scarcity of a therapeutic option is immanent in the system of organ donation: here, we are concerned with a question of *allocation*.

Making choices

The latter context is a classic example of trying to determine how to make an ethically justifiable choice in dire circumstances. Consider the following:

A heart for transplantation has become available. Four individuals are matched as potential recipients, with identical medical parameters in terms of the suitability for each recipient (i.e. we cannot distinguish between the potential recipients on the basis of medical parameters).

- *Potential recipient (A) is a housewife and mother of three young children.*
- *Potential recipient (B) is a policeman who was injured in the line of duty.*
- *Potential recipient (C) is a 57-year-old, long-term unemployed drug addict.*
- *Potential recipient (D) is a sex offender serving a lengthy sentence.*

Each of the potential recipients will die if she or he is not the chosen recipient of the transplant.

The example (for which there is no single right answer, by the way) highlights some important issues in allocation decision-making for a scarce resource: first, in the absence of hard medical parameters, it is eminently difficult to make choices. Secondly, a choice has to be made, otherwise all four will perish. So how does one make a choice in these circumstances? Is it, for example, actually the case that the mother of three is a preferable choice to the sex offender when choosing whose life is saved?

Clinical versus allocation decisions

As we have discussed in Chapter 1, the essense of the principle of beneficence is that a doctor ought to do what is beneficial to his patient. What we are now looking at here, however, is an area in which, at first glance, only a small share of the decision-making is actually up to the doctor 'on the ground'. Most of the decision-making relating to resource allocation seems to happen at an institutional level (i.e. at health system level and in organisations such as NICE).

We have already said that, here, we are dealing with an area in which a perfect result is almost impossible to achieve. Our example above illustrates, in a very crude way, that in the absence of hard, clinical parameters for or against a candidate, an allocation decision has to be made in another way – but how do we ensure that such a decision is just? We will try to investigate this question by looking at a number of different normative requirements which we feel play an important role when determining the fairness of prioritisation and allocation decisions.

Liberty

Those making prioritisation decisions must take into consideration that patients will have different preferences (and will sometimes even have rather irrational preferences). This in principle means that individuals ought to be free to make their own arrangements (outside of the prioritisation context) where an intervention is not available for free on the basis of the relevant health service provider. The same is true where an intervention is not available in the United Kingdom, but (for example) in Belgium. This produces questions in relation to the idea of 'distributive justice': where prioritisation decisions exclude funding for certain interventions, or require patients to travel abroad to avail of these interventions, it may lead to only those wealthy enough having access to these services, which is prima facie an undesirable situation. At the same time, it would not do to prohibit private arrangements (thus interfering with individuals' liberty) purely for the purposes of ensuring that everyone has the same poor chances. The result of these considerations, together with the realities of scarce commodities in the health sector, have in most instances led to a two-tier approach: a fundamental level of services and interventions which are made available to individuals independently of their means, and the additional possibility of making private arrangements (for example, by way of a private health care insurance policy) to purchase services and interventions which go over and beyond this fundamental level. It is obvious that in an ideal world, all the health care provision required by an individual would be made available free of charge and immediately. Anyone who labours that point and refuses to discuss the realities of scarcity in this context is simply being unrealistic: this is an area where tough decisions have to be made in order to at least create a benefit for some.

Efficiency

Where resources are finite, and individuals' health, life and well-being depend on having access to these resources, there is a moral obligation to ensure that the scarce resources are administered efficiently. Waste of such resources deprives patients of much-needed treatment. This argument is similar to that which we discuss in Chapter 9: the validity and effectiveness of biomedical research is an important factor for determining its ethical justifiability. Spurious, futile, poorly designed research is as morally unacceptable as wasteful and disorganised allocation of finite health resources. It is therefore eminently important to ensure that the quality of the interventions and services provided within the first tier of our health system is assured – and this is where much of the work of NICE plays an important role. NICE is, essentially, a regulatory valve which the health system has introduced in order to create (occasionally artificial) allocation pathways. It is obviously desirable that funding goes predominantly to therapeutic interventions which are of the highest possible quality and an institution, with an appropriate mandate, which verifies the quality of interventions on the basis of evidence is a fundamental prerequisite for the ethical justifiability of the allocation system as a whole (otherwise decisions could just be made on the basis of which manufacturer produces an intervention most cheaply, independent of the efficacy of the intervention).

Justice and procedural fairness

We have already briefly touched on the issue of distributive justice. The idea is that distributive justice looks at how resources are allocated among those in need of, or entitled to, these resources to ensure that no inequality occurs (as would be the case, for example, if out of those in need only a certain group of individuals, such as the very wealthy, ended up being able to access a certain resource). Distributive justice is therefore concerned with determining a morally acceptable way in which benefits (and burdens) might be distributed across a population.

Another significant aspect is that of procedural fairness, which is concerned with how decisions come about. A number of parameters can be shown to determine the fairness of a procedure:

1. transparency;
2. democratic legitimation of the allocating institution;
3. stakeholder participation;
4. consistency of decision-making across several instances;
5. due process (i.e. appeals possibilities, etc.).[51]

CONCLUSION

The courts, in the decisions we have seen in this chapter, are generally concerned with this question of procedural fairness, rather than the outcome-based question of distributive justice. This is a departure from a generally consequentialist stance of the courts in that the outcomes of the prioritisation and allocation decisions under review are secondary (or play no role at all). The courts merely need to be convinced that the path taken to reach a decision was correct (hence also the reference to *Wednesbury* unreasonableness, which is concerned not with the decision itself, but with the decision-making process). That said, the approach of the courts also takes less account of the individual – in the sense that it will not intervene in resource allocation decisions based on who the person is or the priorities set by managers, unless they are totally illogical.

Indeed, the use of procedure rather than (other than in extreme cases) the content of the decision allows the courts to make decisions that are at least defensible, but more importantly also enables them to avoid unanswerable dilemmas trying to compare the value of peoples' lives. Certainly, many of the decisions that health authorities have to make contain no right answer, and once we accept the fact that resources are not only finite but inevitably insufficient to fund everything, we must further accept that this means that some people for whom there is a possible treatment will not be able to receive it. Perhaps paradoxically, given that we have said that the courts have departed from a consequentialist approach, this is so that others may receive treatment which should, in theory, maximise welfare. In this sense, the priority is the many rather than the individual.

---

[51] G. Marckmann, 'Verteilungsgerechtigkeit in der Gesundheitsversorgung' in S. Schulz *et al.* (eds.), *Geschichte, Theorie und Ethik der Medizin. Eine Einführung* (Frankfurt/Main: Suhrkamp, 2006), p. 183 (our translation).

ADDITIONAL READING

 ### Law

P. Fennell, 'Substantive Review of Decisions to Refuse Treatment' (2000) 8(2) *Medical Law Review* 129

C. Newdick, *Who Should We Treat? Rights, Rationing and Resources in the NHS*, 2nd edn (Oxford University Press, 2004)

C. Newdick, 'Public Health Ethics and Clinical Freedom' (1998) 14 *Journal of Contemporary Health Law and Policy* 335

K. Syrett, 'Impotence or Importance? Judicial Review in an Era of Explicit NHS Rationing' (2004) 67(2) *Modern Law Review* 289

K. Veitch, 'Juridification, Medicalisation and the Impact of EU Law: Patient Mobility and the Allocation of Scarce NHS Resources' (2012) 20(3) *Medical Law Review* 362

Ethics

J. Butler, *The Ethics of Health Care Rationing* (London: Cassell, 1999)

R. Cookson and P. Dolan, 'Principles of Justice in Health Care Rationing' (2000) 26 *Journal of Medical Ethics* 523

T. Hope, J. Savulescu and J. Hendrick, *Medical Law and Medical Ethics: The Core Curriculum*, 2nd edn (Edinburgh: Churchill Livingstone, 2008), chapter 13

E. Matthews and E. Russell, *Rationing Medical Care on the Basis of Age – The Moral Dimensions* (Oxford: Radcliffe Publishing, 2005)

I. Williams, S. Robinson and H. Dickinson, *Rationing in Health Care – The Theory and Practice of Priority Setting* (Bristol: The Policy Press, 2012)

Case studies from this chapter are available online at www.cambridge.org/hoppe.

7 Assisted reproduction

THE WARNOCK COMMITTEE REPORT

As we shall see, assisted reproduction is regulated in England by the Human Fertilisation and Embryology Act (HFEA) 1990 (as amended), which contains the rules and imposes the regulatory structure that must be followed by clinics providing a service. The Act, however, was born as a result of the report of a committee chaired by Baroness Warnock assigned to look into these issues.[1] The remit of the committee was wide, as it was charged with considering:

... recent and potential developments in medicine and science related to human fertilisation and embryology; to consider what policies and safeguards should be applied, including consideration of the social, ethical and legal implications of these developments; and to make recommendations.[2]

The scope of the report thus covered artificial insemination, surrogacy and new processes of artificial reproduction. Abortion and contraception were, however, outside the ambit of the brief.[3] It is worthy of note that the committee was asked to look not just at existing technology, but also at *potential* developments. Given this, the report would have to construct a framework that would respond to change. The remit of the committee was therefore far wider than that of this chapter, which considers only the issue of assisted reproduction. However, the importance of the wide remit lies in the influence it had over the regulatory framework that it suggested and that was implemented by the 1990 Act. Essentially, the committee faced two particular problems. First, it had to establish a clear and coherent ethical position surrounding not just the moral status of embryos and gametes, but also the type of families that they were content to facilitate. In this respect, the

---

[1] *Report of the Committee of Inquiry into Human Fertilisation and Embryology* (Cmnd 9314, 1984).
[2] *Report into Human Fertilisation and Embryology*, para. 1.1.
[3] *Report into Human Fertilisation and Embryology*, para. 1.3.

committee also had to ensure that there was some sort of enforcement mechanism that would ensure that this ethical position was adopted and maintained by clinics offering services. Secondly, the committee had to create a structure that was flexible and able to respond to change, so that any future technological developments could be brought within the ambit of the Act if necessary.

The framework suggested by the Warnock Committee and adopted by the Act is the one copied by the Human Tissue Act 2004 and the Mental Capacity Act 2005: that is, an Act with general principles backed by an overarching Authority which publishes and updates a Code of Practice. Thus, in order to be able to provide services (or conduct research) within the Act, premises must first have been granted a licence from the Human Fertilisation and Embryology Authority.[4] This licence will only be granted if the clinicians undertake to conform to the Act and the Code of Practice, and a failure to do so may result in the loss of the licence.[5] The Code of Practice is produced and updated by the Authority, which in theory at least allows it to respond to technological developments and to close any loopholes left by the legislation.[6] It has certainly done this diligently, with the latest incarnation being the eighth edition since the 1990 Act came into force, an average of approximately one every three years.

ACCESS TO TREATMENT

Clearly, one of the most pressing challenges facing the Act and its regulatory framework is that of the question of access to treatment. This includes two aspects: first, the question of who the HFEA 1990 will allow to receive treatment; and, secondly, that of how to allocate finite resources to decide between those who might qualify. The first of these questions is the most controversial, as it necessarily involves making judgments regarding what sort of family structures are to be encouraged, tolerated or actively barred from seeking treatment. As we shall see, this is an area where the ability of the Code of Practice to respond to changing social mores can be both easily identified and shown to function.

---

[4] The Human Fertilisation and Embryology Act 1990, s. 9(1) provides that: 'The Authority shall maintain one or more committees to discharge the Authority's functions relating to the grant, variation, suspension and revocation of licences, and a committee discharging those functions is referred to in this Act as a licence committee.'

[5] Section 17(1)(e) of the 1990 Act provides that the person responsible at licensed premises must ensure that the conditions of the licence are complied with. Section 18(1)(c) further states that one of the reasons for revoking licences is if 'the person responsible has failed to discharge, or is unable because of incapacity to discharge, the duty under section 17 of this Act or has failed to comply with directions given in connection with any licence'. Thus, it is appropriate to revoke the clinic's licence if it is unwilling or unable to comply with the terms of the licence.

[6] The Authority itself defines its role, in part, as being to 'ensure the HFEA and the sector keep abreast of new scientific and research developments through continued collaborative working with scientific and professional bodies'. See the 'What We Do' section of the Authority's website at www.hfea.gov.uk/133.html.

The Warnock Committee report was very clear in its view regarding the sorts of families that should be created by assisted reproduction – and that was a heterosexual couple, ideally married:

> ... we believe that as a general rule it is better for children to be born into a two parent family, with both father and mother, although we recognise that it is impossible to predict with any certainty how lasting such a relationship will be.[7]

The result was, in the Act as it was originally designed in 1990, the infamous section 13(5) test for the welfare of the child. The section, as originally constructed, provided that before any treatment could be given, clinics had, as a condition of their licence, to first ensure that 'account has been taken of the welfare of any child who may be born as a result of the treatment (*including the need of that child for a father*), and of any other child who may be affected by the birth'.[8] This was a deliberately discriminatory clause that was designed to make it as difficult as possible for those outside of the imagined traditional, heterosexual family structure to gain access to treatment.[9] Moreover, it was nothing if not an accurate representation of what the Warnock Committee had recommended.

However, section 13(5) was undermined in practice. Some clinics did provide treatment to single women and lesbian couples – although this might, as suggested by Morgan and Lee, have more to do with the financial realities faced by clinics that needed to treat women to survive than a principled stand against discrimination.[10] Even more critically, the Code of Practice undermined the discriminatory message of the Act from its very first edition. Indeed:

> The first edition stated that people seeking treatment were entitled to a 'fair and unprejudiced assessment', and that centres should consider 'their commitment and that of their husband (or partner) if any to having and bringing up a child'. Later, when discussing the situation where the child will have no legal father, it states that since centres are required to have regard for the need for a father they should assess whether there is anyone else in the mother's 'family or social circle who is willing and able to share the responsibility' of meeting the child's needs in this respect. This wording continued in the second edition, although it changed in the third edition, where for the first time clinics are asked to consider the child's environment, demanding consideration of the 'ability to provide a stable and supportive environment' for the resulting child. The fourth edition adds that the Act 'does not exclude any category of woman' from being treated, thus moving even further away from what politicians (and Warnock) intended.

---

[7] *Report into Human Fertilisation and Embryology*, para. 2.11. See also S. E. Mumford, E. Corrigan and M. G. Hull, 'Access to Assisted Conception: A Framework for Regulation' (1998) 13 *Human Reproduction* 2349.
[8] Emphasis added.
[9] See D. Gurnham and J. Miola, 'Reproduction, Rights and the Welfare Interests of the Child: The Times They Aren't A-Changin'' (2012) *King's Law Journal* 29, 29–34.
[10] R. Lee and D. Morgan, *Human Fertilisation and Embryology: Regulating the Reproduction Business* (Oxford: Blackwell, 2001), p. 164.

The fifth and sixth editions of the guidance maintained the same approach (although, curiously, the sixth edition dropped the clause that states that no category of woman is excluded under the Act), and a major revision occurred in 2005, for the seventh edition. Here section 13(5) was further diluted, with clinics told that they must merely take into account the 'welfare of the child' born and any existing children.[11]

Thus, when the HFEA 1990 was amended in 2008, it came as no surprise that section 13(5) was among those amendments, particularly given the criticism that the clause had attracted.[12] The need 'for a father' was replaced by a need 'for supportive parenting', so that the section now reads:

A woman shall not be provided with treatment services unless account has been taken of the welfare of any child who may be born as a result of the treatment (including the need of that child for supportive parenting), and of any other child who may be affected by the birth.

As mentioned above, this will do little to change what was already happening in practice, and indeed it merely places on a statutory footing what had long been espoused by the Code of Practice. In this sense, then, little has changed other than that the Act and the Code of Practice are agreed on the approach to take.

The other issue relating to access is somewhat more prosaic: the fact that the scarcity of resources means that not everyone who wishes to access assisted reproductive treatments can be paid for. Of course, this is principally a problem for the NHS, since private clinics need business to survive and, as long as the welfare provisions described above are complied with, they will treat the patient should they be able to pay the fee. In the NHS, of course, the opposite can be said to be true, and it is not surprising to note that assisted reproduction does not lie at the top of the NHS' list of priorities – although in early 2013 an expansion was announced by NICE and women over 40 years of age will be allowed IVF treatment on the NHS for the first time.[13] Nevertheless, resources remain finite and some limitations have to be put in place. This has led to some women arguing that the limitations are unfair, and seeking a judicial review of the decision not to allow them treatment.

A good example of this is the case of *R* v. *Sheffield Health Authority, ex p. Seale*,[14] where just such an application was made.[15] The case involved a 37-year-old woman who had fallen foul of the health authority's rules, which at the time stated that IVF treatment would be limited to women who were aged between

---

[11] Gurnham and Miola, 'Reproduction, Rights and the Welfare Interests of the Child', 35.

[12] Gurnham and Miola, 'Reproduction, Rights and the Welfare Interests of the Child', 35.

[13] See S. Boseley, 'Health Service to Fund IVF for Over 40s', *The Guardian*, 20 February 2013, www.guardian.co.uk/society/2013/feb/20/health-service-fund-ivf?INTCMP=SRCH.

[14] *R* v. *Sheffield HA, ex p. Seale* (1994) 25 BMLR 1.

[15] For an excellent analysis, see A. Grubb, 'Infertility Treatment: Access and Judicial Review' (1996) 4(3) *Med. L. Rev.* 326.

25 and 34, due to the fact that it was felt that this was how the maximum benefit might be derived from what were unquestionably finite resources (at the time in 1984, the sum allocated by the authority for such services was a mere £200,000). The court essentially held that the matter should be considered in two stages. First, there was the question of whether it was permissible for the health authority to place age limits at all on the provision of IVF treatments. Grubb noted that to argue that it was not, as the claimant did, was 'patently untenable' and bound to fail.[16] Indeed, the implications for the health service if it were not allowed to limit treatments *at all* other than those expressly authorised by the Secretary of State would be both severe and wide-ranging.

Having established this, the remaining question was whether the limitation was reasonable, in the *Wednesbury* sense.[17] Again, the court was not persuaded that this was the case, and accepted the authority's argument that the age range was chosen as this was the time that maximised the chances of success for the treatment. Given the finite nature of the resources, it is difficult to disagree with this conclusion.[18] Thus, just as with cases concerning the allocation of resources in general terms, the courts are extremely reluctant to get involved at all, and will be similarly extremely reticent to question decisions by trusts in this area.

Applicants attempting to use the Human Rights Act to gain access to treatment have met a mixed response. In particular, the cases of two prisoners using Article 8 have, perhaps, left nobody satisfied. In the case of *Mellor*, a prisoner's wife would have been 31 at the time that he was released, so he sought judicial review of a decision not to allow prisoners IVF treatment.[19] The Court of Appeal rejected the application on several grounds, including the fact that in this particular case the age of the prisoner's partner at the time of his release meant that they would still be able to access treatment. However, the court also noted that not only was a limitation of his ability to procreate inevitable due to incarceration – and justifiable under Article 8(2) – but also that the state would be quite correct to factor in issues such as the fact that the resulting child would be brought up by only one parent until the prisoner's release. This provision was considered to be a wholly legitimate part of considering the welfare of the child as a part of a general policy relating to access to treatment.

However, the Grand Chamber of the European Court has held that an effective blanket ban is a contravention of Article 8. In *Dickson*, the prisoner's wife would

---

[16] 'Infertility Treatment', 327.

[17] *Associated Provincial Picture Houses Ltd* v. *Wednesbury Corp.* [1947] 2 All ER 680. Essentially, the test is whether the decision was so ridiculous or outrageous that no sensible person or body could have made it.

[18] As Grubb notes, she appears not to have put to the court her strongest argument, which was that she suffered from a condition that could be cured by pregnancy, thus allowing an argument that there were grounds for the authority to be required to depart from its usual rules. 'Infertility Treatment', 328.

[19] *R* v. *Secretary of State for the Home Department, ex p. Mellor* [2001] EWCA 472.

have been over 50 years of age at the prisoner's earliest release date, so the possibility of founding a family after his incarceration would have been all but extinguished.[20] The Grand Chamber noted that the exceptions to the rule that prisoners should not be allowed access to treatment were so difficult to meet that they effectively amounted to a blanket ban, and this contravened Article 8 as prisoners did not lose their right to a family life merely due to their status as prisoners. This is not a difficult burden for states to comply with as they can still have stringent rules as long as there is *some* realistic prospect of some people qualifying, so the decision in *Dickson* should not be interpreted as being likely to give rise to a flood of successful applications by prisoners to access assisted reproduction services. In this respect, *Dickson* remains consistent with an approach that has generally seen the margin of appreciation and decisions by health authorities and the state respected and not interfered with under normal circumstances, but at the same time recognises that this is different from rubber stamping and that in extreme circumstances the courts will act.

SEEKING TREATMENT TOGETHER

The courts cannot avoid intervening, however, when there is a dispute between parties, and in particular between two individuals who decide to engage in treatment together, but subsequently split up. A good example of this can be found in the case of *Evans*.[21] The claimant had been in a long-term relationship with her partner, Mr Johnston, but a laparotomy had discovered borderline tumours in both ovaries. The advice was that both of Ms Evans' ovaries be removed. After being informed of the diagnosis, Ms Evans and Mr Johnston were taken the very same day to a clinic, where they were further informed that as the tumours were growing slowly, it would be possible for Ms Evans to undergo a cycle of egg harvesting for use after the removal of Ms Evans' ovaries. The clinic, however, had a policy of only freezing embryos rather than eggs (at the time, the freezing of eggs was technically extremely difficult, with sharp ice crystals forming during the thawing process likely to destroy the eggs), so Ms Evans' eggs were fertilised using Mr Johnston's sperm.

[20] *Dickson* v. *UK* (2007) (App. No. 44362/04).
[21] *Evans* v. *Amicus Healthcare Ltd; Hadley* v. *Midland Fertility Services Ltd* [2003] EWHC 2161 (High Court); *Evans* v. *Amicus Healthcare Ltd* [2004] EWCA (Civ) 727 (CA). The cases of Ms Evans and Ms Hadley were heard together, but we concentrate on the former. Only Ms Evans appealed to the Court of Appeal, and she further appealed to the European Court of Human Rights and ultimately the Grand Chamber (*Evans* v. *UK* (2007) (App. No. 6339/05)). She was unsuccessful on each occasion.

The law relating to this area is clear: in such a situation, the parties are deemed to be seeking treatment together.[22] Thus, Schedule 3 of the Human Fertilisation and Embryology Act applies, in particular paragraph 4, which states that:

(1) The terms of any consent under this Schedule may from time to time be varied, and the consent may be withdrawn, by notice given by the person who gave the consent to the person keeping the gametes or embryo to which the consent is relevant.

This means that Mr Johnston had the right to withdraw his consent, which would prevent Ms Evans from using the embryos. Indeed, this withdrawal of consent was possible until the point of 'use', which all of the courts defined as being the actual implantation of the embryo. Unfortunately, Mr Johnston and Ms Evans ended their relationship while the eggs were frozen, and he withdrew his consent for Ms Evans to use the embryos. Ms Evans went to court to argue that she should be able to do so despite his refusal of consent. Given the clear nature of the law, it is unsurprising that Ms Evans lost at every stage. At the Court of Appeal and the European Court of Human Rights, Ms Evans argued that her Article 8 right to a private and family life was infringed by not being allowed to do as she wished with the embryos. On each occasion this argument was rejected on the basis that the same could be said for Mr Johnston, and that was essentially the crux of the case. Whichever way the court decided, someone would have his or her rights infringed, and the question was how the law would decide who that was. The European Court found that English law was not unreasonable in its determination of consent at certain points being the key, and therefore the only course of action was to reject Ms Evans' case.

Nevertheless, the devil in the case is in its detail, and the fact that it would appear that Mr Johnston encouraged Ms Evans to fertilise her eggs with his sperm, despite her initial desire to explore the possibility of freezing their gametes separately. As Ms Evans made clear in a statement quoted by the High Court, she felt that she was convinced not to do so:

At this point Howard [Mr. Johnston] told me not to be stupid and that there was no need for that. He told me that he loved me, that we would be getting married and having a family together. I said 'But what if we split up?' Howard told me that we were not going to and that I should not be such a negative person.

I suggested that we freeze some of the eggs and that if we were still together in a couple of years' time and wanted to use them we could always fertilise them then. He told me again that we would not be splitting up, that our future was together and that he loved me ... I told him that I loved him and trusted him.[23]

---

[22] This is one of the purposes of consent specified as allowable under Sch. 3, para. 4. See A. Alghrani, 'Deciding the Fate of Frozen Embryos' (2005) 13 *Med. L. Rev.* 244, 246–8.
[23] *Evans; Hadley* at para. 47.

Mr. Johnston's version of the same events does not confirm this, but he accepted that some statements were made:

I obviously wanted to reassure [Ms Evans] during this difficult time. I was concerned for her welfare. I cannot recall providing her with any specific reassurances at this time ... I could hardly have done anything else in the circumstances. Certainly, I did not enter into any form of legally binding agreement with [Ms Evans]. I would have only provided [Ms Evans] with assurances, the nature of which are frequently given on a daily basis in any relationship.[24]

Wall J. found that, as a question of fact, some assurances had indeed been given (as he noted, had they not been provided then Ms. Evans would have looked at alternative treatment), although he was also careful to point out that this was in relation to their relationship continuing rather than a guarantee that Ms Evans would always be able to use the embryos.[25] Nevertheless, the courts found that Mr Johnston's right not to have a child with his genes trumped that of Ms Evans to have one with hers. Moreover, as Wall J. noted in the first instance decision, Mr Johnston would 'not be in a position to play a full and proper paternal role', and would thus be a father in name only.[26] On this view, parentage is seen as social in nature, or at least containing a social component.[27]

This view of parentage can be seen to be in contrast to the end result of the case of *Blood*, where the concept of fatherhood was defined in purely biological terms.[28] The facts of the case are that Stephen Blood had contracted meningitis and lay in a coma from which he would never recover. Diane Blood, his wife with whom he was seeking to have a child, somehow convinced the doctors treating Mr Blood to extract some sperm from him before he died and store it at a clinic licensed by the Human Fertilisation and Embryology Authority. However, the Authority refused to allow Mrs Blood to be treated using the sperm, as it had been taken without his consent – a point on which the court agreed, finding that the extraction constituted a trespass to his person. Despite finding the removal and storage of the sperm to be illegal, the Court of Appeal also held that Mrs Blood might be entitled, under EU laws guaranteeing the free movement of goods and services, to take the sperm abroad to seek treatment there. As the Authority had failed to take EU law into account when reaching its decision, the Court of Appeal held that it was procedurally improper and invited the Authority to reconsider its opinion. It did, reversing its decision and authorising the surrender of the sperm to Mrs Blood with a view to her taking it to Belgium where she could be treated. She did so and had two children.

---

[24] *Evans; Hadley* at para. 49.   [25] *Evans; Hadley* at paras. 57–67.   [26] *Evans; Hadley* at para. 252.

[27] See J. Miola, 'Mix-Ups, Mistake and Moral Judgement: Recent Developments in UK Law on Assisted Conception' (2004) 12 *Feminist Legal Studies* 67.

[28] *R* v. *Human Fertilisation and Embryology Authority, ex p. Blood* [1997] 2 All ER 687 (CA). For an excellent analysis, see D. Morgan and R. G. Lee, 'In the Name of the Father? *Ex parte Blood*: Dealing with Novelty and Anomaly' (1997) 60 *MLR* 840.

The court had made it clear, however, that the case should be seen as an exception and that it should not be repeated.[29] However, Parliament was to intervene not just to allow posthumously donated sperm to be used, but for the donor to be listed as the father.[30] Needless to say, this does the opposite of the court in *Evans*, in that it imagines fatherhood as merely a question of biological truth without even a semblance of social context.

PARENTAGE

Of course, how the law defines parentage is a question for the Human Fertilisation and Embryology Acts rather than the courts, as is the question of how the law imagines parenthood in general terms. The statutory position is complicated by the fact that there are currently two sets of provisions relating to parentage: one governing treatment provided before April 2009 (which can be found in the Human Fertilisation and Embryology Act 1990) and another for after that date (which is catered for by the Human Fertilisation and Embryology Act 2008). We consider both below.

Motherhood

While it might seem somewhat overcautious to have to define maternity, a brief thought experiment explains the potential complexities: A and B are a lesbian couple who want a child whom both have some involvement in the process of creating. Thus, while they use donor sperm, A provides the egg and consequently has a genetic link to the resulting child. However, the embryo is implanted into B, who carries and gives birth to the child. How should the law define who is the mother of the child? The approach of both Acts is identical with respect to the definition of motherhood: the child's mother is the woman who carried and gave birth to her, irrespective of any biological link or surrogacy arrangement. Thus, section 27(1) of the 1990 Act and section 33(1) of the 2008 Act contain identical provisions that state that the definition of 'mother' is:

The woman who is carrying or has carried a child as a result of the placing in her of an embryo or of sperm and eggs, and no other woman, is to be treated as the mother of the child.

Thus, in our fictional scenario, B, who carried the child, would be classed in law as her mother. What we can see from the above is that the concept of motherhood

---

[29] This was not to be the case: see *L* v. *Human Fertilisation and Embryology Authority* [2008] EWHC 2149 (Fam).

[30] See the Human Fertilisation and Embryology (Deceased Fathers) Act 2003, which amends s. 28(5) of the Human Fertilisation and Embryology Act 1990 to allow this – but only where consent has been given previously, so it would not have helped Diane Blood.

imagined by the Acts is neither biological nor social, but can instead be termed experiential. Whoever undergoes the experience of childbirth is the mother of the child. The test is nothing if not simple and clear, and although it might be criticised for not taking the social aspect of motherhood into account (in contrast to fatherhood, as we describe below), it is difficult to think of a replacement test that is workable in all scenarios.

Fatherhood

In relation to fatherhood, there are some distinctions between the law relating to treatment before the Human Fertilisation and Embryology Act 2008 and that after. If the woman giving birth to the child is married, under both the 1990 and 2008 schemes her husband is assumed by the law to be the legal father. Section 28(2) of the 1990 Act states that this is the case – even if the sperm is provided by a donor – unless it can be shown that the husband did not consent to the treatment of his wife. Section 35 of the 2008 legislation uses almost identical wording to provide for the same assumption to be made.

For unmarried couples and children born under the pre-amendment rules, section 28(3) of the 1990 Act states that as long as the couple attend treatment together (section 28(3)(a)), then that man will be treated as the father of the child. The 2008 Act, meanwhile, contains a far more formal set of 'agreed fatherhood conditions' in section 37:

1. The agreed fatherhood conditions referred to in section 36(b) are met in relation to a man ('M') in relation to treatment provided to W under a licence if, but only if, –
   (a) M has given the person responsible a notice stating that he consents to being treated as the father of any child resulting from treatment provided to W under the licence,
   (b) W ['a woman'] has given the person responsible a notice stating that she consents to M being so treated,
   (c) neither M nor W has, since giving notice under paragraph (a) or (b), given the person responsible notice of the withdrawal of M's or W's consent to M being so treated,
   (d) W has not, since the giving of the notice under paragraph (b), given the person responsible –
      (i) a further notice under that paragraph stating that she consents to another man being treated as the father of any resulting child, or
      (ii) a notice under section 44(1)(b) stating that she consents to a woman being treated as a parent of any resulting child, and
   (e) W and M are not within prohibited degrees of relationship in relation to each other.

As can be seen, the key appears to be the concept of notice being given, whereas the 1990 Act merely spoke nebulously of the couple seeking treatment together. Thus, the 2008 regulations imagine a far more formal process than the 1990 Act, albeit seeking the same result – that couples seeking assistance to reproduce together should be listed as the father and mother of the child irrespective of whether the eggs and sperm used were theirs or provided by donors. In this respect, then, the two Acts appear to define fatherhood in social – rather than biological – terms. It should be noted that this is both different not just from the concept of motherhood as defined by the Acts, which as we note above is experiential, but also to the biological definition of fatherhood that is inserted into the 1990 Act by the Human Fertilisation and Embryology (Deceased Fathers) Act 2003, which allows a dead man's sperm to be used to fertilise the egg of his partner and for him to be listed as the father on the birth certificate.

This may also be contrasted with the possible view of the courts. In the case of *Leeds Teaching Hospital Trust* v. *A and others*, two couples – Mr and Mrs A and Mr and Mrs B – sought fertility treatment.[31] Unfortunately, an error meant that instead of using Mr A's sperm to fertilise Mrs A's egg, Mr B's sperm was used instead. The error was only noticed when the twins subsequently born were of mixed race. Mr and Mrs A are both Caucasian, while Mr B is black. The case arose as Mr A wished to be registered as the legal father of the twins despite not having a biological link to the children. The court was faced with a choice between prioritising biological or social fatherhood – and prioritised the former. Butler-Sloss P. held that because Mr A had not consented to the fertilisation of Mrs A's eggs with Mr B's sperm, they could not be considered to have been 'treated together' under section 28 of the 1990 Act. This would mean that he would not be assumed to be the father as that section allows. Moreover, the court noted that it would be possible for Mr A to adopt the twins, so he could achieve his aim of being their legal father without changing the birth certificate. This seems like a relatively straightforward decision to follow the law literally and resisting the temptation to be creative, but what is of interest is that Butler-Sloss P. also gave as a reason for refusing Mr A's request the fact that the twins 'also retain the great advantage of preserving the reality of their paternal identity'.[32] Therefore, what can be seen is that the law provides for different definitions of parenthood – experiential, social and biological – in different situations, and that, therefore, there cannot be said to be a consistent approach to such matters.

Same-sex couples

The 2008 Act also provides a mechanism for same-sex couples to have both parties registered as legal parents. This affects lesbian couples, as under the 1990 Act there was no mechanism for recognising a second mother, so the child would

---

[31] *Leeds Teaching Hospital Trust* v. *A and others* [2003] EWHC 259.
[32] *Leeds Teaching Hospital Trust* v. *A* at para. 56. This statement is most startling because at the time there was full donor anonymity, so children conceived using donor sperm were not able to have a similar 'advantage'.

be born with only one registered parent – the mother – and her partner would have to adopt the child to have a legally recognised parental interest. The 2008 Act now provides, under section 42, the same assumption of parenthood for a woman in a civil partnership as is granted to husbands. Moreover, section 43 allows a woman to be treated as a second parent if she seeks treatment together with the mother – thus also replicating the rules relating to unmarried heterosexual couples (subject to similar 'agreed female parenthood conditions' detailed in section 44). Lesbian couples will therefore have identical rights and protections to heterosexual couples, and this is fully detailed within the Act.

SURROGACY

Where the woman cannot bring a child to term, or if the couple comprises two gay men, one way to proceed – particularly if the couple want one or both of their gametes to be used – is to commission a surrogate. This, of course, creates its own problems, not least the fact that the surrogate may change her mind later or be involved in some disagreement with the commissioning couple. The legal framework therefore has to take account not just of the welfare of the child and the needs of the commissioning couple, but also those of the surrogate who, after all, is performing a task that is not without personal risk to help others to have a child.

Types of surrogacy

There are two sorts of surrogacy: 'full' surrogacy and 'partial' surrogacy, depending on whether the surrogate provides the egg. They are defined by the Human Fertilisation and Embryology Authority in the following terms:

Full surrogacy (also known as Host or Gestational) – Full surrogacy involves the implantation of an embryo created using either:
　　the eggs and sperm of the intended parents
　　a donated egg fertilised with sperm from the intended father
　　an embryo created using donor eggs and sperm.

Partial surrogacy (also known Straight or Traditional) – Partial surrogacy involves sperm from the intended father and an egg from the surrogate. Here fertilisation is (usually) done by artificial insemination or intrauterine insemination (IUI).[33]

---

[33] Human Fertilisation and Embryology Authority, 'Surrogacy', www.hfea.gov.uk/fertility-treatment-options-surrogacy.html.

If, as is mostly the case, the creation of the embryo will require some medical assistance (such as IVF), then the terms of the Human Fertilisation and Embryology Acts 1990 and 2008 apply – and in particular section 13(5) of the 1990 Act, which requires that the clinic undertakes a welfare assessment in relation to the child.

Regulating surrogacy

The Surrogacy Arrangements Act 1985 regulates surrogacy, and was passed as a response to the first baby in the United Kingdom to be born as a result of a commercial surrogacy arrangement.[34] In particular, the Act does two things. First, it is clear in that it makes it a criminal offence to participate in a commercial surrogacy arrangement. Section 2(3) defines what is meant by 'commercial' surrogacy:

2(3)   For the purposes of this section, a person does an act on a commercial basis (subject to subsection (4) below) if –
(a)   any payment is at any time received by himself or another in respect of it, or
(b)   he does it with a view to any payment being received by himself or another in respect of making, or negotiating or facilitating the making of, any surrogacy arrangement.

The surrogate may be paid reasonable expenses, and under section 2C (inserted by the Human Fertilisation and Embryology Act 2008) non-profit-making bodies can also charge for reasonable expenses – thus facilitating organisations which specialise in matching potential surrogates with commissioning couples.

The other issue with which the 1985 Act concerns itself is to clarify that surrogacy arrangements are not legally enforceable (under section 1A, which was inserted by the Human Fertilisation and Embryology Act 1990). Thus, none of the parties is bound by the 'contract' into which they enter – whether this relates to the surrogate deciding not to give up the child, the commissioning couple deciding not to take the child once it is born or the commissioning couple paying the agreed expenses.

In terms of parentage, the situation is clear, in that the rules contained within the Human Fertilisation and Embryology Acts 1990 and 2008 described above apply. This is uncomplicated in terms of maternity, as under both Acts the 'mother' is the woman who carried and gave birth to the child. Paternity is less logical, as ascribing the rules in the statute to surrogacy leads to unintended consequences – although these can be resolved using adoption subsequently. For example, where the surrogate is married, not only will she be classed as the 'mother' under the 1990 and 2008 Acts, but her husband will be assumed to be the father, even if the sperm used was genetically from the commissioning couple.

---

[34]   See D. Brahams, 'The Hasty British Ban on Commercial Surrogacy' (1987) 17 *Hastings Centre Report* 16.

What is evident is that surrogacy is seen by the law as something which is not to be encouraged and which is filled with danger.[35] Surrogates may not profit from the arrangement, and none of the parties may consider the agreements that they have made binding. It seems almost as if the law has decided that there are so many interests to balance that it will not bother to attempt to do so beyond requiring a welfare assessment for the potential child – but this is only when the Human Fertilisation and Embryology Act 1990 is involved.

CONCLUDING REMARKS ON LAW

The message sent by the law, as we have seen, is somewhat inconsistent – particularly with respect to parentage, where the legal framework cannot seem to decide whether parenthood should be experiential, biological or social. At different times, each is prioritised. It is therefore impossible to say that the law has a single view of what constitutes parentage, or how it imagines or wants families to be. This is perhaps important because much of the law in this area exists to regulate who can and who cannot gain access to assisted reproductive services, and a view of purpose should surely be expected. When put in this way, the entire notion seems somewhat counterintuitive: as a society we would abhor any attempt by the law to limit the power of couples to procreate naturally, so we must ask on what basis we feel entitled to stop couples (or single people) using medical science to help them to do so. Why does the law feel it right to judge who is or is not fit to be a parent?

This is a particularly pertinent question because the law not only does this, but it does so openly. As we saw, the Warnock Committee had a clear view of to whom assisted reproductive services should be available, and this was eventually reflected in the legislation. The regulatory framework imposed by the HFEA 1990 in the form of the Authority, which was supposed to strengthen regulation and uphold the Act, was ironically the source of it being undermined. The Code of Practice's refusal to enforce the discriminatory elements in section 13(5) meant that, in practice, the more draconian elements were not as strictly adhered to as the Warnock Committee and Parliament would have liked. In the period since 1990, the law has had to catch up with the social mores reflected by the Code of Practice, and we have therefore seen changes to section 13(5) and the rules relating to parentage. The law has become more tolerant and less about imposing its view of families than about

---

[35] For an excellent analysis, see M. Freeman, 'Does Surrogacy Have a Future after Brazier?' (1999) 7 *Med. L. Rev.* 1.

reflecting reality and resolving disagreements. This, we believe, is a positive development.

ETHICS

Ever since the first IVF baby, Louise Brown, was successfully brought to term in 1978, the advances in assisted reproductive technology (ART, which is the umbrella term for the different individual technologies used) have been dramatic, as have the moral objections raised. Some of these objections to this type of technology seem to relate to the actual process used: classic in vitro fertilisation (IVF) in a conventional family setting, where the sperm of the male partner is mixed with the egg cells of the female partner 'in a glass' (which is what 'in vitro' means) caused some uproar, but seems to now have been superseded by technologies which shake our conception of parenthood and genetic relations to the core. In some cases, the sperm quality is too poor to trust them to do the job themselves and another, fairly new, process is used – ICSI (intracytoplasmic sperm injection). An image of this process is, confusingly, what is most often used when illustrating stories of IVF or ART in general: the image of the ovum on one side, being penetrated by a thin needle which then introduces the sperm into the egg's cytoplasm. Using this technology, doctors are able to select the most promising-looking sperm and assist it in actually getting to where it ought to go.

Some objections to these types of technology are of a religious nature, with the argument (usually posited by those who have little or no experience of infertility themselves) going to the fact that infertile couples should simply accept their lot in life and adjust to the idea that they were not 'meant to' have children. These types of argument are, clearly, for the purposes of the discussion of assisted reproduction in this book, not particularly useful as they are based on a conception that there is an overriding entity which decides what ought to be the case and that the existence of this entity absolves those who rely on it from any obligation to rationally justify their views. Suffice to say that the majority of these individuals are unlikely to reject intensive medical care using the same logic. The moral objections become more vocal and frequent where the technology is used in order to give the chance of parenthood to relationship constellations deviating from the heterosexual (married) couple, or where we are discussing the use of surplus embryos for research purposes. Addressing the ethical issues raised by the Warnock Report, the resulting legislation and the case law, we will – in this part of the chapter – look at questions of the moral status of the embryo, questions of access to the technology, conflicting interests, parental identity and surrogacy.

The moral status of the embryo is a suitable starting point for our deliberation of ethics in this chapter. There is a reasonable argument in the context of assisted reproduction that the complexity of the issue is reduced by way of the fact that most questions arise at a point where the embryo is still 'in vitro'. This removes large portions of the question relating to the self-determination of the mother from the equation. It also means that we are not under any obligation to discuss the range of different milestones alongside the development of the embryo to determine at which point something normatively significant happens (i.e. what we earlier referred to as the gradual development of moral status). The embryo (or, more accurately, the *blastocyst*, which is an embryo consisting of less than 100 cells) will only be a few days old and have only recently started mitosis when it is implanted. What we need to look at, therefore, is a relatively straightforward question of whether when we create an embryo, which is at the normatively interesting point in time only a few days old, we also ought to give it a chance to flourish. In other words – do we need to implant all embryos created because they have some sort of right to be given a chance to develop into a full human being? While there are examples of legislation that suggest this is the case (such as in Italy or in Germany, where by law, fertility clinics are required to implant all embryos that are created), the reality of fertility treatment seems to be inconsistent with this view (and, indeed, practice differs considerably from legislation)[36] and decisions, such as the one in *Evans*, have demonstrated that there is the very complex issue of consent up to the very point of implantation to contend with.

This type of approach to treating each and every embryo as in some way 'a holder of rights' (even if they were very limited rights) would also entail questions in relation to the type of chance these embryos ought to be given. First of all, the success rate of IVF is very low indeed. The Human Fertilisation and Embryology Authority gives the following success figures for 2010 and 2011:[37]

- 32.2 per cent for women under 35 (32.3 per cent)
- 27.7 per cent for women aged 35–37 (27.2 per cent)
- 20.8 per cent for women aged 38–39 (19.1 per cent)
- 13.6 per cent for women aged 40–42 (12.7 per cent)
- 5.0 per cent for women aged 43–44 (5.1 per cent)
- 1.9 per cent for women aged 45+ (1.5 per cent)

As we can see, even where the age of the women is thought to be within the bracket that is most promising for successful IVF treatment, there is only a one-third

---

[36] Obviously, the requirement to implant every embryo created, regardless of whether or not the woman actually wants another child, raises superseding issues of physical integrity (i.e. we would have to force the woman to undergo the invasive implantation procedure) and simply be ridiculous and futile in circumstances where the law then allows for an early subsequent termination of the pregnancy.

[37] See www.hfea.gov.uk/ivf-figures-2006.html#1276.

chance of success. Of course, this depends on the exact underlying condition (and obviously there are cases where the fertility problem lies with the man, rather than the woman, and once a blastocyst has been created, the chances are greater), but – on average – more than two out of three embryos will not survive the IVF process. How can we justify such a wasteful process? One plausible counter-argument is that of the aims of the exercise: to create life (and thereby do something which is inherently good). There is no biological possibility that the discarded or spontaneously aborted embryos experience any suffering, and (under the current technical conditions) the death of some embryos is a necessary precondition for the success of some other embryos. If we accept that assisted reproductive technologies are not inherently immoral, and in a situation where all embryos created are implanted, and some perish, there seems to be little that speaks against this process.

This argument becomes slightly more difficult where the embryos perish after having been deselected prior to implantation. In conventional IVF or ICSI treatment, where multiple embryos have been successfully created, the clinic will identify those that are most promising and implant these first. Where there is no actual shortage of embryos for the number of planned cycles, this will automatically mean that the least promising-looking embryos perish because better-looking ones have been selected. Add to this scenario the possibility that other advanced technologies (such as pre-implantation genetic diagnostics, PGD) can be used to identify embryos that have certain genetic variants that the clinic or the parents-to-be would rather not have in their children, and the debate becomes even more heated. Where does the normal process of selection (which is a justifiable exercise aimed at limiting risks and burdens to the woman) end, and the process that leads, purportedly, to the 'designer baby' start?[38] Where the factors to be excluded revolve around those which we would ordinarily view as being those of an 'illness' or 'defect', the discussion is easier than where we are speaking of selecting the sex of the child or the hair colour.[39] Embryos thus perish all the time – some because they are no longer needed for the purpose they were originally created for, some because they are deemed to be unfit for purpose. It is unsurprising that these questions give rise to emotional debate, although it is sometimes difficult to pin down where these issues are genuinely new, and where they are simply a variation of another issue (such as that of discussing certain contraceptive technologies as being akin to abortions – these might also be said to be means of deselecting undesired embryos post-fertilisation and pre-implantation).

Where not all embryos are implanted, other questions come to the fore. Imagine a case where a couple have had five embryos created. Two are implanted during

---

[38] See, e.g., H. Biggs, 'Designer Babies: Where Should We Draw the Line?' (2004) 30 *Journal of Medical Ethics* e5, doi: 10.1136/jme.2003.004465.

[39] Although we acknowledge the very broad and difficult debate in relation to what constitutes normal, or healthy, in medical ethics.

the first cycle of assisted reproductive treatment, three are left over. The couple successfully bring both implanted embryos to term – they therefore have non-identical twins. They decide, on the experience of having two young children, that they want no further children and the three remaining embryos at the fertility clinic therefore become 'surplus'. There are a number of options available at this stage: (1) cryogenic storage for future use; (2) donation of the embryos to other couples; (3) donation of the embryos for research purposes; or (4) discarding the embryos.

Storage for future use, option (1), seems relatively straightforward. The embryos are cryogenically preserved and the couple can access these embryos should they want to use them for some purpose at a later stage (or, if they simply haven't been able to make their minds up yet what to do with the surplus embryos). The difficult decisions contained in options (2) to (4) are, here, only postponed (unless they do opt for another cycle). The donation of surplus embryos for other couples, notwith-standing illegality in some jurisdictions,[40] is an option which will enable those couples to have a child who are unable to produce their own embryos. If done altruistically, this option seems to be the preferable one – unless we subscribe to the view that IVF in general, or the facilitation of non-genetic offspring in particular, are worthy of rejection (a point of view the existence of which is worth bearing in mind, but which plays an insignificant role in any serious debate).

Donation for research purposes quite possibly raises the most controversial ethical issues. Many opponents of this option suggest that what is being done here is to simply use embryos as a means to an end (namely research), rather than to accord them the respect and dignity which they should have by virtue of being a potential future person. This is a variation of a Kantian argument (also see Chapter 1), which suggests that persons should never be used as means to an end, but rather should be ends in themselves. Quite how the leap from blastoycst to person is performed to make this argument work is the subject of some debate.

In order to assess the ethical limits of using embryos as means to an end, it is prudent to look at what the intended use of the embryos in research might be. It seems clear that there is a difference between making surplus embryos available for research in the cosmetics industry and research in the health sector. The type of research which is undertaken using surplus embryos is usually human embryonic stem cell (hESC) research. The aim of this type of research is to unlock the potential of regenerative medicine, which is thought to, inter alia, hold the key to combating crippling neurodegenerative diseases. As long as alternative routes to producing the type of stem cells required for this research are still not determined, hESCs from surplus embryos are an important source of material. The question is now whether

---

[40] In the United Kingdom, embryo donation for fertility use is legal and – of course – regulated by the Human Fertilisation and Embryology Authority. Age limits apply and there must be consent of both gamete donors.

the status of the embryo plays a role in determining whether it may be used for these types of activity. While it is possible to deliberate this question by looking purely at the existence of the cells in question, it may help to look at the realities of how we interact with them. In the spectrum of possible activities, we can – if we subscribe to the view that they must not be *used* for anything other than their original purpose – only elect to store them indefinitely or to destroy them as hospital waste (usually by way of incineration). It is extremely difficult to see how incineration is a more suitable way to give respect to a perceived moral status of these embryos than to make them available for an important societal objective (research).[41] Neither would anyone suggest that the NHS ought to create large-scale cryogenic facilities for the indefinite storage of surplus embryos, without the notion that they might, at some stage, be available for IVF. We are of the opinion that, where the research is of the type that can safely be described as being over-whelmingly in the public interest, and the only alternative is to destroy the embryo as hospital waste, research is the preferable option. One thing is for certain – consensus seems an impossibility and we acknowledge that our view is not without serious opposition.

In our discussion of the law, you have seen that the question of what constitutes an acceptable family constellation has featured prominently. The conventional view of a family consisting of a female mother and a male father (who ought to be married) has been challenged repetitively and this antiquated view has, quite rightly, been reformed in consecutive legislation and delegated instruments. The significant moral arguments that have accompanied this debate have been those surrounding the interests of the child and that of social cohesion.

As far as the interests of the child are concerned, there seems to be little – if any – empirical proof that to not have a father, or a mother, by virtue of assisted reproductive treatment is in any way more detrimental to the well-being of a child than it is for those children who grow up in single-parent environments for other reasons (and we certainly do not outlaw divorce for those couples who have had children, or take the children who have lost a parent into foster care). Also, the presence of a heterosexual configuration of parents does not demonstrably include a benefit to the children that is missing where the configuration is homosexual. The so-called 'no differences paradigm' posits that 'there is no systematic evidence demonstrating that children from same-sex households suffer disadvantages rela-tive to appropriate comparison groups from opposite-sex households'.[42]

---

[41] For a discussion, see N. Hoppe and A. Denoon, 'An Ethical Framework for Expanded Access to Cell-Based Therapies' (2011) 6(3) *Regenerative Medicine* 273.

[42] A. Perrin, P. Cohen and N. Caren. 'Are Children of Parents Who Had Same-Sex Relationships Disadvantaged? A Scientific Evaluation of the No-Differences Hypothesis' (2013) 17(3) *Journal of Gay & Lesbian Mental Health* 237.

The question is reduced, in the context of the law discussed above, to the issue of who should be given access to this type of treatment. To deny homosexual couples access to this type of technology is a significant interference with their personality rights – which ought to be better justified than simply by way of a seemingly empirically baseless assumption regarding what is better for the child. Similarly, the argument in relation to social cohesion is one that ought to be justified more solidly. It is simply a fact of life and reality everywhere across the world that the significant and decisive point is that one human being enters into a relationship with another. The sex or gender of these individuals is only secondary, insofar as this has a bearing on whether the couple is able to reproduce without assistance. Quite why a homosexual couple should be denied access to assisted reproductive technology, while a couple who intend to plan their offspring in relation to their career paths is granted access, is completely unclear. And, of course:

The NHS provides a comprehensive service, available to all irrespective of gender, race, disability, age, sexual orientation, religion, belief, gender reassignment, pregnancy and maternity or marital or civil partnership status.[43]

An argument which seems to follow from this fundamental principle is therefore that it is unnecessary to have the discussion about whether procreation is a lifestyle question or, technically, a health care issue. Some argue that assisted reproduction is not a service that should be subsumed under 'therapeutic', but is much closer to being something along the lines of 'cosmetic'. It seems that this very much misses the point: starting a family and, therefore, by necessity, also procreation, is one of the fundamental tenets of human life. It is also an aspect of life which we generally perceive as being part of the set of choices we make to determine our own lives, and give effect to our own preferences to live the life we want. If we completely eliminated this from the equation, society as a whole would very much only be a medium-term undertaking. There is, therefore, a very good argument to suggest that, initially, we ought to place individuals into the position to make that choice – regardless of the reason why they are unable to do so without assistance.

We have seen that the constellations in this discussion revolve around the life-to-be (i.e. the embryo or the subsequent foetus and child) and the parents (in a social and in a genetic sense). Choices made here are, in some cases, spectacular and have difficult consequences for all those involved. The cases of *Hadley* and *Evans* very much meant trying to determine the lesser of two evils: remove the possibility of being a genetic parent from a woman who, through no fault of her own, was otherwise unable to do so, or force a man to become a father against his will. This question is interesting, particularly if contrasted to the discussion we

---

[43] NHS Constitution, Principle 1, available at www.nhs.uk/choiceintheNHS/Rightsandpledges/NHSConstitution/Documents/2013/the-nhs-constitution-for-england-2013.pdf.

had earlier. If we believe that the embryo has an inherent right to be given a chance to live (and we have already seen that this is difficult as it would entail forcing a woman to have the embryo implanted), then issues of choice in relation to the sperm donor would be irrelevant. Inasmuch as we have argued above that starting a family is an important aspect of planning one's own life, this extends to the negative choice, i.e. deciding against becoming a parent. This type of choice is just as legitimate and therefore, rightly, difficult to regulate against.

As far as the child is concerned, we have not yet discussed what the consequences of being an IVF or ICSI child mean. In some cases, for example, where one of the gametes was donated anonymously, there is the possibility of the child not immediately knowing her father. The right to know one's genetic origins has been the subject of some debate,[44] but in terms of medical ethics, there is one particularly challenging point that needs to be overcome: the issue may initially revolve around the question that there might be, on one side of the balancing scales, a negative consequence to being conceived by unconventional means. On the other side of the scales would be the fact that the child would, but for the unconventional means, not have been born at all. The balance is therefore one between existence (with or without some disadvantages) and non-existence. Where the natural consequence of a rejection of this technology would be the non-existence of the child in question, it is simply inconsistent to argue that it is not in the best interests of that child to have been conceived by way of IVF or ICSI – unless one is seriously taking the position that to not live at all is better than to live as an IVF child.

Finally, we have addressed the legal issues of surrogacy, and with it questions of commercialisation. On a first moral assessment, the act of being a surrogate seems to be one of altruism at its best: making oneself available, at great discomfort, to assist others in being parents is a very selfless act indeed. One consequence of this is that there is a very real question of whether we can or should, from a legal viewpoint, compel the surrogate to actually give up the baby after birth. On one side of the argument are those who are striving for a child of their own and have had to take recourse to a surrogate in order to achieve this. On the other side, there is the surrogate who has spent a great many months bringing to term a child who is intended for others. It is undeniable that there is a real chance that the surrogate will have developed an attachment to the child. At the same time, those for whom surrogacy is the only way to have a family will have staked much of their emotional well-being on being able to raise the child themselves. The ethical issues surrounding surrogacy focus on the objectification

---

[44]   See S. Besson, 'Enforcing the Child's Right to Know Her Origins: Contrasting Approaches under the Convention on the Rights of the Child and the European Convention on Human Rights' (2007) 21 *International Journal of Law, Policy and the Family* 137–59.

(and exploitation) of the surrogate,[45] coercion and reproductive autonomy, the fact that (quasi-)contractual arrangements are made for the delivery of a human being, the question of whether the surrogate is paid for her services (and how much) and issues regarding the identity of the child.

It is, in particular, the commercial nature of the agreement which raises the most widely debated moral questions: should we contract for the production of a child? Is it ethically legitimate to pay for this: and, if so, what can be paid for? Loss of earnings, compensation for pain and suffering, disbursements – when does the pecuniary advantage which is given to the surrogate cross the point of this being a case of the commercialisation of human life?

CONCLUSION

The area of assisted reproduction is replete with interesting and challenging ethical questions. The balancing acts we try to undertake in relation to life (as yet unborn), the rights of women who can only become pregnant by way of this method, the rights of potential fathers to assent or object to becoming a parent, and the societal changes which have found reflection in the law make this a particularly worthwhile and rich topic of discussion, both in terms of ethics and of law. As we mentioned in the concluding comments on the law, the legal framework cannot help but involve itself in taking a position on what constitutes an acceptable family. What we have seen in our ethical discussion, however, is another aspect altogether: the use of the embryo, which to some is a person and is certainly a potential person, not so much as an end in itself, but as a means to an end.

Indeed, during some of the treatments and procedures described, some embryos will necessarily be wasted, and therefore in the balancing exercise that seems to take place in virtually all of the chapters in this book, the law has to consider the fact that the embryo is not nothing and deserves to be respected – even if it is not a potential person. However, this is complicated by the fact that some *do* consider the embryo to be a person, and therefore that some of these procedures should not take place. The law seeks a compromise by rejecting this notion, but placing limits on what can and cannot be done.

Another aspect that some might consider unedifying is the fact that disagreements about embryos (and even babies) can result: such as in the case of Natalie Evans, who had what amounted to a custody battle over the frozen embryos, or surrogates who cannot face giving up the child they were supposed to carry for the commissioning

---

[45] Sometimes discussed as akin to prostitution: see, e.g., A. van Niekerk and L. van Zyl, 'The Ethics of Surrogacy: Women's Reproductive Labour' (1995) 21 *Journal of Medical Ethics* 345.

couple. Indeed, in the latter example, the surrogate may have no genetic link to the baby. These are the sorts of issues on which judges have to make decisions since the law allows the practices that give rise to the conflicts in the first place.

Essentially, this is a topic within which there will never be full agreement, and the law is in a difficult position as whatever it decides will meet with disapproval from some. In terms of the balance of rights, we believe that the law is correct to have relaxed the amount of control that it will exert over access to treatment. As we mentioned in the legal description, it would not dream of limiting the ability to procreate of those who can do so naturally, and so its moral authority to prohibit lesbians, for example, from treatment (as the original 1990 Act did) is morally dubious at best (even ignoring the substantial objections on the grounds of discrimination) – although, of course, this is different from questions of resource allocation. Clinics can make their own decisions. The power rests with them, although financial pressures mean that patients who can pay are likely to find someone to treat them. Again, we believe that this is the right approach, not least because almost all of these treatments and procedures are positive in nature, and the development of that technology should be encouraged. We could say that we are in favour of an approach that, not for the first time in this book, protects the individual rights – not least because it best protects the rights of society as a whole. The conflicts it creates are inevitable and, in our view, an acceptable price to pay.

ADDITIONAL READING

 Law

M. Brazier, 'Regulating the Reproduction Business' (1999) 7(2) *Medical Law Review* 166

M. Freeman, 'Does Surrogacy Have a Future after Brazier?' (1999) 7 *Medical Law Review* 1

D. Gurnham and J. Miola, 'Reproduction, Rights and the Welfare Interests of Children: The Times They Aren't A-Changin'' (2012) *King's Law Journal* 29

E. Jackson, 'Rethinking the Pre-Conception Welfare Principle' in K. Horsey and H. Biggs (eds.), *Human Fertilisation and Embryology: Reproducing Regulation* (London: Routledge, 2007)

C. Jones, *Why Donor Insemination Requires Developments in Family Law: The Need for New Definitions of Parenthood* (Lampeter: Edward Mellen Press, 2007)

R. Lee and D. Morgan, *Human Fertilisation and Embryology: Regulating the Reproduction Business* (Oxford: Blackwell, 2001)

J. McCandless and S. Sheldon, 'The Human Fertilisation and Embryology Act 2008 and the Tenacity of the Sexual Family Form' (2010) 72(2) *Modern Law Review* 175

S. Sheldon, 'Fragmenting Fatherhood: The Regulation of Reproductive Technologies' (2005) 68(4) *Modern Law Review* 523

Ethics

J. Callahan (ed.), *Reproduction, Ethics and the Law – Feminist Perspectives* (Bloomington, IN: Indiana University Press, 1995)

T. Hope, J. Savulescu and J. Hendrick, *Medical Ethics and Law: The Core Curriculum*, 2nd edn (Edinburgh: Churchill Livingstone, 2008), chapter 9

H. LaFollette (ed.), *Ethics in Practice*, 2nd edn (Malden: Blackwell, 2002), chapters 16 and 17

B. Solberg, 'Getting Beyond the Welfare of the Child in Assisted Reproduction' (2009) 35 *Journal of Medical Ethics* 373

B. Steinbock (ed.), *The Oxford Handbook of Bioethics* (Oxford University Press, 2007), chapter 18

Case studies from this chapter are available online at www.cambridge.org/hoppe.

8 Abortion, neonaticide and infanticide

INTRODUCTION

There are few topics that elicit quite so much debate as abortion. Ethical positions frequently depend on the individual's views concerning when life begins, and for those who believe that life begins at conception, abortion is, quite simply, murder. For others, the most important aspect is a woman's right to autonomy over her own body – for them, to legislate against abortion is to turn the woman into little more than a foetal container. Essentially, we have to accept that there is no hope of ever achieving consensus regarding abortion, since too many views depend on what Jonathan Glover terms 'ultimate beliefs' – a set of beliefs that cannot be defended through evidence, and instead simply reflect what a person's instinct tells them about an issue.[1] Thus, if we ask someone 'why' enough times when they answer a question, eventually they will reach the bottom of the barrel of their thinking, and they will respond: 'just because'. This is the fundamental moral belief. We all have them, and they are irresolvable. This is why no agreement is possible on the question of, for example, when life does actually begin. The law via the Abortion Act 1967, as we shall see, reflects this and is designed as a compromise. However, equally predictable is the fact that it is a compromise that rather than making everyone happy, instead satisfies nobody.

There are two common misconceptions that exist regarding the Abortion Act 1967, and both relate to this compromise. First, it is not the case that the Act allows for abortion on demand before twenty-four weeks. Rather, as we shall see, although the definition of when an abortion is allowed at an early stage is wide, it certainly does not allow for abortion on demand and some women can be and are refused abortions on what is known as the 'social ground'. The second misconception relates to the belief that the Abortion Act legalises abortion. While it does do this

---

[1] J. Glover, *Causing Death and Saving Lives* (London: Penguin, 1990), see ch. 2 in particular.

in practical terms, perhaps the more correct way of looking at things is to state that the Abortion Act creates exceptions to the rule that causing a miscarriage is against the law – abortions carried out outside the Abortion Act remain a criminal offence. Thus, an abortion carried out outside of the Abortion Act will be illegal and a prosecution can be brought through the other legislation that exists to protect the foetus. Moreover, the exceptions do not relate to the pregnant woman's desire to terminate the pregnancy, but instead in almost all circumstances they are tied to a risk to her health. The only exception, as we shall see, is that a termination is allowed when there is a significant risk that the resulting child will be severely handicapped.

In this chapter we also consider the issue of the removal of medical treatment from babies born with severe disabilities. Here, the decisions made can be similar to abortion, in that it might be felt that the extent of the infant's disabilities make its life not worth living, and a decision is therefore made to allow it to die either by withdrawing care or by not treating infections that might develop, or by providing 'nursing care only'. In essence, then, this chapter relates to the end-of-life decisions regarding foetuses and newborn infants. It is not difficult to appreciate why the area is so controversial.

THE PRE-1967 STATUTES AND CASE LAW

The foetus, technically, has no status in English law.[2] That is certainly not to say that it does not enjoy protection of the law and, indeed, to terminate a pregnancy is prima facie a criminal offence – as we shall see, the Abortion Act 1967 merely provides an exception to this fact.[3] The first of these protections was Lord Ellenborough's Act in 1803, where abortion was made illegal by statute, and was punishable by death after 'quickening'. This was replaced by the Offences Against the Person Act 1861, which remains in force today. Sections 58 and 59 relate to abortion, and explicitly include the pregnant woman in the list of those who may be liable, thus clarifying that abortions are prohibited for the good of the foetus, not the interests of its putative mother:

58 Administering drugs or using instruments to procure abortion.

Every woman, being with child, who, with intent to procure her own miscarriage, shall unlawfully administer to herself any poison or other noxious thing, or shall unlawfully use any

---

[2] See, e.g., *Re. MB (Caesarean Section)* [1997] 8 Med LR 217; and *Attorney General's Reference (No. 3 of 1994)* [1997] 3 WLR 421.

[3] For a brief account of the pre-1967 statutes, see S. Fovargue and J. Miola, 'Policing Pregnancy: Implications of *Attorney General's Reference (No. 3 of 1994)*' (1998) 6(3) *Med. L. Rev.* 265.

instrument or other means whatsoever with the like intent, and whosoever, with intent to procure the miscarriage of any woman, whether she be or be not with child, shall unlawfully administer to her or cause to be taken by her any poison or other noxious thing, or shall unlawfully use any instrument or other means whatsoever with the like intent, shall be guilty of felony, and being convicted thereof shall be liable to be kept in penal servitude for life.

59 Procuring drugs, etc. to cause abortion.

Whosoever shall unlawfully supply or procure any poison or other noxious thing, or any instrument or thing whatsoever, knowing that the same is intended to be unlawfully used or employed with intent to procure the miscarriage of any woman, whether she be or be not with child, shall be guilty of a misdemeanor, and being convicted thereof shall be liable to be kept in penal servitude.

The first part of section 58, as we can see, relates to the pregnant woman herself. There is a requirement that she administers to herself poison or 'another noxious thing' to cause a miscarriage, or does anything else to that purpose. It additionally requires that there must be the intent to procure the miscarriage. The second part of the section relates to others who administer or 'cause to be taken' drugs, or who otherwise help to provide an abortion. Again, there must be intent to cause a miscarriage. Of note, however, is the fact that for those other than the pregnant woman, an offence is committed whether the woman is pregnant or not. For the woman herself, an offence is only committed if she is actually pregnant, although if she wrongly believed that she was pregnant she would still be guilty of a conspiracy to procure a miscarriage.[4] The next section, section 59, prohibits the supply of drugs or instruments 'with intent to procure a miscarriage'. It is thus a companion section, and taken together they provide sanctions for procuring, supplying, assisting and performing abortions (both medical and surgical). As mentioned above, this expressly includes liability for the pregnant woman.

The Infant Life (Preservation) Act 1929 provides for a separate offence of 'child destruction' if the foetus is viable and a termination is performed outside of the Abortion Act. Section 1(1) of the ILPA provides both the elements of the offence and a defence:

Subject as hereinafter in this subsection provided, any person who, with intent to destroy the life of a child capable of being born alive, by any wilful act causes a child to die before it has an existence independent of its mother, shall be guilty of felony, to wit, of child destruction, and shall be liable on conviction thereof on indictment to penal servitude for life:

Provided that no person shall be found guilty of an offence under this section unless it is proved that the act which caused the death of the child was not done in good faith for the purpose only of preserving the life of the mother.

The penalty (life imprisonment) is the same as under the OAPA, but of note is the personalisation of the viable foetus – which is termed a 'child' for the purposes of

---

[4] See, e.g., R v. Whitechurch (1890) LR 24 QBD 420. See also A. Grubb, 'Abortion Law in England: The Medicalization of a Crime' (1990) 18 Journal of Law, Medicine and Ethics 146.

the Act. Nevertheless, it should be remembered that the ILPA does not apply when an abortion is carried out under the Abortion Act 1967.

A case of significance that both explains the courts' pre-1967 attitude to the legislation, and demonstrates their openness to the medicalisation of abortion, is the 1939 case of *R* v. *Bourne*.[5] Dr Aleck Bourne was a respected obstetric surgeon who performed an abortion on a 14-year-old girl who was the victim of a rape described by the judge as of 'great violence'.[6] He gave himself up to the police and told them what he had done as soon as he had done so, and was charged under section 58 of the OAPA. However, Dr Bourne argued that given that his purpose was to preserve the patient's mental health, the operation was therefore not 'unlawful' (a word present in section 58, but strangely undefined). In his direction to the jury, Macnaghten J. displays a (well-placed) confidence in the doctor, a consequent comfort with deferring to his medical opinion, and wide interpretation of the law to nudge the jury towards acquittal:

A man of the highest skill, openly, in one of our great hospitals, performs the operation. Whether it was legal or illegal you will have to determine, but he performs the operation as an act of charity, without fee or reward, and unquestionably believing that he was doing the right thing, and that he ought, in the performance of his duty as a member of a profession devoted to the alleviation of human suffering, to do it ... Nine years ago Parliament passed an Act called the Infant Life (Preservation) Act, 1929 ... [I]n my view the proviso [in that Act] that it is necessary for the Crown to prove that the act was not done in good faith for the purpose only of preserving the life of the mother is in accordance with what has always been the common law of England with regard to the killing of an unborn child. No such proviso is in fact set out in s. 58 of the Offences Against the Person Act, 1861; but the words of that section are that any person who 'unlawfully' uses an instrument with intent to procure miscarriage shall be guilty of felony. In my opinion the word 'unlawfully' is not, in that section, a meaningless word. I think it imports the meaning expressed by the proviso in s. 1, sub-s. 1, of the Infant Life (Preservation) Act, 1929, and that s. 58 of the Offences Against the Person Act, 1861, must be read as if the words making it an offence to use an instrument with intent to procure a miscarriage were qualified by a similar proviso.[7]

Macnaghten J. then turned to consider the question of what was meant by the words 'for the purpose of preserving the life of the mother' in section 58 of the OAPA. He told the jury that the interpretation of the words must be reasonable, but reminded them that there was no requirement that the woman's life be immediately in peril, nor that the doctor wait until there was an actual risk of death – pre-emptive measures were possible. Thus, as long as the doctor believes in good faith that the abortion was necessary to prevent serious physical or mental harm to the

---

[5] *R* v. *Bourne* [1939] 1 KB 687. For an excellent analysis of the role of the medical profession's influence in this area, and a discussion of *Bourne*, see M. Thomson, 'Abortion Law and Professional Boundaries' (2013) 22(2) *Social and Legal Studies* 191, in particular 198–201.
[6] *R* v. *Bourne* at 687.   [7] *R* v. *Bourne* at 689–91.

mother, it would be lawful to perform it.[8] As mentioned above, the judge was clearly trying to nudge the jury into an acquittal. He succeeded, and Dr Bourne was indeed found not guilty by the jury.

The case highlights several factors, including the problems faced by women and the willingness of the judiciary to medicalise the issue of abortion. It also emphasised the lack of clarity in the OAPA in terms of the amorphous nature of the word 'unlawfully', which gave the court the scope to interpret the statute broadly and more in line with twentieth-century (as opposed to nineteenth-century) thinking on the issue of abortion. In many respects, then, *Bourne* paved the way to the Abortion Act 1967.

THE ABORTION ACT 1967

The background to the Act

Bourne was not without its problems. As Hindell and Simms noted in their excellent account of the passage of the Abortion Act through Parliament, the decision was 'both fragile and ambiguous'.[9] It was fragile because Macnaghten J. had stretched the law to its very limits and, according to Hindell and Simms, might well have been overruled by a higher court.[10] It was ambiguous since so much rested on amorphous judgments regarding doctors' 'good faith' and the definition of psychiatric harm. Thus, 'most doctors remained apprehensive of the law'.[11] It was clear, therefore, that parliamentary intervention in the form of a statute was necessary. Sally Sheldon has identified further factors that contributed to what she terms the 'climate for reform': 'the role of illegal abortions in sustaining high figures of maternal mortality, concern and sympathy for the situation of women facing unwanted pregnancy, an unequal application of the law (with a thriving private sector in the provision of abortion) and a lack of a well-organised opposition to reform'.[12] She further highlights two issues that are fundamental to the passing of the Act – being the protection of medical autonomy and taking women away from the back streets and into medical control – which would seek to appeal to all via the medium of medicalisation.[13] This can be seen quite clearly in the Act itself, as we demonstrate below.

---

[8] It is enough that the doctor *honestly* holds this opinion, and there is no need for her to actually be correct – see the pre-1967 Act cases of *R* v. *Bergman and Ferguson* [1948] 1 BMJ 1008 and *R* v. *Newton and Stungo* [1958] Crim LR 469.

[9] K. Hindell and M. Simms, *Abortion Law Reformed* (London: Peter Owen, 1971), p. 14.

[10] Hindell and Simms, *Abortion Law Reformed*, p. 14.   [11] Hindell and Simms, *Abortion Law Reformed*, p. 14.

[12] S. Sheldon, *Beyond Control: Medical Power and Abortion Law* (London: Pluto Press, 1997), p. 17.

[13] Sheldon, *Beyond Control*, pp. 17–31.

The provisions of the Act

Section 1 and the four grounds for abortion

The OAPA and ILPA remain on the statute books, and therefore a doctor (or indeed anyone else) is prima facie liable to criminal prosecution if she carries out a termination. What the Abortion Act does, however, is to provide exceptions to the applicability of those Acts, and to this end section 5(2) and (1) respectively state that, as long as the other provisions of the Abortion Act 1967 are complied with, no offence is committed under either the 1861 or 1929 Acts. The Abortion Act's answer to the question of how to legalise terminations while in some way placating pro-life campaigners was to seek to present the issue as a medical procedure allowable only to prevent great harm to the pregnant woman and overseen by the integrity of the medical profession. This can be seen in the wording of the Act itself (as amended by section 37 of the Human Fertilisation and Embryology Act 1990):

S1(1) Subject to the provisions of this section, a person shall not be guilty of an offence under the law relating to abortion when a pregnancy is terminated by a registered medical practitioner if two registered medical practitioners are of the opinion, formed in good faith –

    (a) that the pregnancy has not exceeded its twenty-fourth week and that the continuance of the pregnancy would involve risk, greater than if the pregnancy were terminated, of injury to the physical or mental health of the pregnant woman or any existing child of her family; or

    (b) that the termination is necessary to prevent grave permanent injury to the physical or mental health of the pregnant woman; or

    (c) that the continuance of the pregnancy would involve risk to the life of the pregnant woman, greater than if the pregnancy were terminated; or

    (d) that there is a substantial risk that if the child were born it would suffer from some physical or mental abnormalities as to be seriously handicapped.

  (2) In determining whether the continuance of the pregnancy would involve such risk of injury to health as is mentioned in paragraph (a) or (b) of subsection (1) of this section, account may be taken of the pregnant woman's actual or reasonably foreseeable environment.

  (3) Except as provided by subsection (4) of this section, any treatment for the termination of pregnancy must be carried out in a hospital vested in the Minister of Health or the Secretary of State under the National Health Services Acts, or in a place for the time being approved for the purposes of this section by the said Minister or Secretary of State.

(3)(A) The power under subsection (3) of this section to approve a place includes power, in relation to treatment consisting primarily in the use of such medicines as may be specified in the approval and carried out in such manner as may be so specified, to approve a class of places.

  (4) Subsection (3) of this section, and so much of subsection (1) as relates to the opinions of two registered medical practitioners, shall not apply to the termination of a pregnancy by a registered medical practitioner in a case where he is of the opinion, formed in good faith, that the termination is immediately necessary to save the life, or to prevent grave permanent injury to the physical or mental health of the pregnant woman.

The first thing to note in section 1(1) is that *two* medical practitioners need to 'be of the opinion, formed in good faith' that one of the criteria in section 1(1)(a) to (d) is satisfied. An exception to this is provided in section 1(4), where the opinion of only one medical practitioner is required if she 'is of the opinion, formed in good faith, that the termination is immediately necessary to save the life, or to prevent grave permanent injury to the physical or mental health of the pregnant woman'. Thus, the ultimate decision regarding whether or not a woman will be allowed access to an abortion is considered to be a medical one. As noted above, this was a deliberate policy aimed at seeking to achieve a compromise with pro-life campaigners, but it has instead drawn criticism from both sides of the argument. Thus, pro-life groups have highlighted that, particularly in private clinics, there is not just no doctrinal impediment, but also an actual financial inducement in favour of permitting abortions, and they argue that this creates an excessively permissive legal environment that risks allowing abortion by demand via the back door.[14] On the pro-choice side of the debate, authors such as Sally Sheldon have long since argued that this 'gatekeeper' role accepted and performed by the medical profession can also empower doctors who *do* have a doctrinal objection to abortion to be able to effectively veto a pregnant woman's choice to terminate her pregnancy.[15] This may be particularly true in rural areas where access to medical services may be difficult and where alternative providers may be tens of miles away. It is important to emphasise that this requirement is relaxed by section 1(4), which provides that only one doctor need authorise the abortion if it is necessary immediately in order to 'save the life, or to prevent grave permanent injury to the physical or mental health of the pregnant woman'.

Section 1(1)(a) is the most controversial of the provisions. Again, perhaps contrary to popular perception, it is the only ground for abortion that contains a time limit. It was originally set at twenty-eight weeks, but following scientific advances in neonatal care resulting in the effective reduction in the amount of gestation time required before viability, this was reduced to twenty-four weeks as a part of the amendments made by the Human Fertilisation and Embryology Act 1990. It is the only ground for an abortion that contains a time limit – all of the others are permissible at any point in the pregnancy. It is referred to as the 'social ground' as it not only allows for consideration of the welfare of any existing children, but also, under section 1(2), for account to be taken of 'the pregnant woman's actual or reasonably foreseeable environment'. Pro-life groups argue that this is the ground that essentially allows for abortion on demand, and indeed the vast majority of abortions – approximately

---

[14] See, e.g., J. Keown, *Abortion, Doctors and the Law: Some Aspects of the Legal Regulation of Abortion in England from 1803 to 1982* (Cambridge University Press, 1988), in particular chs. 4 and 5.

[15] Sheldon, *Beyond Control*.

98 per cent – are authorised under it.[16] In many respects, there is some truth to this. Indeed, as the *Daily Telegraph* reported in 2012, government investigations found several hospitals less than rigidly following the rules and, for example, performing terminations despite the signature of only one doctor, or authorising them without ever personally meeting the patient.[17] However, it would be wrong to assume that this means that a large amount of abortions are therefore carried out at or around twenty-four weeks' gestation. Rather, Department of Health figures from 2011 show that in 91 per cent of cases the abortion is carried out before thirteen weeks, and in 78 per cent of cases they are performed before the foetus has gestated for ten weeks.[18] Only 1.5 per cent of abortions take place after nineteen weeks.[19]

The next two paragraphs allow for abortion in order to safeguard the life and health of the pregnant woman. Thus, section 1(1)(b) provides for terminations to be permitted when they are 'necessary to prevent grave permanent injury to the physical or mental health of the pregnant woman'. This is a relatively clear and uncomplicated paragraph, and there is little to add beyond the actual wording. That said, it is worth noting that the provision specifies that a termination may be allowed where the injury is *prevented*. It therefore does not have to be present at the time of the termination or beforehand. Section 1(1)(c) is similar, and allows for an abortion to be carried out when to continue the pregnancy 'would involve risk to the life of the pregnant woman, greater than if the pregnancy were terminated'. Again, the wording is uncomplicated but for a couple of exceptions that are worth highlighting: the first is that the abortion may be permitted if there is a *risk* to the life of the pregnant woman. Therefore, the condition need not have manifested itself at the time of the authorisation by the medical practitioners, or even at the time of the termination itself – it need only have been identified in good faith by the doctors who have signed the authorisation forms. Secondly, it should also be emphasised that the paragraph does not mandate that the risk be completely eradicated, only *lessened*. The wording clearly states that all that is required is that the risk to the life of the mother that has been identified is *less* if she has the termination than if she does not.

[16] See Department of Health, *Abortion Statistics, England and Wales: 2012: Summary Information from the Abortion Notification Forms Returned to the Chief Medical Officers of England and Wales* (DoH, 2013), para. 2.8. The report can be downloaded at www.gov.uk/government/uploads/system/uploads/attachment_data/file/211790/2012_Abortion_Statistics.pdf.

[17] See H. Watt, 'Fourteen NHS Hospitals Broke Law Over Abortion Procedure', *Daily Telegraph*, 12 July 2012; H. Watt and C. Newell, 'NHS Staff Routinely Forged Abortion Consent Forms, Inspectors Find', *Daily Telegraph*, 12 July 2012; and C. Newell and H. Watt, 'Abortion Investigation: Doctor Willing to Change Reason for Abortion', *Daily Telegraph*, 24 February 2012.

[18] Department of Health, *Abortion Statistics, England and Wales: 2011* (DoH, 2012). The report can be downloaded at www.gov.uk/government/uploads/system/uploads/attachment_data/file/127785/Commentary1.pdf.pdf.

[19] DoH, *Abortion Statistics 2011*.

Needless to say, this relies heavily on the good faith of the doctors signing the form, and does not contain a time limit.

The final ground under section 1(1) is paragraph (d), which permits abortion on the grounds of serious foetal abnormality. As with section 1(1)(b) and (c), there is no time limit, so an abortion under this ground may be carried out at any time if necessary. It is worthy of note that the wording only requires that two doctors are satisfied that there is a *risk* that the resulting child might suffer from 'some physical or mental abnormalities as to be seriously handicapped'. Needless to say, the key to this provision is the definition of 'seriously handicapped', which is not defined by the statute. It is here that the Abortion Act's medicalisation of the decision-making process becomes most fully apparent since, as we have demonstrated above, all that is required is that two doctors sign the form stating that in their view the prognosis *is* that there is a risk that the child might be born seriously handicapped. Clearly, this is open to what some would consider abuse, and just such a situation occurred in the case of *Jepson*.[20]

Joanna Jepson, a clergywoman, found out that an abortion had been carried out after twenty-four weeks' gestation under section 1(1)(d), where the foetus had suffered from a cleft lip and palate. She argued that this did not constitute a 'serious handicap' under the provisions of the Abortion Act. While the Crown Prosecution Service had investigated this, they had made a decision that no prosecution would be appropriate, and she sought a judicial review of that decision. She was granted leave to apply for judicial review, and West Mercia Police agreed to reconsider the case with different personnel, essentially admitting that their first investigation was inadequate. Nevertheless, Reverend Jepson's victory was somewhat pyrrhic, as not only did the new CPS investigation reach the same conclusion as the first, but in doing so it highlighted the fact that the Abortion Act actually allowed for limited oversight by the law. In a press release subsequent to the second investigation, the CPS spokesman Jim England explained that '[t]he issue is whether the two doctors who had authorised the termination were of the opinion, *formed in good faith*, that there was a substantial risk' that if the child were born it would suffer from a serious handicap.[21] It concluded that the doctors had acted in good faith, and that this was therefore the end of the matter in legal terms.

What this demonstrates is that the definition of 'serious handicap' and, indeed, 'substantial risk' is to all extents and purposes left to medical professionals to

---

[20] *Jepson* v. *Chief Constable of West Mercia Police* [2003] EWHC 3318 (QB).
[21] 'CPS Decides Not To Prosecute Doctors Following Complaint By Rev Joanna Jepson', 16 March 2005, www.rcog.org. uk/termination-pregnancy-fetal-abnormality-england-scotland-and-wales.

decide.[22] Whatever one's views on abortion and the issue of cleft lips and palates, it is undeniable that the medicalisation of abortion has the capacity both to enhance the autonomy of pregnant women and also to limit it. It is for this reason that those at polar opposite ends of the argument – such as Joanna Jepson and Sally Sheldon – at least agree on the undesirability of medicalisation in this context, albeit for different reasons.

Section 1(1)(d) is also particularly controversial for another reason: that it can be said to deliberately devalue the life of disabled people, and that their lives are to be considered not worth living (or a valid reason for the parents not to want the child to live).[23] It is difficult to argue against this criticism, and it is worth noting that it is the only ground for an abortion in the Act that is unrelated to the health of the pregnant woman. Nevertheless, as we discuss below in the section on ethics, this does not affect an argument that relies on the autonomy of the pregnant woman. Moreover, as we discuss below, this is arguably consistent with how the law treats infants born with serious disabilities.

Ancillary issues

There are several ancillary issues that constitute the detail of the Act, and also where the common law has developed around it. The first two of these relate to where a termination may be performed and how much help may be provided by nurses and other staff. Section 1(3) requires that all abortions under the Act are carried out in a hospital or clinic approved by the Secretary of State to do so, other than in an emergency. Section 1(3)(A), added when the Act was updated by the HFEA 1990, allows the Secretary of State to approve 'classes of places', and thus it would be possible if the government so chose to approve GPs' surgeries as a class of place to perform medical (as opposed to surgical) abortions and thus, for example, dispense Mifepristone/RU486 for consumption on the premises. This has not yet occurred, and indeed such a move would not be without its problems. As Emily Jackson notes, the procedure would be that the pill would be taken at the GP surgery, and the patient then goes home for 36 to 48 hours, before returning for the doctor to check whether the pregnancy has been terminated by inserting a

---

[22] That said, a Royal College of Obstetricians and Gynaecologists working party pointedly refused to provide a definition, stating that it would be 'unrealistic to produce a definitive list of conditions that constitute serious handicap' (RCOG, *Termination of Pregnancy for Fetal Abnormality in England, Scotland and Wales: Report of a Working Party* (RCOG, 2010), p. 9). The report can be downloaded at www.rcog.org.uk/files/rcog-corp/ TerminationPregnancyReport18May2010.pdf.

[23] For an excellent contemporary analysis of s. 1(1)(d) and the arguments surrounding it in general terms, see S. McGuinness, 'Law, Reproduction and Disability: Fatally "Handicapped"?' (2013) 21 *Med. L. Rev.* 213. For a slightly older but still searching critique, see S. Sheldon and S. Wilkinson, 'Termination of Pregnancy for Reasons of Foetal Disability: Are There Grounds for a Special Exception at Law?' (2001) 9 *Med. L. Rev.* 85.

prostaglandin pessary; 'for up to two days, then, the drug is acting to terminate her pregnancy and may in fact do so. If "treatment for the termination of pregnancy" is occurring throughout this period, the woman would have to remain in hospital'.[24]

Also, section 1(1) states that the termination must be carried out by a 'registered medical practitioner'. The potential liability – and limitations on the role of – nurses and others was considered by the House of Lords in the case of *Royal College of Nursing* v. *Department of Health and Social Security*.[25] In that case, the RCN sought clarification of the law to protect nurses who were involved in medical abortion – most notably giving pills such as Mifepristone/RU486 to patients to induce abortions. The question for the House of Lords was whether this constituted a breach of the 1967 Act. The majority of the House of Lords stated that it was not, as long as the doctor was in charge of the treatment and supervising. In such cases, Lord Diplock held that procedures would be within the Act if performed by nurses or other staff as long as their role was 'in accordance with accepted medical practice'.[26]

What of staff who do not wish to help to perform abortions for reasons of conscience? Can they conscientiously object and refuse to take part? This is governed by section 4 of the Abortion Act 1967, which provides the following:

(1) Subject to subsection (2) of this section, no person shall be under any duty, whether by contract or by any statutory or other legal requirement, to participate in any treatment authorised by this Act to which he has a conscientious objection:
  Provided that in any legal proceedings the burden of proof of conscientious objection shall rest on the person claiming to rely on it.
(2) Nothing in subsection (1) of this section shall affect any duty to participate in treatment which is necessary to save the life or to prevent grave permanent injury to the physical or mental health of a pregnant woman.

As can be seen from the quote above, section 4(1) states that no one will be under a duty to participate – unless the abortion is necessary to save the life or prevent 'grave permanent injury' to the pregnant woman under section 4(2). The protection of conscientious objection is therefore not absolute, and indeed it does not cover a duty to advise patients, so if a doctor will not refer a patient for an abortion on grounds of conscience, the GMC mandates that she must find a colleague doctor

---

[24] E. Jackson, *Medical Law: Text, Cases and Materials*, 2nd edn (Oxford University Press, 2010), p. 686. We agree with her further comment, however, that in practice the 'treatment' is considered the ingestion of the pill, and the fact that women are sent home some hours after taking it is unlikely to cause legal issues. See also S. Rowlands, 'Abortion Pills: Under Whose Control?' (2012) 38 *Journal of Family Planning and Reproductive Healthcare* 117.
[25] *Royal College of Nursing* v. *Department of Health and Social Security* [1981] AC 800.   [26] *RCN* v. *DHSS* at 828.

who has no such moral objections.[27] An example of such a case is that of *Janaway*, where a Roman Catholic worker at a health centre refused to type a letter referring a patient for a possible abortion.[28] She was dismissed from her employment, and applied for a judicial review of the decision, claiming that her refusal was covered by section 4. The case went all the way to the House of Lords, who rejected her claim. The applicant argued that had the Abortion Act not been in force, helping to refer a patient for an abortion would be a criminal offence, and therefore must be a part of what is covered by section 4. The House of Lords, however, took a narrower view of the clause, stating that section 4 only covered the actual taking part in the treatment, and not the referral. As Lord Keith noted, had Parliament intended that people such as Mrs Janaway be covered by section 4, it would have used wording such as 'any act authorised by this Act' rather than 'participate in treatment' authorised by the Act.[29]

The final issue is that of whether the putative father of any resulting child has a right of veto over a termination. The short answer, according to English law, is that he does not. The two most high-profile examples of challenges to this rule are those of *Paton* and *C* v. *S*.[30] In each case, the man sought an injunction stopping the proposed termination, and in each case he was rebuffed. In *Paton*, Sir George Baker P. provided an excellent account of why this is the case:

> The two doctors have given a certificate. It is not and cannot be suggested that the certificate was given in other than good faith and . . . there is the end of the matter in English law. The Abortion Act gives no right to a father to be consulted in respect of a termination of pregnancy. True, it gives no right to the mother either, but obviously the mother is going to be right at the heart of the matter consulting with the doctors if they are to arrive at a decision in good faith.[31]

Furthermore:

> The only way that [Mr Paton's counsel] can put the case is that the husband has a right to have a say in the destiny of the child he has conceived. *The law of England gives him no such right; the Abortion Act 1967 contains no such provision.* It follows . . . that . . . this claim for an injunction is completely misconceived and must be dismissed.[32]

Some final words on abortion

It is important to remember that the Abortion Act merely provides exceptions to the legal rules that prohibit harming the foetus. Moreover, it is not the case – as is

---

[27] See GMC, *Good Medical Practice* (GMC, 2013), para. 52. The guidance can be downloaded at www.gmc-uk.org/guidance/good_medical_practice.asp.
[28] *R* v. *Salford AHA, ex p. Janaway* [1989] AC 537.   [29] *Janaway* at 566.
[30] *Paton* v. *Trustees of the British Pregnancy Advisory Service* [1979] QB 276; *C* v. *S and another* [1988] QB 135.
[31] *Paton* at 281.   [32] *Paton* at 282. Emphasis added.

frequently asserted – that it allows for abortion on demand. Nevertheless, it is undeniable that section 1(1)(a) has grown to have been given a wider application than was originally intended by Parliament. One of the main difficulties for the law in this area is that it has to legislate for the benefit of the pregnant woman, medical staff who may have issues of conscience and also the foetus, which as we saw is not morally insignificant nor treated as such by the law. However, while *in utero* the foetus is a part of the pregnant woman, and to protect it may mean compromising her autonomy and physical and mental well-being. Once it is born alive, however, this is no longer the case and the rules are different, as we discuss below.

CHILDREN BORN ALIVE, BUT SEVERELY DISABLED

Sometimes abortions fail, and the child is born alive. In these situations, the Abortion Act 1967 does not apply, and therefore the child has to be treated in his best interests – as defined and discussed in Chapter 5 of this book. Indeed, the Abortion Act 1967 provides no defence to murder or manslaughter, and to take steps to kill a child born as the result of a failed abortion would leave a doctor liable in homicide. This is also the case when there is no abortion and a child is born. If it is healthy, or there is a realistic way to restore it to a state in which it may be able to enjoy some quality of life, it will certainly be in the patient's best interests to be treated. However, where the child is born with such injuries or disabilities that there would be no quality of life at all, it can sometimes be said not to be in the patient's best interests (in relation to minors, we refer to applying the welfare principle) to continue to treat, and treatment may be withdrawn. Of course, the difficulty in such cases lies in determining when this might be the case, and unfortunately the law has had several opportunities to consider this very question.

Indeed, the law has undergone some development in the last few years, but essentially cases still rest heavily on medical evidence and opinion. The first thing to note is that, in line with the attitude of the courts that we saw in Chapter 5, the courts will not agree to the withdrawal of treatment lightly. A good example of this is the early case of *Re. B*, where a child was born with Down's syndrome and an intestinal blockage.[33] If the blockage were not rectified by an operation, the child would die. If the operation were to be successfully performed, B would have a life expectancy of up to thirty years. The parents wished to let B die, but the local authority sought to make him a ward of court and seek authorisation from the court

---

[33] *Re. B (A Minor) (Wardship: Medical Treatment)* [1981] 1 WLR 1421.

that the operation be performed. The case went to the Court of Appeal after the judge at first instance had decided that the parents' wishes be respected. In the Court of Appeal, Templeman LJ overturned that decision and held that the operation could go ahead, and that children should only be left to die if it was shown that their life would be 'so bound to be full of pain and suffering' that it would be cruel to allow them to live.[34] In the present case, he held that the case involved a desire to 'terminate the life of a mongoloid [sic] child because she also has an intestinal complaint'.[35] It is difficult to argue with the application of the law in that case, and the test was subsequently refined in the case of *Re. J* to be that it would only be in the child's interests to withdraw treatment if to allow treatment to continue would be 'so cruel as to [make his life] intolerable'.[36] In that case, however, Taylor LJ went on to clarify that the intolerability must be viewed from the perspective of the patient – and it must be remembered that even people with serious disabilities can and do find value and happiness in their lives. It would therefore be wrong to state that the mere fact of a permanent, serious disability will be enough for the courts to authorise the removal of treatment from a child.[37] Essentially, the courts now seem to regard this analysis as inexorably bound up with the patient's 'best interests' to the extent that the latter has effectively taken over.[38]

Indeed, the courts have frequently emphasised that their primary consideration is their own assessment of the welfare of the child.[39] This means that, in theory, it should be willing to overrule the decision of parents, doctors or even both. As we saw in the case of *Re. B*, there are instances where the courts have not allowed a child to die even though the parents did not wish treatment to continue. However, there have also been cases where the courts have sided with parents over doctors. An example of this is the case of *An NHS Trust* v. *MB*, where the court refused doctors' request to remove treatment from a child with spinal muscular atrophy. The parents adduced evidence that there were signs that the child gained some pleasure from being with them.[40] Thus, there were signs that MB did not lead an existence free from happiness, and his life could be said to have value to him. It was noticeable that in this case the court utilised a 'balance sheet' approach reminiscent of the Mental Capacity Act 2005 (which at that time was not yet in force) looking at

---

[34] *Re. B* at 1424.   [35] *Re. B* at 1424.   [36] *Re. J (A Minor) (Wardship: Medical Treatment)* [1991] Fam 33 at 55.

[37] On the subject of a life worth living, see M. Ford, 'The Personhood Paradox and the "Right to Die"' (2005) 13 *Med. L. Rev.* 80; albeit mostly in relation to adults. See also A. Morris, 'Selective Treatment of Irreversibly Impaired Infants: Decision-Making at the Threshold' (2009) 17(3) *Med. L. Rev.* 347.

[38] See, e.g., *Re. Wyatt (A Child) (Medical Treatment: Parents' Consent)* [2005] EWHC 693 (Fam) in the Court of Appeal, where the court stated that best interests should be used rather than intolerability as the test. See also Morris, 'Selective Treatment of Irreversibly Impaired Infants'.

[39] See, e.g., *R* v. *Portsmouth Hospital NHS Trust, ex p. Glass* [1999] 3 FCR 145.

[40] *An NHS Trust* v. *MB* [2006] EWHC 507 (Fam).

the benefits and disadvantages of treatment.[41] Another example of a court siding with parents over doctors is the case of *Re. T*.[42]

This case is somewhat odd, in the sense that the concept of the 'welfare of *the child*' was stretched to breaking point (or beyond, depending on one's point of view). T suffered from liver failure, and required a transplant. The doctors treating him wished to provide it, but the parents, who were also medical professionals, thought it best to let him die. The parents had framed their objections to the surgery in terms of the pain and burden on T, but also, more controversially, that they had recently taken new jobs abroad and they would have to return and give them up if T were to have the transplant. Waite LJ reluctantly decided to follow the views of the parents, stating that this was a case where a genuine difference of opinion was possible, and that in such cases the views of the parents should be respected.

That being said, in the vast majority of cases the courts are swayed by the medical evidence, and thus the cases of *MB* and *T* should be considered exceptional rather than representative.[43] However, the problem is that such decisions do not involve exactitudes and certainties. A good example of this is the litigation surrounding Charlotte Wyatt, who was born in 2003 with what can only be described as a bleak prognosis. The doctors involved in the case felt that it would be best to let her die, while her parents, who held strong Christian beliefs, were 'reported to be awaiting a "miracle"'.[44] In such circumstances, it is unsurprising that the courts sided with the medical professionals and granted an order stating that it would be lawful not to ventilate Charlotte.[45] However, Charlotte's condition improved. What followed was a series of court battles regarding whether it would be lawful to remove ventilation, with the doctors consistently arguing that it would not be in her best interests to ventilate should that be required, and her parents that it would. Charlotte Wyatt remains alive.[46]

What *Wyatt* demonstrates is the difficulty faced by the courts when making these decisions. Indeed, they will only be seen as 'right' or 'wrong' after the fact, and this perception can sometimes relate little to the point of principle used. In this regard, the courts' focus on intolerability and best interests is probably as sound a principle as it is likely to find. Nevertheless, these cases also provide something of a contrast to the law regarding abortion. What we saw with the Abortion Act was a

---

[41] This approach was explained in Chapter 5 of this book.

[42] *Re. T (A Minor) (Wardship: Medical Treatment)* [1997] 1 WLR 242; [1997] 1 All ER 906; [1997] 2 FCR 363.

[43] See, e.g., M. Brazier, 'An Intractable Dispute: When Parents and Professionals Disagree' (2005) 13 *Med. L. Rev.* 412, who also argues that the definition of 'welfare' is too medical in nature – an almost inevitable consequence of following medical evidence too easily. See also R. Heywood, 'Parents and Medical Professionals: Conflict, Co-Operation and Best Interests' (2012) 20 *Med. L. Rev.* 29 for a critical examination of that view.

[44] Morris, 'Selective Treatment of Irreversibly Impaired Infants', 366.

[45] Morris describes the judgment and the legal issues as 'unremarkable' (at 347).

[46] For an excellent account of the legal issues, see S. Elliston, *The Best Interests of the Child in Healthcare* (Abingdon: Routledge, 2007), pp. 163–7.

total deference to medical opinion that is lacking once the child is actually born. While we do not wish to use this as a reason to limit maternal autonomy over abortion decisions, the argument that there is little moral difference between the viable foetus and the newborn baby is a strong one.[47] Of course, the key difference is that the child is not within the woman's body once it has been born – but the courts' differing views relating to their ability to intervene is nevertheless noteworthy. Perhaps it is merely due to the fact that medicalisation is the compromise that had to be made to allow the Abortion Act through Parliament, although if this is the case then perhaps that should be reconsidered in the light of modern attitudes. What might have been necessary then may not be now.

THE CONJOINED TWINS CASE

The cases above have examined what to do with severe disabilities that are a danger only to the infants themselves, but in 2001 a landmark case presented itself involving conjoined twins called Mary and Jodie.[48] The case revolved around the question of whether it would be lawful to surgically separate them. The parents, Roman Catholics from Malta, refused to consent to this. The problem that was to prove most taxing for the courts was that were the operation to be performed, Mary would die, although Jodie would survive. The medical prognosis, however, was that if the procedure was not undertaken, then both would die. This led Ward LJ in the Court of Appeal to use some colourful language, arguing that Mary was in effect 'sucking the lifeblood' out of Jodie; and that 'if Jodie could speak, she would surely protest "Stop it, Mary, you're killing me"'.[49]

Much of the legal analysis in the case is concerned with the criminal law aspects, which do not concern us here.[50] In relation to the topics that are most relevant to medical law, the case is similar to *Sidaway* (discussed in Chapter 4), in that the judges all reached the same conclusion – that it would be lawful to separate the twins – but for differing reasons. Thus, Ward LJ and Robert Walker LJ held that the operation would clearly not be in Mary's best interests (the crux of the issue), while somewhat counterintuitively Brooke LJ held that it could be (given that in both situations she would die, he felt that dying separated would be a 'better' death). Equally, Brooke LJ held that 'the doctrine of double effect can have no possible application in this case',[51] while for Robert Walker LJ the operation would

---

[47] See, e.g. (albeit from a US perspective), C. Wellman, 'The Concept of Fetal Rights' (2002) *Law and Philosophy* 65.
[48] *Re. A (Children) (Conjoined Twins: Separation)* [2001] Fam 147.   [49] *Re. A* at 197.
[50] For a criminal law centred discussion, see M. Bohlander, 'Of Shipwrecked Sailors, Unborn Children, Conjoined Twins and Hijacked Airplanes – Taking Human Life and the Defence of Necessity' (2006) 70(2) *Journal of Criminal Law* 147.
[51] *Re. A* at 218.

be lawful as 'Mary's death would not be the purpose'.[52] So what can we take from the case? As Emily Jackson notes in her analysis, ultimately all of the judges 'appeared to start from the utilitarian presumption that saving one life must be preferable to losing two'.[53] It is difficult to argue with this proposition, although perhaps equally compelling is Ranaan Gillon's view that the court had little moral authority to overrule the wishes of the parents, who 'were neither incompetent nor negligent ... and their reasoning [that as Catholics they could not sanction the death of one of their children] was not *merely* religious, but was widely acceptable moral reasoning'.[54] Indeed, it is interesting to note that had the twins presented at Great Ormond Street Hospital in London, rather than St Mary's Hospital in Manchester, the decision of the parents would have been respected.[55]

Ultimately, it is difficult to sense what would have been the correct moral decision in the case, and both of the above views are worthy of being accepted. It should perhaps be noted that Jodie survived, recovered and left hospital, accompanying her family back to Malta. But that is not the important aspect of this case. What it demonstrates is that, when faced with a decision between death and life, the courts will virtually always find a way to protect life. The views of the parents will be considered, but, if they decide otherwise they will be overruled – however reasonable their justifications for doing so.

CONCLUDING REMARKS ON LAW

The foetus is not a legal person. That is not to say that it does not deserve or is not offered protection by the law – it indeed benefits from this in the form of several Acts of Parliament. Nevertheless, given that it is not morally or legally insignificant, it is perhaps strange that the Abortion Act 1967 so prioritises medical opinion over any other considerations. Furthermore, it should not simply be assumed that this is always to the advantage of the woman seeking an abortion – as Sally Sheldon, among others, has demonstrated.[56] What is noticeable is the way in which the courts have allowed themselves to be far more activist in relation to decisions made *after* the child has been born – overruling both parents and doctors on occasion (although the general trend remains one of deference to the medical evidence). Perhaps this is the correct thing to do – after all, the child is a legal person

---

[52] *Re. A* at 259.
[53] E. Jackson, *Medical Law: Text, Cases and Materials*, 2nd edn (Oxford University Press, 2010), p. 932. See in general pp. 931–7.
[54] R. Gillon, 'Imposed Separation of Conjoined Twins – Moral Hubris by the English Courts' (2001) 27 *Journal of Medical Ethics* 3, 4.
[55] See B. Hewson, 'Killing Off Mary: Was the Court of Appeal Right?' (2001) 9(2) *Med. L. Rev.* 281, 289.
[56] See Sheldon, *Beyond Control*.

and therefore perhaps requires a consideration of its welfare more focussed on it and less on its family. However, there are some who argue (as we argued above and return to below) that there is little moral difference between a foetus in late pregnancy and a newborn baby; or even, to some, with the embryo if one believes that life begins at conception. If this is accepted (and we do not here state that we do accept this), then this difference in approach is, to those people, unjustified. But it is unlikely that there will ever be consensus on such issues. Instead of asking which legal approach is 'right', we should perhaps focus on which is 'least wrong'.

ETHICS

This chapter is one of those which we mentioned at the outset as being particularly controversial. Abortion is one of the subject areas which, traditionally, raises intense emotional and moral issues. One of the reasons for this is that it calls into question the continued existence of something many people regard as particularly worthy of protection: budding life. This is why many discussions of abortion, foeticide and infanticide revolve around the very misleading question of 'when does life begin?'

Of course, the answer to that question is technically very straightforward. Biologically speaking, life begins when the gametes (sperm and ovum) unite and the blastocyst develops – when mitosis happens and cells start separating. The process of building a human has then started and life has begun. It should be clear now why the oft-cited question on when life begins is misleading. Something else is really meant here, namely: 'When does life reach a stage where we ought to, morally and legally, protect its existence?'

In order to answer this question (without immediately resorting to poorly argued personal moral intuitions), a number of proposals have developed over many decades of discussion. These proposals are generally concerned with a certain characteristic which gives the embryo or foetus a special status. The first of these thinks of the embryo as being a member of a certain class – that of being an identifiable human being. While this is the position conventionally taken by those who favour according moral status to the embryo from the word go (i.e. when the sperm and the egg fuse), this theory is not without flaws. One problem is that this position entails that many types of contraception would essentially entail what amounts at least to an abortion and, some extremists would argue, the commission of a homicide offence – essentially, any contraceptive measure that does not involve the prevention of sperm and ovum meeting after sexual intercourse. Conventional contraceptives that work by preventing the successful nesting of the fertilised ovum would therefore be problematic. The second problem with this theory is bafflingly simple: there is a time window between fertilisation of the ovum and the point in time where it is actually determined whether the ovum will develop into multiples (such as twins or triplets) or a single embryo. Therefore, the argument that from conception the embryo can be characterised as a discrete member of the human species is not correct in every case.

A second approach to determining when we might be required to provide legal and moral protection to unborn life is that of identifying it as a member of the group 'persons'. This view posits that mere existence of the embryo is not decisive in according it certain rights. What is, in fact, important is a range of characteristics acquired by the embryo over time. In this case, the characteristic which makes the difference is when the embryo becomes a person. The question when that might be is not likely to be resolved to the satisfaction of all at any point soon. Many follow the point of view that some degree of consciousness is required to become a member of this category (consciousness in the sense of being aware and feeling sensations, such as pain). This point in time is certainly during the period of gestation, so this would entail according rights to unborn life. Others may have differing views of what type of property needs to be present for an embryo to become a member of the group of 'persons', so this view certainly does little to provide a straightforward position.

The third position is one usually referred to as the 'potentiality argument'. The cells we are talking about here, i.e. the fertilised ovum, the blastocyst or the embryo, have the potential to develop into a complete individual. By aborting the embryo, we are depriving a potential person of their life.

Finally, it may be that it is not an inherent characteristic of the embryo that means it is in some way special and worthy of protection, but the fact that the unborn life becomes part of a social web: it is accorded its moral status by virtue of how we view it in the greater scheme of things. This argument goes to the undoubted intuition possessed by most right-thinking people which ensures that we do provide special protection to our offspring.

One of the fundamental issues, therefore, is that of the exact moral status of the life that is being ended. Only after we address that question do we have to question the motives of those who want to end the life. In other words, if an abortion is early on in the pregnancy, does it matter less whether the reasons for terminating the pregnancy lie in the mother's health or in a lifestyle choice (i.e. it being inconvenient to have a child)? The further the pregnancy progresses, the more solidified the status of the unborn life becomes. Certain thresholds are passed and it becomes increasingly problematic to successfully justify a termination of the pregnancy. The two rough categories are those who feel that there is a 'hard' milestone after which a moral status comes into existence (such as conception, implantation, primitive streak development, 'quickening', viability or birth). Others adhere to the view that this is a gradual process, a growing of the moral status alongside the child. While different theories attach meaning to different thresholds in the development of a child, most would probably agree that the passing of time and the continuous development of embryo into foetus and foetus into a child represent a continuous scale, with a corresponding increase of legal protection attaching to the unborn life. Some of these thresholds seem, on closer inspection, somewhat arbitrary.

In 2012, two Australian moral philosophers, Alberto Giubilini and Francesca Minerva, published a controversially debated paper entitled: 'After-Birth Abortion: Why Should the Baby Live?'[57] In this paper, the two academics posited that neither foetuses nor newborns have the same moral status as actual persons and the fact that they are potential persons is irrelevant. When accepting that foetuses are regularly aborted even when they are healthy, the argument can be taken to its natural conclusion, which is that there is no significant moral difference between aborting a foetus and killing an infant. The academic paper was taken up by the popular press, with *The Sun* headlining 'Slaughter Newborn Kids, Say Academics'.[58] *The Telegraph* carried the headline: 'Killing Babies No Different from Abortion, Experts Say'.[59] It is clear that neither *The Sun* nor *The Telegraph* adequately contextualised Giubilini and Minerva's perfectly acceptable moral philosophical paper. It is also obvious that worlds collided in this instance: on the one side, two scholars who did exactly what they should – argue a point all the way to its conclusion, however bizarre, so that we may learn whether the point has validity in the first place; and, on the other side, the harsh court of public opinion which does not accept that in academia, no question is out of bounds, lest we are happy to forsake scientific progress.

What becomes clear beyond a shadow of a doubt is how contentious this particular area of medical law is. Emotions run high and there are numerous conflicting moral views of abortion: from those who feel that it should be an individualistic-ethical decision for the parents (based on their sets of values and desires) to those who feel that there is a case for society to prohibit abortions in any case (based on a societal set of values which suggests that all life is worth protecting).

Even those who favour a macro-level prohibition of abortion will appreciate that those directly concerned have their own interests and desires. A blanket prohibition

---

[57] A. Giubilini and F. Minerva, 'After-Birth Abortion: Why Should the Baby Live?' 39(5) *Journal of Medical Ethics* 261.

[58] G. Wilson, 'Slaughter Newborn Kids, Say Academics', *The Sun*, 1 March 2012.

[59] S. Adams, 'Killing Babies No Different From Abortion, Experts Say', *The Telegraph*, 29 February 2012.

on abortion would disenfranchise the pregnant woman, essentially robbing her of control over her own body. This is a serious infringement of her right to autonomously lead her life the way she wants. This right simply includes decisions in relation to how she interacts with her own body, a right she does not waive by virtue of becoming pregnant. This is certainly the case where the woman's life is at risk, perceivably so in cases where the pregnancy is the result of rape, but should, many would argue, be a fundamentally given entitlement. It is in many ways problematic, therefore, that some jurisdictions view abortion as generally unlawful but tolerated as this criminalises a legitimate choice. At the same time, this line of argumentation is simply only one way to argue for legitimacy of a pro-choice stance in a legal way. It does nothing to establish a moral entitlement on behalf of pregnant women to put their own desires over the developmental potential of the unborn life.[60]

Interesting and complex issues arise where the pregnancy has progressed to a point where the foetus is potentially viable. There seems to be no good ethical argument in favour of an invasive abortion if the birth of the viable foetus can be achieved by way of an equally invasive caesarean section. A late-term abortion is usually only contemplated where the pregnant woman's life or health are at serious risk. If the foetus were viable in these circumstances, we would assume that the choice would be made for a birth by emergency caesarian and a subsequent attempt to coddle the infant in hospital. It is difficult to imagine a medically indicated late-term abortion of a viable foetus.

Another layer of complexity in the ethical debate is added where we leave the ground of elective abortions (i.e. simply wishing to terminate a pregnancy for the purposes of preventing the continuation of pregnancy) and turn our attention to selective terminations. Selective terminations are those where unborn life is terminated on the basis of a pre-existing condition which renders the pregnancy undesirable. This may take place in vitro during the course of IVF treatment, where from a range of available blastocysts, the most viable ones or those that have been checked for genetic defects are selected and the rest are discarded. Sometimes, amniocentesis is carried out in the third or fourth month of the pregnancy and leads to a result which indicates a defect. The majority of pregnancies are accompanied by regular ultrasound examinations and clinical chemistry of the pregnant woman, both of which may lead to an indication of a defect which in turn may result in the question of the termination of the pregnancy. The basis for this type of choice is often manifold: the desire to have a healthy child only, the assumption that certain types of defect diminish the child's quality of life in an

---

[60] R. Hursthouse, 'Virtue Theory and Abortion' in H. LaFollette (ed.), *Ethics in Practice: An Anthology*, 2nd edn (Oxford: Blackwell, 2002), pp. 94–103.

unacceptable way, the ability of the parents to cope. One criticism of this is that it creates different qualitative classes within society: if we decide to terminate pregnancies that would lead to children being born with chromosome disorders such as trisomy 21 (Down's syndrome), does this mean that we automatically assert that we feel that all those who live with Down's syndrome should not have been allowed to be born?[61] The counter-argument is that the termination of a pregnancy works on the assumption that the unborn life has a significantly inferior moral status to actual persons, therefore our decisions in relation to genetically defective unborn life have no bearing on our view of genetically defective actual persons. A strong and plausible position against such a selection is that of social cohesion – regardless of whether or not we apply the same views to unborn life and to actual persons, it is without doubt the case that those who live with this type of disability would feel offended by this type of selection. Any system of justifying pregnancy terminations that completely eradicated the possibility of giving birth to a genetically defective child may well lead to a societal loss of respect for any living person who belongs to this category. This is a threat to social cohesion and goes against the grain of the principles of solidarity which form the basis of our communities.

If we subscribe to the viewpoint that, however his may be justified in detail, the moral status of the unborn develops alongside the unborn herself, it seems intuitively clear that there must be some sort of moral distinction between terminating a pregnancy and ending the life of a newborn infant. Giubilini and Minerva address this very issue when they argue that it is simply accepted that certain health conditions of the foetus have in the past been held to justify an abortion. They continue their argument to the point after birth:

A serious philosophical problem arises when the same conditions that would have justified abortion become known after birth. In such cases, we need to assess facts in order to decide whether the same arguments that apply to killing a human fetus can also be consistently applied to killing a newborn human.[62]

Where is the line drawn – and why? This intriguing question formed the nucleus of what Giubilini and Minerva wanted to debate. Is it the case that we actually genuinely assume that both a foetus and an infant have inferior moral status to an adult? Is an infant not an entity particularly worthy of protecting? The paper attracted scholarly criticism (as well as, of course, very unscholarly criticsm – the authors actually received death threats). While there was disagreement about the solidity of the authors' argument, the fundamental notion that they had identified

---

[61] See, fundamentally, B. Shepperdson, 'Abortion and Euthanasia of Down's Syndrome Children – the Parents' View' (1983) 9 *Journal of Medical Ethics* 152–7; and N. Douglas, 'Ethical Dilemmas of Antenatal Screening for Down's Syndrome in Primary Care' (2010) 4 *Advances in Mental Health and Learning Disabilities* 20–4.

[62] Giubilini and Minerva, 'After-Birth Abortion', 261.

was convincing: if there is no significant difference between two states, why treat them morally differently? Andrew McGee writes:

Many people who believe abortion should be permitted would reject the conclusion that killing a newborn baby should likewise be permitted. The challenge is to explain why the rejection of that conclusion is not irrational.[63]

It may well be that it is not relevant whether there is a significant moral distinction if society has created a distinction on the basis of what McGee calls a rejection of Giubilini and Minerva's conclusion. Aside from biologistic explanations which might centre on the natural way we are inclined to protect our own offspring, there is a societal consensus that killing infants is quite simply something that ought to be avoided. Nevertheless, very difficult decisions sometimes need to be taken in the medical setting, and the case of *Re. A*, with the conjoined twins Jodie and Mary, is one of those. Ward LJ's surprising rhetoric ('Stop it Mary . . .') is of course misleading (as it demands something of Mary she is unable to provide) and hence inappropriate as an indicator of fault. Ward LJ does go on to acknowledge that in this extraordinarily difficult balancing exercise, the best that can be achieved is not a good outcome, but merely the least awful outcome:

I am wholly satisfied that the least detrimental choice, balancing the interests of Mary against Jodie and Jodie against Mary, is to permit the operation to be performed.

In essence, the balancing exercise that was undertaken here was one of life against life, Jodie against Mary. In a seemingly purely utilitarian way, the court ordered the operation in order to cause the least amount of unhappiness, to possibly save one life at the expense of another where to do nothing would have meant the death of both children. The case does not raise the fundamental question we have discussed above: is it morally acceptable to kill infants, more than it is morally acceptable to kill adults? We suggest it is not – it is morally wrong to kill an adult because, inter alia, the act deprives the adult of his future. The same argument can be developed plausibly for an infant, and possibly for a foetus.[64]

CONCLUSION

It is justified, in this context, to ask whether what we are discussing here is genuinely a question of a societal compromise (as the law suggests) or simply the path of least resistance at any given time. In an ideal world, all children are wanted

---

[63] A. McGee, 'There's No Good Argument for Infanticide', Practical Ethics Blog, University of Oxford, 2 March 2012, http://blog.practicalethics.ox.ac.uk/2012/03/theres-no-good-argument-for-infanticide/.

[64] D. Marquis, 'An Argument that Abortion Is Wrong' in LaFollette, *Ethics in Practice*, p. 83.

and are born healthy into happy families. We are not living in a dystopia and still it is safe to say that we are far away from that perfect world. Pregnancies happen for many reasons, and for many reasons they may not be wanted. The law has provided a framework within which it is legally acceptable to terminate a pregnancy, and in providing this framework it has entered into a balancing exercise.

Where the balancing exercise is between the life or health of the pregnant woman and the potential life of the unborn child, the balancing act is one that is relatively straightforward. Where the reasons for a pregnancy termination lie in factors that are less immediately plausible (such as for lifestyle reasons or because the child may have a disability which the parents-to-be feel unable to cope with), the balancing exercise becomes much more complicated. Overall, the sense is that this is a situation where the moral and legal arguments are aimed at producing the least unfavourable outcome in any given circumstances.

The law has not helped by taking a moral position that leaves those on both sides of the debate unhappy. In theory, abortion is strictly controlled and should only be available to safeguard the health of the pregnant woman. This restriction, as well as the medical element to the control criticised by authors such as Sally Sheldon, has drawn the ire of those who believe in a woman's right to choose. Equally, however, the breadth of section 1(1)(a) and the way in which it has been used have met with the disapproval of pro-life campaigners who feel that if it does not introduce abortion on demand in theory, it comes close to doing so in practice.

Of course, the decisions that have to be made are hard, but the law exists in part because someone has to make them. Moreover, such decisions must also be made after the child is born. Here the law has taken something of a pragmatic approach that does not protect life at all costs. Rather, it considers welfare and, certainly in the conjoined twins case where the choice was one dead child or two, employs a utilitarian view. Moreover, as can be seen from several of the cases, the law does not simply defer to parental choice, but actively participates in determining what is best.

Ultimately, however, this is another case of balancing interests. Medical staff may have moral objections to what is proposed, and they must be protected. Equally, pregnant women have their health, well-being and, according to some, right to choose to be protected; while the foetus cannot simply be discarded as incidental or morally insignificant. The law has an unenviable task in protecting all of these interests, which will frequently conflict, and it is thus no surprise that its approach is somewhat pragmatic. However, it clearly seeks to make compromises. As mentioned above, it does not protect life at all costs – either in terms of the foetus or neonates and infants. However, it also does not allow pregnant women to do as they wish, nor defer to parental choice after the child is born. The situation is similar for medical staff, who have a right to refuse to participate as long as there is no risk to the health of the pregnant woman. Essentially, the law tries as much as possible to do what it feels is 'for the best' in all circumstances. Unfortunately, this is as likely to make everyone unhappy as it is to be satisfactory to all.

ADDITIONAL READING

Law

S. Elliston, *The Best Interests of the Child in Healthcare* (Abingdon: Routledge, 2007)

B. Hewson, 'Killing Off Mary: Was the Court of Appeal Right?' (2001) 9(2) *Medical Law Review* 281

J. Keown, *Abortion, Doctors and the Law: Some Aspects of the Legal Regulation of Abortion in England from 1803 to 1982* (Cambridge University Press, 1988)

S. McGuinness, 'Law, Reproduction and Disability: Fatally "Handicapped"?' (2013) 21 *Medical Law Review* 213

A. Morris, 'Selective Treatment of Irreversibly Impaired Infants: Decision-Making at the Threshold' (2009) 17(3) *Medical Law Review* 347

S. Sheldon, *Beyond Control: Medical Power and Abortion Law* (London: Pluto Press, 1997)

M. Thomson, 'Abortion Law and Professional Boundaries' (2013) 22(2) *Social and Legal Studies* 191

Ethics

D. Boonin, *A Defense of Abortion* (Cambridge University Press, 2003)

C. Cameron and R. Williamson, 'In the World of Dolly, When Does a Human Embryo Acquire Respect?' (2005) 31 *Journal of Medical Ethics* 215–20

R. Gillon, 'Is There a "New Ethics" of Abortion?' (2001) 27 *Journal of Medical Ethics* ii5–9

B. Steinbock (ed.), *The Oxford Handbook of Bioethics* (Oxford University Press, 2007), chapters 17–19

S. Wilkinson, 'Eugenics, Embryo Selection, and the Equal Value Principle' (2006) 1 *Clinical Ethics* 146

Case studies from this chapter are available online at www.cambridge.org/hoppe.

9 Organ transplantation and the use of human tissue

INTRODUCTION

Although the utilisation of human organs and biological material of human origin has a long and colourful history,[1] therapeutic interventions such as transplantations to replace a diseased organ have only become medical routine in the past sixty years. Modern uses of human biological material are varied and it is necessary to distinguish these uses if we are to understand the legal and ethical aspects properly. In this chapter, we will look at the use of whole human organs for the purposes of transplanting them to another human (organ transplantation); the use of human tissues for the purposes of transplanting them to another human (tissue transplantation); and the use of human biological material for non-therapeutic purposes, in particular tissue research.

The use of human tissues and organs for transplantation and other purposes has undeniably caused problems for the law, for several reasons. First, there has tended to be a shortage of organs available for transplantation (also see Chapter 6 on 'Resource allocation and prioritisation'). This has meant that there are people who would benefit from transplants who have not been able to receive them due to the simple fact that there has not been a suitable organ. However, studies have consistently shown that there are far more people who would say that they would be willing to donate organs than there are people who *actually* donate them, which results in a frustrating situation where the organs and the desire to donate them are present in theory, but not in practice.[2] Thus, the law has to balance the need for further organs (and encouraging people to donate them) with an equal need to

---

[1] For centuries, so-called anthropophagic medicine played an important role, ranging from drinking an adversary's blood to making balms and lotions from the adipose tissue of the deceased, not to mention the use of human bodies and body parts for research and teaching throughout the history of mankind.

[2] See, e.g., Parliamentary Office of Science and Technology, *Organ Transplants* (Postnote 231, 2004), which can be downloaded at www.parliament.uk/business/publications/research/briefing-papers/POST-PN-231; and

protect the choices of those who do not wish to donate. On a related note, the law has to ensure that people who decide to donate are actually doing so because they want to, rather than because they feel compelled to. This coercion may take different forms, from a simple response to financial inducement (if someone *needs* the money she may consent for that reason rather than because she wants to) to believing that they have to consent given the help that they have already been offered by medical professionals (this would particularly be the case with patients in the NHS who are asked by their doctors whether they wish to donate organs). Finally for this non-exhaustive list, the law also has to contend with interactions not only between doctors and potential donors, but also between doctors and the relatives of those potential donors. Given that donation will in many cases occur straight after the death of the donor, this can lead to difficult situations, in particular where the donor has not made her wishes clear to the relatives.

The law also has to consider other uses of human tissue, such as that of research. Human biological material has increasingly become a matter of interest to many different types of research, in particular large-scale epidemiological studies such as UK Biobank. Such initiatives involve volunteers donating blood, urine, saliva and other samples and agreeing to 'provide detailed information about themselves and … have their health followed'.[3] Through this process, UK Biobank seeks to gather information 'with the aim of improving the prevention, diagnosis and treatment of a wide range of serious and life-threatening illnesses – including cancer, heart diseases, stroke, diabetes, arthritis, osteoporosis, eye disorders, depression and forms of dementia'.[4] The idea is to learn to distinguish better between conditions we develop on the basis of our lifestyle and conditions we develop on the basis of our genetic predisposition. For this purpose, this type of project (and UK Biobank is only an example – there are many across Europe and the world) needs to collect a large amount of samples and information from a large number of people and connect samples and information in a biobank – essentially a repository.

Needless to say, this project carries with it its own legal challenges, not least questions of ownership of body parts and tissue and consent. These issues, alongside questions regarding the use of organs for transplantation, are considered in this chapter because they both come under the remit of the Human Tissue Act 2004 (HTA 2004) and the regulatory framework that it creates. However, in order to fully understand the HTA 2004, it is necessary to know what the legislation was designed

---

E. Mossialos, J. Costa-Font and C. Rudisill, 'Does Organ Donation Legislation Affect Individuals' Willingness to Donate Their Own or Their Relative's Organs? Evidence from European Union Survey Data' (2008) 8 *Biomed. Central Health Services Research* 48.

[3] UK Biobank website at www.ukbiobank.ac.uk/about-biobank-uk/.　　[4] UK Biobank website.

to fix. In this case, it was an Act of Parliament designed as a specific response to weak legislation and some high-profile scandals involving retained body parts.

The inadequacies of the previous legislation, the Human Tissue Act 1961, were exposed by a slew of scandals in the 1990s and early 2000s.[5] The Kennedy Inquiry into infant cardiac surgery at Bristol Royal Infirmary in the 1990s found that organs were being taken from the dead infants for research purposes without the knowledge or consent of their parents.[6] Things took a turn for the worse when it was found by the Redfern Inquiry that this practice was also routinely adopted at the Alder Hey Children's Hospital in Liverpool, again without the knowledge or consent of parents in many cases.[7] A subsequent census ordered by the Chief Medical Officer found that, rather than this practice being limited to these two isolated cases, it was actually endemic in England and uncovered '54 000 organs, body parts, stillborn children, or fetuses that had been retained since 1970'.[8] This was widely thought to be unacceptable, but made possible by the then legislation, which was best described as 'a toothless tiger imposing fuzzy rules with no provisions for sanction or redress'.[9] This is for two main reasons. First, as Skegg notes, section 1(1) of the 1961 Act stated that if a person 'during his last illness' had expressed a request for parts of his or her body to be used for transplantation or research, the 'person lawfully in possession of the body' could authorise the removal of the organs post-mortem. However, it failed to provide a definition regarding who would be in 'lawful possession' of the body.[10] It was generally felt that if a person died in hospital, then the hospital would be in lawful possession.[11] Secondly, and perhaps even more perplexingly, although the 1961 Act specified conditions for the removal of organs and tissue, it never provided for any sanction for non-compliance (hence its toothlessness). Therefore, there was confusion regarding even fundamental questions such as whether any breach of the statute should be dealt with in the criminal or civil courts.[12] It was clear that any new Act would have to address these questions of control and compliance.

The resulting Human Tissue Act 2004 must, then, be seen for what it is: a specific response to perceived weaknesses in the previous statutory regime that allowed

---

[5] For general discussions of the background and the enactment of the 2004 Act, see K. Liddell and A. Hall, 'Beyond Bristol and Alder Hey: The Future Regulation of Human Tissue' (2005) 13 *Med. L. Rev.* 170; and D. Price, 'From Cosmos and Damien to Van Velzen: The Human Tissue Saga Continues' (2003) 11 *Med. L. Rev.* 1.

[6] See the *Bristol Inquiry Interim Report*, www.bristol-inquiry.org.uk/interim_report/annexb1.htm.

[7] *Royal Liverpool Children's Inquiry Report* (London: The Stationery Office, 2001).

[8] V. English, 'Presumed Consent for Transplantation: A Dead Issue After Alder Hey?' (2003) 29 *Journal of Medical Ethics* 147, 147. See Department of Health, *Report of a Census of Organs and Tissues Retained by Pathology Services in England* (London: The Stationery Office, 2001).

[9] M. Brazier, 'Organ Retention and Return: Problems of Consent' (2003) 29 *Journal of Medical Ethics* 30, 31.

[10] P. D. G. Skegg, *Law, Ethics and Medicine* (Oxford University Press, 1984).

[11] D. Lanham, 'Transplants and the Human Tissue Act 1961' (1971) 11 *Medicine, Science and the Law* 16.

[12] See I. Kennedy, 'Further Thoughts on Liability and the Human Tissue Act 1961' in I. Kennedy, *Treat Me Right: Essays on Medical Law and Ethics* (Oxford University Press, 1989).

medical scandals to take place. In particular, there were concerns relating to the lack of enforcement procedures and sanctions in the old law, and also that patient autonomy had not played a prominent role in the law. This was made clear by the then Secretary of State for Health, Alan Milburn, in 2001:

the law will be changed to enshrine the concept of informed consent. The existing law in this area has become outdated. *The Human Tissue Act 1961 does not even contain penalties for breaches of its provisions.* The law has ill served bereaved parents in our country and causes confusion for staff. It must be changed.[13]

What can therefore be seen in the new Act is designed to place the concepts of consent and accountability at the heart of the law. As we detail below, it has succeeded in that aim. It is also worth noting that the Human Tissue Act is also the United Kingdom's implementation of an EU directive (Directive 2004/23/EC on setting standards of quality and safety for the donation, procurement, testing, processing, preservation, storage and distribution of human tissues and cells). Given the impetus provided by the scandals outlined above, the Human Tissue Act came into being well before the deadline for implementation of the directive and goes above and beyond the requirements of the directive in that it also applies to uses for human tissue that are not therapeutic.

THE HUMAN TISSUE ACT 2004

The HTA 2004 received Royal Assent in late 2004, and came into force in 2006. It covers the removal, storage and use of human organs and what it terms 'relevant material'.[14] 'Relevant material' is defined in section 53(1) as 'material, other than gametes, which consists of or includes human cells', which means that it includes blood. Section 53(2) further specifies that 'relevant material' does not include human embryos outside the body or hair and nail from the body of a living person. The removal, storage and use of such materials may only occur for what the Act terms 'scheduled purposes', which are outlined in Schedule 1. Part 1 of Schedule 1 outlines the purposes for which organs and relevant material may be used, as long as appropriate consent has been obtained:

1. Anatomical examination.
2. Determining the cause of death.

---

[13] *Hansard*, 30 January 2001. The debate can be found at www.publications.parliament.uk/pa/cm200001/cmhansrd/vo010130/debtext/10130-06.htm. Emphasis added.

[14] An excellent summary of the Act can be found in M. Brazier and S. Fovargue, 'A Brief Guide to the Human Tissue Act 2004' (2006) 1(1) *Clinical Ethics* 26.

3. Establishing after a person's death the efficacy of any drug or other treatment administered to him.
4. Obtaining scientific or medical information about a living or deceased person which may be relevant to any other person (including a future person).
5. Public display.
6. Research in connection with disorders, or the functioning, of the human body.
7. Transplantation.

Schedule 1, Part 2 lists the purposes for which organs and relevant material *of deceased persons* may be used without consent:

8. Clinical audit.
9. Education or training relating to human health.
10. Performance assessment.
11. Public health monitoring.
12. Quality assurance.

Transplantation is listed in paragraph 7 as a scheduled purpose in Schedule 1, Part 1, and therefore organs may be removed, stored and used for this purpose under the Act, as long as the task is undertaken by a body that has been granted a licence to do so by the Human Tissue Authority (which we discuss below). The accountability requirement was easy to fix, and quite simply some sanctions have been included in the Act. Thus, under section 5(7), a person who does not comply with the Act commits a criminal offence and faces imprisonment for up to three years, a fine or both. The regulatory structure imposed by the 2004 Act is much the same as that accompanying the Human Fertilisation and Embryology Act, in that there is an 'authority' (in this case, the Human Tissue Authority) that regulates conduct. It does so by granting licences, and is backed up by a Code of Practice that allows for unexpected scientific developments and the maintenance of the Act as fit for purpose without constant revision and amendment.[15] Indeed, the two bodies are so similar in form and function that during the drafting of the Health and Social Care Bill in 2011 to 2012, there were proposals to merge the two.[16] The debate surrounding the scandals – which hinged on the medical professionals involved failing to respect the wishes of relatives – led to the Act's emphasis being on consent. This is where we begin our examination.

---

[15] There are currently nine Codes of Practice considering issues ranging from consent to public display. An up-to-date list can be found on the Human Tissue Authority's website at www.hta.gov.uk/legislationpoliciesandcodesofpractice/codesofpractice.cfm.
[16] A review regarding a possible merger was commissioned by the government and was due to report in April 2013. However, as of the time of writing, the report – by Justin McCracken, formerly of the Health Protection Agency – has not been published, although it has been submitted (as confirmed in the House of Lords by Earl Howe on 12 June: see *Hansard*, 12 June 2013, col. 1642).

'Appropriate consent'

The focus of the Act, however, is on consent, and Part 1 of the three-part Act is devoted to this issue. Indeed, none of the actions permitted by the Act may be performed without the existence of 'appropriate consent'. Sections 2 to 4 detail how appropriate consent may be obtained from children and adults. Children are first to be considered, under section 2. Section 2(2) provides that, if the child is competent to make his own decision, then the Act simply states that 'his consent' is required for a live organ donation to be made. This means that the organ may only be removed for transplantation if the child has given informed consent to the procedure (as defined by the common law). However, if the child is not competent to give consent (or, as section 2(3)(c) states, is 'competent to deal with that issue ... but fails to do so'), then someone with parental responsibility may do so on behalf of the child. Essentially, this is no different from the rules relating to consent for minors in the common law, although whether it would be advisable for an organ to be removed for transplant on the basis of consent by the parents and notwithstanding a refusal of consent by the minor is questionable. There is certainly good evidence that, in terms of medical ethics, the dissent of a minor ought to generally be respected even in instances where that minor might not be in a position to give valid positive consent. We will return to this issue in more detail in the discussion of the ethical aspects below.

For minors who have died, section 2(7)(a) states that 'appropriate consent' means the consent of the minor as long as 'a decision of his to consent to the activity, or a decision of his not to consent to it, was in force immediately before he died'. If the child had made no decision, or was not competent to do so, then someone with parental responsibility would be able to make it on the child's behalf (section 2(7)(b)(i)). If there is no such person, or they are unavailable, the consent of a person in a 'qualifying relationship' with the child may be sought (section 2(7)(b)(ii)). We discuss 'qualifying relationships' later in this section. We can therefore see a three-pronged structure for obtaining consent from a minor. If the child is competent, they may provide consent themselves. If not, or if they cannot do so, then someone with parental responsibility may consent on their behalf. If there is nobody with parental responsibility, then a person in a qualifying relationship will suffice. The law therefore attempts to balance the requirement for consent with the socially desirable result of increasing the numbers of donations by providing various avenues for the treatment team to obtain consent. This approach is replicated for adults.

Appropriate consent for adults is covered by section 3. For living donors, the situation is simple: appropriate consent means the consent of the donor (section 3(2)). If the donor is dead, then things are more complicated. Under section 3(6)(a), consent given (or refused) just prior to death may be taken as a valid consent or refusal of consent. If there is no such decision made, then just as with minors there is a structure available for surrogate decision-making. First, the donor may have appointed one or more nominated representatives to make decisions on her behalf. The process of doing so is set out in section 4 of the HTA 2004, and provides that an appointment may be made in relation to some or all decisions for which appropriate consent is required (section 4(1) to (2)). Unless otherwise stated, if there is more than one representative nominated, they may act both jointly and severally (which begs the question of what the hospital might choose to do in the case of fundamental disagreement between two representatives). Under section 3(6)(b)(ii), then, if the donor cannot give consent, the nominated representatives can then do so on her behalf.

If there is no nominated representative, or they are not available (section 3(7)), then consent may be given by someone in a qualifying relationship under section 3(6)(c). Given the fact that these qualifying relationships are used for both minors and adults, and that they constitute a form of surrogate decision-making where the donor has not authorised that such decision-making may take place, this is an important issue, which we now turn to examine.

'Qualifying relationships'

As mentioned above, consent will only be sought from those in qualifying relationships to the potential donor if the donor has not indicated his wishes himself, and if he has not nominated a representative. The concept of 'qualifying relationships' allows the treatment team another opportunity to find someone to consent on the donor's behalf. The theory is simple: people in such relationships will best know the potential donor and are most likely to know whether he would have wanted to consent. The chosen method of achieving this under the Act has been to create a list of relationships under section 27(4):

(a) spouse or partner;
(b) parent or child;
(c) brother or sister;
(d) grandparent or grandchild;
(e) child of a person falling within paragraph (c);
(f) stepfather or stepmother;
(g) half-brother or half-sister;
(h) friend of longstanding.

This list is designed to be hierarchical, so those seeking consent must first seek out someone in paragraph (a). If, and only if, they are not reasonably contactable, or refuse to make a decision, will it be permissible then to move on and attempt to contact someone in paragraph (b). Needless to say, the decision of the person asked must be respected – in other words, if the spouse refuses consent, then that refusal must be respected, and it is not permissible to then ask the potential donor's child for their consent to seek a different answer. Although perhaps superficially attractive, this system is, as we highlight below, somewhat simplistic.

'Appropriate consent' in the Act – fit for purpose?

As we noted at the beginning of this chapter, the challenge for the law is to balance the need to encourage donation of organs with one to respect the autonomy of the potential donor – particularly given the circumstances that convinced the government to create the legislation in the first place. What we find here, however, could be seen as being something of an uneasy compromise. Indeed, what we see with the requirement for appropriate consent is a situation where the legislation introduces layer upon layer of regulations in an attempt to ensure as much as possible that, if the patient might have wished to consent, that consent will be discovered. Nevertheless, perhaps as a consequence of the scandals, this encouragement is somewhat undermined by the Code of Practice. Code of Practice 1 (out of five) covers consent. While it does acknowledge that if the potential donor, her nominated representative or someone in a qualifying relationship has consented to donating an organ it would be legal to do so under the Act, it counsels caution in relation to actually doing so. Thus, paragraph 76 provides that in a difficult situation:

> The emphasis in these difficult situations should be placed on having an open and sensitive discussion with those close to the deceased where the process is explained fully to them. Healthcare professionals should also consider the impact of going ahead with a procedure in light of strong opposition from the family, despite the legal basis for doing so.[17]

It is generally thought that, in the context of organ donation, a treatment team will likely not go against the wishes of the relatives even where clear and express consent from the deceased donor is identifiable. This is generally for pragmatic reasons, but also out of a clear prioritisation of the element of trust in the donation process, which would be eroded by enforced explantations.

While, in the light of Bristol, Alder Hey and the retained organs scandal it is difficult to argue with the notion that the medical profession should err on the side of *not* taking organs if in doubt, there does seem to be something of an over-reluctance to remove an organ if *anyone* objects strongly. Needless to say, this will not be conducive to gathering as many organs as donors would wish to donate.

---

[17] Human Tissue Authority, *Code of Practice 1 – Consent* (HTA, 2009). It can be found at www.hta.gov.uk/legislationpoliciesandcodesofpractice/codesofpractice/code1consent.cfm?FaArea1=customwidgets.content_view_1&cit_id=666&cit_parent_cit_id=652.

The many different avenues for obtaining consent, as outlined above, are most certainly a hybrid of the regulations' aims to ensure strong consent (as a result of the scandals) while at the same time maximising donation rates.

A further issue relates to the operation of obtaining consent from those in qualifying relationships. As we highlight above, these are hierarchical in nature, so that if those in paragraph (a) refuse consent, those seeking consent must accept that and cannot attempt to gain it from someone in paragraph (b).[18] However, for this to be justifiable it assumes that the hierarchy of relationships accurately reflects that in the potential donor's life. The list in section 27(4) takes no account of the fact that the donor might be estranged from certain people. The most obvious example is that parents are included in paragraph (b), while step-parents are much lower down the list in paragraph (f). If, for example, a parent left when the child was very young and did not maintain contact with the family, it is surely incongruous that that person's opinion will take priority over that of the person who effectively raised the donor and will know their wishes best. Furthermore, it is surely the case in such circumstances that the donor would *wish* the step-parent to be consulted before the biological parent. In other words, the Act imposes a relationship hierarchy that is assumed rather than actually reflective of the life of the potential donor. Given the professed concentration on autonomy and consent in the Act, this is unfortunate. This is partially acknowledged in the Code of Practice, but no real solution is offered:

> While the HT Act is clear about the hierarchy of consent, the person giving consent should be encouraged to discuss the decision with other family members – this may include people not on the list, for example, an aunt or uncle.

So, while it should be acknowledged that the HTA 2004 is certainly an improvement on its predecessors, this is not to say that it is perfect. Indeed, just as it is clearly a direct response to the scandals that caused its creation, it might also be argued that the problems within it – and in particular the somewhat inconsistent response to the consent requirements – stem from precisely the same factors.

Incapable adults

Where an adult lacks capacity, any decision to undergo a procedure with the aim of donating organs or material to another person will be subject to the provisions of the Mental Capacity Act 2005. This means that an advance refusal to consent to a donation must be respected, as must decisions made by someone granted lasting power of attorney by the adult in question (although it will be remembered that such decisions are subject to the patient's best interests). Failing this, however, the

---

[18] See also the *Code of Practice 1*, para. 84, which reinforces this point.

Mental Capacity Act's Code of Practice provides that decisions relating to incapable adults donating organs or bone marrow come under the heading of decisions that are 'so serious that the court has to make them', and thus should be referred to the Court of Protection.[19] This means that a donation of this sort may only be authorised if it is in the patient's best interests to do so.

There have been no post-Mental Capacity Act 2005 cases relating to organ donation by incompetent adults so far, but there is one pre-Act authority relating to bone marrow donation. In *Re. Y (Mental Patient: Marrow Donation)*, the court had to consider whether it was in the best interests of a woman who could not give informed consent to donate bone marrow to her sister, who might otherwise die.[20] The problem was that the donation would primarily benefit the donee, with no physical benefit to the donor. Connell J. authorised the procedure, utilising a creative approach to best interests, which he defined widely. Drawing on US authority (*Curran* v. *Bosze* – albeit concerning children), the judge held that benefit might be found in the relationship between the donor and her family.[21] Connell J. therefore quoted Calvo J. in *Curran*, stating that the mere relationship might suffice in satisfying the best interests requirement:

> The evidence clearly shows that there is no physical benefit to a donor child. If there is any benefit to a child who donates bone marrow to a sibling it will be a psychological benefit. According to the evidence, the psychological benefit is not simply one of personal, individual altruism in an abstract theoretical sense, although that may be a factor. The psychological benefit is grounded firmly in the fact that the donor and recipient are known to each other as family. Only where there is an existing relationship between a healthy child and his or her ill sister or brother may a psychological benefit to the child from donating bone marrow to a sibling realistically be found to exist. The evidence establishes that it is the existing sibling relationship, as well as the potential for a continuing sibling relationship, which forms the context in which it may be determined that it will be in the best interests of the child to undergo a bone marrow harvesting procedure for a sibling.[22]

However, Connell J. had to go even further than Calvo J. had done, as the situation in *Re. Y* was different. This is because in *Re. Y* the sisters were not close to each other – the donor's close relationship was with their mother. Thus, Connell J. could not rely on the closeness of the parties, and had to be more creative. He did this by arguing that, were the donation not to proceed, the donor's relationship with her mother would be affected by the death of the donee. This was particularly the case as the donor's mother would then have to look after the donee's daughter:

---

[19] DCA, *Mental Capacity Act Code of Practice* (DCA, 2007), para. 6.18 (available at http://webarchive.nationalarchives.gov.uk/+/http://www.dca.gov.uk/legal-policy/mental-capacity/mca-cp.pdf).

[20] *Re. Y (Mental Patient: Marrow Donation)* [1997] Fam 110. See also an Australian case with similar facts of the same year: *Re. GWW and CMW* [1997] 21 Fam LR 612.

[21] *Curran* v. *Bosze* 566 NE 2d 1319 (Ill 1990).   [22] *Curran* v. *Bosze* at 1343–4, quoted in *Re. Y* at 114.

In this situation, the defendant would clearly be harmed by the reduction in or loss of contact with her mother. Accordingly, it is to the benefit of the defendant that she should act as donor to her sister, because in this way her positive relationship with her mother is most likely to be prolonged. Further, if the transplant occurs, this is likely to improve the defendant's relationship with her mother who in her heart clearly wishes it to take place and also to improve her relationship with the plaintiff who will be eternally grateful to her.[23]

In our view, this case stretches the concept of best interests beyond breaking point – it is not even that the donor would suffer by extension if the donee died, but would do so because their mother would do so. Indeed, the case has been criticised for this.[24] Nevertheless, it demonstrates the way in which the courts can interpret the concept of best interests in a creative fashion to achieve a desired result.

But could this be replicated with organ donation after the Mental Capacity Act? The first thing to note is that in *Re. Y* Connell J. was explicit in his view that the judgment he gave should not be used as a precedent for 'more intrusive' procedures, which organ donation certainly would be.[25] So in theory even under *Re. Y* organ donation might not be applicable (although that is not to say that it might not be if the relationship between the parties was more direct, such as if the donee was the mother herself). In terms of the Mental Capacity Act, as we argued in Chapter 5, the definition of best interests is phrased in language that is far from unequivocal and certainly leaves much room for interpretation. Nevertheless, one segment of the Code of Practice does stand out as particularly pertinent. In demonstrating that when defining best interests decision-makers should be aware that they may only consider the best interests of *the individual concerned*, the Code provides an example of this:

Pedro, a young man with a severe learning disability, lives in a care home. He has dental problems which cause him a lot of pain, but refuses to open his mouth for his teeth to be cleaned. The staff suggest that it would be a good idea to give Pedro an occasional general anaesthetic so that a dentist can clean his teeth and fill any cavities. His mother is worried about the effects of an anaesthetic, but she hates to see him distressed and suggests instead that he should be given strong painkillers when needed. While the views of Pedro's mother and carers are important in working out what course of action would be in his best interests, the decision must not be based on what would be less stressful for them. Instead, it must focus on Pedro's best interests.[26]

This would, we suggest, make it even more difficult to justify a decision to remove biological material such as an organ or tissue from an incapable adult with at best tangential benefit for that individual. Nevertheless, it remains to be seen how the

---

[23] *Re. Y* at 115.
[24] See, e.g., E. Wicks, 'The Greater Good – Issues of Proportionality and Democracy in the Doctrine of Necessity as Applied in *Re A*' (2003) 32 *Common Law World Review* 15, 25–7.
[25] *Re. Y* at 116. This taxonomy of invasiveness was mirrored in the Australian case *Re. GWW and CMW*.
[26] *Mental Capacity Act Code of Practice* (DCA, 2007), p. 69.

courts will resolve such issues and, as we mention above, there is certainly sufficient 'wriggle room' in the Act's definition of best interests for a case such as *Re. Y* to be decided in the same way again. Indeed, the substituted judgment elements of the factors might be held to provide the justification needed to allow the procedure.

OTHER USES OF ORGANS AND TISSUE, BIOBANKING, TISSUE BANKING – LEGAL ASPECTS

As we have seen at the outset, there are other uses for human biological material. Such material might be explanted and stored for future therapeutic use (i.e. in terms of a transplantation). It may also be of particular significance for biomedical research. In this latter case, material obtained from patients or research participants is linked to health information about that person and stored. Generally, the larger the number of samples and data sets in such a repository, the more significant the epidemiological value of the repository. These projects are generally referred to as 'biobanks' and they represent one of the most important contemporary biomedical research tools. An example of such a large-scale epidemiological biobanking project is UK Biobank, where researchers are collecting a very large number of samples, associated health information and ongoing medical data in order to pinpoint whether certain conditions are lifestyle-based or genetically predetermined. As the UK Biobank website explains, samples are taken with:

the aim of improving the prevention, diagnosis and treatment of a wide range of serious and life-threatening illnesses – including cancer, heart diseases, stroke, diabetes, arthritis, osteoporosis, eye disorders, depression and forms of dementia. UK Biobank recruited 500,000 people aged between 40–69 years in 2006–2010 from across the country to take part in this project. They have undergone measures, provided blood, urine and saliva samples for future analysis, detailed information about themselves and agreed to have their health followed. Over many years this will build into a powerful resource to help scientists discover why some people develop particular diseases and others do not.[27]

In ethical terms, the project is controversial, and for that reason it shall be discussed in more length in the ethical analysis in this chapter. With regard to the legality of the project, there are fewer controversies. The storage and use of the samples are legal as long as the premises have a licence from the Human Tissue Authority and the provisions and limitations contained in the HTA 2004 are complied with. The main issue is that of informed consent. Volunteers are asked to provide what is

---

[27] See www.ukbiobank.ac.uk/about-biobank-uk/.

essentially a blanket consent with respect to the use of the samples that they donate, not least because UK Biobank cannot anticipate exactly what they will be used for during what is intended to be a long-term project.[28] However, even this causes more ethical than legal problems, since if the donor agrees to provide the wide consent sought, and can withdraw it at any time, the law is satisfied (largely due to the fact that the Act's engagement with the *quality* of consent sought is quite superficial and not representative of the controversial debate in medical ethics – see section 3(2): appropriate consent means consent).[29]

CONCLUDING REMARKS ON LAW

What we can see here is that the HTA 2004 is very much a product of its history, in that it is a specific response to specific scandals. The subsequent implementation requirement for European Directive 2004/23/EC was forestalled by Parliament's response to the Bristol and Alder Hey scandals and the Act therefore also goes significantly above and beyond the requirements of the European norms. The balance that it seeks to achieve between protecting the rights of patients and ensuring (if not increasing) the rates of organ and tissue donation is perhaps an impossible one. Nevertheless, the Act does the job of closing this previous law's oversights and walking the tightrope as well as it can be expected to. This is another topic where the rapid rate of technological development makes it incredibly difficult for the law to keep pace.[30] Indeed, the issue of biobanks is an example of the sort of challenge that requires legislation to be both flexible and based on sound principles. The Human Tissue Authority and the regulatory framework imagined therein is, again, a sensible method of achieving this.

---

[28] For more information regarding the current consent provisions, see the 'UK Biobank Ethics and Governance Framework' (2007), pp. 5–6, www.ukbiobank.ac.uk/wp-content/uploads/2011/05/EGF20082.pdf?phpMyAdmin=trmKQlYdjjnQIgJ%2CfAzikMhEnx6. See also T. Caulfield and J. Kaye, 'Broad Consent in Biobanking: Reflections on Seemingly Insurmountable Dilemmas' (2009) 10 *Medical Law International* 85; T. Caulfield, 'Biobanks and Blanket Consent: The Proper Place of the Public Good and Public Perception Rationales' (2007) 18 *King's Law Journal* 209.

[29] See M. Sheehan, 'Can Broad Consent Be Informed Consent?' (2011) 4(3) *Public Health Ethics* 226. See also, e.g., M. Hansson *et al.*, 'Should Donors Be Allowed to Give Broad Consent to Future Biobank Research?' (2006) 7(3) *The Lancet Oncology* 266. For good general discussions, see S. Gibbons, 'Regulating Biobanks: A Twelve Point Typological Tool' (2009) 17(3) *Med. L. Rev.* 313; E. Rial-Sebbag and A. Cambon-Thomsen, 'The Emergence of Biobanks in the Legal Landscape: Towards a New Model of Governance' (2012) 39(1) *Journal of Law and Society* 113.

[30] For further reading on fast-moving regulatory targets, see R. Brownsword and K. Yeung (eds.), *Regulating Technologies – Legal Futures, Regulatory Frames and Technological Fixes* (Oxford: Hart, 2008).

ETHICS

The complexities of making organs and tissues available for therapeutic and research use raise a number of interesting legal issues as well as connected ethical issues. In this chapter, we have so far outlined the most prominent legal issues and how the law attempts to deal with them. The fact that much of the current law in England and Wales flows from a spate of scandals surrounding the inappropriate use of human body parts (remember that these uses were not technically illegal) makes this a particularly interesting area in terms of identifying and analysing the ethical issues: after all, it was the general public's *moral* outrage that triggered the development of the current law. This context may therefore be a good example of public moral intuition leading to policy-making, which in turn shapes our legal system – law following ethics.

Some of the ethical issues have already been pointed out above. They can be broadly categorised into individual issues and societal issues, with some overlap between them. The individual issues centre on questions of autonomy in relation to disposing of one's own body and its parts; decision-making by others; the protection of individuals' choices (regardless of whether the choice is for or against donation) and issues of inducement and commodification. The societal issues revolve around inducement and commodification, encouraging donation and enabling biomedical research, resource allocation and trust in research.

From a fundamental point of view, the question centres on whether it is at all morally permissible to 'use' the human body. This issue must be taken seriously when addressing settings such as living donation, where the physical integrity of a healthy volunteer is impaired. The issue is less pressing when dealing with a deceased donor. In this latter context, much hinges on when we think of an individual as dead. The classic concept of cardiovascular death (i.e. the heart stops beating and the blood flow ceases) is not particularly helpful when addressing organ transplantation, as a reasonably transplantable organ needs to be circulated as long as possible. Most jurisdictions have enshrined concepts of brain death or brain stem death, which permit the declaration of death at a point in time where the body is still circulated with oxygenated blood (we address the question of how death is diagnosed in Chapter 11). This has led some commentators to contend that the individual in question is not dead, but dying, at the point when the organs are taken, which in turn raises significant ethical issues. As it seems clear from the evidence that the degeneration of brain function can be shown to pass a 'point of no return' at some stage, we feel that while it would be technically incorrect to deny that death is a process rather than a distinct point in time, the debate around the legitimacy of brain (stem) death is moot. If it is accepted that transplantation medicine is a socially desirable activity, the focus must turn to how this activity can be performed within a framework of moral permissibility, rather than questioning the entire activity on the basis of individual abusive practices.

Transplantation has a long history. The first attempts to graft other people's body parts onto a person lie in antiquity, and generally making use of biological material has an extensive tradition. The questions before us here have therefore featured in literature and discourse in ethics for a considerable time. Much of the debate has its epicentre in the question of whether the human body should at all be at our disposal for purposes other than to provide a vessel for the individual. Immanuel Kant, the influential eighteenth-century German philosopher, is representative for a moral perspective that firmly places the human body in a category of its own, removing it from the realm of the mere movable object that can be treated as any other movable object. He raises a number of objections to this, one being a conceptual one:

Man cannot dispose over himself because he is not a thing; he is not his own property; to say that he is would be self-contradictory; for insofar as he is a person he is a Subject in whom the ownership of things can be vested, and if he were his own property he would be a thing over which he could have ownership. But a person cannot be a property and so cannot be a thing which can be owned, for it is impossible to be a person and a thing, the proprietor and the property.[31]

Kant makes no distinction between the individual and her body.[32] Disposing over one's body and its parts (for example, by giving a kidney to a relative) would therefore be a paradox transaction, as the 'gift' and the 'giver' are identical, although it seems clear that he is also struggling with the limitations of language when describing his objection. The flaw in this particular line of reasoning might lie in Kant's simplistic view of the mechanics of contracts (in a very broad sense). There seems to be no conceptual problem with a party to a contract playing more than one role (in some circumstances a party can contract with itself) and it is not immediately clear why, therefore, a party cannot make contractual arrangements that pertain to its physical entity (think of employment contracts). It is clear that Kant means something else. He elaborates elsewhere and concentrates on the mechanics of using the human body for a purpose other than simply housing the individual: 'So act as to treat humanity, whether in thine own person or in that of any other, in every case as an end withal, never as a means only.'[33]

---

[31] I. Kant, *Lectures on Ethics*, P. Heath (trans.) (Cambridge University Press, 2001), p. 157.
[32] Unlike his sixteenth-century predecessor, René Descartes, whom he criticises, who introduces a famous dualism between individual and body. See also A. Ripstein, *Force and Freedom: Kant's Legal and Political Philosophy* (Cambridge University Press, 2009), p. 177.
[33] I. Kant, *Fundamental Principles of the Metaphysic of Morals [1785]*, T. K. Abbott (trans.) (Buffalo, NY: Prometheus, 1988), p. 58.

The idea here, and we can find this idea entrenched in many commentators' views of using the human body as a resource, is that the human body is something special – and this means keeping it outside the realm we have ordinarily created for movable objects in our real world. What neither the Kantian view nor these commentators provide us with is a plausible reason why that should be the case. The reasons in the past debates vary from fundamentally religious notions to pragmatic ones. Thomas Hobbes, for example, needs the notion of the sanctity of the individual's life to justify his almost dystopic premise of individuals being locked in a no-holds-barred fight for survival and the consequent absence of super-positive ethical norms.[34] John Locke, while strongly advocating the presence of super-positive ethical norms, puts the same view of the body on a solid religious footing, almost going so far as saying that to destroy or interfere with one's own body amounts to an interference with God's property rights.[35] Both approach the subject from the point of view of a prohibition of suicide, but also include in this any alteration or erosion of the individual's ability to fend for herself.

Modern commentators take the approach of wondering whether an increased availability of the human body would automatically lead to exploitation.[36] There are some plausible objections to this argument, of which two are particularly notable: first, the mere possibility that an activity might also result in exploitation does not mean that we automatically prohibit this activity. It merely means that there ought to be a balancing exercise for the risks and benefits associated with the activity and appropriate safeguards should be put in place. It is possible to think of many activities in modern society that give rise to questions of exploitation – few of them are prohibited outright, most are simply regulated. Secondly, the argument that exploitation might be the result and that the scope and consequences of that are unclear essentially amounts to a so-called 'slippery slope argument'. This view contends that the mere unforeseeability of the harm means that the activity is not ethically justifiable, as terrible consequences might flow from it and once started on the course of action in question, we would be unable to stop it. This type of argument is legitimately criticised for its inherent resistance to any empirical counter-argument: it does not (and cannot) base its contention on empirical knowledge about our world and a discussion is therefore difficult, if not impossible. This, in many scholars' view, places the slippery slope argument outside the range of permissible discursive tools. We strongly endorse this view.

The issues we are dealing with here therefore revolve around one central point, which is intuitively plausible: the human body is special and we need special rules to protect the vessel and its helmsman (or woman). This protection is clear and

---

[34] T. Hobbes, *Leviathan* (London: Penguin, 1982).
[35] J. Locke, *Second Treatise on Government* (Indianapolis, IN: Hackett Publishing, 1980).
[36] See, e.g., S. Wilkinson, *Bodies for Sale: Ethics and Exploitation in the Human Body Trade* (London: Routledge, 2003).

unequivocal in instances where the organ or tissue in question is still connected to the individual and that individual is still alive. Any removal would result in physical harm to the integrity of the individual, which in almost all cases is unacceptable. This means that the questions before us arise at a subsequent stage. Before moving on to the question of how medical ethics views and discusses the issues raised by organ and tissue transplantation, it is therefore worth noting that there are conceptual thresholds in this context of which we need to be aware: many of the questions discussed in this chapter only come into existence where the material in question (the organ or tissue) has been separated from the donor. Before this point, the fact that the material is a part of the donor means that it is generally unavailable. Both legal and moral arguments draw a narrow space within which separating these materials from the body is acceptable and the lawfulness of the separation plays a role in whether the material can then be used in the desired way.

The significant distinction that we need to bear in mind here lies in whether the material is from a living or a post-mortem donor. It is fairly obvious that this has an impact on the question of consent, but the distinction also plays a role in discussing the fundamental question of dignity when using the individual's body. From a practical perspective, there is also a technical issue in relation to tissue harvesting. While in the post-mortem context organs for transplantation can in almost all cases only ever be harvested from an individual who has died in an intensive care setting, tissue harvesting can be performed even in cases where the individual has died elsewhere and there has been complete cessation of cardiovascular activity for some time. This, in theory, expands the scope for tissue availability, but the flip-side is that there is a tendency to apportion potential donors in the intensive care setting either to organ donation or to tissue donation. We will return to the significance of this point below. In order to systematically address the ethical issues in this setting, we will initially look at the overall considerations in relation to autonomy and liberty (building on what we have written in Chapter 4). We will then identify the questions specific to material taken from a deceased donor, before looking at those that distinguish the living donor, and issues at a 'societal' level such as encouraging donation, respecting the decision-making of individuals and resource allocation.

Issues of autonomy

As with all other areas of medical law, the subject matter of organ and tissue transplantation revolves around ensuring that the concerned individuals' autonomy is respected. The question of what can be done with an individual's body raises interesting new questions: in particular, can we do with our bodies what we want, or are there limits? Surely, if autonomy is the decisive parameter, the capable and informed individual ought to be able to do what he wants. In fact, society does draw a line somewhere. We can take the example of Eric Lubbock, the fourth Baron of Avebury, as an illustration: Lord Avebury is a Liberal Democrat peer who has been a member of the House of Lords since 1971. In 1987, it was reported that he had suggested that after his death he would like for his body to be turned into dog food for the benefit of Battersea Dogs' Home.[37] This, as you might imagine, caused something of a stir and there was a very public debate about what we can, or cannot, do with our own bodies after death. Another frequently cited example is that of the philosopher Jeremy Bentham, who succeeded in ensuring that his body is preserved for posterity by asking his best friend (who was also his doctor) to embalm him. He had himself put on display in a glass case (he called this his 'auto icon'). His mummified body, clad in his own clothes (and, after expectable degeneration, equipped with a wax head), is being kept at University College London and is occasionally brought into meetings where the minutes record him as 'present but not voting'.[38]

Both of these cases, and quite possibly our reaction to hearing of them for the first time, show us one thing clearly: what happens to individuals' bodies after death is not trivial, but raises numerous emotionally charged issues. Why is this the case? Surely, after our death, the person that was there originally is no longer present – merely the lifeless shell. That lifeless shell is just an object and no longer a living human being who can suffer from maltreatment or whose rights can be trespassed upon. There is certainly no consensus on this issue, with many medical ethics commentators giving strong opinions for and against the free disposability of the body.[39] Some argue that there is a sustained respect for the individual whose body is now all that is left, and that this sustained respect (sometimes linked to the idea that there is a surviving sense of dignity about a deceased person) imposes obligations when dealing with the body. What seems clear is that this is an area where moral issues play an important role and decisions in relation to using, or not using, a deceased's body have a strong ethical component.

Deceased donors

We regulate for the type of decision we might want to make for a time after we are no longer able to make decisions by way of some *inter vivos* provision. A classic

---

[37] N. Hoppe, *Bioequity – Property and the Human Body* (Aldershot: Ashgate, 2009), p. 83.

[38] See www.chem.ucl.ac.uk/resources/history/chemhistucl/hist03.html.

[39] For an overview, see D. Dickenson, *Property in the Body: Feminist Perspectives* (Cambridge University Press, 2007); and N. Hoppe, *Bioequity – Property and the Human Body* (Aldershot: Ashgate, 2009); and M. Quigley, *Self-Ownership, Property Rights, and the Human Body* (Cambridge University Press, forthcoming).

example is that of a simple will, in which we make provisions about how our property might be disposed of after our death. Another such example is that of an organ donor card, which essentially represents a documentation of ex ante consent for our organs and/or tissue to be taken for certain specified purposes after our death (usually for the purposes of helping others, sometimes – such as in the case of body donations – for research purposes). Once we have died, it is up to others to ensure our wishes are respected. This raises interesting situations of conflict where an individual may have decided that she wants to be an organ donor, but the relatives object. Legally, it seems sensible to say that the deceased individual is no longer a person in the legal sense (and therefore not a carrier of (many) rights) and the relatives are persons (and therefore carriers of rights). The relatives can still interact meaningfully with others in a legal sense, whereas the deceased individual cannot. In a pragmatic, and possibly slightly cynical, sense – it is legally much more hazardous for a clinician to disrespect grieving but living relatives than the wishes of a deceased individual.

In the absence of positive law that confers rights on an individual which survive that individual's death, for example in the same way as property dispositions in a will are enforced by law even though the testatrix is no longer around, there is no good legal argument to permit the deceased's wishes to have any effect. There is, however, a moral viewpoint which suggests that there ought to be a healthy measure of respect for the deceased, and respect for her wishes. This can be explained by way of treasuring the memory of the deceased as well as by way of not wishing to cause irritation to surviving relatives. The result is that there is a plausible suggestion that the dignity of an individual does not necessarily disappear automatically with her death.[40]

Our respect for this dignity is signified by the many rituals we have in terms of saying farewell to a deceased person, none of which would be socially necessary or economically sensible if we simply regarded corpses as biohazardous waste material. At the same time, there is a balance that we need to tread to address the fact that the individual in question is no longer a holder of rights: there are instances where respecting his dignity may in fact be in conflict with the welfare of a living individual or legitimate aims of society. There are a number of concepts that seek to address the balance between society's requirements and respect for an individual's *inter vivos* wishes. Some jurisdictions have established classic opt-in systems for organ donation, which are thought to best reflect the desire to respect the

---

[40] In fact, some jurisdictions have enshrined this concept in their interpretation of fundamental rights. In Germany, there is a doctrine which stipulates that, as time passes, an individual's personality rights become weaker, but they still prevail over death initially. For an overview, see E. Klein, 'Human Dignity in German Law' in D. Kretzner and E. Klein, *The Concept of Human Dignity in Human Rights Discourse* (The Hague: Kluwer Law International, 2002), pp. 145–59.

individual's wishes. Opt-in systems require potential donors to have made arrangements during their lifetime to ensure that it is known that their organs can be taken. In the absence of appropriate documentation of this desire, the organs are out of bounds. Narrow opt-in systems foresee that the donor himself must have made and expressed these wishes. Broad opt-in systems also permit that relatives express what the donor would have wanted.

Opt-out systems, such as those in use in Austria or in Spain, confer more responsibility on the individual to make choices. These systems work on the basis that one should express dissent during one's lifetime or there is a presumption that the organs are available for transplantation. The Austrian system is a narrow system, where the views of relatives are (technically) not taken into account, whereas the Spanish system is broader and does take them into account.[41] In reality, it is safe to assume that even in Austria, the relatives' views are factored into clinical decision-making. Germany, where by and large a broad opt-in-style system has been in use for many years, has now adapted to a choice-based system. This means that all adults are at some stage asked to make a choice for or against being a donor by their health insurance companies. In the absence of a choice being made, the individual is treated as though they had opted against being a donor.

A slightly more outlandish system under discussion (but not being practised) is that of conscription.[42] In this system, there is no opt-in or opt-out – everyone's organs are simply available for transplantation. John Harris expands this concept on the basis that there is a moral duty to make one's body available after death:

> Indeed it seems clear that the benefits from cadaver transplants are so great, and the harms done in going against the wishes of those who object so comparatively small, that we should remove altogether the habit of seeking the consent of either the deceased or relatives. This would be another example of a small but significant class of public goods, participation in which is mandatory.[43]

A weaker version of this system is where we permit the taking of an organ against the prior wishes of a deceased individual or their family where we have an identified recipient whose life might be saved this way.[44] This latter approach has much in common with the common law defence of necessity, but also represents a balancing exercise which smacks of a utilitarian approach: weighing the dignity of a deceased against the life of one or more patients.

---

[41] Organ Donation, Statements: 'Opt in or Opt Out', updated November 2012, www.organdonation.nhs.uk/newsroom/statements_and_stances/statements/opt_in_or_out.asp.

[42] A. Spital, 'Conscription of Cadaveric Organs for Transplantation: Time to Start Talking about It' (2006) 70(3) *Kidney International* 607.

[43] J. Harris, 'Organ Procurement: Dead Interests, Living Needs' (2003) 29(3) *Journal of Medical Ethics* 130.

[44] N. Hoppe, 'A Sense of Entitlement: Individual vs. Public Interest in Human Tissue' in C. Lenk *et al.* (eds.), *Biobanks and Tissue Research: The Public, the Patient and the Regulation* (Heidelberg: Springer, 2011), p. 53.

The living donor

Living donation of organs (such as parts of one's liver or one of our kidneys) raises interesting additional questions. As the donor is now an active stakeholder (rather than simply a passive provider of material) she will also interact with other stakeholders meaningfully and her own rights are of particular concern. The donation of an organ is still a surgical procedure that carries the classic surgical risks. In the case of donating a kidney, there is also the additional risk of the one remaining kidney failing and the donor herself becoming a patient in need of a transplanted organ. This means that the balancing of risks and benefits becomes particularly significant here, and we need to bear in mind that the donor is putting her own future health at risk.

This brings to the fore questions in relation to her motives when donating organs or material. There is an assumption that this constellation (live donor and live recipient in the context of a scarce and life-saving resource) is particularly vulnerable to practices of exploitation and undue inducements. Many jurisdictions have stipulated that in order for an organ to be given to someone else, there ought to be a relationship of proximity between donor and recipient (to avoid a market for organs to develop, where matched organs are simply offered to the highest bidder). It is widely assumed that offering financial compensation for parts of the body is wrong, as it commodifies the human body, i.e. converts it from being the special entity that we identified it as at the outset to a commodity that can be traded. Prohibitions of commercialisation can be found in numerous laws, instruments and guidelines. The preamble of the Human Tissue Directive (2004/23/EC) states thus:

As a matter of principle, tissue and cell application programmes should be founded on the philosophy of voluntary and unpaid donation, anonymity of both donor and recipient, altruism of the donor and solidarity between donor and recipient.[45]

Words such as 'voluntariness', 'donation', 'altruism' and 'solidarity' characterise the discussion in this regard. Above and beyond the broad rejection of making human tissue and organs into a commodity, and of preventing exploitative practices, the Directive also cites health and safety concerns:

Voluntary and unpaid tissue and cell donations are a factor which may contribute to high safety standards for tissues and cells and therefore to the protection of human health.[46]

It is fair to say that this quote may well simply be a reflection (and a repetition) of a fundamental tenet of EU regulatory competence, intended to lend legitimacy to

---

[45] Directive 2004/23/EC of 31 March 2004 on setting standards of quality and safety for the donation, procurement, testing, processing, preservation, storage and distribution of human tissues and cells, [2004] OJ L102, 7 April 2004, Preamble, para. 18.
[46] Directive 2004/23/EC, Preamble, para. 19.

what essentially amounts to top-down European regulation of domestic health systems.

Encouraging donation and respecting autonomy

We have seen that transplantation, as a clinical option, is a desirable activity. The transplantation of organs saves the lives and improves the health of thousands of people every year.[47] Encouraging individuals to make themselves available as donors, either during their lifetime or after their death, is therefore of paramount importance. To date, the number of individuals on waiting lists still outstrips the availability of organs.[48] At the same time, an overwhelming proportion of people would be willing to donate – far more than actually carry a donor card.[49] Public engagement, communication and education exercises play an important role in changing this asymmetry. Another extremely important aspect is that public trust in transplantation needs to be fostered. Where practices in transplantation medicine fall below the ethical standard legitimately expected by the public, donation rates tend to drop. This was seen in a particularly dramatic fashion when doctors in Germany altered their patients' clinical chemistry data to artificially move them up on the waiting lists. In some cases, doctors pretended that their patients were receiving dialysis (which increased the urgency) or, astonishingly, simply mixed the patients' blood with urine before sending it to the lab. This led to a dramatic 12.8 per cent decrease in donation rates in 2012.[50] It also led to doctors being arrested and denied bail on the basis that their actions may have led to the death of identifiable individuals on the waiting list (i.e. those patients whose places were taken by the fake dialysis patients).

Not meeting standards in relation to honesty, transparency, fairness and procedural justice results in a public health hazard – an aggravated lack of organs in an already overstretched system. This is to the detriment of individuals (who fail to receive a transplant in time when otherwise they would have) and society (which has to foot the bill for the increased health costs of those who cannot be treated with a transplantation).

Another problem that became apparent in the aftermath of allocation scandals is that of how organs are actually allocated to individual patients. We address allocation issues in more detail in Chapter 6. Suffice to say that systems basing the allocation of an organ on urgency rather than utility are beginning to be the

---

[47] Organ Donation, 'Statistics', updated August 2013, www.organdonation.nhs.uk/statistics/.

[48] See www.organdonation.nhs.uk/statistics/downloads/annual_stats.pdf for the latest statistics.

[49] See S. Morgan and J. Miller, 'Beyond the Organ Donor Card: The Effect of Knowledge, Attitudes, and Values on Willingness to Communicate about Organ Donation to Family Members', Health Communication 14 (2002), pp. 121–34.

[50] C. Metz and N. Hoppe, 'Organ Transplantation in Germany: Regulating Scandals and Scandalous Regulation' (2013) 20(2) European Journal of Health Law 113.

subject of sustained debate: is it better to give a liver to a patient whose life might be saved by the transplantation but who will never leave intensive care, dying three months after the operation, or to an individual who might not (yet) be terminally ill, but who would be able to leave the hospital and lead a normal life?

Biobanking and research with human tissue

One of the uses of human tissue that we have dealt with above is the inclusion of samples (of varying types) in tissue repositories. Biobanks and tissue banks are extremely valuable research infrastructures, with a definite trend towards large hospitals and NHS trusts setting up unified biobanking initiatives. Access to many thousands of samples and associated health data holds the key to providing answers to some extremely pressing questions, such as whether a condition is lifestyle-based or genetically predetermined. It also provides a resource which enables efficient clinical quality control and long-term documentation of samples and information. Most importantly, these tissue collections enable researchers to undertake studies, for which we used to recruit volunteers (who were inconvenienced or even potentially harmed), in vitro, eliminating the risk to volunteers.

The potential of these resources is therefore phenomenal. At the same time, human biological material has to be procured and stored in these repositories. When the material is procured, it is often unclear what type of research will be done with it. This means that at the time of procurement, a proper informed consent is not possible (as the doctors are unable to inform the patient about the exact type of research that is undertaken). Consider paragraph 24 of the Declaration of Helsinki:

In medical research involving competent human subjects, each potential subject must be adequately informed of the aims, methods, sources of funding, any possible conflicts of interest, institutional affiliations of the researcher, the anticipated benefits and potential risks of the study and the discomfort it may entail, and any other relevant aspects of the study.

The type of information required here cannot be provided at the time of recruitment, as the repository itself normally does not conduct any focussed research. It is the intermediary, the supplier of material and data to the ultimate research group. This raises the question of how consent for research with biobanks might be sought. One model is that the initial consent only covers procurement and storage and that the patient has to be re-contacted if and when a distinct research project is identified. In that situation, the patient is then informed of the purpose of the study and an additional consent is sought. Alternative models are those of a broad consent[51] (i.e. a consent to 'research' as a whole, rather than a distinct type of research) and of a waiver of consent (i.e. giving up the right to give, deny or

---

[51] M. Sheehan, 'Broad Consent Is Informed Consent' (2011) 4 *Public Health Ethics* 26.

withdraw consent altogether). The latter is certainly problematic in that it essentially means that there is no consent as, technically, there is no one who has retained the right to give consent. The former does not represent specific informed consent and therefore falls below the threshold we require for normal clinical interaction. From a purely theoretical medical ethics perspective, it seems clear, though, that where the patient understands the scope and consequences of broad consent, or even a waiver of consent, and willingly agrees to this, then to not accept this also smacks of inappropriate paternalism.

Large-scale research infrastructures, such as UK Biobank, have also produced legally and ethically interesting new problems. The greater the integration of the research participants' personal data with the research infrastructure (for example, by way of linking health data from their GPs to the biobank), the weaker the argument becomes that it is not possible to turn that data flow around in order to feed information back to the GPs. Consider this example:

A agrees to participate in a population biobanking project. Blood and some measurements are taken, and she is also quizzed in relation to her lifestyle and any illnesses that might run in the family. During the course of the subsequent analysis of her samples and data, it is discovered that A has a high familial risk of a certain disease, and that current clinical guidelines suggest that she should have check-ups much more regularly than other individuals in her age group.

The biobanking project has a policy of not feeding information back to participants. There might be a number of reasons for this. One, which we have hinted at, is that it is simply technically too difficult for the biobank to relink their database to an individual patient. We are not sure whether, in the light of recent technological developments, this argument is going to be sustainable for much longer. There is also a common-sense argument that suggests it would be unwise for research projects to provide this type of information to participants. If these projects were to identify potential disease parameters and then intervene in the patients' treatment by giving them or their GPs a heads-up, they would simply contaminate their sample, and the research would be useless. Put simply: we need sick people in these cohorts in order for the research to be meaningful.

This very pragmatic reasoning goes hand in hand with another important, and to some extent plausible, position – what we are dealing with here are *research infrastructures*, not clinical establishments designed to diagnose and treat. It is quite simply not the job of the researchers to give clinical advice to research participants.

The area we are discussing here is that of 'incidental findings', i.e. what to do when during research we come across unsolicited information which is clinically relevant to the individual? Is there a duty to act and to prevent harm from occurring? If so, what does that mean for the validity of the research? If not, how do we foster trust in research if we fail individuals when they are most needy? The moral, and legal, dilemmas this poses will become more of an issue as biobanks increasingly use the whole array of diagnostic machinery to gather as much detail as possible about each research participant. Where medical imaging is used at the recruitment stage, it is only a matter of time until the radiologist in charge sees the first suspicious shadow on the images. Will she then really not tell the individual to see their doctor urgently in the interests of not contaminating the sample for the research? And, if so, what does that say about our society – and about our duties towards each other, morally and legally?

CONCLUSION

The ethical position taken by the law in this area can best be described as one resembling squeamishness. Certainly, the 2004 Act does not allow people to do with their organs what they will. This includes both in terms of what may be done with their organs – the uses for which human tissue may be put are limited to those outlined in Schedules 1 and 2 of the Act – and in obtaining adequate permission before doing it. With respect to the latter, the Act and Code of Practice take something of a contradictory position and, as we argue above, it impacts on the ability of individuals to have their autonomy respected. Thus, while the Act authorises the use of organs where the donor has given consent, objections by family members will, following the Code of Practice, cause the medical team to reconsider and not take the organs. This, of course, has two consequences: first, it will mean that a potential donee will be denied a transplant despite the fact that the putative donor was willing to donate the organ. Secondly – and most disappointingly for a piece of legislation that is supposed to be based on consent – the effective right of veto of family members fails to respect the autonomy of the donor. Indeed, it is noticeable that the Code of Practice does not even contain a caveat that states that the medical team will reconsider taking the organ if the relatives feel that *the donor* might have objected. Rather, their objections would appear to be valid even if they are for reasons unrelated to the wishes of the donor.

As we argue above, while this is understandable in some respects given the scandals that formed the impetus for the creation of the 2004 Act, it does nothing to increase the amount of organs available for transplantation (quite the opposite, in fact). Furthermore, the other options described above, such as opt-out systems or even conscription, cannot be considered at this time as a direct consequence of the scandals and the need for time to allow the medical profession to regain the trust of the general public in this area. In many respects this is a shame, but it is equally a level of squeamishness that is inevitable. The dominant principle of the Act, then, is not so much the protection of autonomy, but a desire not to upset anyone.

Here, the law has therefore chosen to balance the interests not just of the patient, the doctor and society, as we have seen before, but also those of the patient's relatives. Perhaps oddly, rather than prioritise the autonomy of the patient, or the utilitarian interests of society (through increasing the amount of organs available for transplantation), the quasi-legal Code of Practice essentially provides a veto that protects the wishes of relatives – even if they do not accord with those of the patient. While understandable given the reasons for the creation of the Act, as we argue above, this is to be regretted. Perhaps at some point in the future the Code of Practice might be modified to take a more directive approach to protecting patient autonomy, which would increase the number of available organs, but it would appear that that time has not yet come. Once it does, it could be argued that, just as we saw in Chapter 2, the protection of the right of the individual patient coincides with the protection of the interests of society as a whole.

ADDITIONAL READING

Law

A. Cambon-Thomsen, 'The Emergence of Biobanks in the Legal Landscape: Towards a New Model of Governance' (2012) 39(1) *Journal of Law and Society* 113

T. Caulfield and J. Kaye, 'Broad Consent in Biobanking: Reflections on Seemingly Insurmountable Dilemmas' (2009) 10 *Medical Law International* 85

A. Cronin, M. Rose, J. Dark and J. Douglas, 'British Transplant Research Endangered by Human Tissue Act' (2011) 37 *Journal of Medical Ethics* 512

K. Liddell and A. Hall, 'Beyond Bristol and Alder Hey: The Future Regulation of Human Tissue' (2005) 13 *Medical Law Review* 170

D. Price, 'From Cosmos and Damien to Van Velzen: The Human Tissue Saga Continues' (2003) 11 *Medical Law Review* 1

D. Price, 'The Human Tissue Act 2004' (2005) 68(5) *Modern Law Review* 798

Ethics

B. Björkman and S. Ove Hansson, 'Bodily Rights and Property Rights' (2006) 32 *Journal of Medical Ethics* 209–14

N. Hoppe, *Bioequity – Property and the Human Body* (Aldershot: Ashgate, 2009)

C. Lenk, J. Sándor and B. Gordijn (eds.), *Biobanks and Tissue Research* (Dordrecht: Springer, 2011)

J. Radcliffe Richards, *The Ethics of Transplants – Why Careless Thought Costs Lives* (Oxford University Press, 2012)

R. Veatch, *Transplantation Ethics* (Washington, DC: Georgetown University Press, 2000)

Case studies from this chapter are available online at www.cambridge.org/hoppe.

10 Research

INTRODUCTION

Patients within a health system, such as the NHS, might interact with health professionals in a number of different ways. The obvious one is that they are patients in receipt of medical treatment. Another regularly occurring context is that of medical research. In this setting, the person participating in the research might either be a patient (and the research is usually into the condition from which the patient suffers) or she might be a healthy volunteer. In any case, where the aim of the exercise is not primarily to improve an individual's health condition, different rules apply. A borderline case is that of experimental treatment being provided to patients, where the treatment is not proven, but the doctor may feel that it could be of benefit. We outline the different types of treatment and experiments here.

WHAT IS RESEARCH? RESEARCH VERSUS EXPERIMENTAL TREATMENT

It is more difficult than it initially appears to get a clear definition of what is meant by research. Indeed, the concept of research must be distinguished from experimental and innovative treatments, and indeed from 'treatment' in general terms. A simple definition is provided by the General Medical Council, who state that research refers to:

an attempt to derive generalisable new knowledge. Research aims to find out what is best practice by addressing clearly defined questions with systematic and rigorous methods. It includes studies that aim to generate hypotheses as well as those that aim to test them.[1]

[1] GMC, *Good Practice in Research* (GMC, 2010), para. 1.

The guidance makes it clear that this might involve and cover both research with human participants as well as records-based research, or research using donated human tissue.[2] Moreover, the definition of research also covers clinical trials. This, according to the GMC, encompasses a wide range of investigations and, for example:

they can test medicines or vaccines, treatments, surgical procedures, devices, or health prevention or care. A clinical trial of investigational medicinal products is a particular type of trial that is governed by legislation.[3]

What can be seen from this definition is that the entire concept of research covers an exceptionally wide area. What we can glean from this, as Hazel Biggs highlights, is that in general terms the 'aim of research is to create new knowledge or understanding', and thus expand knowledge.[4] As the National Institute for Health Research – a body set up by the Department of Health – notes, this new evidence can be used to 'support decision making by professionals' both for individual practitioners and through organisations setting national guidelines such as the National Institute of Health and Clinical Excellence.[5] However, it is important to remember that research does not, and does not intend to, benefit the individual research participant. Rather, a patient who is provided with treatment that is new will not be participating in a 'research' project (as defined here), but will rather be receiving experimental or innovative treatment. Given that this is not 'research', it is not governed by the same rules, and thus doctors are freer to provide it, as long as the patient consents to it or it can be said to be in her best interests, particularly if there are no existing alternative therapies or treatments.

This was considered in *Simms* v. *Simms*.[6] The case concerned two patients, one who was 16 years old (and therefore still, in legal terms, a minor), and another aged 18. Both had probable variant Creutzfeldt-Jacob disease (vCJD), and were not legally capable of making any decisions themselves. There was no existing treatment, and the prognosis presented to the court was that in a short space of time both patients would die. However, there was a procedure being developed in Japan that offered hope, or at least a slowing down of the deterioration of the brain. While it had been tested on non-human animals with mixed results, the procedure had yet to be tested on humans. Indeed, the research was so novel that it had not even yet been published (although it had been submitted to a journal). The parents of both

[2] GMC, *Good Practice in Research*, para. 2.   [3] GMC, *Good Practice in Research*, para. 3.
[4] H. Biggs, *Healthcare Research Ethics and Law: Regulation, Review and Responsibility* (Abingdon: Routledge, 2010), p. 6.
[5] The National Institute for Health Research's research page can be found at www.nihr.ac.uk/research/Pages/default.aspx.
[6] *Simms* v. *Simms; A* v. *A (A Child)* [2002] EWHC 2734 (Fam). For an excellent and comprehensive analysis of the case, see S. Fovargue, *Xenotransplantation and Risk: Regulating a Developing Biotechnology* (Cambridge University Press, 2011).

patients, with the agreement of the hospital, sought a declaration that both patients were incompetent and that the procedure would be in their best interests. In effect, the parents were claiming that the experimental procedure should be treated the same as any other medical treatment. Butler-Sloss J. (as she was then) agreed and granted the declaration.

The reason, the parents argued, that it was in their best interests was because there was no other 'treatment' that would even slow down the progress of the disease. The court therefore undertook a cost/benefit analysis, weighing the risks of the procedure against the potential benefits, despite the fact that both were speculative. Of course, any such analysis will have reached the same conclusion as Butler-Sloss J. given the fact that the prognosis without trying the procedure was so grim. This will be a feature of applications to permit experimental treatment: while the benefits may be undetermined, trying something new may at least offer some hope where there is otherwise none.[7] Thus, while it can be seen that experimental treatment is clearly at least at the interface with research, it differs in the way in which it is intended to benefit the patient rather than simply expand knowledge.

One interesting aspect of the judgment is the judge's consideration of the *Bolam* test. Indeed, a major legal question was whether to provide the treatment would be *Bolam* compliant. Butler-Sloss J. decided that it would be, in the sense that the medical experts giving evidence concluded that they might provide the procedure themselves (and they were found to constitute a responsible body of medical opinion). However, she also warned that there was a distinction to be made between *Bolam* asking whether other doctors might provide the treatment as she had, and using *Bolam* to restrict treatments to only those that had already been tried. The latter would be a barrier to progress:

The *Bolam* test ought not to be allowed to inhibit medical progress. And it is clear that if one waited for the *Bolam* test to be complied with to its fullest extent, no innovative work such as the use of penicillin or performing heart transplant surgery would ever be attempted.[8]

Therefore, for experimental or innovative treatments, *Simms* outlines the process that the courts will undertake. First, they will ask whether there is medical support for attempting the treatment, and if there is, seek the consent of the competent patient. If the patient is incompetent, the treatment will only be provided if it is deemed to be in the patient's best interests, which will involve a balancing of risks and benefits (this will not have changed following the passing of the Mental Capacity Act 2005). But it is important to note that this is classed as 'treatment'

---

[7] See S. Fovargue, 'The (Ab)use of Those With No Other Hope – Ethical and Legal Safeguards for Recipients of Experimental Procedures' (2013) 22(2) *Cambridge Quarterly of Healthcare Ethics* 181.

[8] *Simms* v. *Simms* at para. 48.

rather than 'research'. For actual research projects there is a far greater number of rules, and also significant statutory oversight.

THE LEGAL REGULATION OF RESEARCH

Different types of research

In general terms, if one wants to carry out 'pure' research without human participation, but using human tissue, then the regulatory framework will depend on what sort of research is being conducted. Thus, research using human tissue is governed by the Human Tissue Act 2004, and research using gametes or zygotes is regulated by the Human Fertilisation and Embryology Act 1990. In both cases, the structure for regulation is similar. Research may only be conducted by centres that are licensed to do so, and the licence will only be given if the centre agrees to abide by the limitations of the relevant statute. A failure to do so will result in the withdrawal of the licence. Needless to say, in both cases the consent of the donor of the human material is central to the question of whether it may be used. This is enforced, in each case, by the relevant authority (the Human Tissue Authority or the Human Fertilisation and Embryology Authority), which is responsible for both creating and updating rules and guidance, and also ensuring that these are complied with. In this way, the statutes, which for obvious reasons can quickly become out of date, can adapt to changing circumstances and respond to medical innovations.[9]

Another form of research is what is known as health service research (HSR). This takes information about individual treatments, collates it and seeks to build an evidence base that allows researchers to extrapolate conclusions about best practice and the efficacy of certain treatments. Thus, for example, if patients were treated using different drugs for the same disease, HSR would involve reviewing the information surrounding how many patients fully recovered and how long that took with each drug, and drawing conclusions from that. This research, by definition, requires a large sample group to be statistically meaningful. The problem with this is that it will be a significant barrier to the viability of undertaking this research to require the consent of patients whose information is used. This is because this consent may be difficult, if not impossible, to obtain. Some therefore argue that,

---

[9] A good example of this relates to the changes made by the Human Fertilisation and Embryology Act 2008, many of which concerned research (for a brief overview, see S. Fovargue and J. Miola, 'Key Changes in the Regulation of Assisted Reproduction Introduced by the Human Fertilisation and Embryology Act 2008' (2011) 6(4) *Clinical Ethics* 162).

particularly in a country that contains a health service that is free at the point of use, this consent should not be required, and therefore that such anonymous data sets should be used.[10] However, it is also possible to argue against the use of such data without consent, on the basis that such information should be considered confidential in nature and that, although there might be a public interest in using it for research, the fact that some patients may object to the research project may mean that there are good reasons for requiring consent.[11]

Clinical trials involving human participants are governed by the Medicines for Human Use (Clinical Trials) Regulations 2004, which implemented an EU Directive into English law.[12] The purpose of the directive was to codify the philosophy behind the rules relating to research, and it requires member states to ensure that their legal rules comply with the principles contained in the directive. The directive states that the 'accepted basis for the conduct of clinical trials in humans is founded in the protection of human rights and the dignity of the human being with regard to the application of biology and medicine, as for instance reflected in the 1996 version of the Helsinki Declaration' and is therefore to create EU-wide standards for good clinical practice.[13] The regulations seek to impose upon researchers a set of procedures that should ensure that clinical trials using human subjects are carried out in a way that is both safe for trial subjects and encouraging of good science. The Medicines and Healthcare Products Regulatory Agency (MHRA) has published a useful summary of the regulations.[14] It highlights the fact that in most respects English law already complied with the directive, but identifies the key changes to existing English law as follows:

Pharmacology studies in healthy human volunteers (Phase 1 studies) require authorisation from the MHRA where previously they only needed a favourable opinion of an ethics committee;

Investigational medicinal products (IMPs) must be manufactured to good manufacturing practice (GMP) standards and the manufacturer must have a manufacturing licence; and

Each trial must have an identified sponsor who takes responsibility for its initiation, management and conduct. The Regulations allow a group to collaborate to take on these responsibilities.[15]

---

[10]   J. Cassell and A. Young, 'Why We Should Not Seek Individual Informed Consent for Participation in Health Service Research' (2002) 28 *Journal of Medical Ethics* 313.

[11]   E.g. a vegetarian patient may object to her information being utilised to form the basis of a project that will involve research using animals.

[12]   Directive 2001/20/EC on the approximation of the laws, regulations and administrative provisions of the member states relating to the implementation of good clinical practice in the conduct of clinical trials on medicinal products for human use.

[13]   Directive 2001/20/EC, para. 2.

[14]   MRHA, *Description of the Medicines for Human Use (Clinical Trials) Regulations 2004*, www.mhra.gov.uk/home/groups/l-unit1/documents/websiteresources/con2022633.pdf.

[15]   MRHA, *Description of the Clinical Trials Regulations 2004*, p. 4.

The MHRA also identifies other aspects imposed by the regulations as a consequence of the Directive:

> To establish our ethics committee system on a statutory basis (Regulations 5 to 10, and Schedule 2);
>
> To require all clinical trials to be conducted in accordance with the principles of good clinical practice (GCP) (Regulations 28 to 31, and Schedules 1 and 5);
>
> To provide additional protection for minors and physically or mentally incapacitated adults who are candidates for clinical trials (Regulations 14 to 16 and Parts 3 & 5 of Schedule 1 for incapacitated adults and Regulation 15 and Part 4 of Schedule 1 for minors);
>
> To require sponsors to provide trial medicines free of charge to patients if they are not covered by a prescription charge (Regulation 28);
>
> To provide for inspection by the MHRA for GCP and GMP to help ensure those standards are maintained (Regulations 47 to 52, Parts 2 & 3 of Schedule 7, and Schedule 9); and
>
> To provide for enforcement of these new provisions (Regulations 47 to 52 and Schedule 9).[16]

Essentially, the regulations mandate that: trials must only be carried out at licensed clinics; they have prior ethics committee approval, as well as approval from the MHRA; and adequate provision is made both for considerations of patient safety as well as a risk/benefit analysis of the proposed research. This is made explicit in the statement of principles listed in Schedule 1, Part 2, which are listed as applying to *all* trials:

1. Clinical trials shall be conducted in accordance with the ethical principles that have their origin in the Declaration of Helsinki, and that are consistent with good clinical practice and the requirements of these Regulations.
2. Before the trial is initiated, foreseeable risks and inconveniences have been weighed against the anticipated benefit for the individual trial subject and other present and future patients. A trial should be initiated and continued only if the anticipated benefits justify the risks.
3. The rights, safety, and well-being of the trial subjects are the most important considerations and shall prevail over interests of science and society.
4. The available non-clinical and clinical information on an investigational medicinal product shall be adequate to support the clinical trial.
5. Clinical trials shall be scientifically sound, and described in a clear, detailed protocol.
6. A trial shall be conducted in compliance with the protocol that has a favourable opinion from an ethics committee.
7. The medical care given to, and medical decisions made on behalf of, subjects shall always be the responsibility of an appropriately qualified doctor or, when appropriate, of a qualified dentist.
8. Each individual involved in conducting a trial shall be qualified by education, training, and experience to perform his or her respective task(s).

---

[16] MRHA, *Description of the Clinical Trials Regulations 2004*, p. 5.

9. Subject to the other provisions of this Schedule relating to consent, freely given informed consent shall be obtained from every subject prior to clinical trial participation.
10. All clinical trial information shall be recorded, handled, and stored in a way that allows its accurate reporting, interpretation and verification.
11. The confidentiality of records that could identify subjects shall be protected, respecting the privacy and confidentiality rules in accordance with the requirements of the Data Protection Act 1998 and the law relating to confidentiality.
12. Investigational medicinal products used in the trial shall be –
    (a) manufactured or imported, and handled and stored, in accordance with the principles and guidelines of good manufacturing practice, and
    (b) used in accordance with the approved protocol.
13. Systems with procedures that assure the quality of every aspect of the trial shall be implemented.

It is worth noting that the regulations contain criminal sanctions – including terms of imprisonment – for non-compliance, which is another reflection of how strictly the regulations are supposed to be adhered to. Nevertheless, it is certainly true that the bulk of the regulations is essentially procedural in the sense that the oversight provided by the licensing authorities and the requirement for ethics committee approval are seen as sufficient to protect research subjects and ensure that only valuable and well-planned research is authorised. Despite some instances of serious harm to patients during research projects, such as at Northwick Park, the system appears to work, at least in the sense that no ethics committee has yet been sued.[17]

Given the largely procedural nature of the regulation, it is perhaps unsurprising that once the research project has been approved, there are no restrictions on competent patients volunteering to become subjects. However, informed consent is critical, including informing the patient that they have the right – without sanction – to withdraw from the study at any time.[18] It must be remembered that such research projects rely on healthy volunteers, and that the volunteer participant is taking part in a project that is not going to be of benefit to him – and indeed is not designed to be – while on the other hand inevitably exposing him to some risk. Therefore, in our opinion, there is no reason at all that should be accepted for not informing him of all known risks beforehand.[19] Certainly, any notion of therapeutic privilege (discussed in Chapter 4) or that informing of too many risks may result in the subject placing too much importance on small risks and refusing consent is inappropriate.

---

[17] At Northwick Park in 2006, a research project caused significant adverse events in the participants, and six healthy volunteers suffered multiple organ failure. For an excellent overview, see P. Ferguson, 'Clinical Trials and Healthy Volunteers' (2008) 16(1) *Med. L. Rev.* 23.

[18] This is covered by Sch. 1, Pt 3 of the Medicines for Human Use (Clinical Trials) Regulations 2004.

[19] See J. Miola, 'The Need for Informed Consent: Lessons from the Ancient Greeks' (2006) 15(2) *Cambridge Quarterly of Healthcare Ethics* 52.

Moreover, unfortunately clinical research has a long and undistinguished history when it comes to undertaking research without the consent of participants, as events during World War II and the Tuskegee Syphilis Study, which are but two examples from the previous century, demonstrate. Regard must also be had for people who may be considered vulnerable in this context. Patients may feel that their treatment may depend on their participation, or that they have a moral duty to agree to take part. Equally, employees of clinics or hospitals may feel that they are under pressure from their employers to take part. Thus, the voluntary aspect of consent – somewhat taken for granted in other areas – must be treated most seriously in the research context. Nevertheless, all of this presumes that the volunteer has the capacity to consent to participation. For those who lack that capacity, the rules are different.

ADULTS WHO LACK CAPACITY

Incompetent adults cannot consent on their own behalf, but there is provision in both the regulations and the Mental Capacity Act 2005 that authorises their participation in research projects. Sections 30 to 34 of the Mental Capacity Act 2005 provide conditions relating to the participation of adults who lack capacity in research projects. Under section 30(3), however, a distinction is made between a clinical trial (for which the rules for participation would be governed by the 2004 Regulations) and other research (which would come under the aegis of the Mental Capacity Act). In other words, the Mental Capacity Act framework will only apply to research where the Clinical Trials Regulations do not. For research projects carried out under the Mental Capacity Act scheme, there are a number of conditions attached before the study may be approved. Indeed, section 31 provides that:

(1) The appropriate body may not approve a research project for the purposes of this Act unless satisfied that the following requirements will be met in relation to research carried out as part of the project on, or in relation to, a person who lacks capacity to consent to taking part in the project ('P').
(2) The research must be connected with –
  (a) an impairing condition affecting P, or
  (b) its treatment.
(3) 'Impairing condition' means a condition which is (or may be) attributable to, or which causes or contributes to (or may cause or contribute to), the impairment of, or disturbance in the functioning of, the mind or brain.
(4) There must be reasonable grounds for believing that research of comparable effectiveness cannot be carried out if the project has to be confined to, or relate only to, persons who have capacity to consent to taking part in it.

(5) The research must –
  (a)   have the potential to benefit P without imposing on P a burden that is disproportionate to the potential benefit to P, or
  (b)   be intended to provide knowledge of the causes or treatment of, or of the care of persons affected by, the same or a similar condition.
(6) If the research falls within paragraph (b) of subsection (5) but not within paragraph (a), there must be reasonable grounds for believing –
  (a)   that the risk to P from taking part in the project is likely to be negligible, and
  (b)   that anything done to, or in relation to, P will not –
    (i)   interfere with P's freedom of action or privacy in a significant way, or
    (ii)   be unduly invasive or restrictive.
(7) There must be reasonable arrangements in place for ensuring that the requirements of sections 32 and 33 will be met.

There is a considerable difference between the general principles that apply to competent and incompetent patients. For the former, non-therapeutic research is defined as a study that will not and is not intended to benefit the participant. However, for patients who lack capacity this is not the case, and section 31(2) states that the research project must relate to an impairing condition affecting the participant or the treatment of such a condition. Moreover, under section 31(4), the project cannot be authorised unless it can be demonstrated that 'comparable effectiveness' could not be achieved by recruiting participants who do have capacity. Therefore, not only must the project relate to the incapable adult (and thus actually or potentially benefit her directly), but it must also be necessary to use her rather than a competent volunteer. Even then, under section 31(5) and (6) a risk/benefit analysis must be undertaken to ensure that the burden imposed by the research does not outweigh the benefits that the individual is likely to gain from it. Section 31, therefore, can very much be seen as directly protecting adults who lack capacity – and it is of course both right and necessary that this approach is taken. Moreover, section 31(7) then refers to additional requirements which further augment this protection: section 32 relates to consultation with the potential participant's carers, and section 33 provides additional safeguards which are designed to immediately stop any research to which the subject seems to be objecting:

(1)   This section applies in relation to a person who is taking part in an approved research project even though he lacks capacity to consent to taking part.
(2)   Nothing may be done to, or in relation to, him in the course of the research –
  (a)   to which he appears to object (whether by showing signs of resistance or otherwise) except where what is being done is intended to protect him from harm or to reduce or prevent pain or discomfort, or
  (b)   which would be contrary to –
    (i)   an advance decision of his which has effect, or
    (ii)   any other form of statement made by him and not subsequently withdrawn, of which R is aware.

(3) The interests of the person must be assumed to outweigh those of science and society.

(4) If he indicates (in any way) that he wishes to be withdrawn from the project he must be withdrawn without delay.

(5) P must be withdrawn from the project, without delay, if at any time the person conducting the research has reasonable grounds for believing that one or more of the requirements set out in section 31(2) to (7) is no longer met in relation to research being carried out on, or in relation to, P.

(6) But neither subsection (4) nor subsection (5) requires treatment that P has been receiving as part of the project to be discontinued if R has reasonable grounds for believing that there would be a significant risk to P's health if it were discontinued.

In common with much of the purported philosophy behind the 2005 Act, section 33 is strongly directed towards providing autonomy even for adults lacking capacity, and also towards ensuring that it is their needs and wishes that are protected. To this end, section 33(3) should be noted, in that it provides that the interests of the participant 'must be assumed to outweigh those of science and society'. Thus, the primary aim in recruiting an adult who lacks capacity must be the benefit to her, rather than the importance of the research itself. It is easy to see why this does not apply to clinical trials, and why a separate framework is in place for them.

As discussed above, the 2004 Regulations govern the conduct of clinical trials. The rules to be followed by ethics committees are contained in section 15(7), which states that:

(7) If –
   (a) any subject to the clinical trial is to be an adult incapable by reason of physical and mental incapacity to give informed consent to participation in the trial; and
   (b) the committee does not have a member with professional expertise in the treatment of –
      (i) the disease to which the trial relates, and
      (ii) the patient population suffering that disease,

   it shall, before giving its opinion, obtain advice on the clinical, ethical and psychosocial problems in the field of that disease and patient population which may arise in relation to that trial.

A set of conditions and principles is also contained in Schedule 1, Part 5 governing the use of incapacitated participants in trials:

Conditions

1. The subject's legal representative has had an interview with the investigator, or another member of the investigating team, in which he has been given the opportunity to understand the objectives, risks and inconveniences of the trial and the conditions under which it is to be conducted.

2. The legal representative has been provided with a contact point where he may obtain further information about the trial.

3. The legal representative has been informed of the right to withdraw the subject from the trial at any time.

4. The legal representative has given his informed consent to the subject taking part in the trial.

5. The legal representative may, without the subject being subject to any resulting detriment, withdraw the subject from the trial at any time by revoking his informed consent.
6. The subject has received information according to his capacity of understanding regarding the trial, its risks and its benefits.
7. The explicit wish of a subject who is capable of forming an opinion and assessing the information referred to in the previous paragraph to refuse participation in, or to be withdrawn from, the clinical trial at any time is considered by the investigator.
8. No incentives or financial inducements are given to the subject or their legal representative, except provision for compensation in the event of injury or loss.
9. There are grounds for expecting that administering the medicinal product to be tested in the trial will produce a benefit to the subject outweighing the risks or produce no risk at all.
10. The clinical trial is essential to validate data obtained –
    (a) in other clinical trials involving persons able to give informed consent, or
    (b) by other research methods.
11. The clinical trial relates directly to a life-threatening or debilitating clinical condition from which the subject suffers.

Principles
12. Informed consent given by a legal representative to an incapacitated adult in a clinical trial shall represent that adult's presumed will.
13. The clinical trial has been designed to minimise pain, discomfort, fear and any other foreseeable risk in relation to the disease and the cognitive abilities of the patient.
14. The risk threshold and the degree of distress have to be specially defined and constantly monitored.
15. The interests of the patient always prevail over those of science and society.

This is similar to the principles in the Mental Capacity Act in many ways – particularly the final point, which echoes that of the 2005 Act in prioritising the subject over society – with one exception. Paragraph 7 states that an explicit wish by the subject to refuse to participate or to withdraw need only be 'considered', whereas in the Mental Capacity Act's section 32(4), the expression of such a desire would trigger an immediate obligation to accede to the subject's wishes. This is an unfortunate paragraph that has drawn criticism – and it is easy to see why.

The difference, then, between participants with capacity and those without capacity is therefore one of benefit. For capable research subjects, they understand and consent to the fact that the research is not intended to benefit them. However, with incapable subjects their lack of ability to consent to the procedure means that they must derive some advantage from it themselves which must not be outweighed by the risks to them. Again, it is difficult to argue with such an approach.

MINORS

There is a similar list of conditions and principles in the 2004 Regulations that govern research involving minors and, in general terms, the situation mirrors that relating to adults who lack capacity. The list is contained in Schedule 1, Part 4:

Conditions

1.   Subject to paragraph 6, a person with parental responsibility for the minor or, if by reason of the emergency nature of the treatment provided as part of the trial no such person can be contacted prior to the proposed inclusion of the subject in the trial, a legal representative for the minor has had an interview with the investigator, or another member of the investigating team, in which he has been given the opportunity to
understand the objectives, risks and inconveniences of the trial and the conditions under which it is to be conducted.

2.   That person or legal representative has been provided with a contact point where he may obtain further information about the trial.

3.   That person or legal representative has been informed of the right to withdraw the minor from the trial at any time.

4.   That person or legal representative has given his informed consent to the minor taking part in the trial.

5.   That person with parental responsibility or the legal representative may, without the minor being subject to any resulting detriment, withdraw the minor from the trial at any time by revoking his informed consent.

6.   The minor has received information according to his capacity of understanding, from staff with experience with minors, regarding the trial, its risks and its benefits.

7.   The explicit wish of a minor who is capable of forming an opinion and assessing the information referred to in the previous paragraph to refuse participation in, or to be withdrawn from, the clinical trial at any time is considered by the investigator.

8.   No incentives or financial inducements are given –
     (a)   to the minor; or
     (b)   to a person with parental responsibility for that minor or, as the case may be, the minor's legal representative, except provision for compensation in the event of injury or loss.

9.   The clinical trial relates directly to a clinical condition from which the minor suffers or is of such a nature that it can only be carried out on minors.

10. Some direct benefit for the group of patients involved in the clinical trial is to be obtained from that trial.

11. The clinical trial is necessary to validate data obtained –
     (a)   in other clinical trials involving persons able to give informed consent, or
     (b)   by other research methods.

12. The corresponding scientific guidelines of the European Medicines Agency are followed.

Principles

13. Informed consent given by a person with parental responsibility or a legal representative to a minor taking part in a clinical trial shall represent the minor's presumed will.

14. The clinical trial has been designed to minimise pain, discomfort, fear and any other foreseeable risk in relation to the disease and the minor's stage of development.

15. The risk threshold and the degree of distress have to be specially defined and constantly monitored.

16. The interests of the patient always prevail over those of science and society.

Again, it is worth noting that under point 7 the desire or request of the minor to be withdrawn from the study or to refuse to participate in it at all need only be 'considered'. The list also seems to preclude research that is of no benefit to the minor participant – as point 10 mandates that '[s]ome direct benefit for the group of patients involved in the clinical trial is to be obtained from that trial'. Also noteworthy is the fact that Regulation 2 of the 2004 Regulations defines a minor as someone under the age of 16. Whether *Gillick* would apply is not mentioned, but it should be presumed – given the fact, for example, that the consent of someone with parental responsibility is explicitly required, and that where the child is *Gillick* competent the consent of both the minor and the parent should be obtained – although as we saw in Chapter 5 in strictly legal terms the consent of the parent would be sufficient to make medical treatment legally permissible.

CONCLUDING REMARKS ON LAW

The law relating to clinical research inevitably has to perform a balancing act. On the one hand, research on human subjects is vital in order for medicine to progress, and the interests of society are best served by encouraging it. However, it is at least equally important that people who lack capacity and vulnerable groups are not exploited or used as means to an end. In this regard, then, we see that the 2004 Regulations and the Mental Capacity Act 2005 seek to address this by requiring some form of benefit to the incapable research subject. Yet, this issue is of great ethical interest and import precisely because it directly pits the interests of the individual against the interests of society – and the balancing act is one that is very difficult to perform correctly.

What we can see in the Acts is a tight regulation of researchers. As we shall see below, this is again a response to previous events – in this case, the atrocities committed by the Nazis had a profound effect and resulted in a number of codes and guidelines which sought to eradicate exploitation. We can see this in particular in relation not just to incapable adults, but children too. However, the question must be asked: first, is it ever possible to conduct research without exploitation? By its very definition, research is an information-gathering process the effect of which is ultimately unknown. Only a very thorough consent process will suffice if participants are not to be exposed to risks to which they do not wish to be exposed. Even then, they must be informed that some of those risks will be unknown even to the researchers.

Indeed, there is a particular concern to protect incapable adults and minors: they cannot consent to the risk model described above, and therefore the requirement that they can only participate if there is a chance of them benefiting is absolutely correct in our view. The law takes a protective, deontological position with respect to such participants. Their interests are placed above the interests not only of researchers, but also of society as a whole that might benefit from the research. The needs of the many are thus trumped by those of the individual. We would argue that this would be the right approach even if there had not been a history of research participants being exploited. Given that there is, such rules are indispensable.

ETHICS

It is clear that there is a fundamental friction between the ability to undertake sound research and guaranteeing individuals' health and well-being. London writes:

> By pushing forward the boundaries of knowledge, medical research ultimately aims to improve the standard of medical care available to future patients. On the other hand, medical research requires the participation of individuals, each of whom has his or her own interests and needs. As high-profile scandals in research ethics powerfully illustrate, the pursuit of sound science and statistical validity may require research activities that diverge from – or which are simply antithetical to – the best interest of present participants.[20]

It is the job of research ethics to identify and describe means to protect the clinical trial or other experimentation. The ethics of biomedical research have been significantly influenced by historical events in the twentieth century. In particular, the atrocities committed during the Nazi regime in Germany between 1933 and 1945 gave rise to extensive developments of ethics-based guidance documents. We have seen in Chapter 1 that the approach taken by the law when looking at ethical guidance is to place responsibility for interpretation and application firmly in the hands of medical practitioners. The impetus behind the development of ethical guidance following the Nuremberg Trials, held between December 1946 and August 1947, was rather to remove responsibility from the individual and give firm, and binding, guidance to a profession as a whole. This guidance was manifested initially in the Nuremberg Code, which in 1947 enshrined the following norms:

1. The voluntary consent of the human subject is absolutely essential. This means that the person involved should have legal capacity to give consent; should be so situated as to be able to exercise free power of choice, without the intervention of any element of force, fraud, deceit, duress, over-reaching, or other ulterior form of constraint or coercion; and

---

[20] A. J. London, 'Clinical Equipoise: Foundational Requirement or Fundamental Error?' in B. Steinbock (ed.), *The Oxford Handbook of Bioethics* (Oxford University Press, 2009), p. 571.

should have sufficient knowledge and comprehension of the elements of the subject matter involved, as to enable him to make an understanding and enlightened decision. This latter element requires that, before the acceptance of an affirmative decision by the experimental subject, there should be made known to him the nature, duration, and purpose of the experiment; the method and means by which it is to be conducted; all inconveniences and hazards reasonably to be expected; and the effects upon his health or person, which may possibly come from his participation in the experiment. The duty and responsibility for ascertaining the quality of the consent rests upon each individual who initiates, directs or engages in the experiment. It is a personal duty and responsibility which may not be delegated to another with impunity.

2. The experiment should be such as to yield fruitful results for the good of society, unprocurable by other methods or means of study, and not random and unnecessary in nature.

3. The experiment should be so designed and based on the results of animal experimentation and a knowledge of the natural history of the disease or other problem under study, that the anticipated results will justify the performance of the experiment.

4. The experiment should be so conducted as to avoid all unnecessary physical and mental suffering and injury.

5. No experiment should be conducted, where there is an a priori reason to believe that death or disabling injury will occur; except, perhaps, in those experiments where the experimental physicians also serve as subjects.

6. The degree of risk to be taken should never exceed that determined by the humanitarian importance of the problem to be solved by the experiment.

7. Proper preparations should be made and adequate facilities provided to protect the experimental subject against even remote possibilities of injury, disability, or death.

8. The experiment should be conducted only by scientifically qualified persons. The highest degree of skill and care should be required through all stages of the experiment of those who conduct or engage in the experiment.

9. During the course of the experiment, the human subject should be at liberty to bring the experiment to an end, if he has reached the physical or mental state, where continuation of the experiment seemed to him to be impossible.

10. During the course of the experiment, the scientist in charge must be prepared to terminate the experiment at any stage, if he has probable cause to believe, in the exercise of the good faith, superior skill and careful judgement required of him, that a continuation of the experiment is likely to result in injury, disability, or death to the experimental subject.[21]

The focus of the ethical instructions contained in these paragraphs is clearly on the protection of the 'human subject' (now often referred to as 'research participant'). The reason for this is that during the time of the Nazi regime, medical experimentation ran wild with little or no regard for the human subjects, and in many cases concerned spurious research questions, which entailed great suffering or the death of the subjects with no genuine knowledge generation.

The Nuremberg Code was replaced by the World Medical Association's Declaration of Helsinki in 1964. Again, the focus was very much on protecting

---

[21] 'Trials of War Criminals before the Nuremberg Military Tribunals under Control Council Law No. 10', Vol. 2 (Washington, DC: US Government Printing Office, 1949), p. 12. See http://history.nih.gov/research/downloads/nuremberg.pdf.

human subjects. The 2008 version of the code contains thirty-five norms in three sections. The three sections cover introductory remarks (A), principles for all medical research (B) and additional principles for medical research when this is combined with medical care (C). The Declaration of Helsinki is not binding law, but it attains binding quality by virtue of professional bodies and learned societies being likely to exclude members in cases of contravention. There is, therefore, a concrete sanction attached to non-compliance, the result being an inability to lawfully practice medicine or medical research.

Given that the relevant instruments' focus is on the protection of the individual participant (which is the main focus of the sub-discipline of research ethics), much revolves around questions of consent. Where an intervention is therapeutic in nature, the consent of the individual essentially indemnifies the medical professionals carrying out the treatment. Additional obstacles are put in place, both in terms of law and ethics, where the aim of the intervention is not entirely, or not at all, therapeutic. We distinguish between *experimental treatments* and *experimentation* in this context: *experimental treatments* are still aimed at achieving a therapeutic effect, though by means which have been insufficiently tested to make an exact prognosis on the treatment's efficacy possible. The main thrust of experimental treatments is therefore still to benefit the patient. At the same time, the generation of new knowledge about a disease or an intervention is also part and parcel of this type of treatment.

Human *experimentation* is only aimed at proving the effect of an intervention and there is no primary expectation of a therapeutic benefit for the patient. That is why this type of interaction with patients and research participants is highly regulated: the beneficiary of the activity is not the individual, but society through the knowledge generated. One mechanism which is commonly used to achieve a high level of protection for the research participants is that of a research ethics committee (REC, sometimes referred to as an institutional review board, IRB). The REC will assess study designs before the research takes place and ensure that the study conforms to accepted ethical guidelines. The Declaration of Helsinki states in principles 14 and 15:

14. The design and performance of each research study involving human subjects must be clearly described in a research protocol. The protocol should contain a statement of the ethical considerations involved and should indicate how the principles in this Declaration have been addressed. The protocol should include information regarding funding, sponsors, institutional affiliations, other potential conflicts of interest, incentives for subjects and provisions for treating and/or compensating subjects who are harmed as a consequence of participation in the research study. The protocol should describe arrangements for post-study access by study subjects to interventions identified as beneficial in the study or access to other appropriate care or benefits.

15. The research protocol must be submitted for consideration, comment, guidance and approval to a research ethics committee before the study begins. This committee must be independent of the researcher, the sponsor and any other undue influence. It must take into consideration the laws and regulations of the country or countries in which the research is to be performed as well as applicable international norms and standards but these must not be allowed to reduce or eliminate any of the protections for research subjects set forth in this Declaration. The committee must have the right to monitor ongoing studies. The researcher must provide monitoring information to the committee, especially information about any serious adverse events. No change to the protocol may be made without consideration and approval by the committee.

In particular, the REC will test the study design for a number of parameters:

- the risk versus benefit relation of the proposed research;
- the quality and voluntariness of the consent sought from participants; and
- the quality of the proposed research.

Risk assessment is an important feature of the ethical assessment of human experimentation. It represents a balancing exercise between the value of the generated knowledge, potential benefits for the participants and actual risks inherent in the research. Where the knowledge generated is of little value (for example, the umpteenth verification of the efficacy of a certain drug with no added research question that makes the knowledge generated novel), it is unlikely that even slight risks will be considered appropriate. The more promising the research question, the more likely it is that greater risks are acceptable. In terms of potential benefits, patients participating in studies can, of course, be the beneficiaries of new treatments (as long as they actually turn out to work better than the conventional treatments). More abstractly, sufferers of a certain condition can benefit from research into their condition, even if there is no direct health benefit for them individually.

Risks can, of course, be very real physical risks (from the pain and associated risks of being injected with a needle to taking drugs which might have harmful side effects), but this category also includes social risks, such as stigmatisation and discrimination. Discrimination might occur where a person's association with a certain disease precludes him from enjoying certain things (for example, if genetic analysis shows that a person is very likely to develop heart disease at some point, an insurance company might refuse to insure him, or his employer might terminate his contract). Stigmatisation is an issue both subjectively and objectively: when a person learns of a certain condition, he might feel extremely unhappy with himself. Likewise, if those surrounding him find out about the condition, he might be ostracised.

In addition, the quality of the proposed research plays an important role in determining its ethical justifiability. Spurious, ill-thought-through or poorly run experiments make wasteful, disrespectful, superfluous or risky use of human subjects and should therefore not be permitted, even if the research participants willingly make themselves available for this or any other very dangerous type of research. The risk involved in the research is a very important determinant of whether the research will be allowed (independently of the participant's consent). Hope, Savulescu and Hendrick very helpfully categorise the point thus:[22]

	Research where participants knowingly expose themselves to high risk	Low-risk research where participants do not know they are taking risks	Low-risk research where participants are fully informed	Poor-quality research that is of little value but where participants are fully informed
Libertarian (rights based)	Yes	No	Yes	Yes
Paternalistic (duty based)	No	Yes	Yes	No
Utilitarian (consequentialist)	Yes	Yes	Yes	No

Consent, again, becomes particularly interesting when we discuss research subjects who are unable to give consent, such as children or incapacitated adults. Research with children is extremely difficult, but not impossible – to prohibit it completely would essentially be inequitable to children as a whole as medical treatments would not be available that were systematically tested for them. Instead, adult treatment options would simply be scaled down or used off-label for the paediatric patient.[23] This is undesirable, especially since the old rule still has merit in this setting: children are not simply small adults. Put another way, simply reducing the dosage to allow for the child's smaller body size does not address all of the differences between adults and children. This makes off-label use particularly risky. It is therefore desirable to permit research with children, but the safeguards obviously need to be particularly strict.

The same is true for research with incapacitated adults. Especially in the context of dementia research, there is an overwhelming need to be able to recruit incapacitated patients into trials (otherwise we would struggle to develop treatment

---

[22] T. Hope, J. Savulescu and J. Hendrick, *Medical Ethics and Law* (Edinburgh: Churchill Livingstone, 2008), p. 220.
[23] Off-label means that a drug which has been approved for adults is used for children (or, indeed, vice versa). It may also mean that a drug that has been approved for a certain condition is used to treat another condition. A large proportion of drugs administered in paediatric oncology is off-label, simply because to conduct clinical trials with children is extremely difficult.

options for neurodegenerative diseases such as Parkinson's or Alzheimer's disease). In essence, the individuals we have discussed here are particularly vulnerable and therefore worthy of particular, institutionalised protection. This is achieved by way of requiring REC approval when planning research with patients or volunteers. It should also be clear that research with individuals unable to give consent is only appropriate where the same research cannot be carried out using healthy volunteers who are able to give consent.

The Oviedo Convention (the Council of Europe's Treaty on the Protection of Human Rights and Dignity of the Human Being with regard to the Application of Biology and Medicine) outlines the requirements for research with participants who are unable to give consent:

Article 17 – Protection of persons not able to consent to research

1. Research on a person without the capacity to consent as stipulated in Article 5 may be undertaken only if all the following conditions are met:
    (i)   the conditions laid down in Article 16, sub-paragraphs i to iv, are fulfilled;
    (ii) the results of the research have the potential to produce real and direct benefit to his or her health;
    (iii) research of comparable effectiveness cannot be carried out on individuals capable of giving consent;
    (iv) the necessary authorisation provided for under Article 6 has been given specifically and in writing; and
    (v)   the person concerned does not object.
2. Exceptionally and under the protective conditions prescribed by law, where the research has not the potential to produce results of direct benefit to the health of the person concerned, such research may be authorised subject to the conditions laid down in paragraph 1, sub-paragraphs i, iii, iv and v above, and to the following additional conditions:
    (i) the research has the aim of contributing, through significant improvement in the scientific understanding of the individual's condition, disease or disorder, to the ultimate attainment of results capable of conferring benefit to the person concerned or to other persons in the same age category or afflicted with the same disease or disorder or having the same condition;
    (ii) the research entails only minimal risk and minimal burden for the individual concerned.

Article 6 provides that others may consent on behalf of the person who is unable to give consent (although it also provides that the person may dissent, i.e. express unwillingness to participate, which should then be respected). Both the suggestion that others can in some way validly consent on behalf of a minor or an incapacitated person and the notion of 'minimal risk' have been subject to critical debate.[24] Additionally, the Oviedo Convention has limited direct value, as it was only ratified by a very small number of states. At the same time, it is prudent to

---

[24] E. Emanuel *et al.* (eds.), *The Oxford Textbook of Clinical Research Ethics* (New York: Oxford University Press, 2008), ch. 42.

assume that the court in Strasbourg may include considerations from the Oviedo Convention when interpreting rights contained in the ECHR. Entirely disregarding Oviedo would therfore be foolish.

CONCLUSION

We have seen before that in many cases the law is as it is due to the specific incidents to which it responded specifically. In this case, it is less a single incident and more the fact that throughout history medical research has been carried out on unwilling participants, often to their detriment. The actions of the Nazis constituted the latest in a long line, but such was its scope and horror that it finally seemed to concentrate the mind. What we see in the conventions and legal instruments is therefore a prioritisation of the protection of the individual. The interests of society in medical research being conducted are thus subordinated to the rights of individuals not to be exploited or treated as ends. In terms of the power struggle between scientist and research participant, the former is limited to protect the latter.

However, there is at least an argument that certain types of research, which carry minimal or no risk to the participant, might be authorised despite the absence of consent because in the risk versus benefit analysis there is some potential benefit and little risk. Health service research, which is considered in Chapter 2, and uses medical *information* rather than experimentation on the body of the participant, might be an example of this. Nevertheless, we would argue that to take such a nakedly utilitarian line would be inappropriate, and it is not unreasonable that science spends some time being oversensitive to participants' rights. This is even more the case when one considers that research misconduct and the exposure of unwilling participants to risk and injury did not stop with the Nuremberg Code (to give but one example: the Tuskegee Syphilis Study, which did not end until 1972, involved knowingly not treating syphilis in African-American men, who were also not told that they had the disease, to examine the effect of untreated syphilis).

What we see in much of the legal framework is a system of checks and balances based on process. Thus, RECs exist to assess risk, benefit and scientific validity before the research is carried out at all. The system is not perfect by any means – as the events at Northwick Park demonstrate. Nevertheless, we must also accept that research and experimentation on the bodies of participants is very rarely risk-free, and that the reason for it happening is to find out more about both benefits and dangers. Given this, informed consent becomes key, and at the very least the law has sought to recognise this. The balance of rights and power skewed in favour of participants is, we believe, both right and necessary.

ADDITIONAL READING

Law

H. Biggs, *Healthcare Research Ethics and Law: Regulation, Review and Responsibility* (Abingdon: Routledge, 2010)

E. Cave, 'Seen But Not Heard? Children in Clinical Trials' (2010) 18(1) *Medical Law Review* 1

P. Ferguson, 'Clinical Trials and Healthy Volunteers' (2008) 16(1) *Medical Law Review* 23

S. Fovargue, 'Doctrinal Incoherence or Practical Problem? Minor Parents Consenting to their Offspring's Medical Treatment and Involvement in Research in England and Wales' (2013) 25(1) *Child and Family Law Quarterly* 1

K. Liddell, J. Bion, D. Chamberlain, C. Druml, E. Kompanje, F. Lemaire, D. Menon, B. Vrhovac and C. Weidermann, 'Medical Research Involving Incapacitated Adults: Implications of the EU Clinical Trials Directive 2001/20/EC' (2006) 14(3) *Medical Law Review* 367

Ethics

J. Boomgaarden, P. Louhiala and U. Wiesing (eds.), *Issues in Medical Research Ethics* (New York: Berghahn Books, 2003)

E. J. Emanuel, C. Grady, R. A. Crouch, R. K. Lie, F. G. Miller and D. Wendler (eds.), *The Oxford Textbook of Clinical Research Ethics* (New York: Oxford University Press, 2008)

T. Hope, J. Savulescu and J. Hendrick, *Medical Ethics and Medical Law: The Core Curriculum*, 2nd edn (Edinburgh: Churchill Livingstone, 2008), chapter 14

P. Oliver, *The Student's Guide to Research Ethics*, 2nd edn (Maidenhead: Open University Press, 2010)

B. Steinbock (ed.), *The Oxford Handbook of Bioethics* (Oxford University Press, 2007), chapters 24–7

Case studies from this chapter are available online at www.cambridge.org/hoppe.

11 The end of life

INTRODUCTION

Types of euthanasia and the criminal law – 'killing' versus 'letting die' and double effect

There comes a point in the treatment of some patients when it is clear that they are not going to recover: their injuries are too severe, they are in an irreversible coma, or they are simply too old and nothing can be done. In such scenarios, palliative care becomes appropriate. Palliative care is medical treatment that is designed not to 'cure' the patient of any disease, but instead to try to help her to be as comfortable as possible as she dies. This may include a range of actions and omissions, such as the provision of pain relief (which may shorten life), the withholding of artificial nutrition and hydration or even determinations not to resuscitate the patient should she stop breathing. These are obviously difficult and controversial decisions, and there is considerable disagreement, as we shall see, regarding whether they amount to euthanasia. Before considering the legality or otherwise of euthanasia, it is first necessary to distinguish between the two types of the practice – 'active' and 'passive' euthanasia. The distinction between these two is certainly not as intuitive as it initially sounds. 'Active' euthanasia is the process imagined by most people when they consider the practice, and it involves actively ending someone's life, most usually through the injection of a drug that will painlessly kill the patient. It is called 'active' euthanasia because the doctor will take active steps to shorten and end the life of the patient, and the cause of death will be the act of the doctor rather than the progression of the disease from which the patient suffers. 'Passive' euthanasia occurs when the doctor fails to act to save the life of the patient. This involves withholding treatment from the patient, such as antibiotics or, more controversially, artificial ventilation or nutrition and hydration. The distinction is that in this scenario the patient's disease will kill him, rather than any drug administered by the doctor. Essentially, the difference is seen to be one between killing and letting die, although, as we discuss below in relation to the ethical aspects, this is not without its problems, as recognised by the House of Lords.[1] Put at its simplest, passive euthanasia can sometimes be lawful, while active euthanasia is not. The most pressing problem for doctors wishing to help someone to end their life is, not unreasonably, the criminal law. More specifically, the law of murder provides that it is an offence to undertake an act that causes the death of another person with the intent to kill or inflict grievous bodily harm. Obviously with active euthanasia, where death is not just intended but is the actual aim, this is more than satisfied. It is therefore illegal and can be classed as murder. In English law, there is no defence of 'mercy killing'.

However, to hold that no drug may ever be administered to a patient if it will shorten her life is clearly overly restrictive and can have a prejudicial effect on the ability of medical staff to provide adequate pain relief. For this reason, the principle of double effect may be invoked to allow such treatment to be given to patients. The doctrine of double effect holds that a side effect (death) is not considered to be intended as long as the primary purpose is legal. As mentioned above, this most frequently relates to pain relief which has the side effect of shortening the patient's life, and it provides that the intention in giving the pain relief is therefore the relief of pain (which is legal) rather than the shortening of life (which is illegal and can be classed as murder). The principle is broadly supported, even by those who are pro-life.[2] Nevertheless, that is not to say that it is without its difficulties. We discuss this further in our ethical discussion, but it is, for example, not easy to ask the law to simply disregard as unintended a known and inevitable consequence.[3] Indeed, the operation of the doctrine of double effect rests on an acceptance that foresight of a consequence *can* be distinguished from intending it, and this creates real problems. The reason for this is that, in the general criminal law relating to homicide (medical treatment is undoubtedly subject to this), the House of Lords in the landmark case of *R* v. *Woollin* determined that a foresight of a virtual certainty was determined to constitute intention – which is enough to satisfy the mental element for a charge of murder.[4] The case concerned a man who had, in a fit of rage, thrown his baby onto a hard surface, fracturing his skull. He claimed that he did not intend to kill the child

---

[1] For a classic argument questioning the validity of the distinction, see J. Rachels, 'Active and Passive Euthanasia' (1975) 292 *New England Journal of Medicine* 78. See also, from a pro-life perspective, J. Keown, *Euthanasia, Ethics and Public Policy* (Cambridge University Press, 2002), Pt IV; and from a contrary perspective, see S. W. Smith, *End of Life Decisions in Medical Care: Principles and Policies for Regulating the Dying Process* (Cambridge University Press, 2012), ch. 4. Smith also provides an analysis of Rachels.

[2] See, e.g., Keown, *Euthanasia*.

[3] An excellent dissection can be found in R. Huxtable, 'Get Out of Jail Free? The Doctrine of Double Effect in English Law' (2004) 18 *Palliative Medicine* 62.

[4] *R* v. *Woollin* [1999] 1 AC 82. See A. McGee, 'Finding a Way through the Ethical and Legal Maze: Withdrawal of Treatment and Euthanasia' (2005) 13(3) *Med. L. Rev.* 357.

(this is necessary for a charge of murder) – but admitted that he foresaw that it was a virtual certainty that severe harm might be suffered. The question was whether this foresight of a virtual certainty might be intention (or at least evidence of intention), and the House of Lords held that it could. This foresight is present in many cases of administering pain relief, and nobody is currently suggesting that it is illegal. We can only assume that there is an unspoken exception relating to medical treatment, and indeed we would be surprised if the courts did not uphold it. Nevertheless, the concept of double effect can be seen to be problematic not just in terms of its ethical basis, but also as it sits somewhat uncomfortably with the criminal law.

However, even passive euthanasia is not without legal complication, given that in order to cease ventilation or withdraw artificial nutrition and hydration (ANH), physical acts (in the form of switching off the ventilator or removing naso-gastric feeding tubes) are performed. These would, in ordinary circum- stances – such as if you were to enter a hospital and undertake them – be positive acts causing death, which with the requisite intention would be murder (and otherwise would be manslaughter). Thus, in order to circumnavigate the law of homicide, the courts had to create and adhere to two concepts that are at the very least arguable: that ANH and ventilation constitute 'medical treatment' rather than basic care, and that removal of such treatment is an omission rather than an act. These fictions were created by the House of Lords in the landmark case of *Bland*, the facts of which also demonstrate the difficulties inherent in making law in this area.[5]

Anthony Bland was a victim of the Hillsborough stadium disaster in 1989, which claimed the lives of ninety-six Liverpool Football Club fans. He was crushed and as a consequence suffered hypoxic brain damage. He was some time later diagnosed as being in a persistent vegetative state (PVS), with no prospect of recovery. Lord Keith eloquently described his condition:

Anthony Bland cannot see, hear or feel anything. He cannot communicate in any way. The consciousness which is the essential feature of individual personality has departed for ever . . . In order to maintain Anthony Bland in his present condition, feeding and hydration are achieved artificially by means of a nasogastric tube and excretionary functions are regulated by a catheter and by enemas. The catheter from time to time gives rise to infections which have to be dealt with by appropriate medical treatment. The undisputed consensus of eminent medical opinion is that there is no prospect whatever that Anthony Bland will ever make any recovery from his present condition, but that there is every likelihood that he will maintain his present state of existence for many years to come, provided that the medical care which he is now receiving is continued.[6]

---

[5] *Airedale NHS Trust v. Bland* [1993] AC 789.   [6] *Bland* at 856.

A declaration was sought that, in the light of this, the ANH should be withdrawn and Anthony Bland be allowed to die. In judgments rich in sensitivity and with various levels of analysis, their Lordships unanimously held that it would indeed be lawful to do so. However, in order to do so, the court had to contend with several issues. The first, as mentioned above, was the question of how to circumnavigate the law of homicide. This is where the two arguable concepts were created and applied. The first questionable assertion was that ANH constituted medical treatment. It was put to the court that ANH was in fact basic care, and to define it as such would have ramifications.[7] Indeed, Lord Keith acknowledged that the criminal law makes it clear that once a duty of care is assumed for an individual, basic care must be provided.[8] Thus, by rejecting this view of the status of ANH (which had been defined as basic care in the case cited to the court) and medicalising the procedure, it became possible to remove it as long as there was no legal justification for providing the 'treatment'.[9] It will be remembered from previous chapters that medical treatment may only be given lawfully if the patient consents (if she is competent), or if it is in her best interests (if she is not). Failing this, treatment simply cannot be given. As the House of Lords suggested in *Bland*, in the absence of such a justification to treat, it is not just lawful to stop the treatment, but actually a battery not to do so.[10] In *Bland* itself, the argument was that his best interests were not served by continuing treatment – as we discuss in detail below – and this was made possible only because ANH was defined as 'medical treatment'. This medicalisation is not unproblematic, as we also discuss below in the context of the case of Leslie Burke.

The second assertion, related to the first, is that the process of discontinuing treatment constitutes not an *act*, but, rather, an *omission* to treat. This, as explained above, is critical in circumnavigating the law relating to homicide, as the doctor is not committing a positive act causing death (but, rather, not providing treatment that she has no legal right to continue to provide). As Lord Goff explained:

> At the heart of this distinction lies a theoretical question. Why is it that the doctor who gives his patient a lethal injection which kills him commits an unlawful act and indeed is guilty of murder, whereas a doctor who, by discontinuing life support, allows his patient to die, may not act unlawfully – and will not do so, if he commits no breach of duty to his patient? Professor Glanville Williams has suggested (see his *Textbook of Criminal Law*, 2nd ed. (1983), p. 282) that the reason is that what the doctor does when he switches off a life support machine 'is in substance not an act but an omission to struggle,' and that 'the omission is not a breach of duty by the doctor, because he is not obliged to continue in a hopeless case.'
>
> I agree that the doctor's conduct in discontinuing life support can properly be categorised as an omission. It is true that it may be difficult to describe what the doctor actually does as an

---

[7] See Lord Keith at 858.   [8] Lord Keith at 858.

[9] The case was *R* v. *Stone and Dobinson* [1977] 1 QB 354; see *Bland* at 858.

[10] *Bland* at 883, *per* Lord Browne-Wilkinson.

omission, for example where he takes some positive step to bring the life support to an end. But discontinuation of life support is, for present purposes, no different from not initiating life support in the first place. In each case, the doctor is simply allowing his patient to die in the sense that he is desisting from taking a step which might, in certain circumstances, prevent his patient from dying as a result of his pre-existing condition; and as a matter of general principle an omission such as this will not be unlawful unless it constitutes a breach of duty to the patient.[11]

Although doctors can be under a duty to act as they owe a duty of care to their patients, as Lord Goff noted this would not be the case unless not to act would be a breach of duty. Given that there was no legal justification in treating Anthony Bland, this was not the case and the doctor would thus be acting lawfully. The controversy over this lies in the fact that the removal of life-sustaining treatment – such as the switching off of an artificial ventilator or the removal of naso-gastric ANH tubes – is clearly a physical *act*. This can be contrasted to, for example, not giving the patient antibiotic pills, which is a physical omission. Indeed, as Lord Goff recognised, if what he termed an 'interloper' were to enter the hospital and undertake these very same actions, they would be considered *acts* by the law and the interloper would be guilty of murder if he had the requisite intention to kill or cause grievous bodily harm.

Thus, these two legal fictions, created in *Bland*, have allowed the courts to both circumnavigate the law of homicide, and also, in their view, distinguish the removal of treatment from euthanasia. The latter, in particular, is unconvincing – particularly given that two controversial legal positions had to be established merely to get to this point – as recognised by Lord Goff in the House of Lords:

It is true that the drawing of this distinction may lead to a charge of hypocrisy, because it can be asked why, if the doctor, by discontinuing treatment, is entitled in consequence to let his patient die, it should not be lawful to put him out of his misery straight away, in a more humane manner, by a lethal injection, rather than let him linger on in pain until he dies. But the law does not feel able to authorise euthanasia, even in circumstances such as these, for, once euthanasia is recognised as lawful in these circumstances, it is difficult to see any logical basis for excluding it in others.[12]

Equally, Lord Browne-Wilkinson recognised the fact that the law and what he saw as the moral argument may lead to different conclusions, ending his judgment by noting that:

... the conclusion I have reached will appear to some to be almost irrational. How can it be lawful to allow a patient to die slowly, though painlessly, over a period of weeks from lack of food but unlawful to produce his immediate death by a lethal injection, thereby saving his family from yet another ordeal to add to the tragedy that has already struck them? I find it difficult to find a moral answer to that question. But it is undoubtedly the law and nothing I

---

[11] *Bland* at 866, *per* Lord Goff.   [12] *Bland* at 865, *per* Lord Goff.

have said casts doubt on the proposition that the doing of a positive act with the intention of ending life is and remains murder.[13]

Indeed, it is clear that the decision in *Bland* constitutes their Lordships performing legal gymnastics to achieve what they would define as justice in the face of contrary legal rules. Moreover, it is also clear that even though they engaged in considerable judicial creativity, the House of Lords still felt unable to go as far as they would have liked in the decision. In this particular case, we feel that it is difficult to disagree with their decision to modify the law in order to achieve what they (and we) believe is a more just conclusion.

COMPETENT PATIENTS

Refusal of treatment – Ms B

Whether a patient can lawfully refuse treatment will depend on whether or not they are competent, and whether they are an adult. For children, the law to be applied is that relating to consent for minors, which we discussed in Chapter 5. It will be remembered that the refusal of consent to treatment by a competent minor may be overturned by a consent provided by either parent or by the court. Where the adult patient is competent and actively refuses consent to treatment, however, the law is simple: treatment is unlawful in the absence of consent from a competent patient, and a refusal of consent must be respected. A good illustration of this point can be found in the case of *Ms B*.[14] Ms B had suffered a cavernoma in 1999, which required surgery.[15] In 2001 she suffered a further cavernoma which left her tetraplegic, and respiratory problems which resulted in her being treated with a ventilator, upon which she became reliant. Following the first cavernoma, Ms B had composed a living will that stipulated that were she to suffer from a 'life threatening condition, permanent mental impairment or permanent unconsciousness', treatment should be withdrawn.[16] Following her readmittance to hospital in 2001, Ms B was transferred to the intensive care unit (ICU), where she informed doctors of the existence of the living will. She was told that it was not specific enough to cover her existing situation, and a month later she underwent further surgery to remove the cavernoma. This led to her regaining the ability to move her head and articulate words, but she remained disappointed and asked for the ventilator to be switched off. There

---

[13] *Bland* at 885, *per* Lord Browne-Wilkinson.   [14] *Ms B* v. *An NHS Hospital Trust* [2002] EWHC 429.
[15] A cavernoma is a 'cluster of abnormal blood vessels, normally found around the brain or spinal cord' (see the NHS Choices website at www.nhs.uk/conditions/cavernoma/Pages/Introduction.aspx).
[16] *Ms B* at para. 4.

were initial disagreements regarding her capacity from April 2001, but by August the hospital felt that she was capable, but refused to switch off the ventilator, as they felt this to be unethical.[17]

The case went to court in 2002, and Butler-Sloss P. quickly identified that everything revolved around the balancing of two competing principles: autonomy and the sanctity of life. Both, she said, were worthy of protection – although, oddly, she noted that autonomy was protected by the law, whereas the sanctity of life was of concern to 'society and the medical profession'.[18] It therefore fell to her to choose between them, and the choice she made was in favour of autonomy. She provided a quote from Lord Goff in *Bland* to demonstrate the position that the law must take:

> [I]t is established that the principle of self-determination requires that respect must be given to the wishes of the patient . . . To this extent, the principle of the sanctity of human life must yield to the principle of self-determination . . . and for present purposes perhaps most important, the doctor's duty to act in the best interests of his patient must likewise be qualified. On this basis, it has been held that a patient of sound mind may, if properly informed, require that life support should be discontinued . . . It is simply that the patient has, as he is entitled to do, declined to consent to treatment . . . and the doctor has, in accordance with his duty, complied with his patient's wishes.[19]

Thus, autonomy 'trumps' the sanctity of life. Indeed, the case of *Ms B* should perhaps not be seen as an 'end of life' case, but, rather, as a (very simple) consent case. It is unlawful to provide/impose treatment on a competent patient without her consent. Once Ms B, in a competent state, had expressed her refusal to consent while in a competent mental state, the legal justification for ventilation no longer existed, and it had to be removed, whether the treatment team felt it ethical to do so or otherwise. Ultimately, the choice rests with the competent patient, and we believe that it is the correct course of action.

SUICIDE / ASSISTED SUICIDE – PRETTY, PURDY AND JAMES

Diane Pretty

Since the Suicide Act 1961, it is no longer an offence to commit or attempt to commit suicide. However, it is an offence to help or even merely encourage someone else to do so. Thus, section 2 of the Act provides that:

---

[17] This comes through in the medical evidence: *Ms B* at paras. 54–71. See also para. 97.   [18] *Ms B* at paras. 21–2.
[19] [2002] EWHC 429 at para. 23.

(1) A person ('D') commits an offence if:
   (a)   D does an act capable of encouraging or assisting the suicide or attempted suicide of another person, and
   (b)   D's act was intended to encourage or assist suicide or an attempt at suicide.[20]

Needless to say, this may pose problems for both patients who wish to end their lives and doctors who are minded to help them to do so. Doctors must be wary not just of the injunction not to assist, but also not to *encourage*, not least because under the new section 2(1B), 'D may commit an offence under this section whether or not a suicide, or an attempt at suicide, occurs'; and a person convicted under the Act is liable to imprisonment for up to fourteen years (section 2(1C)). For patients, particular issues may arise for those who find themselves in such a state of disability that they are physically incapable of killing themselves if they find their lives to be intolerable.[21]

   This was the situation that Diane Pretty found herself facing. She suffered from motor neurone disease, a progressive degenerative illness that had already reached the point where she was physically unable to take her own life. When she decided that the time had come to end her life, she wished to have her husband help her to do so. She therefore asked the Director of Public Prosecutions (DPP) to provide her with a guarantee that her husband would not be prosecuted under the Suicide Act 1961. When the DPP refused to do this, Ms Pretty went to court seeking a review of that decision. The case ended up in the House of Lords and then the European Court of Human Rights, which upheld virtually all of their Lordships' conclusions.[22] Her argument was essentially that several articles of the European Convention on Human Rights, incorporated into English law by the Human Rights Act 1998, were incompatible with the provisions of the Suicide Act and that the DPP should therefore properly have acceded to her request. Despite some judicial sympathy for her case, both courts found against her and the decisions of the courts in her case remain important. We consider each of the provisions of the Convention that she attempted to use.

   First, there was Article 2, which provides for a right to life. As Lord Bingham noted in the House of Lords, Ms Pretty's argument was that:

The purpose of the article is to protect individuals from third parties (the state and public authorities). But the article recognises that it is for the individual to choose whether or not to live and so protects the individual's right to self-determination in relation to issues of life and

---

[20] It should be noted that this wording differs from the original, which stated that someone commits an offence if she 'aids, abets, counsels or procures the suicide of another, or an attempt by another to commit suicide'. The new wording of s. 2(1) was added by s. 59(2) of the Coroners and Justice Act 2009.

[21] Indeed, in the criminal law case of *AG* v. *Able* [1984] QB 795, the court held that words such as 'counsel', 'abet' and 'aid' all related to 'helping', and the court would essentially ask whether the defendant 'helped' in the enterprise.

[22] *Pretty* v. *DPP* [2002] 1 AC 800 (HL); *Pretty* v. *UK* (2002) 35 EHRR 1.

death. Thus a person may refuse life-saving or life-prolonging medical treatment, and may lawfully choose to commit suicide. The article acknowledges that right of the individual. While most people want to live, some want to die, and the article protects both rights. The right to die is not the antithesis of the right to life but the corollary of it, and the state has a positive obligation to protect both.[23]

This argument was rejected as stretching the principle beyond breaking point. Indeed, there is something inherently counterintuitive about attempting to utilise an Article that is meant to *protect* life to justify the removal of it. According to the European Court of Human Rights:

Article 2 . . . is unconcerned with issues to do with the quality of living or what a person wishes to do with his or her life . . . [and] cannot, without a distortion of language, be interpreted as conferring the diametrically opposed right [to die] . . . nor can it create a right to self-determination in the sense of conferring on an individual the entitlement to choose death rather than life.[24]

Even if Ms Pretty's argument centred more around the right to self-determination, it was still considered a step too far. Thus, while Lord Bingham accepted that there was not a specific duty on the state to protect her life, it would be 'a very large, and . . . quite impermissible, step to proceed from acceptance of that proposition to acceptance of the assertion that the state has a duty to recognise a right for Ms Pretty to be assisted to take her own life'.[25]

Ms Pretty also tried to use Article 3, which prohibits torture and inhuman or degrading treatment. Her argument was summed up sequentially by the House of Lords:

(1) Member states have an absolute and unqualified obligation not to inflict the proscribed treatment and also to take positive action to prevent the subjection of individuals to such treatment . . . (2) Suffering attributable to the progression of a disease may amount to such treatment if the state can prevent or ameliorate such suffering and does not do so . . . (3) In denying Ms Pretty the opportunity to bring her suffering to an end the United Kingdom (by the Director) will subject her to the proscribed treatment. The state can spare Ms Pretty the suffering which she will otherwise endure since, if the Director undertakes not to give his consent to prosecution, Mr Pretty will assist his wife to commit suicide and so she will be spared much suffering. (4) Since . . . it is open to the United Kingdom under the Convention to refrain from prohibiting assisted suicide, the Director can give the undertaking sought without breaking the United Kingdom's obligations under the Convention. (5) If the Director may not give the undertaking, section 2 of the 1961 Act is incompatible with the Convention.[26]

Again, Lord Bingham rejected the argument. He said that Article 3 was intertwined with Article 2, and that indeed 'a state may on occasion be justified in inflicting treatment which would otherwise be in breach of article 3 in order to serve the ends

---

[23] *Pretty* v. *DPP* at 810.   [24] *Pretty* v. *UK* at para. 3.   [25] *Pretty* v. *UK* at 813.   [26] *Pretty* v. *UK* at 814–15.

of article 2'.[27] Thus, if Ms Pretty were to be given the right to die (as to hold otherwise would be a contravention of Article 3), that may constitute a breach of Article 2.

Ms Pretty also attempted to use Article 8 – the right to a private and family life, also held to constitute a right to self-determination. She submitted that Article 8 'embraces a right to choose when and how to die so that suffering and indignity can be avoided'.[28] Here, the House of Lords and the European Court differed slightly. The House of Lords found that the right had not been engaged at all (although it argued that even if it had been, it would be within the ambit of the exclusions in Article 8(2) to ban assisted suicide). This is because it is 'expressed in terms directed to protection of personal autonomy while individuals are living their lives, and there is nothing to suggest that the article has reference to the choice to live no longer'.[29] In contrast, the European Court held that it *had* been engaged, since English law 'prevented by law from exercising her choice to avoid what she considers will be an undignified and distressing end to her life'.[30] However, it agreed with the House of Lords that the Suicide Act's provisions remained well within a reasonable application of the exclusionary clause in Article 8(2).

Next, Ms Pretty argued that Article 9 (freedom of thought, conscience and religion) had been violated, on the basis that she had a sincere belief in assisted suicide. The House of Lords gave this argument short thrift:

One may accept that Ms Pretty has a sincere belief in the virtue of assisted suicide. She is free to hold and express that belief. But her belief cannot found a requirement that her husband should be absolved from the consequences of conduct which, although it would be consistent with her belief, is proscribed by the criminal law.[31]

Finally, she attempted to use Article 14 (freedom from discrimination). Ms Pretty argued that she was being prevented from exercising her choice to kill herself by her illness, and that the fact that an able-bodied person could kill themselves while she could not constituted discrimination on the basis of her disability. This would at first sight appear to be her strongest argument – indeed, she was correct to say that under the Suicide Act someone who was physically capable could kill themselves without legal recourse, but she was prevented from doing so because of her illness. Unfortunately, as Lord Bingham noted, Article 14 cannot operate on its own, and in order to use it she had to show that she was discriminated against by failing to be able to enjoy a right conferred by one of the other Articles. Thus, because 'none of the articles on which Ms Pretty relies gives her the right which she has claimed, it follows that article 14 would not avail her even if she could establish that the operation of section 2(1) is discriminatory. A claim under this article must fail on

[27] *Pretty* v. *UK* at 815.   [28] *Pretty* v. *UK* at 817.   [29] *Pretty* v. *UK* at 821.   [30] *Pretty* v. *UK* at para. 67.
[31] *Pretty* v. *DPP* at 824.

this ground.'[32] Even if one of the other Articles had been applicable, Lord Bingham held that her claim would still have failed since the 1961 Act conferred no *right* to suicide.

It is doubtful that Ms Pretty was ever going to win the case. Despite the substantial merit in many of her arguments, they were not based on defensible readings of the law. That said, it is perfectly fair to ask how it is that some of the other legal rules bent to accommodate others create a situation that is significantly morally distinct from what she was asking for. Indeed, the DPP has not prosecuted anyone in Ms Pretty's husband's position for assisting a suicide, and the danger for such patients is that by highlighting the issue they actually force the DPP to abandon the 'look the other way' approach, no matter how principled the stand might be. This is what may have been the result in the case involving Debbie Purdy.

Debbie Purdy

Indeed, the case of Debbie Purdy is similar to that of Diane Pretty. Ms Purdy suffers from primary progressive multiple sclerosis, a condition that is incurable and that will progressively deteriorate until she loses all of her physical capabilities. At some point, she wishes to end her life by going to Dignitas in Switzerland, but when that point is will depend on whether her husband can accompany and assist her journey to Switzerland without being prosecuted under the Suicide Act 1961. Where Ms Purdy's case differs from that of Ms Pretty is in the fact that she was not asking for a guarantee that her husband would not be prosecuted. Rather, she wanted the DDP to publish the factors that would be considered relating to decisions regarding whether it would be appropriate to prosecute people in her husband's position. The DPP refused, and so Ms Purdy went to court challenging that decision. Her case was dismissed at first instance and at the Court of Appeal, and she further appealed to the House of Lords.[33] The House of Lords allowed Ms Purdy's appeal on the basis that guidelines relating to decisions regarding whether or to prosecute should be available to both prosecutors *and* the public, and that the two principles of 'accessibility and foreseeability' should be adhered to.[34] The DPP was thus ordered to publish the factors to be taken into account, and subsequently produced guidance to this effect, which was made public.

The guidance itself, entitled *Policy for Prosecutors in Respect of Cases of Encouraging and Assisting Suicide*, divides the decision into two stages: the evidential stage and the public policy stage.[35] These ask, respectively, whether there is enough evidence for a prosecution and whether a prosecution would be in the public interest. Needless to say, it is the latter that is of most interest to us.

---

[32] *Pretty* v. *DPP* at 825.   [33] *R (Purdy)* v. *DPP* [2010] 1 AC 345.   [34] *Purdy* at 395, *per* Lord Hope.
[35] The guidance can be accessed at: www.cps.gov.uk/publications/prosecution/assisted_suicide_policy.html.

Paragraph 43 of the guidance provides sixteen factors that would make it more likely that a prosecution would be in the public interest. They mostly relate to the consent of the patient (so if, for example, the patient is a minor or is incapable of giving consent under the terms of the Mental Capacity Act 2005, it is more likely that prosecution is appropriate). Also, there are provisions that relate to the good intentions of the suspect (such as that prosecution should be more likely if the victim had not clearly communicated a desire to commit suicide to the suspect or if the suspect had a history of violence or abuse against the victim). This is mirrored in the six factors tending against prosecution in paragraph 14. It is made clear in the preceding paragraph that 'the absence of a factor does not necessarily mean that it should be taken as a factor tending in the opposite direction' (i.e. that if the patient is 18 years old then that is a reason *not* to prosecute). However, the total lack of prosecutions and the focus on the patient's autonomy and the good intentions of the suspect suggest that accompanying relatives to Switzerland for genuinely compassionate reasons and in accordance with the patient's wishes will not result in prosecution. Although the DPP at the time, Keir Starmer, argued in *The Times* that the guidance does not essentially legalise assisted suicide, it must be said, even by those such as us who agree with the DPP's approach, that it goes some way to doing so in practice.[36]

This unsatisfactory halfway house encourages challenges to the law, and the most recent challenge to this was presented to the Court of Appeal with regard to three interested parties: Tony Nicklinson (who had died but whose wife borought the case), Paul Lamb and 'Martin'.[37] The case was decided principally on technical grounds relating to Article 8 of the European Convention on Human Rights, and need not concern us here. Of the applicants, Tony Nicklinson, who had died before the case reached the Court of Appeal, had been almost completely paralysed and had unsuccessfully argued in the Divisional Court that given his total inability to commit suicide, a doctor should be able to kill him without being prosecuted for murder.[38] Paul Lamb's argument, according to the court, was essentially the same as that of Tony Nicklinson. Their cases were rejected by the Court of Appeal which, despite having considerable sympathy for the circumstances faced by people in their position, nevertheless did not feel that it could simply change the law in such a fundamental way, and that therefore the judgments in *Pretty* and *Purdy* should stand. Put simply, the court felt that 'it is simply not appropriate for the court to fashion a defence of necessity in such a complex and controversial field; this is a

---

[36] See K. Starmer, 'So Far, We've Got It Right on Assisted Suicide – Largely Thanks to You, the Public', *The Times*, 6 September 2011.

[37] *R (on the application of Mrs Jane Nicklinson and Paul Lamb)* v. *Ministry of Justice* [2013] EWCA Civ 961.

[38] For an excellent analysis of the case in the Divisional Court with regard to both Tony Nicklinson and Martin, see J. Herring, 'Escaping the Shackles of Law at the End of Life: *R. (Nicklinson) v Ministry of Justice* [2012] EWHC 2381' (2013) 21(3) *Med. L. Rev.* 487.

matter for Parliament'.[39] The case of Martin (as he was referred to by the court – it was not his real name) was slightly different, in that he was arguing that the DPP's guidance, developed and published after the decision in *Purdy*, lacked sufficient certainty and that it must be foreseeable to the public whether certain acts were likely to result in prosecution.

Martin's argument was that while the DPP's guidance provided some help to the close friends and relatives of patients who wish to travel to places such as Dignitas, it is opaque in relation to others, such as paid helpers or doctors providing written reports to Dignitas. By a majority of two to one (Lord Judge CJ dissenting), the Court of Appeal agreed with this. It noted that it would be open to the DPP to state in the guidance that doctors and paid carers *would* be prosecuted if they helped patients wishing to die, but that the uncertainty in relation to them in the current guidance was unacceptable. This was presented as merely being in line with the view of the DPP in *Purdy* that the guidance should be clear to all parties – the Court of Appeal merely felt that it had failed with respect to professionals. We can expect, then, that the guidance will be amended soon, but at the time of writing it has not been.

The law in relation to assisted suicide can best be described as reluctantly clear. The courts do not feel that they are the appropriate forum for modifying the law, but equally judges frequently express their sympathy for patients, and it is also obvious that they are trying to provide as much latitude as possible for people who help the terminally ill to die for compassionate reasons. This extends to the DPP, even if his guidance has been declared suboptimal, and perhaps what is most telling is the total lack of prosecutions for assisting people to die at Dignitas. While this may be reassuring for some, it certainly does not amount to much legal certainty.

INCOMPETENT PATIENTS – BEST INTERESTS AND THE MCA REVISITED

Bland and best interests

It will be remembered that the court in *Bland* had to create two legal fictions in order to allow the removal of life-sustaining treatment from Anthony Bland – that ANH and ventilation were medical treatment rather than basic care, and that such removal, even if a physical act, constituted an omission in legal terms. These combine to become important when we apply the normal rules relating to consent

---

[39] *Nicklinson and Lamb* at para. 56.

to treatment for incapable adults: absent the consent of the patient (through an advance directive), doctors may only provide medical treatment that is in the best interests of a patient who is incompetent. Therefore, in order for the House of Lords to find that the removal of 'treatment' could be authorised, it had to be determined whether this was in the best interests of the patient. The problem for the House of Lords was that, quite understandably, the judges were reluctant to find that death was in a patient's best interests; therefore, they once again had to become creative.

Lord Goff held that the key was how the question was phrased, and found a way to formulate it so that the correct answer could be found:

> The correct formulation of the question is of particular importance in a case such as the present, where the patient is totally unconscious and where there is no hope whatsoever of any amelioration of his condition. In circumstances such as these, it may be difficult to say that it is in his best interests that the treatment should be ended. *But if the question is asked, as in my opinion it should be, whether it is in his best interests that treatment which has the effect of artificially prolonging his life should be continued, that question can sensibly be answered to the effect that his best interests no longer require that it should be.*[40]

Thus, it would be lawful to cease to treat not if it were in the patient's best interests to do so, but instead if it were not shown to be in the patient's best interests to continue to treat. Given that, in the words of Lord Keith, in Anthony Bland's condition it was a matter of 'complete indifference [to him] whether he lives or dies', to continue to treat could not be said to be in his best interests.[41] While ingenious and not without logic, it should be noted that this way of looking at things is different from the way in which the concept of best interests was applied to other areas such as sterilisation, where the question was always whether it was in the best interests of the patient to *undergo* the sterilisation, not whether it was in her best interests not to be sterilised.

The use of the concept of best interests brought forth another issue, which was that of *Bolam*isation. The decision of the House of Lords in *Bland* was in 1993, four years after the decision in *F* v. *West Berkshire Health Authority*, discussed in Chapter 5, and at the height of *Bolam*'s influence. Thus, the way in which *Bolam* was interpreted was very much in the way that limited the court's ability to involve itself in what was seen as medical decision-making. Nevertheless, it could not be denied that the facts of the case constituted issues that went beyond the law. As Lord Browne-Wilkinson noted, 'behind the questions of law lie moral, ethical, medical and practical issues of fundamental importance to society . . . [and] the law regulating the termination of artificial life support being given to patients must, to be acceptable, reflect a moral attitude which society accepts'.[42] This would suggest that fully

---

[40] *Bland* at 868, *per* Lord Goff. Emphasis added.   [41] *Bland* at 858, *per* Lord Goff.
[42] *Bland* at 877–8, *per* Lord Browne-Wilkinson.

delegating decision-making responsibility to the medical profession might not be appropriate (not least because the issues being decided upon cannot be said to constitute matters of technical medical skill), and indeed there was some disagreement among the judges regarding how the ultimate decision should be made. For Lord Mustill, an undiluted use of *Bolam* would be inappropriate, since 'the decision is ethical, not medical, and . . . there is no reason why on such a decision the opinions of doctors should be decisive'.[43] This view was not shared by Lord Browne-Wilkinson, who held that *Bolam* simpliciter should apply and seemed to regret the fact that the courts had become involved at all:

> In the past, doctors exercised their own discretion, in accordance with medical ethics, in cases such as these. To the great advantage of society, they took the responsibility of deciding whether the perpetuation of life was pointless. But there are now present amongst the medical and nursing staff of hospitals those who genuinely believe in the sanctity of human life, no matter what the quality of that life, and report doctors who take such decisions to the authorities with a view to prosecution for a criminal offence. I am not criticising such people: they are acting in accordance with their own moral standards. But their actions have made it extremely risky for a doctor to take a decision of this kind when his action may lie on the borderline of legality.[44]

Indeed, it would always be the case that the key would be not so much the test itself, but *how* it would be applied. In *Bland* itself, such an application was unproblematic since all parties (doctors, relatives and the court) wanted the same outcome: that all treatment be withdrawn and Anthony Bland allowed to die. However, this would not always be the case, and the disadvantage of using *Bolam* in an undiluted fashion was highlighted in the case of *Re. G*, decided less than three years after *Bland*.[45] G had been diagnosed as being in PVS following a motorcycle accident. His condition, assessed by five neurologists, was said to be even more severe than that of Anthony Bland, and the hospital felt that it was not in G's interests to continue with the life-sustaining treatment (in this case ANH). However, some of G's relatives, and in particular his mother, did not agree with this assessment and refused to accept that his condition was hopeless. The question for the court was therefore how to arbitrate this difference of opinion.

A simple application of *Bland* would inform the court that ANH was classed as 'medical treatment', and that it could be withdrawn if it were not in the patient's best interests to continue to receive it. This would be decided by reference to the *Bolam* test as it was interpreted at the time of the case (in this case, it was still pre-*Bolitho*). In order to judge the reasonableness of the withdrawal of treatment, the court was directed to BMA guidance on the matter issued in the wake of *Bland*.[46]

---

[43] *Bland* at 898, *per* Lord Browne-Wilkinson.   [44] *Bland* at 880, *per* Lord Browne-Wilkinson.
[45] *Re. G (Persistent Vegetative State)* [1995] 2 FCR 46.
[46] BMA, *Guidelines for the Treatment of Patients in a Persistent Vegetative State* (BMA, 1993).

Paragraph 5 of that guidance considered what to do in the event of disagreement on the part of relatives:

It is good practice for the doctors to consult the wishes of people close to the patient but their views alone cannot determine the treatment of the PVS patient. People close to the patient may be able to throw light on the wishes of the PVS patient regarding the prolongation of treatment and this is likely to be helpful in decision making. Treatment decisions however must be based upon the doctors' assessment of the patient's best interests.[47]

What this makes clear is that, despite it being 'good practice' to consult relatives (although this suggests that this is not compulsory), the ultimate decision is medical and made by the head of the treatment team. Thus, it was enough that the relatives' views were taken into account – there was no duty to accede to their wishes. The judge in *Re. G*, Sir Stephen Brown, held that as long as this had occurred, *Bolam* was satisfied and the ANH could be discontinued. The power, as with so many other *Bolam*ised issues in the mid 1990s and before, was with the medical profession.

   Since *Bland*, the withdrawal of treatment from patients in PVS has been routinely authorised by the courts. This has even been the case where there has been some disagreement over the diagnosis of PVS.[48] Such patients are deemed to lack an interest in continuing to receive treatment, and this is now seen as legally uncontroversial. One exception to this general rule can be seen in *An NHS Trust v. J.*[49] In that case, Sir Mark Potter refused to authorise the removal of treatment requested by both the treatment team and the patient's relatives because there was a very slim chance of a new drug improving his condition. Indeed, the judge authorised an experimental use of the drug despite the relatives not agreeing to this course of action. The drugs produced no improvement, and at a later hearing the cessation of treatment was authorised.

   Nevertheless, when the courts have identified treatment as being futile, the assumption seems to be that continued treatment is not in the patient's best interests, and they have even shown themselves willing to overrule the views of the patient's relatives. This approach, and its attendant problems, can clearly be seen in the case of *Aintree* v. *James*.[50] David James had cancer, and while in hospital he developed an infection which considerably worsened his condition. This necessitated a move to the Critical Care Unit, where he suffered a second significant deterioration in his condition, and was placed on a ventilator. Shortly afterwards, he lapsed into a coma. The treatment team felt that continued treatment was futile, and that three particular procedures (resuscitation, invasive support for circulatory problems and renal replacement therapy in the event of renal failure)

---

[47] BMA, *PVS Guidelines*, para. 5.
[48] See *Frenchay Healthcare NHS Trust* v. *S* [1994] 2 All ER 403; *Re. H (Adult: Incompetent Patient)* [1997] 38 BMLR 11.
[49] [2006] EWHC 3152 (Fam).   [50] *Aintree University Hospitals NHS Foundation Trust* v. *James* [2013] EWCA Civ 65.

would therefore not be in Mr James' best interests. They sought a declaration from the court to this effect, and requested that a 'do not attempt resuscitation' (DNAR) order be placed on his chart.[51]

At first instance, the court refused to grant this. The hospital appealed, and the Court of Appeal overruled the judge at first instance and granted the declarations sought. Two particular aspects are worthy of note. The first relates to the concept of futility. Ward LJ in the Court of Appeal held that the key question related to whether the three procedures would be futile or overly burdensome on the patient. He stated that the best way to answer this question would be to define what the treatment was supposed to achieve, and then to judge whether it was possible to do so. Ward LJ identified six possible goals for the treatment and came to the conclusion that the correct one was the sixth, 'to secure therapeutic benefit for the patient, that is to say the treatment must, standing alone or with other medical care, have the real prospect of curing or at least palliating the life threatening disease or illness from which the patient is suffering'.[52] He concluded that, considering the concept of benefit widely in this way, the three procedures could be considered futile under this definition of their goals.

The second aspect worthy of note is the question that follows from the first: if treatment is futile, is it in David James' best interests to continue to provide it? It will be remembered that the Mental Capacity Act's definition of best interests contains a significant element of substituted judgment, and that the patient's ascertainable wishes and feelings constitute an important consideration. This created an obstacle for Ward LJ in coming to the conclusion that the treatment was not in Mr James' best interests because all of the evidence suggested that despite his illnesses, Mr James was a happy man who took enjoyment from life and wished to continue to fight to live. Indeed:

The evidence provided to the Court is of a man who continually fought against his medical conditions, cared substantially about his friends and family, and appeared to be generally happy despite his medical outlook. He appeared to maintain a good sense of humour over his situation (based on the jokes about the nurse's singing and going to the pub with his friend). Indeed, the most striking part of the Court's description of David James is how little negative reaction he appeared to have about his medical issues.[53]

Ward LJ's solution was to project on to David James views that were not really supported by the evidence, but instead based on a somewhat more objective view of his interests. Thus, Ward LJ held that if he were competent and considered his position, he 'would have to recognise the futility of treatment, that treatment would

---

[51] A good précis of the facts can be found in S. W. Smith, 'Aintree University Hospital NHS Foundation Trust v James [2013] EWCA Civ 65' (2013) Med. L. Rev., forthcoming.

[52] Aintree v. James at para. 35.   [53] Smith, 'Aintree University Hospital NHS Foundation Trust v. James'.

be extremely burdensome to endure, and that he would never recover enough to go home'.[54] Furthermore, the 'harsh reality' was that his position was 'hopeless'.[55] This allowed the Court of Appeal to conclude that the three procedures would not be in Mr James' best interests and allow the declarations sought by the hospital.

This is problematic for several reasons. First, it is difficult to see on what basis the Court of Appeal determined that David James would not wish to have treatment continue given that all of the evidence provided from family and friends suggested the opposite. The danger is that such an approach encourages a conflation of a patient's best interests with his best *medical* interests, which as we highlighted in Chapter 5 was one of the aspects of the pre-Mental Capacity Act law that the Act sought to correct. Indeed, Ward LJ was open in his declaration that in this case his best medical interests must take precedence.[56] Secondly, as Smith notes, the court seemed to think that the only rational course of action for David James was to avoid painful and burdensome treatment, yet this 'only follows if the requisite aims were the avoidance of pain and burdensome treatment'.[57] Again, there is nothing to suggest that this was David James' own aim – and indeed if we adopt this test then it is difficult to see what treatment would *not* be included in this category of futility for patients in PVS/irreversible comas. The decision in *Aintree*, in terms of its ultimate conclusion, is not one with which we necessarily disagree. Nevertheless, it is somewhat difficult in the sense that it defines futility widely and reattaches medical interests to best interests. We argued above that, since *Bland*, withdrawal of treatment in PVS cases has become virtually routine, and this case adds to that view but extends it to non-PVS comas, particularly if future courts adopt Ward LJ's reasoning.

However, it is not quite correct to say, either ethically or legally, that a person in PVS (or other sort of irreversible coma) does not have any interests beyond those that are medical. The former we consider later in this chapter. As to the latter, the case of *Ashan* v. *University Hospitals Leicester NHS Trust* provides food for thought.[58] In that case, a woman lapsed into a PVS state due to complications following a hysterectomy. The council proposed to send her to a nursing home, but the family disagreed, and wished to have her at her own home, so that she could receive the spiritual benefits of her religion – even if she were in a state that rendered her unable to be conscious of them. The question was, essentially, which place would be most consistent with her best interests. Despite the case being decided before the Mental Capacity Act 2005 came into force, the judge was aware of it and his decision bore it in mind. He held that even if Ms Ashan could not appreciate her surroundings, this did not mean that she could receive no benefit or enjoy any

[54] *Aintree* v. *James* at para. 47.   [55] *Aintree* v. *James* at para. 47.   [56] *Aintree* v. *James* at para. 47.
[57] Smith, '*Aintree University Hospital NHS Foundation Trust* v. *James*'.   [58] [2006] EWHC 2624.

interests. Thus, given that she would probably have wanted to be cared for by her family in the home environment, the family's wishes would be consistent with her best interests. Thus, a person does not lose all of their 'interests' just because they are not conscious of them, and indeed this is a principle that carries with it logical extensions. For example, a patient in PVS might have an interest in remaining alive to 'witness' the birth of a child in the family – even if she is not conscious to appreciate the fact. Interpreting the concept of interests more widely, the family may have an interest in the patient remaining alive so that the baby can 'meet' the patient (who may be a grandparent). Such meetings might be little more than symbolic, but then this is also the case in *Ashan.*

Nevertheless, the courts have been far more active with regard to patients who are not in PVS, even if the sum total of their experience of life cannot be said to be pleasant. An example of this is the recent case of *W* v. *M and others.*[59] Here, the patient was in a minimally conscious state (MCS). This, while not PVS, is not far from it, being described by the judge as:

> a state just above that of vegetative state, but which also involves extremely significant limitations on consciousness with a quality of life that many would find impossible to accept were they able to consistently express themselves with full competence.[60]

An application was made to the court by M's family, supported by the treatment team, to cease to provide ANH when it was thought that she was in PVS. However, during medical examinations required as a part of the application to the court, the diagnosis changed and M was said to be in MCS instead. Needless to say, this was of significance. As Baker J. noted, had M been in PVS, the issue would have been unproblematic and it was uncontroversial that treatment be withdrawn. Indeed, he noted that in PVS cases 'the balance [of interests] falls in one direction every time – in favour of withdrawal'.[61] However, given that the patient was not in such a state, defining her best interests would be more difficult (or, put more precisely, it was far harder to declare that she had no interest in continuing treatment). As Mullock has noted, 'M possessed the ability to derive some benefit from her life and so a careful balancing exercise was required in order to determine whether it was in M's best interests to have ANH withdrawn'.[62] The official solicitor, on behalf of M, had argued that this should not involve going through the 'checklist of factors' in section 4 of the Mental Capacity Act, since given that M was in a stable medical condition, withdrawal of treatment was inappropriate. This was rejected by Baker J., who insisted on using the checklist to ascertain whether it would be in M's best interests to continue to receive treatment.

---

[59] [2011] EWHC 2443 (Fam).   [60] *W* v. *M* at para. 34.   [61] *W* v. *M* at para. 35.
[62] A. Mullock, 'Deciding the Fate of a Minimally Conscious Patient: An Unsatisfactory Balancing Act?' (2012) 20(3) *Med. L. Rev.* 460.

As Mullock notes, the balancing exercise was difficult because it was unclear just how much joy and pain M was receiving through her life as it was. Given this, it might be expected that M's ascertainable wishes and feelings about her life might take on even more than the already considerable significance placed on them by section 4(6) of the Mental Capacity Act. Here, the family (in the form of M's partner, sister and mother) were unanimous and unequivocal: M would not have wished to continue living in a minimally conscious state. She had had occasion to reflect on the matter when relatives were taken into residential care, and had previously said that she would rather have died than be in a condition such as that of Anthony Bland. However, Baker J. noted that the views of the family regarding the patient's wishes were not to be considered determinative under the Act, and held that he could not find that there was no interest in M continuing to receive treatment. She therefore remains alive in MCS at the time of writing. This is a decision that disappointed Alex Mullock:

> On balance however, M's views seem quite clear. She stated them on more than one occasion and in relation to different scenarios and so it is unfortunate that Baker J chose to effectively disregard this evidence. Moreover, in view of the fact that Baker J himself described the condition of MCS as one which involves, '. . . a quality of life that many would find impossible to accept', his objective view of life in MCS, coupled with the clear evidence from M's family should arguably have enabled him to accord more respect to M's autonomy.[63]

We agree with her analysis, although we also note that Baker J. was at pains to note that there were aspects of her life from which M might take joy, and that now that the new diagnosis was made more might be done to ensure that this was maximised. Yet, Baker J.'s judgment seems somewhat muddled, as he also authorised a DNAR order, and said that if M got an infection it would be for the family and treatment team to decide whether or not to administer antibiotics. How her life was sufficiently intolerable that no effort should be made to save it, but not so that she should be kept alive, he did not say. Nevertheless, the important aspects to the case are twofold. First, in the absence of PVS – which includes a total lack of consciousness and no prospect of recovery – the courts will not merely rubber stamp applications to withdraw ANH. Although MCS is barely above PVS in terms of quality of life, the fact that there is *some* consciousness was enough to elicit some caution in Baker J. – just as it should. Secondly, the Mental Capacity Act's new definition of best interests should not be oversold. Here, Baker J. took what seems like a clear indication of what M would have wanted, but still did not accede to what were assessed as being her wishes. Moreover, this was not due to the fact that other parties might disagree with the decision, but instead because *in the opinion of the judge* her interests lay in treatment continuing.

---

[63] Mullock, 'Deciding the Fate of a Minimally Conscious Patient', 466.

While such caution is both sensible and to be welcomed, it does seem that what has developed is something of a disconnect where patients in PVS will almost routinely have withdrawal of treatment authorised, while for others, even in states close to PVS, withdrawal of treatment is resisted even if it is shown that it is what they would have wanted. What this perhaps demonstrates is that perhaps it is not what the legal rules are that is important, but rather how they are interpreted by judges – something that also seems to be evident in the decision of the Court of Appeal in *Aintree* v. *James*.

LESLIE BURKE – DEMANDING TREATMENT

Indeed, the decision in *W* v. *M* and the approach taken therein can be contrasted to that in *Burke*,[64] a case that eventually found its way to the Court of Appeal. Leslie Burke suffered (and, at the time of writing, continues to suffer) from spino-cerebellar ataxia. This is a degenerative neurological disorder, and he has been confined to a wheelchair since 2004. The nature of the disease is that, eventually, he will become totally dependent on others as he will lose control of most functions, including the ability to swallow, at which point artificial nutrition and hydration would be necessary. At this point, despite his physical disabilities, he would retain full cognitive functioning, including the ability to feel pain. The end point of his illness would come as he would lapse into a coma from which he would not recover. The case arose from a different perspective from others in this chapter as Burke was concerned that GMC guidance, issued in the wake of the *Ms B* case described above, gave doctors the right to remove the ANH from him before he fell into the coma – and therefore while he was still conscious.[65] He was essentially concerned that he might be forced to die in what he considered to be a horrible and painful way, and that the GMC guidance would allow doctors to decide to remove the ANH at an early point despite his objections. He therefore asked the court to declare that the guidance was unlawful.

In particular, he objected to paragraphs 32, 38, 81 and 82. As we demonstrate below, paragraph 16 is also relevant. Paragraph 32 informs consultants that 'it is your responsibility to make the decision about whether to withhold or withdraw a life-prolonging treatment'. Paragraph 38 states that where the doctor was unsure about how to proceed, while she should consult 'another clinician', the decision regarding the withdrawal of ANH ultimately remained one to be taken by the

---

[64] *R (on the application of Burke)* v. *GMC* [2004] EWHC 1879 (first instance); *R (Burke)* v. *GMC* [2005] EWCA Civ 1003 (Court of Appeal).
[65] GMC, *Withholding and Withdrawing Life-Prolonging Treatments: Good Practice in Decision-Making* (GMC, 2002).

treatment team. In paragraph 81, doctors are informed that, 'even when the patient's death is not imminent, the withdrawal of ANH might be felt to be appropriate. In such "sensitive" cases the doctor is advised to "consult" the treatment team, those close to the patient, and a "second or expert opinion from a senior clinician"'. Finally, paragraph 82 advises that in the event of irreconcilable differences of opinion, either with the patient's family or indeed within the treatment team, it may be necessary to obtain legal advice with a view to seeking a court ruling.[66]

Paragraph 16 was also relevant:

Applying these principles may result in different decisions in each case, since patients' assessments of the likely benefits and burdens or risks, and what weight or priority to give to these, will differ according to patients' different values, beliefs and priorities. Doctors must take account of patients' preferences when providing treatment. However, where a patient wishes to have a treatment that – in the doctor's considered view – is not clinically indicated, there is no ethical or legal obligation on the doctor to provide it. Where requested, patients' right to a second opinion should be respected.

At least in prima facie terms, it is clear that Mr Burke's point is valid – the GMC guidance does grant ultimate responsibility to the treatment team. It is also worth noting at this point that the legal fictions created in *Bland* conspire to remove decision-making power from Burke: ANH is considered 'medical treatment' rather than basic care, and to remove it is an omission rather than an act. In theory, then, and applying *Bland*, it is not unreasonable for the doctor to make the final decision regarding whether to treat – as the matter is defined as medical in nature. Of course, the case is unusual in that Burke was not refusing treatment, but rather *demanding it*. When put in such terms, it is equally not unreasonable to suppose that the GMC guidance (and the law) will not order doctors to provide medical treatment that they do not consider to be clinically appropriate. On the other hand, all of this is contingent on accepting that ANH does constitute medical treatment, and to many the notion that a man who is conscious might be dehydrated to death despite this being contrary to his wishes is repugnant.

At first instance, in a wide-ranging judgment, Munby J. found for Burke. He held that the GMC guidance was subject to judicial review, and that it must conform to the law. In terms of how to treat patients in a position such as that of Mr Burke, he said that the sanctity of life, dignity and intolerability must be balanced:

If the patient is incompetent, the test is best interests. There is a very strong presumption in favour of taking all steps which will prolong life, and save in exceptional circumstances, or where the patient is dying, the best interests of the patient will normally require such steps to be

---

[66] For an overview, see J. Miola, *Medical Ethics and Medical Law: A Symbiotic Relationship* (Oxford: Hart, 2007), pp. 173–81.

taken. In case of doubt that doubt falls to be resolved in favour of the preservation of life. But the obligation is not absolute. Important as the sanctity of life is, it may have to take second place to human dignity. In the context of life-prolonging treatment the touchstone of best interests is intolerability. So if life-prolonging treatment is providing some benefit it should be provided unless the patient's life, if thus prolonged, would from the patient's point of view be intolerable.[67]

He also noted that previous cases considering best interests had noted that they did not only encompass best *medical* interests, and that therefore it was open to him, upon performing this balancing act, to find that irrespective of the doctors' opinions it was not in Mr Burke's best interests to remove ANH. He found further justification in the European Convention on Human Rights' Articles 3 (prohibition of torture) and 8 (right to a private and family life – held to encompass a right to autonomy):

if article 3 embraces, as in my judgment it does, the right to die with dignity and the right to be protected from treatment, or from a lack of treatment, which will result in one dying in avoidably distressing circumstances, then the personal autonomy protected by article 8 means that in principle it is for the competent patient, and not his doctor, to decide what treatment should or should not be given in order to achieve what the patient believes conduces to his dignity and in order to avoid what the patient would find distressing.[68]

Thus, Articles 3 and 8 would prevent ANH being withdrawn from a patient who was competent and wished for it to continue, and Munby J. concluded that this would also be the case if the patient was incompetent but sentient and had, as Burke had, expressed a wish for it to be continued. Only when he fell into the coma and became insentient would it be appropriate to remove ANH even if he objected. On that basis, he found for Burke and declared several paragraphs of the GMC guidance to be contrary to the law. This can only be considered a creative judgment, and one which was sure to be controversial. Even though many will be able to sympathise with what Munby J. was trying to achieve, it creates the wider problem of allowing patients to demand treatment that the doctor does not consider to be clinically appropriate.[69]

The Court of Appeal recognised this fact, and reversed the judgment, finding that the GMC guidance did, in fact, comply with the law. David Gurnham describes Munby J.'s judgment as being 'swept aside' by Lord Phillips MR and Waller and Wall LJJ, and this is certainly a fair description.[70] Indeed, their Lordships were almost at pains to deconstruct Munby J.'s judgment at every point, sometimes

---

[67] *Burke* [2004] at para. 116.   [68] *Burke* [2004] at para. 130.

[69] It should be noted that in this case ANH was regarded as 'medical treatment' – as it had been in *Bland*. Had it not been, the courts might have been able to make a distinction between demanding medical treatment and demanding basic care. As the law stands, Mr Burke's argument had to relate to treatment and was thus always likely to fail eventually.

[70] D. Gurnham, 'Losing the Wood for the Trees: *Burke* and the Court of Appeal' (2006) **14** *Med. L. Rev.* 253, 253.

'to the point of rudeness'.[71] The Court of Appeal took a far more narrow view of how doctors and patients interact, rejecting the first instance engagement with 'rights'. Thus, their Lordships emphasised the lack of desirability in allowing patients to dictate what treatment they should be provided, and considered this an infringement of medical expertise. The patient, for her part, may refuse the treatment offered (or choose between options if there are any), which in turn will protect her autonomy. Thus:

> The doctor, exercising his professional clinical judgment, decides what treatment options are clinically indicated . . . If, however, [the patient] refuses all of the treatment options offered to him and instead informs the doctor that he wants a form of treatment which the doctor has not offered him, the doctor will, no doubt, discuss that form of treatment with him (assuming that it is a form of treatment known to him) but if the doctor concludes that this treatment is not clinically indicated he is not required (i.e. he is under no legal obligation) to provide it to the patient although he should offer to arrange a second opinion.

This is, in our opinion, unduly restrictive, and we agree with Charles Foster's description of it as a return to doctor knows best.[72] Moreover, the Court of Appeal did not seem willing to engage with Burke's central argument – that he might face a lingering death that he would be conscious to suffer – dismissing this concern as unrealistic given that (in their view) there was no indication that his treatment team intended to act in such a way. While we agree with the Court of Appeal on their wider point that patients should not be allowed to demand treatment, we cannot help but note that this situation is a direct result of the House of Lords in *Bland* defining ANH as a medical treatment. While it served a purpose to do so, the ramifications have been felt by Leslie Burke as an unintended consequence. Indeed, we accept the argument that it *is* different from ordinary medical treatment, and feel that it should have been acknowledged as such.

CONCLUDING REMARKS ON LAW

The courts have developed the law in this area with a sense of disconnect between what the law requires and what they want to do themselves. As we can see from the case law, they are broadly sympathetic to the idea that adults who wish to die should be allowed to do so, as in the case of Ms B, and indeed they have provided as much leeway as possible to those who wish to be assisted to commit suicide. Indeed, it is at least arguable that they have bent the law as much as they possibly can without allowing it to break – and following *Purdy*, the DPP's guidance and

---

[71] Gurnham, 'Losing the Wood for the Trees', 257.
[72] C. Foster, '*Burke*: A Tale of Unhappy Endings' (2005) 2 *Journal of Personal Injury Law* 293, 298.

Act and omission

The distinction drawn between an act and an omission for the purposes of the law is clearly a legal fiction. In *Bland*, the court essentially decided that when a lay person disconnects life support equipment, this amounts to an act (which amounts to a homicide offence), but when a medical professional does so, it amounts to an omission (which is acceptable where the necessary prerequisites are fulfilled). While there is very limited ethical mileage in discussing the exact definitions developed by their Lordships in *Bland*, the fact that they felt able and compelled to bend the law to very near breaking point is very interesting indeed. It is clear that an unwavering, literal application of the law would have led to an unfair result – it would have essentially eliminated the ability of medical professionals to withdraw life support where it was clear that there was no hope of recovery.

This would have led to a number of bizarre consequences: individual patients may have had to remain on life support indefinitely (until equipment failure, or multimorbidity that started affecting other functions than those that can sensibly be sustained by way of life support equipment). The other extreme is that in cases where it was potentially the case that health deterioration would reach the point of therapeutic hopelessness, doctors might decide not to even start a patient on life support because they would never be able to take the patient off that intervention if it proved unsuccessful (possibly denying life support to every patient below a better than average chance of recovery). It is unlikely that their Lordships in *Bland* had these consequentialist aspects fully in mind when making their decision, which was aimed at achieving fairness in an individual case. Nonetheless, they achieved a right result using means which are very difficult to explain to a lay person. At the same time, the correctness – or at least legal theoretical inevitability – of their approach might be deduced from the fact that other jurisdictions (such as Germany) have independently enshrined the exact same legal fictions.

Clearly, the distinction between act and omission, by itself, already suggests that there is a significant normative difference between these two. The medical ethics debate opens up additional categories to discuss different sets of actions. Active and passive euthanasia essentially correspond to the definitions we have seen above. 'Indirect euthanasia' is commonly used where the doctrine of double effect, discussed below, is meant. 'Assisted suicide' is used when we refer to patients availing of others to essentially carry out what they can no longer do themselves: end their own lives. The significant parameters we might have to take from this segment of the debate are these: who does what when, and whether the patient is still able to decide herself.

Double effect

The doctrine of double effect is a philosophical notion which can be traced back to Thomas Aquinas, who postulated that when an activity is aimed at achieving outcome X, acquiescing to the fact that Y is a likely secondary outcome, this is morally less significant than if we were to aim directly at Y. This separates the issue into one of intention (X) and foresight (Y). The distinction is by no means trivial, but much hinges on it actually being workable, for if we are unable to distinguish between what was intended and what was a by-product, we may well be left with a doctrine which is interesting in philosophical terms, but of limited utility for legal decision-making.[74]

Sanctity of life

We have referred to the notion of 'sanctity of life' in this chapter when seeking to illustrate the courts' endeavours to protect life for no other reason than the fact that 'life' per se is worth keeping. This places the concept firmly into the realm of an ontological tenet of how certain fundamental entitlements come into existence at all. In other words, if we accept that human life is in some way in a special category that ought to be protected at all costs, euthanasia of any flavour (and while we are at it, abortion, too) is simply ethically unacceptable. The phrase has been used in bioethics literature for a surprisingly long time.[75] Heike Baranzke writes:

According to George Khushf's literature search (1996) it seems that Presbyterian preacher John Sutherland Bonnell was one of the first who started the phrase's bioethical usage. In his plea against euthanasia, entitled 'The Sanctity of Human Life' (1951 p 201) he contributed only a single sentence with the phrase: 'Christianity has never ceased to emphasize the sanctity of human life and the value of the individual, even the humblest and lowliest, including the afflicted in mind and body.' Without explicating the phrase's origin and its logic of argumentation Bonnell used it as a self-evident prohibition against killing innocent humans.[76]

There is, in fact, no good moral reason why – without further qualification – human life should be regarded as sacrosanct (in the sense that it should not be touched). Obviously, life is a prerequisite for interacting and realising all of the preferences we consider to be fundamental in order to accept an individual as a protagonist in life. At the same time, it is easy to think of numerous circumstances in which we

---

[74] C. Foster, J. Herring, K. Melham and Tony Hope, 'The Double Effect Effect' (2011) 20(1) *Cambridge Quarterly of Healthcare Ethics* 56.

[75] See, e.g., H. Kuhse (ed.), *P. Singer: Unsanctifying Human Life. Essays on Ethics* (Oxford University Press, 2002); and R. Dworkin, *Life's Dominion: An Argument about Abortion, Euthanasia, and Individual Freedom* (New York: Vintage Books, 1993).

[76] H. Baranzke, '"Sanctity-of-Life" – A Bioethical Principle for a Right to Life?' (2012) 15 *Ethical Theory and Moral Practice* 295, 296.

feel, legally and morally, entitled to deviate from the notion that we should not end a life.

Right to die

The argument in relation to a purported 'right to die' essentially goes to a question of autonomy: does the effect society gives to the autonomy of a moral agent reach to the point where he is allowed to end his own life? This question is by no means trivial because it actually calls into question the fundamental basis for being an autonomous agent in the first place: your own life. Is one allowed to extinguish that basis of one's agency in the first place?

Clearly if, as requested in the case of *Burke*, we actually established a positivated right to end one's life medically, we ought also to discuss who would be the person giving effect to that right. Would we expect nurses or doctors to 'pull the plug' or push a pillow on patients' faces?[77] Can we compel an individual to kill another individual (even if it is with the best of intentions, i.e. to end intolerable suffering)? It seems clear that we cannot easily (or at all) do this. It is also fairly clear that this conclusion does nothing to stop us from assessing the other normative aspects of the end of life: we could assert that, morally, there is a 'right to die' without simultaneously also coming up with the answer of who will help us realise that right.

Slippery slope arguments

We have said before, and we do not hesitate to say again, that slippery slope arguments ('once you do A, then it is a slippery slope to B') are inadmissible in serious medico-legal and medical ethics debate. These types of arguments reject fundamental tenets of scientific discourse: because they concern events that may or may not occur in the future, they are not open to either falsification or sensible verification. Nonetheless, we encounter them the whole time, not least when judges are wary of making wide-ranging decisions.[78] In the context of facilitating euthanasia, these types of arguments are usually concerned with assuming that to allow very sick individuals to end their own lives automatically opens the door to society, as a whole, making normative arrangements to end the lives of those whom we feel have a poor quality of life. While it is always good to be wary when ending lives, this is clearly a far stretch of the euthanansia debate in the cases we have discussed here.

---

[77] Sadly, for a long time, the practice of suffocation did play a role in clinical reality.
[78] See quote above from *Bland* at 865, *per* Lord Goff.

Best interests

When discussing ending treatment for individuals who are no longer able to express their own wishes, the courts have resorted to applying the same rules that we apply in cases where any medical treament is administered to those unable to give consent: is the treatment likely to be in the best interests of the individual in question? What the phrase 'best interests' means is clearly rather variable: we have no doubt that in some of the cases we have discussed above (such as those of Tony Nicklinson or Diane Pretty), it was evidently and manifestly in the best interests of those concerned to decline life support at some stage. This is easy to determine because the individuals concerned said so themselves. Why should this be different in instances where the advance directive was purportedly deficient, or where no advance directive was made at all? The point, we think, is that it is inappropriate to deduce from what those able to express themselves wanted that this is precisely what everyone in that situation would want. And, as is so often the case with irrevocable decisions, the courts prefer to err on the side of life.

From the perspective of medical ethics, it is the case that there is a strong presumption that the patient's autonomy extends to being able to design the path she takes to death in much the same way that she is allowed to direct the way in which she lives her life. This is still true in instances where the patient has made arrangements prior to becoming incapacitated, but is obviously fraught with difficulty where we have to make assumptions about her purported wishes. Where there is no evidence of the patient's wishes in one way or another, the argument can no longer plausibly be said to be about her autonomy – rather, it may turn into an argument that hinges on her dignity (i.e. the attempt by those close to her to ensure that she has a dignified death in the way in which she 'would have wanted').

Another problem when approaching the question of whether we are entitled to end our own lives purely on an autonomy basis is that, surely, this does not only extend to those who are irrevocably ill. Physically healthy individuals may feel the need to end their lives and if we exclusively deploy our argument in relation to autonomy, then this must also be available to perfectly healthy individuals. The nightmarish scenario often cited in medical ethics debates here is that of the lovesick 15 year old – would we say that she is able to avail of the same service as Debby Purdy wanted to access in Switzerland? The point defeats itself if argued to its end point, as the lovesick 15 year old can end her own life, but it still illustrates significant deficits in relying purely on autonomy in this setting.

Finally, it is also interesting in this context to discuss whether the actual act of ending the life of the person in question is one that is inspired by the autonomy of the person in question (as manifested in the ways we have discussed above) or one that is in some way extrinsically motivated. By extrinsic motivation we mean that we assess, externally, that it is actually much better for the person to be dead than to live in the state they are in. The latter seems to be a case of the courts or the doctors assuming that the quality of life of the individual is so inferior to the fundamental standard we might be entitled to expect from life that it is better to be dead. This is, of course, fraught with considerable difficulties because it substitutes a (generally) white, middle-aged, middle-class judge's notion of what is acceptable for that of the person whose life is at stake. The one fact which seems undisputable, and which bolsters the courts' fictional interpretation of the law in *Bland*, is that it would in any case be legally and ethically unacceptable to carry out any type of treatment which the patient does not want or would not have wanted. This includes life-sustaining treatment where no such treatment is wanted – it simply boils down to a question of evidence in law, and a question of theory in ethics.

CONCLUSION

Butler-Sloss LJ in the *Ms B* case stated that the law had to balance patient autonomy and the sanctity of life. She was absolutely correct, but it has to do far more than that. First, it has chosen to concern itself with questions regarding slippery slopes. Whether we accept the validity of such arguments, it is perhaps unsurprising that the courts – who base their decisions on precedent and extending principles from one case to another – should have this at the forefront of their minds in such cases. The courts have also had to deal with a disconnect between their own views regarding the end of life and the limits of the law. As we saw in *Bland*, the courts will try as hard as possible to find a way to allow the disconnection of life-support treatment and do so to the point of bending the legal rules to breaking point. More widely, we can see in the lack of prosecutions of people helping relatives go to the Dignitas clinic in Switzerland a lack of appetite on the part of the DPP to prosecute. In essence, then, the law appears in theory to be somewhat different from its practical application. Nevertheless, in ethical terms this does not need to be the case. The law does not view the sanctity of life to be an inviolable principle – nor indeed one that trumps autonomy, as we saw in the case of Ms B.

   That said, we can see that autonomy is not an unlimited principle either. Thus, the law still prohibits (in theory) assisting suicide and euthanasia. The point made by Diane Pretty, among others, that her disability prevents her from ending her own life and to deny her help constitutes discrimination is a strong one in ethical terms. It makes no sense that a person who wishes to die can end their own life, but cannot obtain help to do so.

There are also, however, issues of medical power to consider. On the one hand, we can fully understand how some doctors – who see their role as protecting rather than ending life – would not wish to be involved in helping patients to die. It would clearly be wrong to force them to do so, although nobody is suggesting doing so. However, it would also be an error to pretend that all doctors strive to keep patients alive all of the time. Decisions regarding the removal of ANH or artificial ventilation are based on the patient's best interests, and as we have seen in Chapter 5 there were long periods where this was essentially a medical construct. Even since the passing of the Mental Capacity Act 2005, there remains a large medical element in such decisions and, as we argue above, judicial approval for withdrawing treatment in PVS cases is virtually routine. Moreover, as can be seen in the case of *Burke*, where medical professionals do not believe that continued treatment will be in a patient's best interests there is no duty – legal or, according to the GMC, ethical – to provide it, even if the patient wants it. As we note, this is in wide terms the correct approach, but we must accept that the medical profession treats the sanctity of life in the same way that the law does – as a concept with limits.

Cases at the end of life are difficult and emotive. The law has had to struggle through, at various times trying to reach decisions that require a modification of the law in order to do what they think is right rather than what a literal interpretation of the law would allow. The same approach has been taken by the DPP in assisted suicide cases. This is perhaps an example of judges taking the approach that it considers ethically correct in individual cases, and it is difficult to criticise them for doing so.

ADDITIONAL READING

 Law

J. Finnis, 'Bland: Crossing the Rubicon' (1993) **109** *LQR* 329

M. Freeman, 'Denying Death Its Dominion: Thoughts on the Diane Pretty Case' (2003) 10(3) *Medical Law Review* 245

D. Gurnham, 'Losing the Wood for the Trees: *Burke* and the Court of Appeal' (2006) **14** *Medical Law Review* 253

R. Huxtable, *Law, Ethics and Compromise at the End of Life: To Treat or Not to Treat?* (London: Routledge, 2012)

J. Keown, 'The Case of Miss B: Suicide's Slippery Slope?' (2002) *Journal of Medical Ethics* 238

J. Keown, 'Restoring Moral and Intellectual Shape to the Law after Bland' (1997) **113** *Law Quarterly Review* 481

S. Michalowski, 'Relying on Common Law Defences to Legalise Assisted Dying: Problems and Possibilities' (2013) **21**(3) *Medical Law Review* 337

S. Ost, 'The De-Medicalisation of Assisted Dying: Is a Less Medicalised Model the Way Forward?' (2010) 18(4) *Medical Law Review* 497

S. W. Smith, *End of Life: Principles and Policies for Regulating the Dying Process* (Cambridge University Press, 2012)

G. Williams, 'Assisting Suicide: The Crown Prosecutors and the DPPs Discretion' (2010) 39(2) *Common Law World Review* 181

Ethics

E. Garrard and S. Wilkinson, 'Passive Euthanasia' (2005) 31 *Journal of Medical Ethics* 64

T. Hope, J. Savulescu and J. Hendrick, *Medical Ethics and Law: The Core Curriculum*, 2nd edn (Edinburgh: Churchill Livingstone, 2008), chapter 12

J. Keown, *Euthanasia, Ethics and Public Policy – An Argument Against Legalisation* (Cambridge University Press, 2002)

H. LaFollette (ed.), *Ethics in Practice* (Malden: Blackwell, 2002), chapters 1–4

B. Steinbock (ed.), *The Oxford Handbook of Bioethics* (Oxford University Press, 2007), chapters 12–16

Case studies from this chapter are available online at www.cambridge.org/hoppe.

12 Concluding remarks

For those who have dipped in to one or a few chapters of this book, we hope that we have managed to pique your interest to find out more, and indeed that you have gained some insight into the complexities of the legal and ethical rules that emerge in the areas of medical law covered by this book. For those who have read all of the chapters: we hope that this is the case for you too, but would like to add some final words regarding some of the themes in this book.

The first of the two strands that run through the book is the question of a balance of rights and interests. Medical law and ethics involves, inevitably, a relationship between doctor and patient. Sometimes their interests will conflict. Thus, in Chapter 3 regarding errors and fault, the law and ethics have to balance the right of the patient for compensation for harm with a duty not to unfairly punish doctors. Equally, we saw in Chapter 8 how the law can make certain exceptions in the case of abortion so that medical staff do not have to participate in procedures that are contrary to their moral and ethical views – although, quite rightly, this is subject to the health of the pregnant woman not being at risk. Other examples can be found in virtually all of the chapters, which is inevitable given that there will always be a relationship between the two parties where the behaviour of one will have consequences for the other. The law cannot help but try to be fair to both parties.

However, a further feature of many of the chapters is the way in which the rights and interests of third parties – and beyond – may be relevant to the law. For example, in Chapter 5 we saw that the interests of parents and their right to parental control have to be considered in relation to their children. This may, at times, cause conflict with medical professionals, particularly if they are refusing consent to, for example, life-saving medical treatment. But at other times this can also put them in conflict with their own children. In the same chapter, we saw how the law will, albeit to a lesser extent, take into account the views of the friends and relatives of adults who lack capacity. Perhaps more controversially, the law has to balance the rights of pregnant women and their foetuses – not just in terms of the health of the woman, but, potentially, when the woman simply does not want to have a child. Such balancing exercises are ubiquitous in this book, and perhaps we need to accept that sometimes a balance that is acceptable to all parties simply cannot be achieved. It is therefore inevitable that the law has to take sides. At times, such as in relation to children, the law takes control and, if anything, facilitates the work of doctors. At others, such as with organ donation in Chapter 9, we see the views of relatives given priority and organs not taken if they object, even if the donor herself has consented to the organs being taken. There is, of course, a reason for this: in this case the organ retention scandals that resulted in a statute being enacted which did not seek to maximise organ donation, but instead minimise the chances of such scandals being repeated.

A final category of interests that we see on several occasions in this book is that of the interest of society as a whole. As we argued with regard to confidentiality in Chapter 2, there are times when the law adopts what appears to be a deontological position in protecting individual rights, but actually does so for the wider purpose of protecting the wider interests of society. This is the opposite of the approach taken by the Human Tissue Act 2004 discussed in Chapter 9, as we mention above, but it goes to show that the interests of society are not insignificant. At other times, such as in relation to research in Chapter 10, there are also interests wider than those of the individual and a legal approach that relies solely and completely on individual patient autonomy would be too simplistic and would not be of overall benefit. Another example of this, needless to say, is the question of access to assisted reproduction, where the law prohibits certain people from procreating in a way that it would not consider appropriate for couples conceiving naturally.

If we accept this proposition, then we accept that sometimes it might be necessary to overrule the choice of the patient. This brings us to the second major theme in the chapters: power. A significant issue in many of the chapters is who decides. Who should decide whether to treat an adult who lacks capacity? Who should decide whether to remove artificial nutrition and hydration from a patient in a persistent vegetative state? Who should decide whether to sterilise such an adult, or to provide treatment to a 17 year old refusing consent to the procedure? Again, in almost all of the chapters, we must try not just to balance interests, but also to determine who makes the ultimate decision. The law has to consider issues beyond mere autonomy and thus, for example, prohibits assisting suicide, as we saw in Chapter 11. Equally, as mentioned above, it essentially facilitates the medical treatment of minors, even if this is contrary to their wishes and those of their parents.

In fact, much of medical law since its inception as a subject has centred around issues of medical power. This relates not just to obvious matters of technical medical skill, but also intrinsically ethical issues. This process was encouraged by the fact that medicine is a respectable profession. This might explain why, for example, access to abortion was medicalised. Yet, nothing exemplifies the ebb and flow of medical power within the law as much as the *Bolam* test. As we saw in Chapter 2, the test was principally designed to assess reasonableness, but as we saw in relation to informed consent, best interests and other issues that are *ethical* in nature, *Bolam* grew way beyond its intended limits and, at one point, was almost ubiquitous in medical law. The decision of the House of Lords in *Bolitho* heralded something of a change in attitude by the courts and legislators – and again this was not limited to negligence. Thus, just as we could identify a process of *Bolam*isation, from the middle of the 1990s onwards there is also a discernible process of de-*Bolam*isation, where the unquestioned medical power of 'old' *Bolam* has either been modified or removed from *Bolam* completely.

For example, with informed consent the courts have progressively moved away from *Bolam* and now essentially determine the materiality of risk through the eyes of the reasonable patient rather than the doctor. Equally, the Mental Capacity Act 2005's definition of best interests – which began life as a component of a Law Commission report that was in part an expression of the *Bolam*ite decision in *F* v. *West Berkshire Health Authority* (see Chapter 5) – replaces *Bolam* with an approach that is based far more on what the patient would want (although, of course, this is not unconditional and elements relating to welfare remain). In both cases, the driving force behind the changes was an increased identification of the issues as ethical in nature and a similar increase in desire to protect patient autonomy. This may be considered somewhat ironic, given that at the height of medical power ethical issues were essentially given over to professional ethics to resolve, whereas now they are increasingly the domain of the courts.

Indeed, what is undeniable is that the general direction of medical law has been moving away from *Bolam* and medical power, and towards a more (though not exclusively) patient-centred model that seeks to allow patients to make their own decisions as much as possible. This is, of course, tinged with limiting notions of welfare and, at times as we have seen, overriding wider social interests. Nevertheless, medical power in medical law today is far less than it was twenty years ago.

A consequence of this has been that the law is making more decisions. Given that autonomy is almost always qualified, the law has to choose when to qualify it. Which begs the question: is it consistent in how it does so, and can it therefore be said to be a consistent ethical approach to medical law? The answer, in short, is 'no'. Although we can identify a general shift towards autonomy, this is far from universal. Thus, for example, in Chapter 2 we see how individual rights are respected not in their own right, but because they fit in with a utilitarian goal. In Chapter 5, we demonstrated that the law still contains a paternalistic streak and that the autonomy of competent minors can easily be overruled if it conflicts with their medical interests, while welfare considerations have been used by the courts in cases such as *A Health Authority* v. *E* to trump the clearly identifiable wishes of the adult patient who now lacks capacity. Equally, in Chapter 9, the Code of Practice defers to the views of relatives who object to organ donation even if that infringes the autonomous choice of the patient. The law relating to research, which we discuss in Chapter 10, is in many respects a reaction to the atrocities committed by the Nazis and the subsequent codes and guidelines.

Rather, what we see in many of these legal changes is a reaction to specific events or trends. With the Human Tissue Act 2004 and the legal regulation of research, as we note above, the organ retention scandals and the Nazi atrocities respectively caused the reaction. With the Abortion Act 1967, there was a more gradual shift in attitude and medical backing for change (exemplified by cases such as *Bourne*). The exception to this is de-*Bolam*isation, where the courts seemed to come to the conclusion themselves that 'old' *Bolam* needed to be changed. In other words, perhaps the most plausible description of the law's ethical position is that it is 'pragmatic'. A good example of this is the Mental Capacity Act and its equivocal language that allows the court to respect autonomy as much as it likes, or to prioritise welfare if it so chooses in any individual case.

This might sound unreasonable, or at the very least unsatisfactory. But it might be said that if the law is about making the correct individual decision rather than ethical consistency, then such latitude is not just to be accepted, but even welcomed. Whether or not the law should be ethically consistent as a whole is a complex question that merits further research. This is outside of the scope of this book (although, instinctively, we do not think that it has to be ethically consistent as a whole, although each topic should strive to be as much as possible). For our part, we would merely state that in most cases we can understand why the statutes are as they are and the cases decided as they were, and do not envy those who have to make the decisions in them.

INDEX